WHAT IS SCRIPTURE?

WHAT IS SCRIPTURE?

A Comparative Approach

WILFRED CANTWELL SMITH

FORTRESS PRESS   MINNEAPOLIS

Prior versions of chapters 3 and 4 have appeared elsewhere: chapter 3 as
"Scripture as Form and Concept: Their Emergence for the Western World," in
Rethinking Scripture, ed. Miriam Levering (Albany, N.Y.: SUNY Press, 1989);
and chapter 4 as "The True Meaning of Scripture," in the *International Journal
of Middle East Studies* 11 (1980): 487–505.

WHAT IS SCRIPTURE?
A Comparative Approach

Book design by Publishers' WorkGroup
Cover design by Tom Baker

Library of Congress Cataloging-in-Publication Data

Smith, Wilfred Cantwell, 1916-
    What is scripture? : a comparative approach / Wilfred Cantwell
Smith.
        p. cm.
    Includes bibliographical references.
    ISBN 0–8006–2782–2 (cloth) : — ISBN 0–8006–2608–7 (paper)
    1. Sacred books.   I. Title
BL71.S55   1993
291.8'2—dc20

                                                                93–27795
                                                                    CIP

Manufactured in Great Britain   (cloth) AF 1–2782   (paper) AF 1–2608
97   96   95   94   93   1   2   3   4   5   6   7   8   9   10

To, and with, Muriel

CONTENTS

Preface   ix

1. Introduction: Presenting the Issues   1

2. A Particular Example, to Illustrate   21

3. Scripture as Form and Concept: Historical Background   45

4. The True Meaning of Scripture: the Qur'an as
   an Example   65

5. The Bible in Jewish Life?   92

6. The Hindu Instance   124

7. The Buddhist Instance   146

8. The Classics: Chinese and Western   176

9. Brief Further Considerations   196

10. Conclusion: Scripture and the Human Condition   212

Notes   243

Acknowledgements   368

Index   370

PREFACE

FOR TWO OR THREE THOUSAND YEARS NOW, and in many cultures and civilizations, communities have treated particular texts in a strikingly special way. The notion scripture has been called into service to cover the several instances. "Scripture" is a Western term, one that previously specified the Bible as revered by Jews and (differently) by Christians; it has as yet hardly been re-conceived to do justice to what we now know of differences among varying centuries, let alone among diverse communities, treatments, and texts. Neither the similarities nor the disparities among distinct instances have been adequately pondered. On close inquiry, it emerges that being scripture is not a quality inherent in a given text, or type of text, so much as an interactive relation between that text and a community of persons (though such relations have been by no means constant). One might even speak of a widespread tendency to treat texts in a "scripture-like" way: a human propensity to scripturalize.

What are we to make of these matters? Most communities have traditionally propounded theories to interpret what has been going on in the particular case of their own scripture. Seldom have they sought to explain other cases, or to understand the matter in general. Academics have studied the various texts carefully; rarely have they considered the human involvement with them. Many have taken for granted that of course religious communities have scriptures; few have asked: why?

One fact is clear, and is made vivid from a comparative perspective: that the role of scripture in human life has been prodigious—in social organization and in individual piety, in the preservation of community patterns and in revolutionary change, and of course in art and literature and intellectual outlook. Given the variety, it is not easy to develop a conception of scripture that will not over-simplify. Given the power and the persistence, it is not easy to develop a conception of scripture that will not under-estimate its wide-ranging importance in world history, to the present day.

For a time Westerners, including secularists, consciously or inadvertently depended on their understanding of the Bible for expanding their sense of scripture around the world. We have reached a stage where we may rather use our new awareness of the world situation to attain a greater understanding of the Bible and of much else both in the West and in other cultures.

The aim of this book is to call attention to the issues, and to offer for discussion some proposed solutions.

Part of the thesis advanced is that to move towards a modern understanding of scripture is to enhance our understanding of what it means ultimately to be human—what it has meant, and could or should mean.

CHAPTER 1

INTRODUCTION: PRESENTING THE ISSUES

MOST OF US HEAR the word "scripture" without stumbling over it. Using it, we give the impression, even to ourselves, that there is understanding of what the term means; that we all know what scripture is. On reflection, it turns out that this is hardly the case.

Our presentation will endeavour to make the point that the matter is altogether more elaborate than we have supposed, the questions deeper, and the solutions more far-ranging. Moreover, our study will, we hope, make apparent that for those responsibly concerned it is important that the issues be recognized; and for the world at large, that they be resolved. At the end, lines are here developed along which, we venture to suggest, a possible understanding might be found. Equally significant, major implications are considered even for those not directly concerned with scripture, but pondering modernity[1].

Whether readers will feel that the proposals here finally set forth are promising, is less significant than that the issues be addressed. Our primary purpose is to invite a consideration of the field.

The matter is presented here in historical, and in comparative, context. This is because our present situation is new. New in this respect as in others, it has arisen in the course of an historical process in which we are caught up, wittingly or no. One element of its current phase is that we can now begin to see the development in which we participate; and can understand ourselves in terms of it. In fact, we can now recognize that our situation cannot be fully understood in any other way. Self-consciousness is central: corporate historical self-consciousness. Secondly, another aspect of our newness is the inescapability now of a comparative perspective. History has

1

placed all of us on earth in a pattern of intertwining strands, and we are aware of plurality. We cannot but be aware of it, dimly or vividly. Here too we do well to sharpen our awareness. For what each group of us on earth does, and is, increasingly affects the future of us all.

By "history" I mean not the past, but rather an on-going process. The present is just as historical as the past, in this sense; as will be coming centuries also. Human history is a process that, having begun no doubt long since, continues today, with a future that is currently being fashioned (in part, by each of us).

Scripture is a reality and a concept inherited from the past, and involved in the general novelty and in the pluralism of our modern world. Yet understanding of it has not kept pace either with the evolving situation currently nor with what we today know of the situation in the past. It is time that we forged a new conception.

Nor has our modern understanding of what it means to be human come as yet to terms with modern knowledge in this area.

For scripture has been and is different from what we have come to imagine. This is so in especially two crucial matters: it has been more important in more ways to more people than we have acknowledged; and it has been, is, more varied than our understanding has recognized. We shall here consider variety first. The other matter— the extent to which scripture has been an element more integrated in human life than is appreciated by current ideas either of scripture or of the human—will emerge as we proceed. It will become evident that we need an enhanced and more subtle notion of scripture, and a more sensitive awareness of what it means to be human.

In the West, several things have happened to the idea of scripture in modern times. One is epitomized in the nineteenth-century controversy over, one might say, the first chapter of Genesis, and in the transformation that that involved in the West's understanding both of scripture and of the universe. We live in the aftermath of that crisis. A certain minority of Christians, it turns out, has not accepted its results, which others assumed to be firmly secured. This threatens to become more troublesome than the majority has been prepared either to expect, or intellectually to comprehend, or socially and politically to deal with. Even otherwise, even for those who have adjusted, the results of the crisis have largely been negative so far as the concept scripture is concerned.

In the century that began about 1850, substantial sections of Western society turned away or drifted away from religion and from thinking about scripture at all. In many cases they replaced an earlier concept of scripture as signifying the Bible as the straightforward, even literal, word of God with, in effect, no clear concept of it. Others reduced the term to simply a synonym for the Bible—as the proper name for a certain book or books. The majority of practising Christians, on the other hand, especially Protestants, have retained the Bible as a serious component of their Christian life, not only in church services. Much the same, or even more firmly, has been true for practising Jews. Yet in both cases the role has been less central than before, and the conception much less clear. The range of ways of understanding what is meant by thinking of the Bible as "scripture" has been wide. Those that pass as being liberal or non-"Fundamentalist"[2], in the era this side of the great Biblical controversy, have had in common most notably the negative quality of not ascribing to scripture the metaphysical or other-worldly status that that controversy did much to demolish. Secularists, also, in the same time-period have developed quite novel references for the term "scripture", without having thought through their hastily contrived notions, as we shall observe in a moment.

Yet positive results of the new outlook have also been major. This present study takes as its starting point both the world-wide perspective that has opened up, recognizing the pluralism of scriptures, and the revolution wrought in Western understanding in modern times of the Bible as scripture, along with the impressive achievements of interpretation since that revolution. Our aim is to move beyond these to a still newer and more comprehensive vision, especially by adducing a more dynamic sense, and a more human one. One of the conspicuous achievements of the modern West in a related area is the mighty movement of historical-critical scholarship in its study of Biblical texts. We say "a related area" because this movement has concerned itself with those texts in their original form and meaning, their ancient setting and background: with constructing a view of the historical situation out of which they arose, and with the meaning that the words had when originally uttered. There is the paradox, however, that at that historical point those texts were not yet scripture. Only later did the practice arise of treating these writings in a scriptural way, and a concept scripture emerge. These texts became scripture presently—in a process that we shall explore in one of our chapters here; and we shall endeavour to understand what was entailed. Modern Biblical scholarship for a time made a point of setting aside any concept of "scripture", and prided itself on studying these texts as simply historical documents; treating them like any other such. Our concern here, in contrast, is deliberately with their role as scripture: a subsequent role, over many centuries. We would hope to clarify what it has involved; shall try to understand what it means to see that these texts have had that additional attribute. Their being scripture, once they had become so, has given them in the life of society and in personal piety a role rich, complex, and powerful.

A newer trend in Biblical scholarship has been to apply to scriptural texts some ideas and methods from literary criticism, such as structuralism and the like. To treat the Bible "as any other literature" is to deal with the texts in their post-scriptural phase—just as "historical" criticism studied them in their pre-scriptural phase. The texts' role in human life as scripture—rich, complex, and powerful, we have said—was during the long centuries in between. Furthermore, it is not yet over.

To observe that role at all accurately is to recognize its fundamentally historical character: its quality of changing over time—and place; of being ever enmeshed in the particular contexts of those in whose lives and societies the role has been played. To observe the situation accurately is to recognize that that coalescence with the actual—the many diverse actuals—that fact of continuous change, that active participation as an integrated part of the flux of an on-going historical process, are not an accidental modifying of some higher or more stable reality. These matters are not something that we must set aside or get beyond or behind in order to understand scripture itself, uncluttered by the vicissitudes. Rather, it is they that are responsible for this or that given text's being scripture; they that constitute scripture's essential character.

The change has taken place at many levels, has been of many sorts. Striking is the variety, at differing times and places, in the interpretation of a given scriptural verse or chapter or section. One might illustrate this profusely from virtually any sacred text. To put us in a position to wrestle with the issue generally, we devote our next chapter to one particular instance, chosen from the plethora available. Even at it we shall look in a selective way, certainly not an exhaustive one; yet the example will suffice to illuminate the kind of thing that has been going on. However stable a text might be (and there are instances when these themselves have decidedly not been stable), if it be a scriptural text the interpretation of it has varied.

To illustrate this, the particular work that for that chapter I have there selected is a Jewish and Christian instance: one specific book from the Bible. One could have picked virtually any other sacred text. This one particular book, although once of great consequence in Jewish and in Christian life, is today little noticed. The book of Genesis, of course, was the focus of monumental controversy last century and early in this, and the slow, painful, radical re-interpretation of it has been an heroic and/or humiliating task of the two communities. The Gospel of John has been interpreted in a considerable range of ways; it is so pivotal for Christian life that a theologically teasing issue arises, once one recognizes, as today we must, that to choose any one of the proffered understandings to the exclusion of the many others comes close to being arbitrary.

Similar considerations apply to the world's other scriptures. Doctoral students these days do careful dissertations studying an historical sequence of interpretations over various centuries of the Bhagavad Gita; of one particular word of the Qur'an; of the Lotus Sutra over one particular century in one specific country, Japan—to mention three done at Harvard University lately[3].

The implications are far-reaching of this matter of divergent readings of a same passage. We shall be exploring its crucial significance in human history. It is by no means the only sort of variety, however, even within a given body of accepted writings. Another variation of importance has been attained by difference of emphasis accorded to portions of a particular scripture. In the Christian Church, to take rather recent examples, it was a consequential innovation when the rise of the Social Gospel in late nineteenth-century America and elsewhere, and continuing on for several decades, developed a new focus on the Old Testament prophets. One might cite also the shifts from the Gospel of John to the other three, the "Synoptics". Even more reverberating were those from the Gospels generally to the Epistle to the Romans, associated with the name of Karl Barth. Sociologists and political scientists have to give weight to such historical changes.

Similarly in the Buddhist case: not only have old movements shifted direction, but new movements have arisen, as attention has been newly given to one or another particular scripture—or *sutra*, as they call them. What distinguishes one Mahayana sect or denomination from another is often, and explicitly, the specific *sutra*, out of the ample supply to hand, that it has selected to focus on, and is inspired by.

In the Qur'an, certain verses affirm the constant direction of all events and actions by God, while certain others proclaim human initiative, freedom, and responsibility. Historically it is possible to discern in Islamic life not only individual emphases, and instances of judicious balance, but also long-range developments. The decline of power, affluence, and cultural creativity of the Muslim empires from the seventeenth-eighteenth century was accompanied by a marked tendency to highlight the passages setting forth divine control—giving rise then to the Islamic "fatalism" (*qismat*, "kismet") widely reported by outside observers during the early colonialist period. During the early Muslim centuries, on the other hand, it was the human-initiative passages that were more stressed. At the present time, once again verses of this other group have re-iteratedly and effectively been being cited—giving enthusiasm to the Islamic "resurgence" now. Although an array of mundane factors has, of course, impinged in these instances, it is evident that the movement in neither the one direction nor the other would have been nearly so potent as is the case, had it not been scripturally inspired.

The mention of Asian texts introduces us to a further major development in the understanding of what scripture is. Two developments, one might say: one more obvious, the other more subtle. Or we may speak of one move, one that has had a superficial impact which is clear and certainly substantial, and that also has quietly had deep implications which have proven even more radical.

Over-all, the shift has been from specific to generic: from the Western word "scripture"'s designating the Bible to its being predicated of a broad series of texts around the world. The Qur'an came to be recognized as the scripture of Muslims; the Tao Te Ching as scripture for Taoists; and so on. From Oxford from 1879 a fifty-volume set entitled *The Sacred Books of the East*[4] was published—an important event in Western civilization. It was widely received, and has been reprinted a number of times since; and books with titles like "The Scriptures of the World" appeared presently, and have been in the hands also of school children for a good while now[5].

Bringing into one's purview the scriptures of traditions and civilizations other than one's own has meant newly incorporating within the concept material of a drastically diverse kind, enlarging the horizon to include a range of hitherto undreamt-of breadth and complexity, which the word is being asked now to accommodate. Moreover, it is not merely that in content the world's scriptures diverge among themselves radically. That is evident enough, although the diversity has not been digested in a new concept of scripture (strain though it be for the old concept). They diverge also in the conception of what kind of thing is involved. This is so at a number of levels. Perhaps none serves to illustrate this more immediately than the matter of writing, something that our word "scripture" quietly posits, or presumes.

It is not only this English term that signifies what is written down. In this it follows or parallels all its counterparts in Western languages: the cognates *scriptura, scrittura, l'Écriture*, of course; and *die Schrift*; in the preceding Greek *he graphe, hai graphai* (for instance, within the New Testament); the Hebrew *ketuvim* (this last regularly for the later components of the Tanakh, or Old Testament, much less often to include its earlier, more basic, elements). Similarly the word "Bible" in all its forms, the Greek *biblia*, the Hebrew *sepher* and *ketab*[6], signify "book" (a word that itself has quietly changed its meaning virtually every century for the past twenty-five). In India, in contrast to all this, the most sacred and awesome of all of what the West calls its various scriptures, the so-called "Veda" (*sruti*), has been oral/aural throughout, emphatically; the prohibition against writing it down has been fierce. Again, in Iran the Zarathushtrian "scriptures", Avesta and such, were oral for centuries, and writing when eventually introduced was at first considered little more than a supplement, until outside pressure impinged, as we shall see in a later chapter.

Arising out of the West's becoming aware of this sort of variety has been an instructive sequel: a gradual recognition then that such variety has in fact obtained also in the West's own heritage, as it has developed over time into what we have now. For even in the Jewish and Christian cases, whence we get our word, the oral/aural dimensions of scripture in the life of those involved turn out on inquiry to have been indeed central—and in many ways more significant, more intimate, more profound, than the written. This fact had been obscured to modern sensitivity both by the massively print-oriented quality of culture in our "Gutenberg era"—especially among intellectuals—and further by the specific term "scripture" used to designate the subject of our study here.

The world-wide and also the Western reach of this oral/aural matter has been made vividly clear in a forceful recent study[7]. Presently the new awareness will take hold.

When a century ago that fifty-volume set of world scriptures was entitled "Sacred Books of the East", the editor (Max Müller) did not hesitate to call them "books", one may readily imagine. As we have remarked, the word "Bible" originally designated books, and the word "scripture" designates what is written. The word *Qur'an*, on the other hand, signifies not what is written but what is recited. Those who know Hebrew will recognize the Semitic root *q-r-'* occurring in, for instance, Isaiah 40:3: "A voice *crying* in the wilderness"—"proclaiming", one might say. The Qur'an is the sacred book *par excellence*, no doubt; yet equally, it represents (as do other scriptures also, but perhaps less strikingly in this double fashion) divine revelation as spoken and heard[8]. The Qur'an is received as divine, and effectively enters men's and women's lives, chiefly as rendered orally[9].

The Bible, too, over much of its life, and not only for those many who were illiterate, has been heard, as well as—until recent centuries much more than—received through the eyes, off the page. The Jewish term *miqra* used for their scriptures[10] is from the same root as *qur'an*. On the Christian side, the Protestant Reformation, in stressing the Preaching of the Word, and in rejecting what it called the idolatry of the mediæval Church's images, constituted it has been said a shift from the visual to the aural for at least northern Europe's primary apprehension of the divine. The new emphasis on the Bible was part of this. When the 1611 King James Authorised Version of the English Bible certified on its title-page that it was "Appointed to be Read in Churches", this did not mean that anyone who had a private copy should repair to the local church building whenever he or she wished to peruse its pages. Rather, in the Biblical case also, the oral recitation, proclamation, of God's Word, in the hearing of the people—but also more quietly, often from memory, in the privacy of one's personal life—means that the word "scripture" in its etymological sense is not a fully accurate, fully revealing, term for our phenomenon. Might one say that no Christian service, from baptism to burial, let alone the weekly gathering on Sunday[11], is formally authentic without an oral presentation, a public reading aloud, from Scripture?

In the world-wide prevalence and usage of sacred texts as a generic human (or divine?) matter, one finds, then, a double involvement. One may think of two broad types into which one might classify the various instances: those where reciting, or reading out loud, is primary; and those where the written form is. In several cases (though not all) the alternative form is then secondary. In several cases an historical shift can be traced from the one to the other, slowly over the centuries, or more rapidly. In some cases, perhaps most notably only with the Qur'an, the two have been quite conjoined.

Intellectually, they are to be distinguished. Yet even the distinction has been less sharp in earlier ages, and is today in other cultures, than is the case in the modern West[12].

There are many other ways too, in addition to this illustrative aural/writing issue, in which scriptures differ, of course, among themselves, as well as each differing in the way that it has been itself received by differing groups or eras within its own community. Some scriptures have at some times served as an unrivalled force binding a society together into a strongly cohesive unit; at other times they have served to strengthen an individual's capacity and courage to stand against his or her society, or served to lift the individual above or out of the mundane course of events in which societies play their primary role. With some groups or at some times a role in liturgy has been dominant, or even exclusive; otherwise such a role may have been minimal. Some religious movements have been exuberant in the translating of their scriptures[13], while others have often tended to regard the language involved as untranslatably holy[14]. Some scriptures have fortified, or generated, a sense of history. (It could be argued that the Bible, with its tale of human history stretching from a long-ago beginning to a final culmination in glory yet to come, and its presentation of the historical process as the primary arena of the activity of God, has been the single most important source of the West's historicizing orientation.) Others have inculcated a sense that the movement of history is ultimately irrelevant[15].

We mentioned, further, a more subtle novelty that crept into modern perceptions in this realm, and we turn now to that.

For it is not only that the term "scripture" has, with this cosmopolitan awareness, come to refer to a wider range of matters. The way in which it is thought of as referring to them—or even, to any one among them—has also changed, rather surreptitiously. This shift has constituted another element in the on-going historical process. It too demands from us awareness, intelligence, and responsibility. It consists in the series of changing categories lying behind conceptions that the Western word "scripture" has served to express. One may say, the sequence of presuppositions included in that term's meaning over the past century or two. Given the importance of these matters in the West's religious and intellectual life, the development is significant. When we say that the term has been important, we mean that the concept with which it was associated was quite central in the life of both the Jewish and the Christian communities (in different ways). When the meaning of the word changed, the associations that earlier went with that word and had given it weight and prestige tended to continue for a time—somewhat vaguely no doubt, indeed with gradually increasing vagueness or confusion, as is customary in such matters. Yet the time has come to clarify the issue, primarily in our own minds. We can no longer reasonably go on in our sharply altered situation without coming to terms with the change, and deciding on our next move. Persons involved in a process do well to become conscious of the process, and to recognize their responsibility in its current phase.

The nineteenth century began, one may say, with the Western word "scripture" designating the Bible, whereas in the twentieth it has come to designate not only it but also the Bhagavad Gita, the Buddhist *sutra*s, and so on. Involved in this development, we wish here to emphasize, has been not only a shift from singular to plural, and from less to more material covered, but alongside that and indeed therein a shift from a transcendent to a positive, even to a positivist, meaning. (Throughout this book, as elsewhere, I use the notion "transcendence" to include immanence[16].) However surreptitious, this shift has had major consequences. We do not contend that the change in word usage alone has caused the change in meta-physical meaning; the two went hand in hand, mutually re-enforc-ing each other and attesting to each other. Our contention is simply that it is important to recognize what has happened.

For the sake of simplicity, let us focus on the usage in English by Christians, in order to elucidate the transformation. "Scripture" used to signify the Bible, understood as The Word of God. To use the term was to characterize a particular book as given by God to hu-mankind. "Revealed by Him" was the regular concept*. This is what we meant in saying just now that the word had a transcendent meaning: explicitly it denoted a work of divine provenance. Then its meaning was broadened—and became less lofty. After the furore of the Darwin and Huxley controversies—over evolution versus the Book of Genesis—there came to be, certainly, considerable ques-tioning among Christians as to that divine dimension. The affair was carried much further, however, when the term was applied to the sacred texts of other communities. Along with unclarity as to

---

*It has been suggested that I should change this wording to avoid the problem in English (peculiar to that particular language; in many other languages it does not arise, especially in the possessive) of using a masculine pronoun in relation to God. A scholar, however, must be fastidious in not misrepresenting other people's views for the sake of making them conform to his/her own. In this case, the reference is specifically to what used to be the case. It is simply wrong to suggest or to imply that it was not customary to use the phrase that I have cited. In all other cases, similarly, a comparable suggestion was advanced, even to the point of modifying quotations. To me it is unthinkable to falsify a direct quotation simply on the grounds that I or my readers do not like what its author actually wrote. Later in this work readers will notice that my own personal practice is in fact to refer to God as "He/She/It"; and indeed I find the modern practice of simply "He/She" here conspicuously biased. My familiarity with the Hindu Goddess tradi-tion, and serious appreciation for it, give a richness in the use of the femi-nine pronoun for the divine—apart from the role of my own mother in my religious development, as I look back on it (though she herself would have been startled by these innovations), and now my relations with my wife. Richness to the neuter is given by my sensitivity to the Hindu *Brahman* tradition, and the unrivalled philosophy of religion that India classically produced—apart from my personal sense that truth, justice, and other such "things" are divine, if one is to use theist language at all; it will be observed that I am at many points inclined to speak of "The Transcendent" where others might speak of "God". (Cf. further our chapter 2 below, note 15.)

one's own Bible, no longer seen as unequivocally God's Word, Christians came to speak of other texts—which most Westerners never had held to be of divine origin—as nonetheless admittedly scriptures. By using the term they indicated that they meant now something altogether this-worldly: a text that some people have regarded as authoritative, or something of that sort.

The difference is stark between seeing (and feeling) something to be divine, and seeing (or feeling) it as something that people have historically (and without good cause?) thought of as divine. The former is a metaphysical judgement, the latter a sociological one.

In this transition, one's own involvement, or that of one's community, tends to get turned around. For Christians, the Bible begins to be seen not as a book inherently authoritative, but as one that one's group has chosen to regard as authoritative. Whether this regarding, even this choosing, was for good or ill reason—and even if it was once for good reason, is it so still—are questions that begin to press. "The Veda is the Hindus' scripture; the Bible is ours" leaves one vulnerable to the query, "Why is it ours?". The word "scripture" has come to designate a text of special status, but a status that now is conferred upon it by men and women, not by God or the universe.

This shift from transcendent to positive or positivist meaning came not only with scripture. This sort of move characterizes the development of Western culture over the past century or two more or less across the board. One might say that scripture is one instance only of this transformation; except that for our concerns here that "only" is insouciant. The shift has mattered; in a great many other areas, and also in this one. A civilization in process of losing its spiritual moorings is in trouble—unless it can retrieve them, or find alternatives to them, in a new vision. The link between the de-transcendentalizing of a concept and the emergence of its plural can be illustrated from other instances. Culture, civilization, religion, value, are among these. The word "culture" used to designate a certain quality of living, the adjective "uncultured" testifying to this by denoting its absence; it has come to designate one or another, rather, of sets of mores, indifferently, without assessment of worth. "Value" used to specify morally something of transcendent, cosmic, significance; "values"—the plural has become prevalent only in this century—specifies whatever someone or some group rightly or wrongly imagines to be of worth. That so-and-so's values may be without value is an interesting new possibility. Crucial is again the self-involvement. If one comes to think of one's own values as whatever it be that one chances or has been led to think of as valuable, then one's ethics is precarious.

We move on from this rather monumental matter to an apparently more minor one, which serves primarily to indicate that the historical situation turns out to be yet more complicated; and odd. Here too history has been steadily at work, with things constantly in motion, from of old. While the shift to the plural around the turn of the century was fateful, on further reflection it turns out that the singular had itself been a Protestant matter—not altogether, yet also not negligibly. During the Middle Ages there had been a gradual movement from *ta Biblia*, a plural in Greek, to *Biblia*, a singular in Latin. That is, perception moved from "the Books" to "The Book"—not merely in the grammatical sense but more substantially in the slow development from a collection of writings to a single volume bound between two covers (a development strengthened, of course, after Gutenberg)[17]. This culminates with the Reformation's *sola scriptura*. Also, the concept "canon" signified at first, and for long, a list of authoritative writings[18]. In both the Jewish and especially the Christian cases it was a matter of several centuries before agreement had become widespread and firm as to what items were included in each community's list. In fact the first official Church pronouncements formally defining the limits of the Canon are post-Reformation—at Augsburg and then Trent in the sixteenth century for the Protestant and Roman Catholic Churches, at the Council of Jerusalem in the seventeenth for the Orthodox.

Even then, the place of the Apocrypha (another plural) was rather vague[19]. It was the early nineteenth century before the King James Authorised Version was regularly printed without them, in such a way as to constitute the Bible as Protestant piety knows it today[20].

To "read in the Scriptures" (Matthew 21:42) seems perhaps a more common Christian phrase from New Testament times on for several centuries, if not until relatively recently, than to "read in Scripture".

What we see here is a long process in which "the Scriptures" used to designate a plurality of Biblical books or passages, or even what we today call "verses", whose content was the significant point, whereas later with Protestant bibliolatry developing one finds increasingly the singular "scripture", designating the book itself as a specific entity, which as a single bound volume became a central religious symbol. Even differentiating among the diverse Protestant Churches, the sociological observation has been made that in the Sunday service, "the more Bishops, the fewer Bibles"[21]. In other words, whereas in some cases vestments and rituals and such are the visible carriers of aura, in other cases the Bible as a physical object is the manifest emblem of authority and awe. Many an evangelical preacher is to be seen holding, or even waving, a (usually closed) Bible in one hand while preaching.

Again, this unitary perception has been dissolved of late in critical Biblical scholarship. The modern academic mind lives by analysis, is suspicious of synthesis if ever it pauses to notice it, and in this particular case has left it long since behind. The historical-critical method has made a point of correlating each part of the Bible not with the other parts but one by one with extra-Biblical data in each separate instance. Indeed the Bible as such is not currently recognized as an academic subject of study; Ph.D.'s are normally given at most either in Old Testament or in New Testament, as distinct fields[22].

To sum up this point: there has been a long-range historical process wherein the plural "scriptures" used to signify the array of texts that the Church recognized as loci of God's communicating to humankind His will and His truth; then came a stage when the singular was in vogue signifying at least in part the empirical object containing those texts or more theoretically the conceptual entity of which they were parts; then the plural again, this time designating the mundane series of the world's collection of texts, which one does not venerate but notes that other people somehow do. More recently, each of the "units" constituting that collectivity is itself fragmented, in novel ways.

A further sort of variety, certainly important, is that a given scripture has at times served to raise to impressive heights the spirits of those engaged with it; at times to keep alive an effective relation to the accepted moral norms of the particular culture; at times to proffer excuses for, or even to instigate, obtuseness, oppression, and wickedness. Few informed observers, whatever their standards for assessment, could disagree that the historical effect of scripture has been, and is, sometimes and in some cases good, at others bad, and at still others an elusive mixture of the two.

Confronted by the range of the world's scriptures, by the diversity of interpretations of specific texts, by alterations of emphasis among parts of a specific scripture, by deep changes in the usage of the word and in the conception that it articulates, by ambiguity in social and moral consequence, one asks: what are we to do in the face of this variety?

Or, to remain closer to our historical orientation: perceiving as we do today a diversity of ever-changing and intertwining processes, in which this concept has been, and we now are, involved, how are we responsibly to construct the next stage of conceptual development? Do we know how to deal with the great variety, even intellectually?

There are several ways of ducking this problem, of avoiding the challenge. Some are contrived by religious people, some by academics. None is convincing. Of the various devices that the academic world has developed, enabling it not to wrestle with the issue, one has been quietly to abandon the notion of scripture. An eminent Biblical authority at Yale stirred up quite a tempest a few years ago by publishing a book under the title *Introduction to the Old Testament as Scripture*[23]. The two last words troubled his fellow scholars. For the academic study of these texts had long since, and on principle, and proudly, treated them as any other literature. Indeed, it studied the texts, Biblical or Vedic or whatever, primarily as historical documents to be used chiefly for reconstructing the ancient situation out of which they came. That they were "scripture" had ceased not only to matter to such scholars, but had in fact virtually ceased to mean anything. There were a few brave exceptions, of course—their numbers growing recently[24].

Those that are not the brave exceptions, those other, narrowly focussed scholars, a critic might teasingly perhaps call antiquarians, or academic fundamentalists who never question the current secularist dogmas. Like them, religious folk avoiding pluralism, diachronic and synchronic, achieve their comparable narrowness of focus by affirming flatly that only one scripture is significant (namely, their own: Qur'an for Muslims, Bible for Christians, and so on) and only one interpretation (presumably, also, their own; or in any case their own type of interpretation).

More liberal theologians, however, but also more wide-ranging intellectuals, are confronted by the still unanswered question: how are we to understand the notion scripture, now that we know what we do know of its multiform variety. A number of quite divergent texts have been put together in the constructing of a given scripture; a number of quite divergent scriptures have been cherished around the world, and have played immensely significant, yet varying, roles in human history because of being treated as scripture; and each of them has then demonstrably been read in a number of divergent ways, ways that have differed from century to century, region to region, village to town, study to palace.

No theory of scripture, we suggest, no meaning assigned to the term, no concept to accompany it, will serve that does not do justice to this variety. Moreover, and this is my second basic point, alongside variety: no understanding of scripture will serve that does not do justice also to the sheer richness and depth with which human life has been imbued over long stretches of time for most human beings and societies, through their use of, their involvement with, their scripture. This richness and depth are difficult to exaggerate. They could be illustrated from the role of the Qur'an in various eras of history, or of the Gita, or of the Chinese classics, and many other instances.

When we say that in a given passage some people have heard this, some that, it might be contended that preferable would be to acknowledge, with deference to eisegesis, that some have read into it this, some that. Indeed it would be difficult to construct an historically sound understanding of scripture without recognizing that people in their diversity have poured into whatever text played that role for them—people have imposed on that text, if one will—much of their deepest concerns, aspirations, fears, hopes, outlooks, feelings. Yet it would be a blunder to note this without recognizing further—and this is what cries out for understanding—that even in these cases, having poured these in they have then received them back profoundly fortified and strikingly enhanced: their hopes activated, their fears assuaged, their choices strengthened with courage, their feelings enriched and deepened.

One way and another, scripture has played a major role in human history, not only in individual and corporate piety and moral sensibility and intellectual vision, but also in law, family relations, literature, art, economic patterns, social and political organization, social and political revolutions, dress, linguistic usage, and otherwise—a role too momentous by far for us not to have a theory of it, not to construct a concept to go with the term. Requisite, indeed, is a new conception not only of scripture, but of the human: a new understanding of ourselves as creatures whose being has generated and sustained, and been sustained by, this curious affair. Rather than continuing to use the word "scripture" loosely, almost vacuously, or leaving it unused in careful, serious discourse, we are challenged to come up with a conception consonant with what we now know of its historical dynamic.

This is so, whether we be sheer intellectuals trying in the university to understand the human scene, or whether we be theologians or other thinkers playing some role in the religious life of the community.

As my own contribution towards this, in the final chapter of this study I make certain proposals. In addition, from time to time as we go along I proffer some observations pertaining to the general question, as well as comments on the particular matters under consideration. As remarked above, however, the primary purpose of this study is to call attention to the issues; and in the course of the work I set forth material indicating the sort of evidence on which a treatment of the matter nowadays must be grounded—or with which at least it must come to terms. Whether from that evidence the inferences that I derive, or see as emerging, readers will find compelling, or adequate, or indeed legitimate, each will decide. In any case, that is less germane than that the evidence be pondered. Surely the historical data must be taken into account also in alternative, or supplementary, proposals that may be brought forward.

At this stage already, we here propound one basic thesis. If not immediately self-evident as stated, it will be seen as we proceed to be well nigh incontrovertible, so manifest will become the solid and far-reaching grounds on which it rests. It is this: that "scripture" is a bilateral term. By that we mean that it inherently implies, in fact names, a relationship. It denotes something in a particular relation to something else. (Some philosophers of languages are beginning to discern that something of this sort is perhaps the case with all terms? This is rather at the level of "implies", however, than of "denotes"; some instances are more obvious than others. Our concern here is where the relationship involved is relatively overt.) No plant is "objectively" a weed: the term designates any plant that grows uncultivated in a situation where it is unwanted by human beings. No person is a husband in and of himself; he is a husband in correlation with another person, in this case a wife. No one is a king except in relation to a certain society and form of government; no building is a temple except in relation to a given community of persons. Fundamental, we suggest, to a new understanding of scripture is the recognition that no text is a scripture in itself and as such. People—a given community—make a text into scripture, or keep it scripture: by treating it in a certain way.

I suggest: *scripture is a human activity.*

More accurately: it has been so, in a world-wide fashion, and for a very long time now. Things were not always thus: we examine scripture's rise in the Western case in one of our chapters here. Yet world history certainly shows that there has been for centuries a human propensity to scripturalize.

The human involvement is central. We take it as a firm sequel to modern historical awareness that the quality of being scripture is not an attribute of texts. It is a characteristic of the attitude of persons—groups of persons—to what outsiders perceive as texts. It denotes a relation between a people and a text. Yet that too is finally inadequate. As we shall see more fully later, at issue is the relation between a people and the universe, in the light of their perception of a given text.

People's attitude here involved, constituting a work as scripture, has not been everywhere the same. The classical attitude of Muslims to the Qur'an is not the same as any one of the various classical Christian attitudes to the Bible. (It has been more distant from most Roman Catholic than from some Protestant. Indeed, we shall be considering later the perception that in many respects it comes closer to the Christian attitude to the person of Christ than to the Bible.) It is somewhat closer to the classical Jewish attitude to the Torah; although, as we shall be noting later, that in turn is to be seen in terms of the duality of relation to the Written and to the Oral Torah, on the one hand, and in relation to the Jewish attitude to the rest of the Jewish Bible, on the other. Hindu attitudes to the Bhagavad Gita, to the Ramayana, and to the Veda are, and are meant to be, diverse. All this is in addition to the diversity towards any one scripture over time, and also from region to region, class to class, temperament to temperament. It is apart, too, from the issue of variety of interpretation.

"Attitude", however, crucially important though it be for under-standing what has been going on here, is perhaps not quite the right word. (Nor, again, is the word "text", as we shall later ponder. Scriptures are not texts!) It misleads insofar as it may suggest any sort of passivity, or subordination; as if the text were to be thought of first, as a given, with people's response to it subsequent and derivative. That the text is preserved, is noticed, has to be explained first; it is the prior fact. No doubt, their scripture to a mighty degree makes a people what they are. Yet one must not lose sight of the point that it is the people who make it, keep making it, scripture.

Scripture, we repeat, is a human activity. It is an on-going and important one. It has been more significant than many others—than art, for instance. Yet it is like other such human activity at least in this: that it has been strikingly varied.

Although the artistic dimension of our life, the capacity to gener-ate art, is not irrelevant, a closer analogy is with the capacity to respond to art, the æsthetic dimension. Yet there are grounds for being somewhat ill at ease with that comparison in any case. No doubt art too through human history has been varied; and cannot be understood in itself, only in relation to persons. Yet it has other-wise been less significant than scripture, less consequential. We men-tion it because we shall return to this, not only noting that scripture and art have, of course, been closely interwoven at many points throughout history, but also propounding a new dimension of the relation between the two that may prove constructive.

Language in the form of poetry comes under the heading of art; language in the form of scripture comes under a heading that it is our task to discern.

This study, then, will present and explore the historical point that there has been and is a human activity of treating a work or works as scripture. It is something that most people, at most times and places, have done. Yet after all, it is a surprising thing to do: to take a piece of literature and evidently to elevate it to a very special status, and then to live one's life, individual and corporate, accordingly. (Even those who feel that there is no problem in the case of their own scripture, have still the question about the rest of humankind.)

Does any of us quite know just what is that status?

Do we understand what has been going on here?

This present study rests on a conviction that it is possible to move, carefully, towards such understanding. Let us see what materials are available to illumine the matter, and what progress we can make.

CHAPTER 2

A PARTICULAR EXAMPLE, TO ILLUSTRATE

IN OUR ENDEAVOUR towards understanding scripture, a first step may well be a clarifying in our minds of where to look; of what is there that awaits, and invites, being understood. We have remarked that a text becomes, and continues as, scripture by being related in certain ways to certain people, at certain times and places. Important, accordingly, is to consider that relation. We must give our attention not only, nor even primarily, to the text but to the people, and to the way that their lives have been formed or modified or enriched or limited by their appropriation of and involvement with that text at specific times. We must strive to understand how the forming, modifying, enriching, limiting, come about; and in what the appropriating and the being involved consist. What have those people done to the text in rendering it scriptural; and what has it done to them?

Scripture is a human, and an historical, fact. We may say: is a human, and therein an historical, fact—intimately involved with the movement, the unceasingly changing specificity of historical process, its grandeur and its folly.

Even those who regard one particular scripture as God-given, or as transcendently absolute, must recognize that without a human response to it, without a community reception and preservation of it, it is otiose. As we shall later explore, to insist that scripture is a human doing, a human involvement, is not necessarily to rule out *a priori* the possibility of its being also divine. To recognize that it has been inescapably historical is not to exclude on principle the thesis advanced by specific groups that in their case it is (we would say, has been) also of timeless significance and worth. Not only for those who participate in one or another of its instances but also for observers, the study of scripture raises questions of an interrelation between time and eternity, of humanity's historically participating in transcendence, of a link between the human and the divine. These issues we leave aside for the moment, to attend first to the empirical situation, the historical human involvement out of which the matter comes to our notice. At that level, it is manifest that scripture is something in which in various forms human persons and groups have around the world and over the centuries been actively engaged. To that engagement we address ourselves.

This may be illustrated by a particular example. Many suggest themselves. One might consider how certain Buddhist texts are treated in the specific context of a particular convent in present-day Taiwan: what their role as scripture in fact means from day to day for those Buddhist nuns[1]. One might examine perhaps the evolving role of the Bhagavad Gita in the life, public and private, of M. K. Gandhi; and might compare it carefully with the role in his life of the New Testament, and of Veda (the Vedas)[2]. One might elucidate the meaning of scripture for the perhaps first person ever to compose a scripture consciously, Mani, and then for the Manichee movement that he launched: tracing the development of that meaning from the movement's founding in the third century in Mesopotamia over the subsequent millennium or so, from Africa and Europe to China[3]. In the chapters that follow we shall be introduced to salient facets of the multiform fact of scripture in several of the major cultures of humankind where it has been significant: major instances that have constituted scripture as historically, and therefore for modern thinkers also theoretically, momentous. First, however, for illustrative purposes we here choose as one example a particular Biblical book, The Song of Songs, and shall note a selected variety of ways in which it has established a claim on our attention, as grounds for our legitimately calling it scripture. The choice of this work is somewhat random but not quite arbitrary: one may hope that this instance is for many readers neither so remote nor so familiar as to be unrewarding.

Certainly in the Middle Ages in the West this work was not peripheral, as it has largely since become. On the contrary, it was decidedly a favourite, and played in religious and social life a central role. Apparently more mediæval Latin manuscripts of The Song of Songs are extant than of any other book of the Bible, from either Testament. Evidently it was copied more often in the monasteries than any other. From only one of the four Gospels (that of John) and from the Psalms were more surviving Christian sermons preached[4]. On the Jewish side the ringing affirmation of the renowned first-and-second-century Rabbi 'Aqiba continued to reverberate, repeatedly quoted: "The whole of time is not worth the day on which The Song of Songs was given to Israel. All the Writings [ketubim] (Hagiographa), are holy; The Song of Songs is the holy of holies"[5].

The Middle Ages took this book seriously!

We must rise to an awareness of how prevalent, central, beloved, and inspiring this little book was, over several centuries. The work was pored over, carefully pondered, elaborately annotated, and eloquently preached; we moderns are little equipped to grasp the extent to which people were stirred, their spirits mightily encouraged. If presently we look at individual commentators, whose positions as we shall see differ among themselves and, even more, differ rather dramatically from modern interpretations, we must not imagine that they are idiosyncratic. Each was warmly welcomed and deeply appreciated, long meditated upon, widely cherished. Each was influential; each is representative.

Another reason for choosing this work as an instructive introduction for an understanding of scripture generally, before we go on to look at the matter more widely, is that it is a sector of scripture that has served so for two distinct communities. In many cases, literature on which one group has conferred—or: in which it has discerned—scriptural status, other religious groups have treated no differently from secularists. Our purposes are furthered by our noting a work that has in this special category served two religious visions, the Jewish and the Christian. It has done so in ways revealingly diverse —as well as engagingly comparable.

In fact, in this particular case we may look as well at a third group at that time involved: namely, the philosophers—admittedly, a relatively small party. In many other instances also of scripture around the world the work of philosophic minds has introduced a distinguishable and at times divergent interpretive stream. Yet in the mediæval West and the classical Islamic world the philosophers are particularly interesting as constituting a somewhat more distinct and self-conscious tradition, and a more inter-religious one, than is often the case.

Thus there are three classes of instances of the mediæval role in the West of The Song of Songs in the lives and the understanding of those by whom it was cherished. The differences among the three, and the similarities, as well as the substance of each individually, will help us to see what has been going on in this matter of scripture.

Specifically, we shall note representative writings from among the three groups, particularly the first two. Our first will be the moving commentary of Rashi, acronym of the eleventh-century French Rabbi Solomon ben Isaac of Troyes, one of the greatest leaders and most influential thinkers of European Jewry[6]. Next, we shall look at the sermons on this text by one of the greatest Christian figures of mediæval times, St. (and later also "Doctor of the Church") Bernard of Clairvaux[7]. Our third, the philosophic position, much less widespread and historically less significant, is interesting for our purposes in itself and for the light that it throws on the other two[8].

One of the few ways in which, in their interpretation of The Song of Songs, the three groups agreed with each other—and with a modern critical reader—was in seeing it as a love-song. Indeed, one can hardly imagine any possible reading of the work that would not recognize this as its fundamental character. After all, the opening verse[9] reads "Let him kiss me with the kisses of his mouth: for thy love is better than wine"; and nowhere from that start to the ardent finish—"Make haste, O my love . . ."[10]—is there a change of tone. They diverged strikingly, however—from each other and from modern critical reading—in their view of what sort of love, and whose love for whom. In each of the communities there were—and were known to be[11]—several interpretations. Many of them are by any historical standard major. The chief Jewish reading saw The Song as depicting the love of God for the Jewish community, or nation; and as delineating that community's national history over the centuries. The chief Christian view presented it as declaring Christ's love for the Church, or for the soul of the individual Church member. The mediæval philosophers read it as setting forth the love of the active for the passive intellect—a salient issue in philosophic thought at the time (and still today in an almost unrecognizably different form a central question for the meaning of human rationality). Let us glance at each of these in turn.

In observing, as we have done just now, that Jewish reading saw in the fervent work a presentation of God's love for that community and a sketch of its national history, a modern outsider is inclined to think of these as two motifs, and to be interested both in how the second came to be perceived as embedded in the apparently quite unhistoricizing Song, and in how the two were combined.

Typical is Rashi's understanding of chapter 2 verse 6, which the King James Authorised Version renders: "His left hand is under my head, and his right hand doth embrace me". For Rashi, and for the multitude that responded eagerly to his commentary, this verse affirms God's loving support of the Jews in the desert after the Exodus from Egypt, including such matters as His providing *manna* for their nourishment. In his Introduction, Rashi remarks that King Solomon—titular author of the work—was imbued by the Holy Spirit (*ruah ha-q-qodesh*) with the capacity also to foresee the future of the Jewish people. At various points in his commentary Rashi presents the text as envisioning the Babylonian Exile, the building of the Second Temple, its destruction by the Romans, the subsequent diaspora of the Jewish people with their suffering then a series of exiles, and so on. Beyond this, he read and presented The Song as referring to events not only future to Solomon as its author but future also to them as its readers, culminating in their final triumph at the coming of the Messiah; all undergirded by the sustained and sustaining care of The Most High.

Outsiders regularly recognize that the Jews' sense of community is strong. Those outsiders sometimes fail to appreciate, however, how utterly integral and even primary this is in the religious vision and feeling: how far the sense of participating—loyally—in the group (and of being participated in by it) is not a consequence so much as a foundational component of Jewish faith[12]. Furthermore, outsiders sometimes fail to appreciate how far, for the Jew, the community of which he or she is a member exists also in time, stretching down through past centuries and on into the future. For many others, and even for some Jews now in our anhistorical unspiritual age, the very word "community" has come to connote simply synchronic rather than also, and even primarily, diachronic group involvement.

When we speak, therefore, of The Song of Songs' being heard (as it was at the very least once a year in the synagogue service at Passover), or being read, by mediæval Jews as depicting the love of God for their nation, and as portraying that nation's history over the ages, this was not two motifs, as an outsider might be tempted to suppose, but one: a statement of God's love for His nation from its inception through to its final redemption. The reader thus participated in the *Heilsgeschichte* herein recognized as the loving deed of a gracious God. That reader was embraced in it, we may say. The Jewish sense of community and history clearly underlay this reading, and contributed to it; but in turn was preserved, heightened, vivified by it.

In addition, it was modified by it, as was many another component of their outlook on life by further aspects of their reading of The Song. Speaking of the impact of our work on the Jewish attitude to the community's central theme, the "Law", a modern Jewish scholar writes of "the Rabbis['] . . . allegorical treatment of the Song of Songs. . . . To the Jew, the text and its Midrash infused a feminine quality of love and warmth into a life of rigor and unending duty. In Aggadic Midrash the imagination ranged freely, . . . converting law to love and ritual to caress. The Bible was no longer only the guide and master of the Jew; it was his intimate companion, his alter ego."[13]

Apart from the material discerned in The Song, in its functioning as scripture in Jewish life, also to be noted is the sheer fact that it is, and was felt to be, a Song, fervent and strong. Reputed as composed shortly after "The Golden Era of Jewish history began when Solomon ascended to the throne of his illustrious father" King David[14], in celebration of the completion of the glorious Holy Temple, the poem was cherished in later ages as resonating with praise to God and joy in serving Him[15]. The whole universe sings to God's glory. Human beings must overcome evil, inward and without, to be able to hear this true music of the spheres, but meanwhile may delight in verbal songs of divine praise, among which this of Solomon is emphatically the grandest. In it God Himself is seen to delight.

Nor is it a merely passive matter, the hearer or reader listening to expressions of ecstasy—of the love between God and Israel. As is fundamentally the case with religious symbolism generally, it activates as well as represents, elicits as well as reveals. Rabbis reported that the intimacy with God that The Song both signifies and generates enabled those who read it with genuine understanding to perceive the created world around them as, and to turn their own lives into, a pæan of rapturous praise.

(Although modern skeptics might have reservations as to whether it was specifically scripture that did the "enabling" here, one could not question at least that it helped.)

The historicizing vision so prominent in Jewish reading of The Song differs from Christian tendencies at the time, which felt it, as we shall be observing presently, as simply contemporary: a here-and-now presence of the divine. One might wonder whether this may have had to do with the sorrowfulness of Jewish life at that time, under oppression and under the constant threat—or actuality—of persecution. Verse after verse was read by Jews as reminding them of the flourishing of their community in the Golden Age of a happier past, in the land of Israel from which they were currently wrenched far away but whose idealized memory and their relation to it were kept vivid in their minds and hearts by this particular scripture as indeed by the general complex of their religious and communal life. Comparably this scripture was read too as promising them a still happier future in the magnificent redemption of their nation—and through them, some added, of the world—at the coming Messianic age.

This sense of continuity through time, of participating in a community in long-range motion, did not exclude the here-and-now. Awareness of past and future as "ours" did not crowd out the present but enriched it. (Many moderns, in contrast, absorbing a different spirit from current culture, have so distanced themselves from their heritage, from previous times, that these are felt as radically "other". They perceive history not as an on-going process in which they are currently participating but as a fixed and alien era of "the past" to which their "identity" consists in their not belonging.) The Song was one of the important ways in which mediæval Jews appropriated to themselves—were enabled to appropriate—a richness in their lives without which those lives would have been bleak; in some cases, unrelievedly so.

Nonetheless, a modern reader of their commentaries cannot but be struck not only by the richness attested but also by the bleakness evinced. Particularly noticeable are re-iterated references to dire sinfulness, as presumably the grounds for current suffering and alienation from God. Rashi, for instance, repeatedly speaks of the current situation of Israel, in Exile, as that of the virtual "widow" of a living husband, constantly remembering God's love from their former life together[16].

By reading, cherishing, reverencing it, by recognizing it as scripture, not only were Jews assured of solidarity with their fellows[17] and of the solidarity of their fellows with them, and that their life had depth and meaning and richness, both in personal and in cosmic terms. More substantially, it was—became—a matter not simply of assurance but of fact. By their recognizing it as scripture, an historian observes, the solidarity was actually there; and their life did in fact have depth and meaning and richness—certainly at the personal level, and if the historian be perceptive, also at the cosmic.

It is not, however, simply that the sinfulness is now, the joyous intimacy between God and Israel was long ago. The nation's sinfulness in the making of the Golden Calf at the time of the Exodus is mentioned often, as the interpretation of many a verse; but also the present exuberance of rejoicing in the Lord, and of His exulting in His continuing love for His great—and only—favourite, Israel.

The way that The Song was heard and read is evidence not so much that mediæval Jewish life was dismal, as that it would have been dismal without scripture.

Christian reading of The Song was in some ways strikingly similar; in others, subtly and significantly different. Let us look at Doctor-Saint Bernard, the work's most influential expositor in the mediæval Christian world, as was Rashi in the Jewish.

When Bernard died, the unfinished eighty-sixth in his series of eloquent and elaborate *Sermones* ("discourses"?[18]) on The Song carried the exploration of this text into though not to the end of its second chapter. We may note first of all that these do not constitute a formal commentary on the text, like Rashi's. Rather, as the title suggests, they were essays proffered as homiletic pieces.

Despite the incompleteness, there is more in his forceful material, as in Rashi's, than we can cover or summarize in brief compass, of course. Yet it is not unfair to select for primary attention one point: that Bernard sees in the Song, and writes so that his readers may see, the setting forth of human destiny as joyous union with God—a union attained in love, of God and of one's neighbour. Most moderns see in that same Song rather—some would say: merely—an ardent poem of love between the sexes, indeed of passionate attraction between particular individuals. Bernard is of course quite aware that that is a possible reading, but is also fully confident that it is a misreading due to those readers' limited vision, limited experience, limited love of God and of humankind more widely; yet due also to their sorely inadequate appreciation of the divine nature already within themselves waiting to be developed. He would not be surprised that the worldly outlook that tends to be brought by modern secular predispositions to this and to all reading would obscure the true import of this text. He would be sorrowful that even religious readers today tend to approach it with an orientation presuming a polarity between the divine and the human. Bernard yields to few in acknowledging human wickedness; and he urges an utterly honest recognition by each of us of our personally wretched condition. He reverts to this often. Yet he insists that, far from being basic, it is a foreign overlay disfiguring the fundamental likeness to God that is the original and eternal nature of each human person[19]. The aspiration to rise to a merging with God, in glorious communion, of which the union of the bridegroom and the bride in the Song is a metaphor, is not merely legitimate, even though the soul be "burdened with sin . . . ensnared by the allurements of pleasure . . . caught in mud . . . afflicted with sorrow, wandering and straying . . ."[20]. The aspiration is, even, almost inescapable: How should that soul fail to have such boldness and confidence in God, when it discerns within itself His image?[21].

This does not mean, however, that for him humanity is divine. He distinguishes the two; at times grossly, so vividly does he feel, and presume that his readers or hearers will of course feel, the terrifying contrast between us in our floundering sinfulness and God's majesty and splendour. At other times, however, the distinction is subtle, rather: as, that Christ *is* the image of God; we human beings are created *after* the image of God[22]. Again: when a human person is united with God, they two become *unus* though not *unum*: the latter term applies only to God and Christ.

Despite all this, Bernard would "proceed with caution" in his reading of The Song, stressing the "mystery" in which the wisdom in "this sacred and mystical utterance" is hidden[23]. He is very conscious, and keeps reminding his readers, that the magnificent truth proffered in this scripture is beyond our firm comprehension. Nonetheless he finds in the work not merely confidence but encouragement to press on to explore: a confidence and encouragement that his sermons made contagious.

Bernard reads The Song, then, and guides his audience to reading it, as invitingly affirming the glorious heights to which humanity may rise, and indeed is intended to rise. Yet in no wise does his exposition suggest that realizing these aspirations will be at all easy; let alone, in any fashion automatic. The contrast drawn between the actual situation and the potential is stark. What The Song expresses, and encourages, in the midst of deeply troubled life, is constant yearning. What it offers is firm and unflustered hope. What it prescribes is rigorous discipline, for the journey from where we in mundane fact are to where rightly we should be and where God's flowing mercy and abounding love are ready, despite our own incapacity and unworthiness, to take us.

Accordingly, for Bernard the message of this scripture, in addition to the vision of a final mystic oneness, is of careful moral refinement and realistic spiritual growth. These are ancillary, yet quite explicit, and integral to the whole: specific practical steps towards the ultimate goal. Thus for him the verse[24] that in the King James Authorised Version reads "By night on my bed I sought him whom my soul loveth" refers, of course, to the soul's longing for and active seeking of the Lord, and means in general that modesty and reticence are being enjoined in contradistinction from any ostentatious piety[25]. (In his exposition of the passage he cites quite naturally as parallel Christ's admonition in the Gospel of Matthew to pray to the Father in secret[26].) It means in particular that the best place for one's devotions is in the privacy of one's own room ("if we pray when others are present, their approbation may rob our prayer of . . . its effect"[27]), and that the best time is the wee small hours, when others are quietly asleep (those others whom ironically we moderns might be inclined to call "less dreamy"!).

Similarly, the beloved being said to be "among the lilies"[28] inspires him to quite an interesting array of thoughts, of which one is to exhort himself and his hearers or readers to "take care to have lilies in your soul, if you wish to have him who dwells among the lilies dwelling in you"[29], declaring that one's actions, one's endeavours, and one's desires should be such lilies. He goes on to discriminate between the colour and the fragrance of this flower, and to elaborate on that. These two he sees as signifying for actions, for instance, inner quality and overt reputation respectively—rather in the fashion of the more recent "Let justice be done and be seen to be done"[30]; though Bernard cites rather Romans 12:17[31]. He develops the distinction nicely and stresses that it is certainly better to have inward purity without good report than *vice versa*; the latter alone is no virtue. The combination of both is, however, best; is necessary to constitute a lily, colour plus fragrance[32].

Bernard, then, was not that kind of mystic for whom union with the Absolute is a substitute for moral striving and conformity to obligation, nor even an alternative to them. For him it is, rather, their result, and their reward. *Transformamur cum conformamur* [33]: we are transformed into God's likeness as we are conformed to His will. Accordingly, he finds in what to us is the passionate imagery of The Song not only the depiction of a promised glory but also the details of the exacting route that will lead to it.

I mentioned his coalescing of a passage from the Gospel and a verse from The Song. This is quite typical of his, and of his era's, reading of Scripture as a total coherence. At times he (whose intimate and ready familiarity with the entire Bible is striking) includes in a single passage citations or phrases from a half dozen books of the two Testaments[34]. At every point he assumes, and assumes that his readers will assume, that the entire Bible presents not merely a coherent, but a single (though not a simple!) message. The meaning of any part of it is illumined, or even perhaps in some sense is for readers determined, by the meaning of other parts and of the whole.

Given his understanding of what scripture is, such a view is of course altogether reasonable; and we shall be observing that something of the sort is common also for other bodies of scripture and other communities across the world. In fact, we may find ourselves inferring that part of what it means to regard a body of literature as scriptural is to recognize it as an integrated unity. In Bernard's case, this general consideration is fortified or supplemented by—or: underlies—his personal mystic propensity, tending towards seeing all things as coherent and ultimately one.

Even in regard to scripture, the unity that he saw was—in line with what we found in our first chapter above—not that of a book. Like others in his era, he did not know, did not perceive, presumably had never seen, the Bible as a single volume. Rather, unity for him lay in what the various books that he knew as scripture had to say: the unity of God's message to humankind.

A further matter arises here, in Bernard's reading of this work. No doubt, to treat a piece of literature as scripture is *a priori* to rule out contradictions, or even serious divergences. These can be at most apparent, or preliminary. Yet there is involved at the same time another quality that one might regard as over against this, yet from another perspective may be seen as part and parcel of the same matter. The very elevation that lifts the whole above such human mundane failings as inconsistencies also means that the right meaning of any given passage is, as Bernard recurrently attests, so lofty as to be perhaps beyond our reach.

As previously observed, what is proffered in scripture is transcendent truth. The words that we read are "deep in mystery", and present us with a mystery that we must struggle to explore—that it is our privilege to explore. This is a point that Bernard makes often[35]. Furthermore, in line with this he is quite conscious of the fact that the task of human discerning of the meaning often means in effect a choice. The reader is free, one might say, to choose how to interpret an ambiguous passage, except that that freedom is constrained by the vivid awareness that it is at the best possible meaning that one is striving to arrive. (A modern critical reading, in contrast, searches not for the best meaning, in a metaphysical sense, but for the most probable meaning in an historicizing one.) An example of his diffidence: Bernard may remark that "there is no answer" to a question as to who is being addressed in a particular passage[36], and then add "unless perhaps" it be so-and-so; but he then continues, "I think it better to suppose" that it is . . . [37]. Again: "If anyone thinks that this should be understood . . . in the sense that . . . , I do not dissent"[38]. His tentativenesss appears regularly: "I do not think it would be wrong to say . . ."[39].

His total confidence about God's love, and about the strict moral obligations that this entails, go along with a humility about his own (or any human being's) ability to apprehend them—let alone, to live up to them. Both the confidence and the humility are given strength by his reading of scripture.

If we turn next to the restricted circle of mediæval philosophers' reading of the Song, we may note that the variety of interpretations was of course less. The work was in some instances seen as indicating "the mysterious harmony of the universe"; or "the union of the divine soul with the earthly body"[40]. The primary and most significant view, however, was as we have remarked that it depicted love between the active and the passive intellect.

Aristotle's rather elusive positing of these as two distinct matters[41] had presently become explicit and was developed within the general Greek legacy to the Muslim world and to Europe of perceiving the universe as rational, and human beings—alone among living things—as participating, at least potentially, in that cosmic rationality. By the time with which we are here concerned, this movement of ideas had meanwhile been enriched (some would say, merely: had been modified) by the neo-Platonic outlook, with which indeed for some thinkers it had merged (though Plotinus himself had not used these particular terms). By this stage the Active Intellect was regarded as a primary cosmic principle, equated in some cases (especially among the Arab philosophers) with God or the first reality and in any case viewed as the prime emanation of the Absolute. It was further seen as that which turns the potential intellect of each of us into whatever particular intelligence, awareness, we may severally attain. Plato had emphasized our love of Truth; and Aristotle—as the famous opening sentence of his *Metaphysics* asserts— the universal human "impulse to know". *Philosophia* means "love of wisdom". In this reading of The Song, however, Truth also loves to be known; and Wisdom ardently meets more than half way those who pursue her. This enhanced the neo-Platonists' vision of Truth's, or The One's, or this Active Intellect's, unceasing exuberance downwards towards the rest of the universe and us. Thus The Song provided for those thinking in this fashion an image of fervent mutuality in the love that helps define philosophy. The Active Intellect, which is the cause of the intelligibility of things, is indeed active. The aspiration of those of us that are intellectuals to know, to pursue the truth, not merely is supplemented but is preceded and is sustained by a force greater than we individually—or even collectively. The final goal is an apprehension through the mind of—is one's mind being apprehended by—all that truly is: a transcending of one's solipsistic self in a union with the no longer other.

What are we to make of these three sorts of reading of The Song, all starkly alien to modern sophistication? Let us consider first their positive significance, in so far as we may be able to discern something of the sort. We will then reflect more negatively, critically assessing what price the mediævals paid for such treasures as they may have found in the work treated as scripture. Throughout, we bear in mind that our purpose in this present study is to move towards understanding not what is the real or correct meaning of this particular text—nor of any other[42]—but rather, what does it mean, and in this case what did it mean at this period in this part of the world to these groups, to have a scripture, to read a text scripturally.

Relevant here is the statement, "We read the Gita not in order to understand the Gita. Rather, we read it, if we are Hindus, in order to understand the world, and our life within it; and if we are historians, in order to understand how the world has been seen by Hindus, to understand what the Gita has been doing to people these two thousand years or so as under its influence they have gone about their daily business, and their cosmic business"[43].

Something similar is to be noted with regard to our approach to the role of The Song of Songs in mediæval Jewish and Christian and philosophic life. Rashi's and for instance Ibn 'Aqnin's works[44] were formally commentaries on the text, whereas Bernard's was rather, as we have noted, a set of homiletic discourses inspired each by a verse or phrase, in systematic sequence; these discourses therefore were each written (or preached?) explicitly for moral and spiritual edification. Yet this formal distinction makes little substantial difference. All three aimed at proffering not, in the fashion of modern exegesis, "the meaning of the text", but the meaning of the universe, of world history, of human life: of the readers' own lives as they read, or as they set forth about their affairs after reading. They aspired to *that* meaning considered in the light of the words here proffered. Considered in the light of "the text", one might say, except that on reflection it becomes clear that this too will not do: we shall be arguing that the idea of a text, as an object to be understood, is modern and impersonal and subordinating, characterizing present-day culture's objectivizing orientation to the world[45]. Their intent was rather to discern that meaning in the light of what God had to say to them.

There is a difference, obviously, between two attitudes that we may imagine towards a telegram that a person away from home may receive, and that reads, let us suppose: "Dear Jane. Come home at once; Mother critically ill. Dad". In the one case we may picture the recipient's reacting to the news with whatever emotional response and practical steps may apply in the particular instance. In another case, we may envisage attention's being given to the text, with the applicable questions then being, rather: first, of course, is it a hoax, or a forgery; if genuine as text, was it nonetheless composed some years ago by someone else's father and sent to *his* daughter Jane, it being somehow retrieved and delivered now to quite another person of the same first name, but otherwise in a drastically different situation and to whom the message has no relevance; and so on. No one could argue that whether the telegram is genuine, and whether the situation that it addresses is indeed the recipient's situation, are unimportant issues. Yet neither would one suggest that the two orientations to the telegram do not diverge.

It is manifest that each of the mediæval writers that we have considered, and—we may presume—their readers also, brought to their reading of Scripture their particular complex of presuppositions. We too bring our complex of presuppositions to our reading of the same text, or of any text. We differ from them not in this point, but simply—yet it is not simple!—in that our presuppositions are different ones. It is not that we do not have them, nor that they are not powerful in determining how we read. There is one potential difference in this matter, as yet actualized however among but few: namely, that today our awareness of historical development and of cultural diversity means that we may, with effort, become to some degree self-conscious of our particular worldview, recognizing it as one among others, and to that extent may transcend it. Thereby we may forge a new outlook that is aware of the particularity of our former one, and to some extent aware therefore of its limitations and bias, as seen now in the light both of that very particularity and of newly discerned obviously possible alternatives. At its best the new outlook will be aware also of the on-going movements in which those others and one's own take their respective places. Ideally we reach towards a new outlook subsuming the positive qualities of our own prior view and positive qualities from the significant alternatives.

Such transcending, however, is not easy. Self-criticism seldom is. Yet it is greatly rewarding.

To apprehend aright, however, what was going on in Rashi's or Bernard's or other such reading of The Song, it is requisite that we note not merely the ideational presuppositions of each, important though these be, but also the whole range of the writer's Jewish or Christian or philosophic involvements and sensitivity and commitments and aspirations. This last is as important as any of the others. For each writer, his understanding of the work is a function not only of where he was coming from but also of where he was going. His reading can be understood only as an activity—within his religious life: as a moment within the process of his spiritual development.

May we not say, then, that for a work to be scripture means that it participates in the movement of the spiritual life of those for whom it is so. At times they poured into it, but also then they got out of it, the highest, best, fullest to which their mind or imagination or heart could rise.

It is not only that their life shaped the meaning that scripture had for them. The further, and more noteworthy, point is that for each, that scripture and the meaning that it had for him or her, the fact of its being scripture, shaped them. Too, it shaped then the course of history. The first point has recently been fairly widely recognized: that the ambience of the time affected—almost, effected—the way that a sector of scripture was understood. With our modern self-conscious awareness of cultural diversity, of the specificity to time and place of all our ideas, this point can be fairly clearly grasped. The second point, on the other hand—that the understanding of each part of scripture, and of the whole, not merely affected the lives of those who read but to a significant degree determined them, and effected, certainly affected, the course of history: this has been less adequately explained. It is at least equally important for our endeavour in this present study to understand the enigmatic role of scripture in human affairs.

Not only are the earnestness and fervour striking, even the exaltation, with which these writers approached their reading of The

Song; or shall we not more accurately also say, with which they came away from such reading. Also striking, in for instance the case of Bernard, is the poetic mood in which—his discourses on the work are lively evidence—he lived his life. That poetic mood stands in contrast with the prosaic mode in which most of us moderns live ours. We are inclined to dismiss as romantic or sentimental, if not sheer fancy, his reading The Song and finding in it not a mundane love-lyric but an expansive invitation to rise to love of God and love of neighbour and to abide there, in that simultaneous contemplation and action; and finding from it a firm re-assurance that this is not merely possible but inherently right and humanly proper, that anything else is an aberration. Certainly a sophisticated modern does not find it easy to converge with that vision; or at least, not with this way of formulating it and of being re-assured of it. Yet neither must we be swift in ignoring these nor in relegating them to a bygone era irrelevant to a comprehending of the human condition, or even of our condition. It repays us to strive to understand and indeed to appreciate how it was that so intelligent and learned an administrator saw The Song so, and saw the world so; and made available to a growing public an ability to agree and to applaud, to cherish, and to be uplifted. Clearly we have here, and in Rashi and the philosophers, a revealing illustration of what it meant, in the thought and lives of an age, to have a scripture, to relate to a work scripturally; a forceful indication of the richness that this effectually signified.

An historian, seeking to understand the development of Western civilization and the life of its people over a long period, or any philosopher or humanist or social scientist seeking to understand the human condition, neglects then at serious cost the role of this Song in this phase of human affairs. The treatment of this work—and we have selected out only two main types and one rather peripheral one from among several comparable treatments in the Middle Ages—brought a richness and depth into people's lives that have little parallel in the twentieth century, when this way of reading it has largely been replaced, often by no reading at all or no diligent reading, or else by another sort of treatment altogether. Let us turn now to an example of this last, as our next way of viewing the work: the modern academic.

It can be equally assiduous, equally solid, involving the same or even perhaps greater devotion to the text, certainly elaborate annotation. Yet it is based on quite another set of presuppositions. It involves another, radically divergent, "approach", as current jargon has it. To illustrate it, one may select a comparably impressive work from this new orientation: the recent volume on The Song of Songs in the Anchor Bible series of commentaries, by the Yale scholar Professor Marvin Pope[46]. It is a seven-hundred-page work of modern historical-critical scholarship, a work of certainly the same first-rate quality in its line as Rashi's and Bernard's works are of first-rate quality in theirs. One comes away sure that it is the product of several years of painstaking effort and very close attention to the text. It too takes its place in the development of a substantial historical tradition, going back to Spinoza[47] and the Enlightenment—and carrying forward that development to new levels.

The other authors that we have cited illustrate similar major historical developments: in the Rashi case going back probably to Rabbi 'Aqiba and others in the first-to-second century and in any case to the accepted interpretation as evinced for instance even in the authoritative "translation"—actually in this case a homiletic and decidedly allegorizing paraphrase[48]—of the Bible into Aramaic known as the Targum (in its present form, probably seventh century)[49]. Bernard's sense of The Song goes back at least to Origen in the third. Origen's powerful and still today entrancing commentary proved seminal[50].

The Pope volume investigates the text, of course, in the original Hebrew—and not the languages in which, as scripture, it is or has been chiefly read—giving elaborate heed to variations of manuscript and variations among early translations in a range of other early languages, now otherwise mostly forgotten. Not only so, but it considers the work also in the light of still more ancient sources that may well have impinged on its Biblical form. (It has been found that these were many, and curious.) It attends too to other considerations that may illuminate the situation out of which the Song as it was eventually formalized arose; or that may illuminate the distinguishable parts out of which it was eventually put together. The study simply does impressively well what modern Biblical scholarship in general is expected to do and does.

As usual, the primary thrust is to reconstruct as accurately as may be the "original" meaning of the text, of the passages and verses one by one, of the genre, and so on. Yet Pope's differs from most instances of this sort of modern study in one important new way. In this presentation the work being investigated is not placed entirely at a great distance in time from ourselves (a distance notoriously difficult to bridge). For there is in addition one substantial section that presents and analyses the history of interpretation over the intervening centuries: in early and then mediæval and in modern times. This last—the modern—is thereby seen in several cases as continuous with one or another of the multifarious earlier types of meaning that The Song has had for its readers, but in other cases as introducing relatively new emphases, including, for instance, feminism.

The more usual academic study of the Bible in modern times has presented Biblical theology with a tantalizing dichotomy between what the text meant and what it means today, or can reasonably or homiletically be taken to mean[51]. Placing oneself rather within the on-going process of its role as scripture, a further category of thinking, "what it has meant", transmutes the problem significantly.

In addition to our three mediæval and one modern academic instances of varying ways of treating this sector of Scripture, there is a fifth to which also we would draw attention. It is earlier, and might be called the original usage of the work, except that once again under modern historical-critical analysis the concept of "original" tends to crumble. Let us call it simply one prevalent early treatment of the material, before it became part of the Bible[52]. There is some argument that the work developed out of remarkably early, or surprisingly distant, predecessors (Egypt, Syria, Babylonia; and developing even since Pope's work, South India[53]; scholars argue against each other on these points). In any case, it has been shown that this work (or at least large parts of it) at one time was, or was treated as, what we today would call a somewhat run-of-the-mill love-song. There is indisputable evidence that it was sung irreverently in taverns[54] in the first century A.D.[55] (No explicit reference to God occurs in The Song—despite the mediæval commentators' finding implicit references from or to God in virtually every verse.)

Also, the work was slow in being accepted into the canon, and then came in only under considerable protest[56].

We moderns, then, find ourselves invited to ponder these five ways of looking at The Song of Songs. We must remember that there have been others; yet these are probably the most important historically, and in any case will well serve to point our concerns there. Before we reflect on them in their stark mutual difference, let us consider for a moment also their less obvious interrelations.

Were it not for what Rashi and Bernard represent—the mediæval Jewish and Christian cherishing of the Song, and of the Bible generally; and their discerning in it of metaphysical, theological, ultimate human, worth—then modern scholarly studies such as Pope's would not be being written, or published, or read. It is the Western legacy of an erstwhile sense of the Bible's supreme importance that has generated the prodigious effort of modern Biblical scholarship, even though that scholarship itself does not share or support a notion of importance, or worth; let alone, of metaphysical status, or theological or salvific role. Take away mediæval notions of the Bible, and modern attention to its parts would neither have arisen nor continue to be funded. Again, that The Song of Songs grew out of a secular love-ditty sung in taverns, or again perhaps out of formalized Ancient Near Eastern fertility cults or even pagan funeral-wake ceremonies, is something that we know only because modern Biblical and historical scholarship has in turn unearthed it. Moreover, our ability to see mediæval Jewish and Christian interpretations in relation to each other, which at the time appeared contradictory and mutually divisive, is also a function of a modern intellectual outlook, that of comparativist history.

Nonetheless, despite such intertwinings, one's primary stress must be on the fact that these various visions have been disparate. They represent five distinct phases in a complex and on-going historical process. The others lack the historical erudition of Pope, and his sense of particularity and of change over time. Pope lacks the abandon and lilt of the tavern song: one is not surprised that his work is serious, is in prose, is devoid (almost!) of music; it lacks, of course, also the cosmic reach of either the Jewish Rashi or the Christian Bernard: the ontological godliness and moral uplift. These last two writers lack the qualities both of their early predecessors and of their late successors, of course; they lack also an authentic appreciation of each other's vision. Neither calls his reader's attention to the other community's position or the way that The Song serves that community's spiritual life[57]. And the tipplers in the taverns, we may be sure, were unaware of or were drowning out any of the other interpretive perceptions.

What are we to do in the face of this variety?

Most moderns are either unaware of it, or have of late been turning from it. They have been moving away from variety of interpretative method in principle, choosing only one view. For "Fundamentalists", this is whichever one historical position they like to deem orthodox; and to it they will cling. For others, especially among intellectuals, the one view has usually meant siding with the likes of Pope. We are with him, most of us, not merely in accepting the kinds of question that he asks, and of finding that he reports; but many also in rejecting what he rejects, of the other perceptions of the work, particularly the mediæval devotional readings. These he thinks of as historically interesting but often "bizarre"[58]. Most moderns dismiss them casually as obviously barking up a wrong tree. Modern Biblical scholarship in principle as well as in practice has tended to assume that to read The Song or any other book in the Bible—let alone, the Qur'an or the Lotus Sutra—with the view that God is speaking to *us*, personally, *now*, in and through that text is ("was") to adopt an orientation remote and irrelevant, if not benighted. The mainline Church, and liberal Jews, to a large extent accepted, heroically after a profound struggle, the positive side of Biblical scholarship's outlook, without thinking through the negative implications; and with but little to propose as to how to supplement the position. Secularists and academics accepted it, with no reason to query or to amplify.

We will come back to this issue in due course. For the moment, we wish simply to suggest that the richness and depth of the mediæval readings, their moral and spiritual strength, deserve notice. Has their loss not meant an impoverishment of modern life? We may repeat the remarks made above: that in mediæval life—both Christian and Jewish, even if in separate ways—The Song of Songs was "prevalent, central, beloved, and inspiring. . . . people were stirred, their spirits mightily encouraged". This work succeeded in convincingly attesting that God loves us, cares for us, is close to us, and one might venture to say yearns, certainly delights, to have us love Him, to live close to Him. Such facts are hardly negligible.

Manifestly, we today cannot go back to those earlier interpretations. We have lost the innocence that was one of the foundations on which the imposing edifice was built. (It was by no means the only foundation!) By now that innocence has been lost, or become not that but ignorance—or ignoring. Those moderns who deliberately choose it and opt for it seem a menace to the rest of us and to society at large—and spiritually a menace to themselves. A religious stance that excludes intellectual integrity is ill. Rather, one accepts Pope's questions, and answers, not only totally, in principle, but joyously. I have cited his work because it is a sheer delight of brilliant modern scholarship. About its historical information one is surely enthusiastic; I reject nothing in, subtract nothing from, his thesis. Add to it, however, we decisively should. Much remains to be done.

One welcomes with delight the innovative move of including in an authoritative study of an ancient text a survey of that work's spiritual reception over the intervening centuries; a move that points in a direction for future major developments. The new vision that will inform the next great step in this realm will ask new questions. It will build on the wide range of historical data that we now have, but in taking these seriously it will incorporate new sensitivities, and involve new orientations.

The richness of those intervening centuries is surely no small attainment. Nonetheless, if we today must not fail to recognize that attainment, equally we must concede that it was reached by a route not open to us now. We are not able, for instance, to follow Jewish commentators in their "gematria": applying to the Biblical words calculations constructed by giving to their individual Hebrew letters the arithmetic value assigned to each in the mediæval Hebrew notational system (now known to have been first introduced into Jewish life and thought several long centuries after the Bible itself had been completed), and then toying with implications of that number or equating that word with some other word of the same numerical value. Thus in the opening verse, "Thy love is better than wine", the word for "wine" (Hebrew *yayin*, spelled y-y-n; these letters, if read as representing numbers rather than sounds, signify 10+10+50, or 70—one might compare Roman "LXX") was at times taken as meaning the "seventy nations"—the various peoples of the world, other than the Jews themselves. The verse was accordingly presented[59] as affirming that Israel, the beloved of God, is more precious in His sight than all the rest of humankind. Rashi[60] and many others interpret "wine" often as connoting, rather, Torah[61], "the delights of Torah"; some went on to mention the seventy facets of Torah exegesis as involved in that equivalence.

Nor can we go along with Rashi in interpreting love as signifying God's overflowing love that includes His merciless slaughtering of the enemies of Israel; nor with Bernard, in his anti-Semitism, his casual yet firm assumption that Christians are spiritual, Jews earth-bound and lost.

Again, few today are capable of reading " . . . he shall lie all night betwixt my breasts"[62] and feeling as does Rashi that this designates the Tabernacle where the divine presence may dwell amid the Holy Ark's staves[63]; or are capable of following Christian expositors in feeling that the two breasts of the bride designate the Old and New Testaments[64], or alternatively—though is this perchance a whit less remote?—the two great commandments, love of God and love of one's neighbour[65]. Nor are most of us willing to go along with Bernard's denunciation of corporeal love as inherently sinful[66], to be on principle vehemently rejected[67]. (Moderns are more likely to feel pity for the sort of unhappy position that was evidently his[68].)

And so on. Hardly a paragraph of mediæval writing on this work fails to alert a modern reader to the major time-gap and the formidable cultural chasm separating that writing from us, for all its evidence of majestically worthwhile personal engagement.

Modern mystics, and indeed various earlier ones such as Teresa of Avila and certainly John of the Cross, may happily identify love between a man and a woman with the ultimate cosmic love spoken of theologically as between God and the human; may feel that erotic love at its highest not merely is symbolic of, but finally converges with, divine. In this vein one may see the inclusion of The Song of Songs in scripture as indeed attesting to such symbolism, and such convergence. Bernard, in sharp contrast, saw and felt the two loves as not merely diverging but as relentlessly at war with each other.

The particular illustration that we have selected, therefore, the mediæval Song of Songs, we said at the beginning might seem an arbitrary choice. In many ways unique (but then, so are all scriptures), it also may perhaps serve to exemplify some at least of the problems for our day of scripture as a category. It does not itself, of course, provide any solutions. It will have served its purpose if it makes us sense more clearly the elusiveness of these.

Two points, we may say, it suggests. One is that in the past, scripture has played certainly a mighty and often an enriching role in human life over the centuries. The other is that in the present, new ways of being involved with it and incorporating it into modern life are required if a role of even remotely comparable might and richness is to be continued or in some fashion recaptured. One might infer that evidently an alternative road to a similar goal will have to be found or constructed; or a different destination sought via scripture; or the notion surrendered that scripture is still a significant category. Before coming to those sorts of conclusion, however, on the basis of a single instance however illustrative—let alone, before pondering possible alternative routes or alternative goals or probing for possible future significance in this category—we must look more comprehensively at the world situation; and must lay a basis for understanding more thoroughly what has been going on in human life in this matter.

Complex that situation has surely been; and in motion. Let us explore further salient aspects of its variety. And first, let us inquire into how scripture arose in the first place as a significant human involvement.

CHAPTER 3

SCRIPTURE AS FORM
AND CONCEPT:
HISTORICAL BACKGROUND

WE HAVE LOOKED at how a particular piece of scripture served a particular people at a particular time. There are other scriptures, other peoples, other times, and we have emphasized that they must be taken into consideration before a general conception is formed of the place of scripture in human life. This will hold our attention in later chapters. Here we turn, however, to a question seldom asked, yet logically prior. How does it come about that there are on earth such matters as scriptures, to play the diverse yet apparently related or comparable roles that we find them playing? The question has historical dimensions and—as we shall be exploring in more focus in our concluding chapter—human, cosmic, ones. Here we may take time to look at the former, the emergence in time.

Taken for granted for some while now in the West has been that of course many religions have scriptures. Of course these differ, one knows, in what they have to say; and both the immediate background and the outcome of each scripture's saying this or that have been observed. The fact that all of them are there at all has been less studied.

Everything that exists on earth, however, has come into existence historically. It is rewarding, as one considers the panorama of human affairs, to take nothing for granted, inquiring rather into the process by which things that exist have come to be. This turns out especially so of matters so massively important in human life as scripture has widely proven itself to be. There is value, certainly, in noting how things with which we are familiar and that we take for granted, partly because they have been with us for a long time, have in fact changed (evolved, degenerated) over time—and are still in process now. Important also is to recognize how it happened that the affair got started.

Our inquiry here is into the historical process by which the notion of scripturalizing arose, a couple of thousand years ago in the Near East. (To Far East developments, only partially related and much less crystallized, we allude in later chapters.) That Western process can be seen as coming to a head, as it were, over thirteen centuries ago in the Qur'an. It can be seen as constituted, gradually, of many strands, some of which go back very far, others were later than is often sensed. Let us see whether our understanding is furthered by our becoming more conscious of that process.

It is illuminating to begin with the seventh century A.D. as the virtually culminating stage of the process, and to trace it then backwards in time.

"Islam . . . is pre-eminently a . . . religion of the book", says the phenomenologist van der Leeuw[1]; and any who study Muslim history or any facet of Muslim life can document that characterization richly. The notion of a parallel between the Muslim Qur'an and the Christian Bible, as two instances of the genus scripture, is of course an approximation; yet it is only a first such. Closer to the truth of the two situations is an analogy between the role of the Qur'an in Islamic life and thought, and the role in Christian life and thought of the figure of Christ[2]. For Christians, God's central revelation is in the person of Christ, with the Bible as record of that revelation. Counterpart, in the Islamic scheme of things, to the latter, the record of the revelation, has been Muslim *hadith*, the so-called "Tradition", a secondary group of materials in the Islamic complex— decisive, yet secondary. Both sophisticated Muslim thinkers and comparativist Western scholars are beginning to accept this: that the genuine parallel is between the Qur'an and Christ, as the two paramount motifs[3].

Qur'an is to Muslims what Christ is to Christians. It is difficult to exaggerate the centrality, and the transcendence, of the Muslim scripture for Muslim faith. Other communities have produced sacred books; in the Islamic case it was the sacred book, rather, that has produced the community. Muslims, from the beginning until now, are that group of people that has coalesced around the Qur'an. Muhammad is important in the Islamic worldview because he brought the Qur'an; he derives his significance from that fact. The Muslim world protested when in the nineteenth century the West called its religious movement "Mohammedanism", as though he were primary. For Muslims, God is primary; their relation to Him (*iman*) is mediated through the Qur'an. For them, this scripture stands uncreated, pre-existent. The Word of God is eternal, is an attribute of God Himself; and like His other attributes, "it is not He nor is it other than He"[4]. Apart from these theoretical considerations—these theological parallels to Christology—the practical role of the Qur'an in Islamic life, individual and corporate, has throughout been central: not only in what the West calls law, and morality, piety, and liturgy, but in economics, in social polity, in art—especially calligraphy—, in grammar, and so on.

Muslims pay Jews and Christians the compliment of calling them also "People of the Book", by which they mean that these groups have what approximates, whether closely or in partially distorted fashion, to religion in its true and proper form—as distinct from pagans and idolators who, without divine revelation in this form, this book form, are lost.

We begin with these remarks not in order to speak about Islam, but in order to speak about scripture. The Islamic instance represents the notion *par excellence* of scripture as a religious item; and our thesis here is that it does so as the culmination of an historical process to be discerned in the Near East, gradually solidifying over the centuries. Scripture as a form and as a concept gradually emerged and developed in the Near East in a process of consolidation whose virtually complete stage comes with the Qur'an.

Many scholars have of late been reconstructing the story of this matter of scriptural consolidation in the circumscribed instance of the Bible—considering it there, as it were, internally. Here we are endeavouring to see the emergence of the Bible's context. For the process in which it was (better: in which the two Bibles, Jewish and Christian, were) involved—in which, one might better say, their coalescences were in due course involved—appears as having transcended their particular formation.

We are already suggesting that the process transcended that formation in time at this end by emerging in a more developed form in the seventh century A.D. in the Islamic movement. It transcended their formation in time at the other end by having been launched, scholars have of late recognized, in Babylonia and pre-Israelite Canaan in the second millenium B.C., as we shall remark later. It transcended them religiously, we can see if we note (moving backwards now from the Qur'an) the later Zarathushtrian and the Manichee and the Mandæan and the Babylonian and the Ancient Egyptian. It transcended them also culturally, if one takes into account, as it turns out that one must, the Alexandrian grammarians' canonizing of what we in their wake call the classics of Greek literature, at roughly the same time as, or a little before, the emergence (in the same town) of the Septuagint. One could readily argue that these, including the Greek Septuagint, had an influence on the development of a Jewish notion of scripture and then later a Christian one—or *vice versa*: influences, if one is to use that word, were active in both, or let us say all, directions. Yet rather than arguing that, we shall suggest rather that all the variegated parts of these several developments can best be understood as various details within one over-all process—which we are calling the emergence of scripture as form and concept for the Western world.

When we say that in the Qur'an this process culminates, we do not mean to suggest that it altogether stops at that point. Almost a thousand years later the Granth Sahib, the scripture of the then emergent Sikh community in India, the form of it and the concept of it and its place in the personal piety and corporate polity of the Sikh community over the next three or so centuries, until today, were manifestly influenced in turn by the Qur'an: by scripture as a form and a concept in the religious life of the Muslims with which the Sikh movement emerged as continuous[5]. That movement was continuous also, in another way and perhaps less closely, with the Hindu. Even closer to our own day, Joseph Smith in the United States with his Book of Mormon, for example[6], illustrates that the notion was still generative as recently as the nineteenth century, although in the twentieth it has become somewhat problematic even for older traditions.

Yet none of these instances carried the development any further. Qur'an and Bible have served as models for subsequent instances, but there has been no advance in form since the Qur'an. In, probably, the ninth century A.D., or in any case substantially after the

Muslim conquest of Iran, a Zarathushtrian book states that Zara-thushtra "brought the religion" and engraved the twelve hundred chapters of it on tablets of gold[7]. Indeed, for a time modern scholars thought that the writing down of the Avesta occurred after the rise and dominance of Islam: partly in imitation, partly under Muslim pressure, as a Zarathushtrian response to explicit Islamic recognition of the higher status, political and economic as well as spiritual, of communities with a scripture[8]. More recently, it has been recognized that that process in the Zarathushtrian case had in fact begun somewhat before the rise of Islam; but not long before. In any case, it came to fruition only after the arrival of the Muslims, and under their influence. A rendering of the Avesta into some sort of written form can nowadays be discerned as attested incipiently at least in the sixth century A.D. (Its language was by then no longer spoken; a script was invented for the purpose; and a Pahlavi—that is, a ver-nacular—translation of some parts of it also appeared in written form.) Yet its consolidation into a recognized holy book seems definitely to have followed upon the establishment in Iran of the Islamic outlook[9].

This raises an issue of an emerging bilateral relation or inter-mingling of two scriptural streams. As we observed in our introductory chapter, the Indian and Iranian mode of what the West has called scripture has been oral/aural, not written. While the two modes are jointly in evidence among Zarathushtrians certainly after, and incipiently before, their meeting with the Islamic movement, one must note that also in the Western case their juncture had not been absent, by any means. Not only did certain steps in the long-drawn-out process in Iran occur under the influence and stimulus of the Qur'an, but perhaps also *vice versa*. The Qur'an can be seen not only as continuous with the Biblical tradition of a written sacred book (it itself makes that continuity explicit), but also as continuous with the more distinctively oral/aural tradition that for long had characterized the Iranian (and the Hindu) case.

In this double involvement, written book and oral recitation, the Bible also had to some degree already been participating, as it has continued to participate, in both the Jewish and the Christian cases. We noted that the word *qur'an* signifies what is recited, declaimed, read aloud; it appears[10] that the term is from *qeryana*, the Syriac word used in the Near Eastern sector of the early Christian Church for what today in the West in the service is called the lesson (French *leçon*, "recitation"), or for "reading the lesson", to use that erstwhile tautology. Thus the double involvement can be discerned on each side incipiently before the seventh century. Yet the Islamic is the instance where the two are most clearly fused, both in practice and conceptually.

In the period before the Qur'an developed, it is not clear how far we are seeing mutual influences of two originally distinct streams, and how far simply a natural and independent tendency to move from either primarily written or primarily oral traditions to a supplementary expression of the other sort. With the Bible, in that activity in the Church service and in general, the oral was perceived as deriving from something written. On the other hand, for a thousand years what we with some uncouthness call Zarathushtrian "scriptures" were primarily recited, chanted, incanted: "murmured", as the outsiders' reports of Persian matters in this connection regularly put it[11]. The Persian terms themselves[12] are, rather: to learn by heart, to memorize; but apparently this memorizing was regularly done out loud (as as one observes still today among, for example, Bombay Parsis). Even if the Avesta was in some fashion and in some part written down in still pre-Islamic times, yet it seems not to have been thought of as a *book* until post-Islamic, a couple of centuries later[13]. As has been true also elsewhere at times, at first writing was perceived as simply a mnemonic device, to facilitate or to ensure that the oral rendering be accurate. The oral form was clearly primary; and for many centuries it had not been supplemented.

One must note, also, that in some situations a text might be treasured in written form yet effective in the community chiefly in oral/aural ways.

Thus it seems reasonable in this matter to see the Qur'an, with its persistently and solidly dual mode[14], as culminating a Near Eastern process of which the written strand seems perhaps somewhat more characteristic of the Semitic background, with the recitation aspect, prominent in both, yet more exclusively prominent in the Indo-European, and specifically the Iranian.

However that particular matter may be, in general the world into which Islam and the Qur'an emerged was one in which already religious communities had each its scripture—in some form. This was the situation in the Near East in the early seventh century A.D.;

and indeed it was so also already in the sixth, although one must not imagine that situation to have been static. In the sixth, the Babylonian Talmud was completed; probably towards the end of that century[15]. This process had closed in for the Jewish community of Jerusalem a good century and more earlier: its Talmud was "brought to closure" some time around the beginning of the fifth[16]. In these two cases also, it is interesting to note, the authoritative or "canonical" form of the Talmud, as a consolidated text, was the oral version. For several centuries the written form remained peripheral: altogether secondary[17].

In the fourth century much was going on in the long process of scripture development, throughout the area; and it is interesting to see how far the process had got by that time. This was the century during which the Christian community made substantial (although certainly not yet final) progress in coalescing a new, supplementary, scripture—or, scriptures—for itself, in the form of what it came to call a New Testament[18]. (It was in Greek, as were also its earlier scriptures, which thereupon became its Old Testament: the Septuagint.) Also in the fourth century the vigorous Manichee movement formalized its seven books of scripture[19], paralleling—it seems, consciously—its explicit rival contenders for a following. The Manichee movement was up-to-date from the start in these and other formal matters. Its founder Mani is presented already in the third century (although the text may be apocryphal, perhaps from the fourth) as saying that other founders of new religious movements wrote no books, but rather left that to their disciples, citing Zarathushtra, the Buddha, and Jesus[20]. He himself will make no such mistake, he is reported as affirming. He sees to it that his message, he himself will commit to writing.

Mani's move here seems to suggest that already in the third or fourth century the idea was getting around, at least to perceptive minds, that religious movements have each a book, that a new religious movement must have a new written book. (Such an idea could hardly have occurred to Jesus.) On more careful scrutiny, however, the stage reached at that point is not yet so clearly advanced. To have the message of one's group's original leader preserved intact in written form and thus available is not yet to indicate necessarily how formally scriptural, how sacred, how consolidated, that writing is perceived as being (as, for instance, Wittgenstein's followers, keen to publish posthumously their master's words, of course know[21]). Even to revere what someone says, and then to have it written down, is not yet necessarily to have a holy book. And as we have said, it seems to have been in the fourth century, rather than the third, that a Manichee canon is fairly well congealed, though doubtless in the third the process may have got underway. In any case, the transition from valuing a written account because it made available treasured material, to treasuring the book itself, was gradual.

In both centuries, what interests us here is the wider context in which this transition was proceeding. In that wider context the Manichee emergence and development are not merely a symptom, though they surely are that, but also an active and activating participant. They influenced the others, as well as *vice versa*. It is from the fourth century also that we have our earliest documentation of the Mandæan[22] thesis, important later, that their scriptures were affirmed to be, as books, pre-existent[23]. This important idea they expressed in a form considerably less firm and developed than is found in the Qur'an later, and still later and more elaborately in Muslim theology and folklore. They acknowledged, also less clearly than in the Islamic pattern, that other communities' scriptures were pre-existent also. Their position was in line with the movement already in evidence for some while now among the Jews—at whose position we shall be looking presently—that ultimate truth and wisdom were available to them as handed down in their tradition and treasured, and gradually that the words in which that truth and that wisdom were expressed were indeed of ultimate worth, and in due course that the books (in gradually developing phases of that concept) in which those words were ordered, were themselves ultimate, cosmic.

The idea of pre-existence was a Semitic time-related way of saying something regarding the supremacy and non-contingency of certain matters in human life discerned as transcendingly valuable[24]. Metaphysics was developed by the Greeks as another way of saying the same sort of thing. (Modern Western culture has no agreed way of articulating such a perception, after several centuries during which scripture—developed in the process at which we are here looking—provided one accepted way of affirming it.)

At another historical source for the pre-existence notion we shall be looking presently: second-millenium-B.C. Babylonian and Canaanite motifs that are a forerunner of this form—namely, the idea that there are books in Heaven from before creation with humanity's destinies inscribed in them; and that the Saviour had had privileged access to these books, bringing their contents (later, it was said, bringing the books themselves) down to earth to share with his fellow humans.

Meanwhile, we note that at the end of that same fourth century a centralizing and systematizing Christian Pope in Rome (where the use of Greek for Biblical texts had continued well into the third century) decided that it would be helpful to have a coherent unified Latin version of the Church's scriptures. (It would hardly yet be correct to say, "of the Bible".) He asked Jerome to work on it. This laid the basis[25] for what became in the sixth[26] to ninth[27] centuries and later[28] what we know as the Vulgate—which for something like a thousand years then *was* the Christian Scripture for much of the (Western) Church. This version had no predecessors in Latin as a unified, boundaried, authoritative entity, a Scriptural book. (Various parts of it, no doubt, had predecessors: this and that discrete writing, in this and that divergent wording—especially scattered in North Africa.) Nor did the new version itself yet constitute such an entity, although it did much to further the process[29].

Before the fourth century, as we have remarked, the Scripture of the Christian movement was in effect the Septuagint[30], more or less what is now "the Old Testament" but in Greek. It was a product of Greek Alexandria of the third to first centuries B.C. and later; of which, more below. For like the Manichee, but with a much narrower, much less pluralist, awareness, the Christian movement too emerged into a world where its religious milieu—namely, the Jewish—already possessed scriptures, if not yet a scripture. One can see the situation in action from the numerous references in the pages of the Gospels, and, to a lesser extent, in the Epistles to what is written. Yet the Old Testament as one knows it today was only partially in mind, had only partially coalesced. The re-iterated phrase "The Law and the Prophets" illuminates that it was partial, naming but two out of the three groups of writings later constituting a canon; or occasionally (Luke 24:44) the Law and the Prophets and the Psalms. More often, there is a reference simply to what is written by Moses. (Jesus seems to have envisaged Moses as literally writing out the

Pentateuch, by hand?). The consolidating process was in Jesus's day unmistakeably underway, yet had progressed by then only to a certain stage. It had gone far enough, however, that the idea of a religious community's having sacred writings was in due course adopted, appropriated, absorbed—almost unwittingly.

Of course we have such treasures from the past, early Christians felt (had no reason not to continue to feel). The only significant person seriously to question the idea was Marcion, in the second century, who saw the new Christian movement as substantially different from the one out of which it otherwise unselfconsciously felt that it had come, yet from which by now (second century) it had become sharply alienated. It is sufficiently different, Marcion suggested, that it need not conform to previous dispensations in the matter of scriptures; just as it need not in other matters, such as law (nor even, implicitly, in monotheism?). Even he, however, does not seem to have suggested no scripture at all. His thought was not that, but the striking idea that rather than continuing to have the Jewish scriptures, the Church should generate a new scripture of its own.

It is an anachronism, however, to think of him as advocating simply "the" (or even "a") "New Testament", as one used to be told. He proposed a set of writings in some ways distantly comparable to, yet sharply distinct from, that as yet quite unformed corpus. (One would, indeed, virtually have to say that such a thing was as yet non-existent as a corpus—nor "even as an idea"[31].) What he proffered comprised two parts: an *Instrumentum*, and *Antitheses*. The former was constituted of an abbreviated Lucan gospel and selected letters of Paul, drastically amended; the latter was his own composition, a kind of commentary on the former[32].

Marcion's movement was not without result. It became indeed a movement, especially in the third century but enduring in Syria into the tenth: he and it were more than idiosyncratic. The result was not what he had in mind; yet one may see his movement as playing a significant role in the process that concerns us. The dominant Church did not drop the Jewish-scriptures idea, but adapted it rather. It did so with a *tour de force*, some might say: one accomplished over the next couple of centuries. There are partial parallels later in principle, though not in practice, in the Qur'an; a thousand years still later the Sikh scriptures emulated this again in a minor fashion[33]. Yet in the end it could be contended that Christian scripture is the only instance in world history where one movement explicitly incorporates the scripture of another as such within its own, adding things new but making the old part and parcel—even though in ways to this day never fully clarified[34]: a somewhat subordinate part and parcel, heavily re-interpreted. It accomplished this more or less during the fourth to sixth centuries, as we have said. It was moving gradually towards this already in the third.

That was the century also in which for the Jews there culminated a two-hundred-year process in their first consolidating of what had for a time been somewhat diffuse oral legal traditions into the systematized and later written Mishnah[35].

It was in the third century, too, that the Corpus Hermeticum was completed[36]. Also, and relatedly, in process at this time was a certain coalescing, though yet incomplete, of texts for a movement that is still alive and well in modern America, India, and elsewhere: namely, astrology. The world history of astrology is complex but not unmanageable. Few of us have realized how interconnected has been its elaborate and widespread development around the world; what a coherent historical process it has constituted, from Egypt in Hellenistic times[37] into Western Civilization generally, also eastward to India, and thence, along with the Buddhist missionary movement, to China and on[38]. The chief Sanskrit translations and popularizing texts appear from the second and especially third centuries A.D.[39]. The important Hellenistic work *Tetrabiblos* of the second century A.D.[40], and the fifth-century compendium of Hephaestus of Thebes[41], are among texts that helped to give this movement partially systematized coherence in the West. Yet neither the movement, nor these or others of its writings, ever attained a status of the same order as the scripturalizing communities that we call religious, and their texts. Maybe we should not have introduced this item into our discussion here; but it could be deemed perhaps legitimate to note that things were going on at this time some of which did, and some did not, attain a degree of consolidated specialness for which words such as "sacred" serve. It seems clear that the astrology movement, although incorporating materials from earlier Babylon, emerged basically in the area and period that here concern us and developed then into a world-wide affair with considerable influence in the history of humankind since, as a more or less coherent system of ideas—and yet, it never became a community, and never generated scriptures. Of these last two facts a possible interrelation would perhaps be worth exploring. It may remind us too that, despite nineteenth-century Western interpreters' tendencies, religious movements are substantially more than systems of ideas, are not just what people "believe".

The second to the seventh centuries A.D. in the Near East, then, show us the Scripture movement in process of consolidating. The various new religious movements of that time and place each participated in that over-all process. They did so in ways—and this focusses our thesis here—that varied at least as much, one gets the impression, *with the century concerned as with the particular movement under consideration*: the Christian, the various Gnostic and later Mandæan, the Zarathushtrian (not exactly a new movement), the Manichee, various minor groupings, and finally the Islamic. This phase begins with the Jewish movement already to some degree possessed of a scripture—or more accurately, of scriptures. In their case, additional ones were still being added. For one basic element of what presently became the conception of scripture was already there, the fact of inherited texts treated as highly special, and indeed of cosmic quality. Another element, the fact of a specific and closed entity with fixed boundaries, integrating these, was yet to be attained. Reputedly or symbolically the latter, the consolidating, culminated for the Jews in the so-called Council of Javneh (Greek, "Jamnia") at the end of the first century A.D.; actually that consolidating occurred later—perhaps considerably later[42]—after having developed very gradually over many preceding centuries. The story of that long gradual development is nowadays being studied and told with increasing care and emphasis[43], and we leave the telling to others.

For we will not here trace further back, step by step, our story of this Near Eastern process in its incipient stages over the series of preceding centuries, noting how in the B.C. period each one of the specific movements participated in the over-all context, or contributed to it[44]. Rather, we content ourselves with calling attention to a few salient issues, bearing in mind once again the general context within which the development, early and late, seems to have been dynamically involved. In that context, we note specifically three matters: the Greek classical tradition, and especially Alexandria; a particular motif from Babylon and early Canaan, namely the idea of celestial-tablets or divine books; and the general tradition of writing.

The Greek tradition is fairly perspicuous. Crucial for us is the emergence, in what we therefore have come to call post-Classical times, of a formal concept of classics. One Heraclides Ponticus already in the middle or more probably late fourth century B.C. adjudged Aeschylus, Euripides, and Sophocles to have been the Athenian tragedians of salient worth; and presently those three, and they alone, were not merely read but cherished. The others, and one gathers that there had been several, were forgotten, their texts are lost, and these three were launched on the career of elevated status with which in Western culture they have been honoured ever since[45]. For other types of work the process occurred a little later than this, especially in the third century B.C., and especially in Alexandria, where the *grammatikoi*—the word itself is illuminating: "those concerned with what is written"—carefully edited accurate texts, carefully adjudicated which writings should be included in their canon (it is hardly reasonable, surely, to call it other than that), and established a corpus of what we now recognize as "the Greek Classics"[46]. (With the term *grammatikoi* here one may compare its first cousin *grammateis* serving Hellenized Jews, and appearing for instance in the New Testament, for the Jewish experts in *their* inherited and systematized religious patterns who are known in the English translations as "the scribes"[47].)

There is a complication here: for those Alexandrian classics were the product not only of the so-called classical Greek age; they included Homer (also Hesiod). Already in what we today call classical Athens the *Iliad* and *Odyssey* had become a privileged tradition: semi-scripture, one may say, of the oral type[48]. Alexandria in the third century turned them carefully into scripture of the written type, thus enabling them presently to serve like the writings (*sic*[49]) of Plato, Aristotle, and the dramatists, as ideal literature also for the non-Greek-speaking phases of Western civilization since that time[50].

To the important role in the life of the West of this "classical" literature—a role that for certain periods may be perceived as in a sense at least semi-scriptural for that life—we shall return in a later chapter below. There would seem no question but that they deserve to be—insist on being—included in our topic.

The Alexandria milieu is context for our concern here also in another way. At virtually this same time, Greek-speaking Jews there and in upper Egypt were involved in important connected developments. In the early third century B.C. at the services in their Egyptian synagogues, "the five" components of the Pentateuch were being recited in Hebrew followed by a rendering in Greek. Later that century a separate Greek version of the five appeared, as in effect almost a book, a formal entity. By the end of the next century the view was promulgated that that translation, the so-called Septuagint, had itself been miraculous[51]: a scripturalizing step, conspicuously. By that time (when Hebrew was no longer current even in Palestine, let alone in Egypt), further Hebrew writings, "the Prophets", were becoming substantially canonized in Palestine, and gradually the Septuagint was enlarged by such new additions (though not exactly the same ones as the Hebrew counterparts). By the first century A.D., early or late, pretty much the whole of what Christians later came to call the Old Testament, except maybe Qoheleth (Ecclesiastes) and perhaps The Song of Songs, was in the Septuagint. We mention all this partly because it would seem that a canonizing process, especially if one thinks of it as in part an integrating of former disparate or at least independent components into one reified entity, is unavoidably hastened by the translation matter. Before a notion of canon has been formalized or finalized one in fact decides what to translate[52], what to incorporate into the, in this case Greek, repository, into one's liturgically functional as well as revered and normative ("sacred") book.

In this double sense—that is, for both classicists and Jews—Alexandria played a highly significant role in the scripturalizing process. The Septuagint became not merely a translation, however. In due course it incorporated within itself additional writings composed originally in Greek. That is, it not only participated in the scripturalizing process, but materially contributed to it, carrying it forward. Another way of putting this point is to say that the Greek-speaking Jews continued the process begun by and now inherited from their Semitic-speaking ancestors[53]. Moreover, as we have seen, it was the Septuagint that became the scripture of the Christian Church. (It was not until the Reformation that the Hebrew version began in effect to replace it—for that one sector of the Western Church—as the "original" for its Old Testament[54].) Adding to the scripture extra works composed *de novo* in Greek was of course continued further by Christians' eventually incorporating into their Bible the "books" constituting a New Testament.

Yet there is more: a third or even fourth way in which Alexandria, and its developing of the classical tradition, are significant in this story. For it provided still another element without which scripture is not a viable operating concept or form—or at least, not for material previously unscripturalized. For this Greek city at this time developed the pattern of interpreting allegorically ancient texts whose literal meaning is out of tune with newer conceptions. That pattern too it inherited from "classical" Athens. Hellenistic thinkers developed it carefully, specifically the philosophic interpretation of Homer and Hesiod[55]. Jews in this environment appropriated, absorbed, this; with the result that by the end of the B.C. era Greek-speaking (by which one means, Greek-thinking) Jews introduced this immensely consequential orientation into, also, Biblical interpretation; or we may say, into interpretations that made a Bible continuingly possible. Specifically, Philo of Alexandria was evidently the first to do so; but we all know that he was not the last. In this practice he was adopting tendencies quite familiar to his fellow Hellenizing Jews. Put another way: he was inserting the on-going development of Biblical interpretation into the larger transcending context of the process of the development of classicized or canonized ancient texts[56].

We shall be considering in a later chapter subsequent phases in the rich elaboration of the Greek classical tradition. Here we turn to our second concern for the B.C. period: namely, the concept of heavenly tablets. Some years ago a parallel was noticed between a Tablets-of-Destiny idea, attested in Babylonian cuneiform and coming from probably well before 1000 B.C., and the notion, even the phrasing, of revelation serving in the Qur'an. The scholar who spotted it set to tracing the outworking of the idea, and found it running as a continuous thread, showing itself here and there through the maybe two thousand years or so of intervening religious history in the region[57]. Not every one of the details in his argument carries conviction; yet in general it is evident that he was on to something major. The Semitic high gods Samas and Adad were depicted in ancient sources as giving inscribed tablets ("of the gods, . . . with the mystery of the heavens and the earth") to a mythical king[58] on earth. Again, Hammurabi (late third or early second millenium B.C.) is represented as having been given the law code by the god Samas[59] (god of justice[60]); and in a land where, unlike Egypt, there is virtually no stone, copies of that law were written out in the usual manner on clay tablets but the original was cut in diorite, and set in the temple of Marduk. Thus the law was symbolically perceived as representing the cosmic order, not merely a mundane[61]. It is striking that not merely the notion but indeed the actual word, *l-w-ḥ*, in both its Arabic and Hebrew forms, is the same for the celestial tablets on which the Qur'an is eternally inscribed[62] and for the tablets of revelation given to Moses on Mt. Sinai[63].

The West has in its own way been heir to the idea of revelation adumbrated here, but elaborated with further related elements. Involved here is the ancient Mesopotamian Assembly-of-the-Gods notion, a divine gathering at which on New Year's Day in a book (*sic*) the events of the coming year on Earth were written (*sic*). Outstanding human individuals could become decisively important to their fellows if they could somehow ascend to heaven and become privy to what is in that celestial book. An alternative was that one of the gods, preferably their chief, might take the initiative and show or give the book or parts of it to such a person. Recently it has been shown that such an idea of a Divine Council, with a special human person somehow having privileged access to its proceedings, obtained also in pre-Hebrew Canaanite lore; and it has therefore been argued that it may have been with that source rather than directly with Babylon that later Hebrew ideas were continuous[64]. If we speculate as to the situation in Israel in, say, 1000 B.C., we may suppose that in a given village there was no book and perhaps nobody was literate but that around the campfires at night tales were told and vividly received of Moses and his divine tablets received at Mt. Sinai, written by the finger of God.

The Qur'an as divine revelation is a late yet fairly exact culmination of the process that begins with this divine knowledge cut in stone and made available to humankind. Less fully yet not negligibly, the Bible as we know it, considered as a revealed book, is a development from this campfire imagery. Later on, Moses came to be thought of as having received at Sinai not only "the ten words" cut in stone, but five whole books known today as the Pentateuch; and still later, as having received these latter in writing and as well an oral instruction (Hebrew: *Torah*) "finally" cast in codified[65] form by Judah ha-Nasi shortly after 200 A.D. as the Mishnah; and eventually in more ample form as the Jerusalem Talmud by 400 or so, or still more amply as the Babylonian Talmud by at the latest 600, as we have seen. This latter date is that by which the other stream from this tradition, the Christian, had almost completed its similar development from the same source, by giving to its scriptures, by then fairly well (though not yet quite) consolidated, a status that recaptures in many respects these notions of a divine book vouchsafed to earth. Those growing up in the early years of this century in conservative Christian or Jewish homes inherited some such view of the Bible as a divine writing sent down among us. In this historical sketch we have already noted such a view also with the Gnostic-Mandæan material; to some extent with the Manichee; and by the ninth century A.D. with the Zarathushtrian.

Hindu, Buddhist, Chinese scriptural conceptions, teasingly similar in other ways, have little of these particular notions.

It may be noted that the idea of the Qur'an as a written book in addition to its being known as an oral recitation, and comparable notions in other Western traditions of "scripture" as something written even when in practice functioning as something spoken, and the relation between written and oral/aural generally in this matter, have one basis in this conception of their having been written in heaven.

Our brief historical survey (brief survey of "the pre-history" of scripture) is virtually done; yet we may close with just a word about the third matter that we indicated that we would consider: namely, writing as such. A study of scripture should begin, perhaps, rather with language, that distinctively and profoundly human characteristic. Modern linguists have studied its prose dimension, not much its poetry; even less, its scriptural mode. That question, however, we leave aside until our final discussions; with it, we shall in part conclude. Here, a brief historical observation about writing. Today great numbers of us are so literate, have become so familiar with writing and with books, that we have forgotten the aura that once surrounded this mysterious contrivance.

Writing emerged in the Near East about 3000 B.C., in Egypt (hieroglyphic) and in Mesopotamia (cuneiform)[66]. For long it was the prerogative of a circumscribed élite, of temple and palace; of bureaucracies. Somewhere about 1500 to 1200 B.C., the alphabet was invented[67]—a step in the direction of democratization. From then on, what the bureaucracy thought important could be preserved, as before, but smaller and unofficial groups could now do the same if they were serious about it. A significant step was taken, or is illustrated, in 621 B.C. in Israel: the Josiah reform[68], triggered by the discovery of a book in the Jerusalem temple. Whether the work (basically, today's Deuteronomy) was composed and surreptitiously lodged in the Temple in order to be discovered so, as was contended for a time, or was rather, as more modern scholarship[69] tends to prefer, found there perhaps inadvertently, does not affect our argument. In any case the book was in fact composed, and in fact set forth innovating ideas, and in fact became cherished and consequential. Illustrated here is a transition from writing as a way of fixing the *status quo* to writing as the manifesto of a dissident group; from writing as recording to writing as propounding.

Prior to this, writing served to make permanent what was already established, authoritative. Here, by contrast, the idea was to establish what was newly written. This begins the process to which we have all become heir: writers who write (*sic*) new ideas to change the course of history.

The revolutionary nature of this was masked. The new ideas could prove revolutionary only insofar as they seemed traditional. The work that was discovered was ascribed to Moses (who had died some six centuries earlier) as a so-called "prophet" figure. What a brilliant, what a consequential, forgery or misunderstanding!—consolidating the outlook of the eighth- and seventh-century-B.C. Hebrew prophets in a written document. Instead of something being written down because it was important, this message was considered important because it had been written down.

Probably the discovery was not simply a hoax. The book, although in novel fashion forward-looking in the sense of proposing innovations, was also in traditional fashion backward-looking not only in that its programme for reform was couched in terms of ancient authority, specifically Moses, but also in that the author or authors did genuinely feel, it seems, that their programme was reviving or reforming (in the literal sense of forming once again) inherited traditions from of old. (There is some evidence that this appeal to a reconstructed picture of a community's earlier age being presented anew as a model for the present, for inspiration and aspiration, reflects in an innovative way a new mood of attention to the past that was emerging at that particular period—around the seventh century B.C.—not only in Palestine but rather widely in the Near East, from Egypt to Assyria and Babylonia[70].) Reformers, as the word itself affirms, have traditionally presented themselves as re-establishing a pristine past while actually proposing a novel future. Thus not merely, at this historical stage, was writing as such not yet conceived as an instrument for introducing newness; also, newness was as late as the Protestant "Reformation" in Europe not yet conceived as desirable in moral and spiritual life.

We should remark at least briefly, in this hastening survey of the ancient period, on a Persian development in the matter of written language: the massive Behistun or Bisitun inscription in Iran[71], of about 500 B.C.; a decisively imposing statement in three languages incised on the vast rock-face, wherein the Emperor Darius proudly asserts his accomplishments, desiring all to remember them and to be impressed. May Ahura Mazda, he proclaims, protect and reward him who preserves, punish and curse him who destroys, this[72]—a sentiment echoed often by scripturalists later[73]. On a much smaller scale, this strand in our process is continued in the Safaitic inscriptions in the Arabian desert half a millenium or so later[74].

In fine, our suggestion is that the emergence for the Western World of scripture as a form and as a concept is a rich and complex process, deserving more attention than certainly we have been able to give it here. It is a form and concept playing a prodigiously important role in human lives and societies throughout Western, and Islamic, history ever since; and the process is fascinating and rewarding to study. The West has long tended to derive its concept of scripture from the Bible; it is not amiss to suggest that we are now in a position where our understanding of the Bible, and of much else across the world, may begin to be derived from a larger concept of scripture.

We close this historical survey, simply observing that scripture has been an amazing idea, an astonishing form. Moreover, we return to the remark above that the concept of scripture has not seriously developed since the Qur'an in the seventh century A.D. This is surely also an astonishing fact: needing nuance, yet a grave fact for at least the West. It constitutes a luxury that we can no longer afford. Our world needs a new concept of scripture. (The movement that began with Spinoza[75] with his new orientation to the Bible texts, and that has grown into the massive and important academic enterprise calling itself historical criticism, has hardly yet provided that new concept. The result of its immensely illuminating work has been to dismantle for Western culture its inherited notion of scripture, leaving it with a focus on content but without form; or at best, given the new concern with canon, with some incipient sense of a form but still without a concept.)

Before we tackle this formidable matter of a new concept of scripture, however, we must look more closely not only at a major though not widely known instance of Western scriptural involvement once the form and concept had jelled for this civilization, but also then at non-Western cases, with their diverging patterns.

CHAPTER 4

THE TRUE MEANING
OF SCRIPTURE:
THE QUR'AN AS AN EXAMPLE

IN OUR SECOND CHAPTER, we remarked that we were endeavouring to ascertain with regard to The Song of Songs not the "true meaning" of its text, or of its discrete passages, but rather the historical meaning among certain groups at certain specified times. We stressed that those readings, though illustrative, and important though they were so far as they went, nonetheless remained particular. This particularity is in addition to the fact that not only The Song has been and is but one among many diverse sectors of the Bible, but also that the Bible has been and is but one among many scriptures of our human community. That specific investigation, then, may have been—and we trust, was—helpful as an introductory step, serving to open up both the depth and the width of our task. Yet issues remain unresolved; further steps obviously remain to be taken.

Our third chapter, again, dealt with historical emergence, without raising questions as to the significance of what emerged.

In pursuit of historical meanings, however, we do not wish to evade the question of true meaning. Nor, in pursuit of the historical meanings of a particular scripture do we wish to set aside our fundamental concern, to apprehend as nearly as we may truth about scripture generally, as for long an almost world-wide human fact. On the whole, this latter issue we defer to the concluding chapter of our study. Parts of it, nonetheless, implicitly accompany us at every stage of our inquiry, growing out of our treatment of specific matters. In this present chapter, we venture to address the question of how historical meanings relate to the true meaning of a particular scripture, paying illustrative attention to a specific case: the Qur'an[1].

The Qur'an has been and is the scripture of a limited—though vast—sector of our race: the Muslims. For them, it has represented ultimate truth. For them, its true meaning has indeed been that cosmic truth. Others nowadays recognize that it has been and is the scripture, whatever that may mean, of Muslims. For such observers, it represents an involvement of peoples to whose ways—to whose seeing and thinking and feeling and doing—they have thought and felt and seen themselves as outsiders. Muslims have felt the scriptural quality more vividly; outsiders have of late studied its historical vicissitudes more critically. For both, a reconsideration interlacing scriptural and historical may prove helpful in illuminating our generic question.

Yet our task is not simple.

"Religion is poetry plus, not science minus"[2] is a *bon mot* to some of whose implications we shall return later, for more elaborate pondering. The relation among prose, poetry, and scripture will be occupying us from time to time throughout our study. Yet already this aphorism is relevant. The historical or historicist interpretation of religious matters not long ago was seen as leaving something out; indeed, as subtracting. In our own day, in contrast, a more mature historical and historicizing view is being attained that enables us to enhance, rather than to reduce, our apprehension of humanity's spiritual life; and this we may see in the scripture matter. Academic intellectuals are no doubt prosaic folk, or at least aspire to prose. Unless careful, in the study of religion they can find themselves thereby missing the poetry; let alone, the 'plus' beyond it. In the critical study of poetry as a form of literature, the aim of scholarship formulated in prose is to deepen our understanding of poetry; in the critical study of religion, we may share such aspiration. Fortunately, movement in this direction has begun. Sensitivity and discernment are gradually increasing. With these, and with the newly acquired massive array of historical data—an array far beyond anything available to past generations—we should manage to forge new conceptions more capable of doing those data justice; more adequate to our rich and subtle material, including the deep human involvements.

In our addressing that global problem, this study rests on the conviction that the matter of scripture may prove illustrative; and with regard to scripture, let us see whether the specific instance of the Qur'an may serve to illuminate globally.

The problem in "true meaning" may be formulated simply. Any given passage in scripture has tended, one may observe, to be interpreted in more than one way. What are the criteria then for determining the proper interpretation? What does it mean to say that the true meaning of such-and-such a word, or verse, or chapter, in the Qur'an for instance, is thus-and-so; and that other readings are less correct, or even are altogether fanciful?

This question has been addressed internally by most religious communities; certainly by Muslims, and indeed by various sub-sections among them: including, in the Islamic case, the classical Sunni colleges (*madrasah*s), various groups of Sufis, the orthodox Shi'ah, the Isma'ilis, and so on. These have developed principles of scriptural interpretation, rules of exegesis, and the like; and especially, have worked with either explicit or implicit underlying theories that determine or express their basic orientation, even though within each set a lesser or greater degree of individual variation persists. The Western scholarly world, too, developed its own view. There came to be a modern academic position—held with force, and executed (as were also the Muslim ones) with brilliance.

Our suggestion is that none of these is any longer convincing. All are beginning to be seen as starkly idiosyncratic, and limited; one might even say, demonstrably inadequate. The time has come to move on to a significantly new orientation. We today both can and must develop a quite new sense of what constitutes the meaning of scripture—any scripture: Bible, Upanishads, or whatever; and for any reader: Buddhist, Christian, or sceptic; humanist, Marxist, academic. These last, academics, are explicitly engaged in the pursuit of truth; others less explicitly may well be equally or more seriously concerned to attain it. All are in a position today to take a substantial step forward towards delineating what constitutes the true meaning of scripture—in part, by learning from each other. The most promising solution is one that is continuous with each of the careful yet partial theses that have been advanced thus far, and subsumes most of them, but moves beyond all.

We begin with observed data: the givens of historical reality, in this case concerning the Qur'an. The particular observation that concerns us is that that scripture, both as such and any given passage within it, has meant many different things to many different people at different times and places. This has been the case for the Qur'an, among Muslims—as for The Song, we incipiently saw, among Christians and Jews; and for the others. This starting point is important. Its focus on the historical does not in itself, however, rule out ahead of time a possibility that through the observed materials the human beings involved may have been, as they report, in touch with a reality transcending history. What we can affirm is that the relation to transcendence, whether putative or real, has taken place within history, and has observably been conditioned by the historical situation. It is to be understood historically.

Not only what we study is historical, however; so, too, is our study of it. Students, inquirers, academics, also participate in the historical process: at a particular time and place, coming out of a particular background and moving forwards to a situation less determinate. The pursuit of truth, too, takes its conditioned place in an historical development. Scripture, whatever else it may additionally be, is an historical phenomenon. The understanding of scripture, whatever else it may additionally be, is also an historical phenomenon. The understanding of scripture that is becoming possible, truer than any that have gone before, is possible because we can now construct it on the basis of a new critical awareness of what has gone before.

If one of the great achievements of the recent past was the development of historical consciousness, the great step today is to acquire historical self-consciousness. (Also, in addition to historical criticism the great imperative is to develop historical appreciation.) In the second part of this chapter, accordingly, we will look at the modern West, to become critically aware of its current movement of understanding: to see the West and its ideas as participant in the historical process.

First, however, let us look at what has been going on on the Islamic side.

The starting point here is that Muslims have held the Qur'an to be the word of God. One may not agree with them; yet that hardly justifies dismissing the fact as not important, not relevant. We shall see in a moment that there was a phase in outside academic study when this naive error was in fact made, of so dismissing it, deeming the point irrelevant, or downright distracting. Western students of the Qur'an tended to be either Christian or Jewish on the one hand, or secularist, perhaps atheist, on the other; and accordingly in both cases to hold firmly that the Muslim view of the matter—the transcendentalist view, one might call it—was manifestly silly or perverse, and anyway was wrong; and therefore must be discounted. Even the "therefore" here has become for us absurd; a form of nineteenth-century logic (or early twentieth-) that in the *late* twentieth century is palpably a mistake. We shall return to this. For the moment, we simply insist that to understand the Qur'an as scripture one must recognize it as scripture. In the first instance this is meant not as a cosmic category, but as a human one. The error of which we speak was one that the West made in its first handling of non-Western cultures and religious groups generally. In this case it derived from inheriting a tradition according to which a scripture was conceived as something sent down, maybe verbatim, from another world, and imagining in line with this that if a given text is not in fact divinely revealed (but only imagined to be so) then it is not scripture. The Qur'an therefore was seen by the West as not truly scripture; certainly not primarily scripture; and in effect, as not scripture at all. It was studied and treated not as scripture, but as any other book[3].

In other words, the West had no adequate understanding of scripture, at that point in Western history. It had concepts for ordinary human books, and for divine books (neither of them perhaps fully adequate concepts, though for the moment we let that pass). It had, however, virtually no concept for books that people treat as divine whether or not they in fact be so. One might virtually say that it had as yet no intellectual, as distinct from theological, concept of scripture. As we saw in our introductory chapter, it presently began to use the word "scripture" for these without pondering what in these cases it meant. In their attempted understanding of the Qur'an, accordingly, Westerners have tended to omit from serious consideration its most conspicuous, and historically its most consequential, characteristic. If we do not understand the Qur'an as scripture, we come close to not understanding it at all, one may surely say.

We cannot understand the Qur'an, and its role in human history, without an adequate understanding of scripture as a major matter in human affairs, individual and social; and in turn we cannot develop a serious concept of scripture, obviously, unless it be one that comprehends, *inter alia*, the Qur'an.

It is as an historian, not yet as a theologian, that one insists on this. At the sheerly observational level, one can hardly over-estimate the central significance of this spiritual quality of the text, as an active force in an imposingly large sector of human history.

For Muslims, the Qur'an has been received as the *ipsissima verba* of God Himself: God speaking to humankind not merely in seventh-century Arabia to Muhammad, but from all eternity to every man and woman throughout the world—including the individual Muslim as he or she reads or recites it or devoutly holds it, or vividly or dimly or even unconsciously remembers a passage or phrase from it. It represents the eternal breaking through into time; the unknowable disclosed; the transcendent entering history and remaining here, available to mortals to handle and to appropriate; the divine become apparent. To memorize it, as many Muslims have ceremonially done, and even to quote from it, as every Muslim does daily in his and her formal prayers and otherwise, is to enter into some sort of communion with ultimate reality. The memorizing does this in a fashion that I have suggested may be formally compared with the Christian eucharist[4]. Certainly, to obey it is to leave the purely natural and to enter upon that realm where the mundane and the transcendent meet: an instance of the almost universal human awareness, formalized especially in the Semitic consciousness, that the other things in our life we share with the world of animals and nature, but the moral imperative, righteousness, mediates to us something higher, more ultimate.

On the one hand, physical copies of the Qur'an have been treated always with formal reverence. On the other hand, the content of the book is, ideally, the source not only of the religion of Islam in general and of every part of it in particular, but also of the whole life of the community in motion. There are many written commentaries on the work, as we shall be noting presently. In a wider sense, the life of the Prophet has been regarded as essentially a commentary on and exposition of the Qur'an. Moreover, the whole of Islamic history might in some ways be regarded as at least ideally an elaborating and implementing of its meaning—however limited by human failing. Or, to move from ideals to actualities, Islamic history might be seen (must be seen, even by the down-to-earth outside observer) as the on-going interplay between human and mundane distractions, on the one hand, and on the other the corporate Muslim attempt to work out in practice the meaning of the divine word. Islamic "Law" (*shari'ah*) is thought of as implicit within it, educed from it formally. In recent times, even modern science has by a few speculative minds been seen as a kind of commentary on particular parts of the scripture.

Wherever the Islamic movement has spread, the Qur'an has been studied, copied, interpreted, and sometimes translated. The chief field in Muslim Qur'an scholarship has been exegetical commentary—*tafsir*—phrase by phrase. The first great exponent of this art, after various less impressive though certainly significant forerunners, was the historian and exegete al-Tabari, early in the ninth century; but he was not the last. His mighty work in many volumes is still in use today and is still imposing; yet many hundreds of other Muslims have written expositions and interpretations since. There have, indeed, been some major, and many minor, commentaries in each succeeding century—first in Arabic, in subsequent centuries in many varied languages. Certainly in our own day, the publishing of careful, serious, and provocative commentaries continues.

To write a commentary in any age is to suggest that extant interpretations are to some degree inadequate; even though attitudes to the tradition vary widely. The writing of formal analytic or exegetical *tafsir*, however, is but one among several ways in which Muslims have set forth one or another specific interpretation of their scripture, or of specific verses within it. Every theologian, jurist, mystic, heresiarch, nationalist, agitator, philosopher, has tended over the centuries, and across the Muslim world, to incorporate an interpretation of the Qur'an or (more usually) of individual parts of it into his system: sometimes in a distinctive way, slightly or markedly. And indeed every individual worshipper, quoting this or that verse from the Book in their daily prayers, as they must, sees and feels in that verse something that is surely far from simple. For every such worshipper, that "something" is in part a function of the meaning for it purveyed to them by their milieu, in which this or that school of tradition predominates; and something, further, that is in part a function of their own personal capacity, insight, sophistication, piety, temperament, and the like—and indeed also of their knowledge of Arabic.

71

Without waiting for a fully developed concept of scripture, then, we may readily make a few elementary observations, which may suggest some, at least, of what is involved. For example: if the Qur'an be read as the word of God, as it has been read for fourteen centuries now by Muslims (they perceive it as the word of God and then they read it), then for any given word or phrase or passage that may demonstrably or conceivably mean either of two or more different things, the meaning that a particular reader or group will choose, and will regard as the right one, will on principle be the best possible meaning, in his or her or their best judgement. If he or she be a follower (*muqallid*), accepting some particular authority as decisive in these matters (for example, if a Muslim living this side of the thirteenth century accepts Baydawi's commentary as determinative), then in practice the text has for that person only one acceptable meaning: the one proffered by that authority (not that Baydawi did not on occasion register alternative possibilities). If, on the other hand, one be oneself an original thinker, or if one be confronted with divergent authorities, then a choice is necessarily made; and it would be irresponsible, and indeed blasphemous, not to hold that the meaning that God intended is the better, or the best, of the two or more that might seem to be possible. The range of "possible" may be small; but within it, one chooses the highest. A scholar confronted with a mundane text rightly chooses among possible readings the most probable; the man or woman of faith, confronted with a scripture, rightly chooses the most exalted. The scholar, also, must recognize that for such readers that is the most probable. (Otherwise that scholar is a poor historian.)

If you yourself are a Muslim writing a commentary; or are a Sufi *pir* master instructing your *murid* disciple; or are a conscientious jurisconsult deciding a tricky point of law; or are a modern Cambridge-educated Muslim reflecting on contemporary life; or are a twelfth-century Shirazi housewife practising your private devotions in the solitude of your home; or are a left-wing leader of the ninth-century slave revolt of the Zanj protesting against what seem to you the exploitation and hypocrisy of the establishment—in all such cases the correct interpretation of a particular Qur'an verse is the best possible interpretation that comes to you or that you can think up. I do not mean that you concoct it cunningly or contrive it irresponsibly. On the contrary: you are constrained by the very fact of your esteeming this as the word of God to recognize as the most cogent among all possible alternatives that interpretation that in your judgement is the closest to universal truth and to universal goodness. You choose not what is the best for you, but what in your judgement is the closest to what is good and true absolutely, cosmically. (Your sense of what it signifies may inhibit acting on what you would prefer, or are strongly impelled, to do.)

One does not know these days whether any given one among one's readers may believe in God or not; but one must submit that for those who do not, this argument then should be that much the more cogent. Those who reject any "supernatural" realm in our universe, far from being able to dismiss concepts such as 'God', 'revelation', and the like, have to wrestle with them the more earnestly. If the term 'God' does not refer to a transcendent being, ultimate source of all that exists, ultimate truth, ultimate authority for all moral obligation, but is no more than a construct of the human imagination, then one must recognize it as a concept that conceptualizes, unifies, and animates whatever the persons who use it know or can discern or imagine of truth, goodness, worth, within this universe and within social and personal life. If the concept 'God' be in one's private view a figment of human fantasy, either in general or in the case of the more particular Muslim conceptions, then surely—one must plead—recognize that it is an exceedingly important figment, one that has for a few thousand years been consequential on a stupendous scale. Some philosophers have argued lately that it is a meaningless concept; but anyone who takes history seriously cannot be that superficial, or—to put it bluntly—that wrong. The Muslim concept of God has been massively meaningful. It is then the business of the historian to ascertain and to make evident what it has meant to many millions of people at various times and places on our planet. The Muslim affirmation that it is God who speaks in the Qur'an becomes, for those amongst us that are humanist or naturalist or other non-theist, simply a quaint yet notably powerful way whereby theists encapsulate in this symbolic form at the very least their capacity for, and their sensibility to, beauty, truth, and justice (to use terms from Greece); or, more elaborately, to beauty, truth, and justice around them, and integrity, decency, and responsibility within. It is historically evident that in the dynamics of the centuries the symbol has shaped for them that capacity and that sensibility; and evident that in turn these have shaped the Muslim's interpretation of the symbol. Islamic history has in significant part been and continues to be the story of that double interplay.

Indeed, has the whole history of religion not been in significant part the story of the ever lively dialectic between human beings' capacity on the one hand to derive from or through their inherited symbols the vision, the norms, the wholeness, the drive by which at best they live, and on the other hand to invest in those same symbols the highest aspirations, the noblest dreams, the truest ideas and grandest feelings to which their minds and hearts have in fact been able to rise?

As an outside observer sitting on the sidelines, one may because of one's own predilections or prejudice or wisdom be inclined to pass a judgement that they would have been able to rise higher had they had other symbols, or no symbols at all. Yet that sort of speculation should not stand in the way of observing that nonetheless the historical fact is that this is the way that they did live, these the symbols in interaction with which they rose to whatever heights they at various moments did rise, and in terms of which they articulated that rising.

A symbol-system begins to wane, and presently collapses, when its symbols prove no longer capable of receiving and holding and activating the highest and best that a given people can imagine.

Yet this is in passing. We do not propose here to advance a general theory of symbols. All that we would urge is a comment on an observed fact. The fact is that the Qur'an has in the course of fourteen centuries, and over a large expanse of our planet, meant different things to different people. The comment is that those different things have been in part a function, of course, of events in seventh-century Arabia; in part a function, of course, of the varying mundane circumstances of their own time (differing economic and social status, differing interests, differing temperaments, and so on . . .)—circumstances that have limited and in part determined people's capacity to interpret, and to discern truth and goodness. Yet those varying meanings have been in part a function also, since it has been a scripture, of the inner pressure on all of us to reach out and upwards to discern truth and goodness, to push on beyond one's limitations. Unless one hold (against, surely, the evidence of human history) that human beings have no tendency to aspire to truth and to goodness, then one must recognize that in the Islamic instance this tendency has been oriented in considerable part to and through the Qur'an.

Of course, as with all of us, in every civilization, this aspiration had to take its place within a welter of other pressures, choices, social structures, distractions, all of which not merely competed with but modified it. The human ability, among Muslims and the rest of us, to discern what is true and good has at times been strikingly limited or woefully distorted[5], even apart from an ability to live up to or even close to what they so discerned. Those who find the history of human apprehension of truth and goodness discouraging, can make a powerful case. (Evident too throughout has been the relative ease with which we have all noticed other people's shortcomings, overlooking or under-estimating our own.)

When we say that the Qur'an and various parts of it have meant different things to different Muslims, we are not suggesting that the history of Muslim Qur'an interpretation is chaotic: that every one was totally free to read into the text whatever whimsies might appeal to him or her. We are not even suggesting that within certain constraints each read into it whatever he or she could summon the ingenuity to make seem plausible. There is something of both of these on the fringes of scripture interpretation in all traditions throughout the world. Nonetheless one is well aware both that, in the Islamic case, on the one hand the formal constraints were rigorous, and that on the other hand internal discipline, sincerity, and often humility, were common.

No doubt, among the constraints on personal judgement as to the best and highest interpretation has been one's sense of community —currently, and stretching through time. Not everyone has felt that his or her own immediate assessment of what is right and good is necessarily better or more trustworthy than the group's. As we have elsewhere elaborated: of all the major religious movements in human history the Islamic has been the most systematic, the most coherent. It has been characterized by a quality that modern jargon calls authoritarian—though that way of putting it tends to miss the point that this has in almost all instances been freely and gladly accepted.

"Loyal" would be an alternative description. Nonetheless: however patterned the system, however rigorous the order within which they choose to live, human beings are complex, subtle, unique, in the Islamic as in all cases. Each person has been a personality, less or more distinctive. Each intellect has been active, less or more creatively. And even within the boundaries of what might appear to be a fixed position, the amount of movement should not be under-estimated.

Let us take one example. Discussed with some vigour has been whether the so-called "night journey" and "ascent to heaven" of the Prophet Muhammad mentioned in the Qur'an[6] should be taken figuratively or literally. Both views were propounded. Each was sincerely held, and ably defended. Over the course of the centuries, the position came largely to prevail that a metaphorical or figurative interpretation should not be accepted. This tended at a certain point in history to get formulated by saying that the journey and the ascent were real—in Arabic, *haqq*.

That was fine. Nonetheless, incorporated into that eventual orthodox consensus was the recognition that the pertinent Qur'an verse could be interpreted as indicating either that Muhammad was awake or that he was asleep when he made that Night Journey and Ascension—or was somewhere between the two. The act of dreaming, after all, is also real[7].

Moreover, along with the orthodox view, if you are a mystic or have been influenced by the Sufis, if you feel that reality is primarily spiritual, if for you truth in the religious realm is basically a matter of a transformation of the person, if spiritual growth or decline is a more fundamental fact of each human life than are such minor and comparatively unreal things as physical ups and downs; then of course you may agree that the ascent of the Prophet to heaven was real, but by "real" you may mean what someone else less perceptive of spiritual inwardness would call metaphorical. That is, two people may agree that a given matter spoken of in the Qur'an is real, but they may have different notions of what reality is, and therefore, of what is being affirmed about that passage of scripture, and in it. That this has in fact happened in Islamic history can be documented quite precisely from the texts. That these different positions have been taken; that words have been interpreted in these various ways; and so on—these are historical facts for which we have concrete empirical evidence.

At another level, interpretations of this one particular verse gradually constituted in Muslim life—and art—a lavishly embroidered series of imaginatively embellished constructs, the ramifications of which have been traced not only throughout Islamic history but even as far afield as not only the imagery but even the basic structure of Dante's *Divine Comedy*[8]. (It would be obtuse not to recognize that the Qur'an has played a role in world history, not merely in Islamic.)

We may confine ourselves, however, to the Muslim tradition itself. Once again, neither in the case of this verse nor in general is the matter chaotic. It is possible to trace connected movements of ideas, developments, institutional trends, and the like. There is a history of meanings, which can be demonstrated and explained. The history of how the Qur'an has been understood, or any part of it, can be studied, like the history of anything else.

We could go on, but enough. Let us turn now to Western interpretations.

If the prime fact about the Qur'an, in historical reality, for a time escaped the West's capacity to grasp and to digest—the fact of its having existed for thirteen centuries and more primarily as scripture—the second historical fact about it did not escape the Western academic's notice; namely, that it had been interpreted differently by different groups at different times. This fact was known and recognized. Yet it too has not been grasped, and certainly has not been digested. Rather, it too tended for a time to be dismissed.

For the academic West's first scholarly reaction to the observed fact of the Qur'an's being interpreted differently in different times and at different places by different people, was to fasten on one century, and one place, and one person: holding that the text's real meaning was its meaning in the seventh century, in Arabia, for Muhammad, "the man who wrote it". The importance of this decision has not been fully recognized; nor its historical quality, its particularity. We can learn a good deal by taking it seriously. Our thesis contends that history must always be taken seriously; and so also must the views of intelligent leaders of thought within it. If we can understand with some depth and some exactness the position that was here being set forth, in the academic West—the Muhammad theory of the Qur'an, we may call it—we shall have made significant progress in our pursuit of truth. Our present study would not be being offered if this position on the matter appeared still valid, or adequate. Yet we wish to emphasize the importance of this Western interpretation; and to interpret *it* in turn. Embedded within it, covertly, were a view of history, a view of religion, and a view of language, to which it will be rewarding to give close heed; as well as its having been characterized by an absence of a view of scripture.

A major first step this was, in the process of scholarship. Some excellent work was done; one must not fail to be impressed by it. Over against the Muslim view that the Qur'an originates in the mind of God, Western scholars were resolute that it originated, rather, in the mind of Muhammad and in the milieu in which he lived. They set out to demonstrate this, to investigate it, to document it with precision, depth, and elaborate analysis. They succeeded brilliantly. In careful studies of the Prophet's life and times, of Arabic and of foreign vocabulary, of currents of ideas, international contacts, social conditions, economic developments, and much else, the historical situation of that period was assiduously reconstructed. Within that reconstruction the Qur'an was shown to take its accepted place.

The work was on the whole magisterially done. It was on the whole incontrovertibly valid. So far as the text itself was concerned it was on the whole illuminating of the process of its emergence as, in due course, a book (the first in Arabic) and of the meaning that its various parts may be mundanely seen to have had in the environment in which they first arose. We must pay our tribute to the scholarship that effected this. The quarrel is only with any concomitant assumption that once one has ascertained or reconstructed *this* view of the Qur'an one has therein discovered its true meaning, historically. That generation of scholars, no matter how formidable, has definitely not left our generation with the problem of scriptures' meaning fully solved.

In this historicist interpretation were embedded, we have suggested, a view of history, a view of religion, and a view of language. Let us look at each in turn.

An intellectual outlook strong in Western academic thought at that time (and for some, still dominant) may be called "analytic". The modern Western university as such has often been excellent at analysis, but seemingly less good at synthesis, and indeed less concerned with it. This matter was even formalized in philosophy when some for a time explicitly held that truth is analytic, or is arrived at analytically.

In the historical realm, a dominant mood was to think of history as the past. The historian's outlook had an orientation backwards, and indeed historiography was thought of as the knack of intellectually contravening time's arrow and threading one's way in the opposite direction back along the one-way street of humankind's historical development.

Taking this and the analytic predilection together, an attitude prevailed whereby the task of an historian was often understood as that of considering anything extant at any given point in the historical process and discerning the parts out of which it was composed, ferreting out where each had come from, tracing the various elements of any complex back to their respective sources. Thus anything was thought to have been understood when it had been broken up intellectually into its components, and deemed to have been understood historically when the lines here converging had been traced back to their various origins.

One should not under-estimate how powerful was this view: powerful both in the sense of enabling a deal of accurate, and illuminating, material to be discovered, and displayed, and also in the sense of powerfully colouring, however unconsciously, the outlook, the worldview, of those generations. Much truth was attained via this route. Yet like all human ventures, it was limited, even flawed. That it is the human condition to live by half-truths would be a formula a whit simplistic; but whether we can up half-truths to, might one say, a three-quarters level, or whether all percentages for all the fluctuations are of a much, much lower order, one hesitates to aver. This much we do know: that it is historically naïve to be other than humble in one's asseverations. Intellectual inquiry is an art, of combining confidence about what one knows with humility about its feeble approximation to full truth on the matter.

It will be noted that we ourselves, however persuaded that this way of going at historical understanding is but a first step, attempted in our preceding chapter something of the sort with regard to scripture in the West generally. We did so feeling that that could be illuminating. Yet there are serious limitations to the outlook. History is not the past; history is process. The study of history is the study of process. To understand history is to understand movement—forwards.

In analysing an historical datum into parts, the older view tended to overlook or anyway not to interpret the process that went into the synthesizing (a process obviously crucial, historically). An historical account of anything that separates out its elements and traces each back to its source is not so accurate a description of what actually happened as is one that looks at exactly the same facts but the other way around, and makes intelligible the historical process by which those disparate items from here and there were at a given moment creatively put together, to constitute something new. It is the integrating of parts into a whole that is historically interesting; and that was historically significant—stupendously so in the Qur'an case. Moreover, after something has been put together, its subsequent career is to be ascertained and understood. After all, one has hardly explained the Qur'an if one explains, however meticulously, what went into it, but does so in a way that neglects, that leaves uninterpreted, even incomprehensible, perhaps even unnoticed, what came out of it, and for fourteen centuries has continued spectacularly to come out of it in expanding waves from Spain to Indonesia, from Kazakhstan to central Africa.

The outlook here criticized, under-playing the process of construction and the success of integrations, while neglecting subsequent emergences, one might uncharitably call "studying history backwards"[9].

The earlier tendency to ask about causes more than about effects was conspicuously true of the Qur'an. One instance is that regularly translations in English, French, and the like published by the West quietly re-arranged the *surah*s (chapters) in chronological order, evidently taking for granted that Western readers would of course be interested in the form of this work before it became a scriptural book for Muslims, not after. Scholars wrote books on the sources of Muhammad's ideas, and for a time there was, for instance, quite an argument as to whether he had taken more from the Jewish or from the Christian side. There was relatively little inquiry, to follow up that particular example, as to how it was that once the Qur'an and the Islamic movement were launched, persons from these two earlier communities came in great numbers (many millions), in subsequent decades or centuries, to prefer the Qur'an's way of putting things previously known to them in Christian or Jewish forms—and accordingly became Muslims[10]. As of scripture at large, the significance of the Qur'an lies in part, no doubt, in the background and its mundane sources; but so far as actual history is concerned, that significance lies in much greater part in its prodigious and continuing force in the lives of men and women and children since, as over a large sector of the globe and over a long course of centuries they have in its light dealt with their changing problems and have confronted creatively a fluctuating series of varied contexts.

The point is illustrated in many, almost all, aspects of Western study; but perhaps in none more tellingly than in the verbal meaning of the text. We have remarked that Muslims have throughout been writing commentaries on the meaning of their sacred word. In the West there was until recently strikingly little attention paid to this voluminous literature, on the grounds that Muslims—being dupes, as it were, of the notion that this was scripture—of course could not understand that text so well as could a Western scholar free from that limitation. Besides, this commentarial literature was relatively "late" (a derogatory term): most of it comes from the third Muslim century on, and therefore it could be disregarded. The later it was, the more dismissible. A new interpretation introduced, let us say, in the eighteenth century seemed to these observers not relevant to an understanding of the meaning of the text. Illustrated here is a cavalier attitude to history, specifically to on-going history (yet surely history is nothing if not something that on-goes!). The eighteenth century is just as important in the eyes of God, a theist might say, as is the seventh; it should be just as important in the eyes of an historian. These men (we say "men", for there were virtually no women among them) saw the Qur'an as a seventh-century Arabian document. They simply failed to see and to note the historic fact, vivid to us if we be sensitive, that it is equally a ninth-, and a fourteenth-, and an eighteenth-, and a twentieth-century document, actively; and that it has been intimately involved in the life and history not only of Arabia but of Nigeria and Sumatra, Northern India and western China.

The Qur'an has played a role—formative, dominating, liberating, spectacular—in the lives of millions of people, philosophers and peasants, politicians and merchants and housewives, saints and sinners, in Baghdad and Cordoba and Agra, in the Soviet Union since the Communist revolution, and so on. That role is worth discerning and pondering. The attempt to understand the Qur'an is to understand how it has fired the imagination, and inspired the poetry, and formulated the inhibitions, and guided the ecstasies, and teased the intellects, and ordered the family relations and the legal chicaneries, and nurtured the piety, of hundreds of millions of people in widely diverse climes and over a series of radically divergent centuries.[11]

We cannot, then, set aside this development and freeze the object of our interest to one moment of its large course, that initial moment, with not a moving picture of its dynamic and variegated life but a single frame, magnified, and held fixed and motionless, so that all its details could be minutely studied[12].

That historians, of all people, prosecuting what has generally been called historical criticism of a scripture, should be so static in their vision, may seem odd. Indeed we have perhaps presented this interpretation of the position as though it were a whit ludicrous. Yet not to understand it would itself be anhistorical. That way of looking at the world, and of analysing historical movements, is intelligible when seen as arising when and where it did, and as functioning in its particular cultural setting. It too is to be understood historically. Today, with a more informed awareness and a more cosmopolitan vision, we can see the earlier contribution as falling nicely into place in the historical development of Western scholarship and Western civilization generally, and can see that it has been indeed a major contribution. Yet it is one beyond which it is our privilege now to move.

Our second issue with regard to the West's understanding in recent centuries in this area, beyond the particular sense of historiography, has to do with the era's views on religion. Muslims themselves have often sensed in Western Islamics scholarship an hostility out to undermine their faith. In some instances that scholarship has been built on sheer fascination (and on the Western drive to know). In other cases there may indeed have been a conscious or more usually unconscious antipathy, or at least disdain, seen in attempts to break up the Islamic religious system, intellectually. Involved here is the point that Enlightenment rationality was founded, in significant part, on a critique of religion; and Western academic mentality was for a good while inherently skewed against an intellectual understanding of human spiritual traditions, especially as institutionalized. (To some degree the same disintegrating perspective was brought to bear, even within the Church, on the West's own scripture, the Bible.) Relevant, too, is the point that the modern analytic mode of thinking has itself been inherently oriented away from human wholeness, and creativity, and synthesizing vision. The religious dimension, after all, has been the primary locus of humanity's endeavour to see things whole—and to achieve integration, wholeness, oneself. This has been so with special force in the Islamic case, where a central emphasis has been on *tawhid*, unifying.

Moreover, Western religious mentality was inherently intolerant of "religions" other than its own. Thus Christians and Jews, on the one hand, secularists on the other, however polarized at home, joined forces *vis-à-vis* the rest of the world in a conviction that their religions were benighted, even illegitimate. Few in the West today have any inkling of how arrogant and derogatory was the nineteenth-century attitude to Asian religious life[13].

Linking the critique of religion generally with the perception of history generally, we turn to note a dominant attitude on religious history of the West internally. The sense that the study of history was a search for origins, that in these matters the pursuit of truth was a quest for the pristine, colours a good deal of the intellectual vision of an era, now drawing to a close; yet especially, one may feel, it has coloured interpretations of religious history.

Embedded here was what might be called "the 'big-bang' theory" of religion. This contrasts with a "continuous creation" view, which we proffer as substantially less inadequate for interpreting human religious developments here on earth. By "the 'big-bang' theory" we mean the outlook, predominant last century and early in this, that perceived each of the so-called religions of the world as a particular entity, an object, introduced at a particular time and place, usually by a so-called "founder", with éclat; with subsequent generations of "believers" living at increasing distance from that originating explosive moment as its echoes reverberated down the centuries. To understand any given religion in this scheme was therefore to go back to that first creative moment, reconstructing it in historical imagination or with historical scholarship as accurately as feasible. This view was applied to history generally; but as we have remarked, especially to religious history. In both realms it leads to the genetic fallacy. To understand the role in human life of oaks, one must study more than acorns.

One may speculate that the whole historicist orientation probably derived to no negligible degree from the West's own religious experience out of, specifically, the Protestant Reformation. That innnovating movement, and its critique of the religious institutions and practices and theories of its day, affirmed a thesis that the true form of Christian life and thought was to be found at the historical beginnings. "Back to the original" was a major element in the Reformers' vision. No doubt their own personal piety, and that of the massive movement that they launched, were oriented to their contemporary scene. The first-century Christ whom they preached, and the long-since-composed Bible that they read and made popular, played a burning role in their lives as immediately present realities. They were no antiquarians! Nevertheless, over against the Roman Catholic Church and its long history, the Reformation repudiated in principle Christian development through time; and located Christian truth historically in, rather, its earliest appearance. In this Protestant worldview, Church History was not the locus of spiritual truth, except in its initial moment. "The original is the true."

This way of thinking was tacitly transferred to the West's growing awareness of other religious life outside its own culture. "Buddhism" was seen as a religion formulated and proclaimed by the Buddha. (The massive over-simplification, indeed gross distortion, of such a notion is apparent to anyone today familiar with Buddhist religious history, not only in China and Japan, but even in India. More conspicuously than most, the Buddhist religious life has been ineluctably a movement, not a system[14].) "Hinduism" was studied with preponderant emphasis on the Rig-Veda, its earliest manifestation (a matter at whose scriptural aspects we shall be looking in a later chapter). And so on. In the Islamic case, the whole complex and its development were perceived in terms of a conceptual scheme that saw Muhammad and his immediate followers as having injected into the stream of mundane history in the seventh century in Arabia an allegedly supernatural something, a religion that the West last century called Mohammedanism, comprising the Qur'an and various other elements, certain doctrines, certain rituals, and the like, the several elements being bound together into a rather closely knit and even rigid pattern. This was seen as constituting a neat package for export, which then was indeed carried far and wide across the lands and across the centuries. Admittedly the task of wrapping it up ready for long-distance shipment and making sure that it would endure intact across the ages took a certain time (a few generations, a few centuries), and involved incorporating into the package various elements largely borrowed from other cultures, or extraneous bits and pieces that got stuck to it inadvertently; also, it was found like other religions to have accumulated in use accretions of various sorts as time went on, so that every now and then reformers might be expected to arise to undo the wrappings and to clean off the adhering foreign matter. The core of the affair, however, was thought of as that original seventh-century entity. And the validity of the whole enterprise was thought of as a question as to whether that original entity did or did not come from outside history as alleged.

We shall later argue that faith, whether one's own or others', can be seen more truly and interpreted more cogently when conceived in terms of a transcendent dimension on the one hand, and ever-changing historical form on the other; that to live a life of faith is for any given person—oneself; or one's neighbour, next door or across the world or across the centuries—to participate in an on-going historical process in and through which one is open to transcendence (to the divine, if one uses that vocabulary). In any case, at the historical level the dynamic context of participation is incontrovertible. Some years ago I argued in my *Meaning and End of Religion* that human religious life, in all its diversity of forms, can be understood best, and perhaps understood only, always in terms of two components: a cumulative tradition, and personal faith. However one may think about, or elect not to think about, Muslims' faith, there can be, for anyone who is in any degree informed, no question but that their cumulative tradition has been dynamic, evolving, diverse. It cumulates. Islam in the fourteenth century has not been the same as in the tenth. Islam in Indonesia has not been the same as in Timbuktu. Islam in the royal court, or the scholar's study, has not been the same as in the village. The differing parts of the whole have been interlinked, in dynamic interplay, but yet they have not been identical, nor have the linkages been fixed. Historically the

Islamic fact has been, and continues to be, a surging, onward movement; no doubt beginning in some sense in Arabia in the seventh century, but developing over great expanses of the earth and over great tracts of time; rich, complex, pulsating, variegated; not a system but a process.

To say that the real meaning of the Bhagavad Gita is its original meaning is like saying that the word "manufactured" really means "made by hand". I am fascinated by etymologies; but I would be an obtuse historian not to recognize that the meaning of words is always in process. To use any word is to participate at a given point in the on-going historical process of its meaning. To read any text, or to hear any pronouncement, is to participate not only in this general process but also, more strictly, at two particular points, that of its being uttered or written, as well as that of its being heard or read.

This brings us to our third matter, which has to do with language, and changing views of language. I subsume the historical-process matter, which obtains here as everywhere else, and move on to that issue of participating at at least two points: the community aspect of language, and the Muslim-community (*ummah*) aspect of the Qur'an as scripture. (Community here includes, of course, community over time.)

In our concluding chapter below we shall return to this issue of language, which of course is pivotal for an understanding of scripture generally—and, indeed, for an understanding of being human. On both counts, the time has come to move beyond the great step that was taken in the nineteenth century and has been developed in this, of envisaging language objectively—impersonally. Language, as we shall observe, is not an object, but a human quality. To see it as an object can be helpful only if one moves on to reconstruct also its inherent link with persons; re-integrating into one's apprehension of it both its always individualist and its always communal nature. Language is, fundamentally, something that people do, and are. It too is a human activity.

Language, no less than anything else human—and much more than some—is a mystery. Anything that one can say or think about it is an over-simplification. Yet we must strive over time to be a little less superficial than we were before. Language is an entrancing and marvellous human quality whereby what is going on in the mind and heart of one person can in part be shared in the mind and heart of another or others—whereby some degree of community, however slight (yet it may even be paramount), is established between or among them. It is a quality magnificent and always impressive; yet as a device it is always at least slightly imperfect. What is communicated to the hearer or reader is sufficiently close to what is intended by the speaker or writer that we do well to be awed and to be grateful; and yet they are in principle never exactly the same—and especially not in important or subtle or deep matters. Since the meaning for any person of any term or concept, let alone of any phrase or sentence or text, is incorporated, and preferably integrated, into that person's total experience and worldview, is or becomes part of that, therefore that meaning can never be exactly the same for any two persons (even though in a particular case the difference *may* be so small as to be in practice negligible), nor for any two centuries (and here the difference may be quite significant), nor for any two regions. For two quite differing cultures, similarity cannot but be sadly partial.

Accordingly, every sentence has always in principle at least two meanings: what it means to the person who speaks or writes it, and what it means to the one who hears or reads it. It is a fact of observation that the two may converge closely, or diverge slightly or much. The convergence or the divergence may in certain cases be studied, and even measured. If there be hundreds of readers, or thousands, or millions, the matter becomes quite complicated. (Human history—human living in society through time—*is* complicated!)

The rise of modern individualism in the West tended to stress the meaning that a writer put into a given sentence. Central or basic was deemed to be the meaning of the individual person who said or wrote something: his or her intention[15]. (Academics in particular were much caught up in this—though its hold has begun to loosen.) It would seem to pertain little, if at all, in the case of poetry. Archibald MacLeish, it will be remembered, affirmed: "A poem should not mean / But be"[16]. Poetry no doubt comes closer to the scriptural situation than do other forms of language, as we shall be considering more carefully in later chapters[17].

With regard to the Qur'an, the assumption that the meaning of its words and phrases is simply what the author meant by them was another form of the historical fallacy that it is fundamentally or exclusively a seventh-century document—for those who assume in addition that its author was Muhammad and not God. What has made the Qur'an scripture, however, is precisely that for Muslims it has been received as the word of God. Not to take this seriously, whatever one's own view of the authorship[18], is to foreclose its meaning as scripture; is to give up from the start any attempt to apprehend its scriptural quality.

Any item of language, we have contended, as understood involves participation by at least two—and possibly many—persons. If a sentence means something, this is always a short-hand way of saying that it means something *to somebody*[19]. What it means, to a given person or given group of persons, is an empirical question, an historical question. There are norms prescribing what a word means or should mean, but those norms are themselves always in the minds or hearts of certain people or groups of people at certain times and places. Further, they are operative insofar as people consciously or unconsciously support or follow them. Language is a human quality; and it exists at all and is significant not in itself, but because it is a symbol for the meanings of persons. It is not a self-subsistent reality; and insofar as meaning is associated with it, that meaning is not inherent. By this one is saying quite straightforwardly that it does not inhere, is not contained within it or within its parts. Meaning exists only inside the consciousness—or the unconscious—of living persons.

(As remarked, however, this matter will occupy us more fully in chapter 10.)

We are ready now to close by addressing directly the question raised in this chapter: the true meaning of the Qur'an as scripture. Our suggestion—indeed our affirmation—is that the Qur'an has meant whatever it has meant, to those who have used or heard it or appropriated it to themselves; and specifically, that the Qur'an as scripture has meant whatever it has meant to those Muslims for whom it has been scripture. Every passage has meant this or that to so-and-so in such-and-such a place at such-and-such a time. The historian can in principle document that it has in fact meant to some degree similar and to some degree different things to different people at different times and places; and can document what those similar things and different things have been and are. The observer with Muslim friends may report what it means to them. We may therefore add together all of these to form a dynamic complex. We spread them out before our minds over the array of the historical process to arrive at the total meaning thus far, as a coherent concept. (This scripture will have future meanings too, we may be sure; these have not yet been determined.) This sequence of various meanings, whatever these have been, is real, is empirical, is a complex of intelligible historical facts. The links among them, the interconnections, the influences, the processes of change, the divergencies, the persistences, the communal life, the communal pressures, the force of traditions, can all in principle be traced. Thus we leave out nothing that Muslims have seen in it. Why should we? Only prejudice, not historical fidelity, can omit the nuances and the reverberations that Muslim reading of it has evinced.

The real meaning of the Qur'an is not any one meaning but is a dynamic process of meanings, in variegated and unending flow. The true meaning of scripture is the solid historical reality of the continuum of actual meanings over the centuries to actual people. It is as mundane, or as transcending, or both, as have been those actual meanings in the lives and hearts of persons.

We would emphasize that it is usually both—and more: that the scripture, being treated as such, is dimly or vividly recognized as meaning not only such-and-such but at the same time more even than that, more than the reader or hearer has as yet discerned. Scripture has sustained the human awareness of a transcending reality, and the human instinct to reach out after it, at the same time as it has proffered the sense that that reality is within reach, and indeed that it is such-and-such.

Any scripture—Gita, Bible, a Buddhist Sutra, or whatever—and any verse or term within it, means what it in fact means, and has meant, to those for whom it has been meaningful.

The only person, it would seem, who may reasonably dispute this conclusion, is the devout Muslim. He or she might well hold that— while our interpretation here may be cogent, and to him or her persuasive, for other scriptures around the world—nonetheless the true meaning of the Qur'an is what God means by it: the true meaning of any word or verse is the meaning in the mind of God. To this, he or she might well go on to say, the various meanings that history evinces in the process of their earthly development constitute an on-going and ever-varying approximation. (Among Muslims, there has been the "Holy Tradition" [*hadith qudsi*] presenting God as saying that "when someone recites or reads the Qur'an, that person is, as it were, entering into conversation with Me and I into conversation with him or her"[20]. Even theologically, it is seen as a bilateral affair, as well as a continuing one.)

That Muslim position deserves to be taken seriously. Far from dismissing it, we shall strive to incorporate into our final theory its discernments (not necessarily involving the particular concept "God"). Equally significantly, we would trust that the Muslim could incorporate our analysis into his or hers. After all, he or she might say, God must be a pretty good historian. Presumably He is more aware than are any of us of the complexities and the fluidity of human life lived in our historical flux. We contend that the Muslim community's perception of the Qur'an as scripture through time must be recognized as basic—whether or not one see it as simply a line, or as the base of a triangle with God always at the apex: an ever-expanding triangle. Similar considerations apply in the Christian case—certainly to their own scriptures, and also potentially to a Christian view of others'[21]. If God has something to say to human beings through scriptures, this is the way that for good or ill He/She/It has said it—has had to say it.

It is hardly obstreperous to suggest that if God acts in human history, it was not only for a moment long ago. This could happily be discussed with the participant or theologian, Islamic, Christian, or generic. For the observer, we proffer our submission: that the meaning of the Qur'an is the history of its meanings—a dynamic, rich, creative, continuing complex; one that is deeply intertwined with the lives of several hundreds of millions of persons over many centuries and many lands.

This is the meaning that it is the business of scholarship to uncover; and that an outside observer who would understand the Qur'an (or anyone who would understand our common humanity) must postulate as the goal of his or her apprehension[22]. An alternative way of formulating our thesis would be this, which correlates with our general affirmation—recognition—that the study of religion is the study of persons. The meaning of the Qur'an as scripture lies not in the text, but in the minds and hearts of Muslims.

Moreover, this is not fancy interpretation; it is a statement of observable fact.

CHAPTER 5

THE BIBLE
IN JEWISH LIFE?

THERE WAS A TIME when Christians, in particular, and various others including Western secularists, imagined that the Church's Old Testament was the Bible for Jews. This is misleading, and not merely over-simplified. A number of reasons may be given for rejecting the equation; a number of steps must be taken to approach more nearly an understanding of the place of scripture in Jewish life. To come to an appreciation of how distinctive that place has been, how divergent from presumed Christian parallels—and from secular assumptions—will in addition help us to refine and to enlarge our sense of scripture generally.

First, of course, it distorts to under-estimate either the significance of the title "Old Testament" for Christians, or its inappropriateness for Jews. (Some Christian groups, beginning recently to appreciate the latter point, jeopardize or evacuate the former one—robbing Peter to pay Saul—by irresponsibly dropping the title "Old Testament" in academic and also in liberal Christian usage, even liturgy.)

Although the matter is much more complex than a question of names, as we shall be noting, nonetheless we may begin by considering also that particular issue. One point is that for Jewish life even the word "Testament" is unhelpful here. The term has changed its meaning since first used by the Church, as we have previously noted. The alternative English translation, "covenant", of the same original would serve better. It would still not quite suffice, however, since it has a specific sense in Jewish outlook that is other[1].

More deeply problematic is the designation "Old".

For no engaged community is their scripture old as distinct from contemporary. It is new every morning. As a living force in their lives, it has functioned as an ever-fresh source of timeless truth; not of antiquarian. In a theist case such as the Jews', as they have read it they have heard God speaking directly to them there and then[2].

Nor for them is it old in the sense of former, preliminary, superseded. This is of course crucial, though the last of these three epithets—"superseded"—applies even in the Christian case only with qualification.

For Jews it has, indeed, been old in the sense of enduring. It has stood the test of time. This was all the more important before the modern days when the latest, most recent, most up-to-date became all the rage, with legacies from one's ancestors denigrated. This scripture has been seen as of long standing, authentic, genuine; not the product of nor modified by human whimsy or passing fashion, not faddish: abiding from of old, and sure to perdure long into the future. ("The Enduring Covenant" would serve better than "Old Testament", certainly.)

Apart from "Old Testament", however, there is a subtler question as to whether even the word "Bible" be altogether appropriate. It is from the Greek, and has been more generally if not basically a Christian term[3]. (Even for Christians, it has changed its meaning significantly every few centuries.) Modern Jews speaking English adopted it for a time. More recently they have been turning rather to a word of their own, taken from Hebrew literature of the past few centuries: *Tanakh*[4]. This is a Hebrew acronym for the three levels in which in Jewish perception are grouped and tiered the "books" that Christians more readily perceive as at one level all within a single category, one of their two, one Testament[5]. *Tanakh* is constructed from the initials of the Hebrew names of the three: the Law, and the Prophets, to use the traditional English names (although the Jewish and Christian Bibles include different books under "Prophets"), and the "Writings". (More technically, these may be named: the Pentateuch, the Prophets, and the Hagiographa.)

A point at issue here is that for Jews there have been three matters involved in that complex perception. Should one carry this further to say, explicitly: there have been three matters involved, not one? The matter is particularly subtle. The triliteral acronym *Tanakh* inherently poses the question, without quite answering it.

The answer, certainly the historical answer, is not a 'yes' or 'no', so much as of varying degree. I have not ascertained to what extent in Hebrew literature the term has been in successive centuries construed grammatically as a plural, to what extent as a singular. As we have seen, the word "Bible" itself derives from an original plural, and in Christendom "the scriptures" yielded during the Middle Ages gradually (never totally) to the singular "scripture". The relatively late emergence of *Tanakh* in Hebrew testifies to a parallel development, and in English it is fully a singular. The historical process is complex, and requires careful illumination: the process by which a people comes eventually to perceive the various elements that we nowadays call their scripture comprehensively, as a single identifiable entity. Still more elusive is appreciation of their situation in this realm in the period before the process has been completed.

Even among Christians, the term "Bible" has come into general use a good deal later than "scripture(s)". "Bible" has become a proper noun, whereas "scripture(s)" is ascriptive. "Tanakh" too is a proper noun, is the name of a book. "Torah" has become that to a degree only; it retains more—for the sensitive, much more—of its loftier senses, such as its original connotation of what God has to say to us: something of which the book is a record, or is an instance; even, a reminder of His saying it. In evidence here is that human process reiterated through history, whereby gradually the focus of attention becomes the symbolic forms themselves, more and more identified with, in extreme cases even replacing, what they symbolize. The human sense of transcendence is elusive unless embodied; yet it can become diminished when embodied too whole-heartedly. Observers, especially outside observers, must be especially careful not to miss the full scope of what has been going on, by insensitively using delimiting terms, or adopting inapt analogies.

Among the more decisive differences between the Jewish "Bible", whatever one call it, and the Christian Old Testament is the order of the books constituting them. The two begin in the same fashion. This is important. Opening with the creation of the world has given the vision of each community a cosmic context for their life and faith. Or—remembering that in other parts of our world the human consciousness of living in a cosmic context has taken other forms—one should rather say: Jewish and Christian scriptures' opening with God's creating of the world has given a form—in these two cases, an historicist form—to that human contextual consciousness of a cosmic context. In contrast, the two scriptures end quite divergently. In the Jewish case their Bible closes with II Chronicles and the edict of Cyrus, "Let them go up" to Jerusalem; in the Christian case, their Old Testament closes with Malachi and the prediction of a coming messianic figure[6].

Thus are the two communities' starkly divergent visions—of themselves, of human history, and of the divine—each served by, grounded in, perpetuated through, their respective patterns of "the same" scripture.

There are more minor differences, which though of some significance need not detain us. Yet another sort of difference is by no means minor. Even when a text is identical it has been read differently by the two groups[7]. This has been conspicuous over the centuries regarding messianic passages[8]—and passages that one community while not the other receives as messianic, such as the Suffering Servant portrayals in Isaiah[9]. We have seen it at work with less momentous import in the case of The Song of Songs. A dramatic instance is the story of the Exodus from Egypt.

This story has on occasion served both communities as a paradigm and inspiration for social hope, and on occasion for radical political activism. The former may be seen for instance among the African-American community, as their spiritual "Let My People Go!" warmly attests. Striking examples of the latter for Christians are during the seventeenth-century English Revolution, and the eighteenth-century American. Among Jews, the chief instances of its role in socio-political history have been in the Maccabean Revolt and the Zionist movement[10]. Further, the Exodus image of a people's journeying out of a situation of hardship through difficulties but under divine guidance to the Promised Land played a role difficult to over-estimate in the European migration to the United States, for both Christians and Jews.

Yet the two groups have differed in their symbolism for their central and most intense religious affirmation, of redemption and salvation. For Christians, this is set forth in the story of the Resurrection, re-activated annually at Easter. The Jewish counterpart is the story of the Exodus, re-activated annually at Passover. The role that these two have played over the centuries in the life, corporate and individual, of members of the respective communities is parallel. Appreciating what has historically been involved is needed to understand this particular Exodus scripture—or scripture generally; or shall we not say, these two, Christian and Jewish, deeply comparable yet conflictingly divergent instances of operative scripture.

As historians we do not know what happened on the Nile or at the Red Sea (or Sea of Reeds) or Mount Sinai three thousand and some years ago. Nor does it much matter. As historians we do know, and it does matter, that in modern times, and in mediæval, in a great range of places outside the Near East, chiefly in Europe and now in America, mediæval and modern Jews have in some measure found through their retelling of the scriptural story and their re-enforcing it with their observance each year of the Passover Feast—a symbolic celebration enabling them the more powerfully to appropriate and to internalize that sector of scripture—liberation from sorrow and threatened despair. They have to some degree been lifted out of the isolated individualism and loneliness to which all human beings are vulnerable, to find joy in community and to find grace.

The fact that the story has become scripture, and has continued as such, has meant that it has functioned in this decisive way in the lives, corporate and individual, of Jews, making available to them, as other forms have made available to others, the ever-renewed re-establishment and ever-enlivened continuance of their group, and the recognition and assurance that God—to use their theist term—loves us; and not only loves us but does something about it, so that our lives are transformed.

Again, what has been important has been not the text as such, but at the very least, what the text says: the story of which the text provides a record, a reminder. (The modern theological emphasis on story is an attempt to recapture this, for our new age.) Nor is it yet the story as such that has been of significance, so much as the event, the happening, the doing, of which the story, in turn, serves as a record, a reminder: the rescuing of a people in bondage and setting them on the road to triumph. Nor indeed is it merely that event, what happened. It is not simply the facts, as the *engagés* Jews have felt the matter; not simply the symbols, as we today might; not simply the fictions, as sceptics might—decisive though all these surely have been. Rather, and finally, the reverberating force of the whole affair has been twofold. First, the participants in that event have been seen and felt not as distant people of long ago but as they themselves, members of one continuing community. (The continuity, and the sense of community, are effected by the very awareness that is both engendered and expressed in this scripturalizing.) Secondly—or one may say, simultaneously—for them the doer of this great doing was, and is, God. For them, at work in these events was, and is, the power behind and within the entire universe, active on their behalf and bounteous.

To understand the Book of Exodus as an ancient or literary text, or both, is one thing. To understand it as scripture is of another order; and is the modern task. How the text came into being, and what empirical data lie behind its development as a text, is one type of inquiry. The relevant empirical facts pertaining to this Book, however, are those that over many centuries since have been giving it significance because it has been treated scripturally by one sector of our race.

As one interim step in exploring these aspects of the matter, let us revert for a moment to the question of names. The Passover reliving of the story of the Exodus brings that question into play. The fact is that neither "Bible" nor "scripture" nor "*Tanakh*" serves well as designating the central matter in Jewish life through the centuries in the realm that is our concern. There can be no doubt but that, for Jews, the most important concept here, to keep for the moment at this nominal level, has been "Torah". A primary task is to understand what that word has signified among them.

In fact, the term has had various meanings. This has been so not only at differing times and for diverse Jewish groups, but virtually in principle for all. To put the point in summary fashion: Torah may stand for something manifestly less than Bible; or, for something substantially more than Bible; or, it may signify indeed Bible; or finally—and more significant than any of these—it may refer to something other than Bible. Let us look at each of these four in turn. In each of the cases other than the third, it represents something more important to Jews than does the Bible. Without question it is the central Jewish concept in this realm.

In general, of course, the most important, the most central, Jewish concept is 'God'. In the mystic movement it has been affirmed that God and Torah are one[11]. Others without going that far have seen the relation between the two as certainly close. A near second in Jewish consciousness to the idea of God (some observers—especially non-theists—would say, logically prior to it or anyway functionally paramount) is the sense of peoplehood, of the Jewish community. The relation between this and Torah has again been seen as close. The Jewish community is indeed that group of human beings to whom Torah (or: the Torah) has been vouchsafed. Torah in all its denotations, given by God, received by the Jewish people, serves as the link between these two[12].

First: Torah as less than Bible. This word "less" is uncouth; since while the Torah in this particular sense forms a quantitative part of an objectively larger whole, yet it is not, cannot be, in any other sense "less". We are referring to the established usage in which the word Torah is the designation specifically for the first five books of the Bible—known traditionally to both Jews and Christians as "the five books of Moses". Thus the word Torah supplies the T of *Tanakh*; it is one part of scripture. It is the name for the first, and for them the highest, of what we have called the three tiers of writings that for Jews make up their Bible: the *Humash* or "Pentateuch"[13]. The Torah scroll, on which the five books are written, is the most sacred physical object in a synagogue. It is housed in an "ark", which at a certain point in the service is ceremonially opened to display that scroll, announcing the most holy moment in the service, which for many is the reading of the prescribed passage from it for the week, although others would feel that the high point of the service is their touching of that Torah scroll with the tassels of their shawls as it is formally carried around the congregation.

Thus in this case Torah constitutes expressly one section of the Bible.

Although without question Torah is and throughout has been the most important of the three, yet for many centuries the three sections collectively have been revered and have been treated together. In the synagogue service the reading of Torah just mentioned—in a set passage—has been "completed" by a reading (with different intonation) of a set passage from one of the other two sectors, the Prophets[14]. The relevance of the latter to the former has often been developed in the sermon. An interesting example is provided by the first chapter of Genesis, with its opening words on God's creating of the heavens and the earth; for this the "completing" or complementing (*haftarah*) passage in the prescribed lectionary is Isaiah 65: 17ff., with as its opening words—from God—the counterpart prophecy of something yet to come: "Behold, I create new heavens and a new earth"[15]. Thus together the two readings induce the worshippers' understanding of today as situated within a rounded context, divinely framed, of past, present, and future history; and understanding of all history, all human existence, as taking its place between—to translate now from theist to Greek terms—actual and ideal, related to both.

The particular passages that have made up this ritual lectionary complement (*Haftarot*, often with also the "Five Scrolls" for festival days) have together constituted another Biblical sector, often published along with the Pentateuch as a joint book[16]. A major modern Jewish source looking at the situation through history stresses the "sharp distinction" that must be made between the Pentateuch and "other sections of the Bible"; and speaks of the latter as having been "merely . . . secondary" for the most important purposes[17]. The source goes on to say that the moralizing haggadists, for their homiletic purposes, "Athough their main preoccupation was also with the Pentateuch", yet gave more attention than did the legalizing halakhists to such other parts of the Bible as were included in the public readings.

There are still other Biblical sectors that were not publicly read in the service at all.

Furthermore, often the Torah in this narrower sense has been given prominence without the other sectors. For example, with the introduction of printing in Europe, of the first six printed Hebrew texts five were of this Pentateuchal Torah, in each case with one of the established commentaries[18].

The supremacy of Torah in this particularized meaning over other parts of the Bible was retained often by perceiving those other parts virtually as explanatory elucidations of it, expansions setting forth its depths of meaning. In mediæval times, those other parts were often included in the concept *Qabbalah*, the tradition[19] that has come down. On occasion it was said that they could be interpreted in the light of those first five books, but never *vice versa*[20]. Nonetheless, one must recognize that historically the "five books of Moses" constituting this Torah in the restricted sense were in fact heard or read, as one might expect and as we shall be noting presently, very much in the light of later understandings[21]. (This is pointed up strikingly in that following the Prophetic period Moses was thereupon known as "Moses the Prophet"; and from the Rabbinic period on, as "Moses our Rabbi".) Another way of putting the observation is that later developments were in theory considered to be elaborations of this Torah, but to some degree were taken as in practice substitutes for it.

Or again, one may say that this small written Torah was perceived as a condensation of the later developments; so condensed, subtle, deep, that persons not steeped in the subsequent lore—non-Jews, certainly; but even those within the Jewish community not Talmudic scholars—could not be expected to understand it.

This leads to our next two meanings for the word "Torah": its signifying the Bible as a whole, and its signifying much more than the Bible.

The former need not detain us long. The usage has been not uncommon, yet informal. It has been widely recognized; yet it would appear to have been little developed, to have been given little precision or attention[22].

That Torah encompasses more than the Bible, on the other hand—our third consideration—has been not merely standard and explicit, but overwhelmingly formative. For ever since the third century A.D. or so, Jewish religious life has been established on the firm foundation that Torah is in two forms, Written and Oral (as we shall presently explore). The latter—the bulkier part—was seen as also in due course having been written down, as Mishnah[23], and was developed in subsequent Rabbinic work, most pivotally the two Talmuds. It continued to be called the Oral Torah on the theory that both Torahs had been given to Moses, the one in written form or to be written down forthwith, the other, larger, Torah to be transmitted by word of mouth, as it then was for several centuries. (Even when it became written, this was at first simply a device to facilitate its being memorized, was a subordinate form to its primary existence as an oral text[24].)

The wording "both Torahs" tends to be that of outsiders, or of modern educated Jews, who observe the conspicuous difference between them, historical and in content, and have assimilated this duality into their consciousness. The normal Jewish phrasing has been rather "one . . . Torah in two forms": "the one whole Torah of Moses, our rabbi", as the Talmudic sources say[25]; or as a modern Jewish scholar puts it, "The written Torah and the oral Torah together constitute a single whole Torah—the full and exhaustive statement of God's will for Israel and humanity"[26]. "Torah", then, in this which has in many ways been the dominant meaning of the term among Jews, is the name for the full revelation given, as they see it, by God through Moses to the Jewish people, and constituting—as everyone must see it—their most precious, most sacred, and of course most distinctive, most constitutive, treasure.

So forceful has been this enlargement of the meaning of "Torah", and so dominant has in fact been the Talmudic vision, that the transition is eased to our final sense of the term: its referring to something other than any document or set of documents.

Intermediate is the usage, quite prevalent from later mediæval times, whereby "Torah" has signified not a particular set of writings, but a somewhat amorphous body of material. It presupposes the particular set, but wanders on from there. Included are the Pentateuch, the Bible as a whole, the two Talmuds (in theory; in practice usually only one or the other, most commonly the Babylonian), and various supplementary works (the second- and third-century *Baraitot*, the twelfth-to-fourteenth century *Tosapot*) but also such further compositions as Rashi's enormously influential commentaries, on the Babylonian Talmud and on the Bible. (Printed editions of this Talmud, from the first in Venice 1520–23, have included its text in the middle of each page along with the *Tosapot* on the outside margin and Rashi's commentary on the inside[27]. Similarly, printed editions of the Hebrew Bible without Rashi's commentary on each page—or, less often, that of Ibn Ezra, David Qimhi, Nachmanides—have been rare.)

Nor has the process stopped; still today new works are added to the array. "Holy books" may signify Torah, but they do not constitute a designated, delimited corpus[28].

Torah here is the substance of what God has to say to Israel, or to humankind—"to us", Jews would put it. The texts connoted by it are whatever texts are recognized as facilitating one's hearing, understanding, personalizing that divine self-disclosure.

I have called this connotation of our term "intermediate", introductory to our next major sense, which has to do with something other than books, because the above already verges on the matter at issue in that final, and highly important, meaning of "Torah" that we must now consider. For it is not that these supplementary writings have themselves as such been deemed to be of divine provenance. Rather, what they have to proffer has been received as setting forth the content or meaning, elaborating the detail, of that divine self-communication.

What this leads us to next I have called "our final sense" in that in our present survey we are approaching it after having noted the others. In fact, however, it is the original or fundamental meaning of the concept, and has been an underlying sense supporting the others, giving each of them what substance it has had. It is final, for Jews, in the philosophic sense, of ultimate, both ontologically and teleologically: primordial truth and goodness, divinely made known as the highest wisdom and chief end of human life, the goal and destiny of the race.

Exploring this "final" meaning, then, will help us towards our final understanding of scripture.

We have begun by suggesting that our endeavour in this study is to apprehend, if we can, and to elucidate, if possible, what it is that evidently characterizes certain works as "scripture" for certain people. What is that quality that apparently elevates those works to this special status? In the present instance, we are addressing rather the preliminary question of Torah; this has the advantage both of being the term that Jews themselves have more readily used, and— as we shall see—of helping us to move towards reversing the way our question has been framed: away from asking what elevates certain texts to the status of scripture, in the direction of our discerning, rather, how the human sense of living in mutual relation with cosmic reality has been brought down to earth and become ensconced for a particular people in a verbal text, or at least correlated with it. We may find this easier to attain by focussing in the Jewish instance on their concept, "Torah", rather than on the recently elaborated and until now rather secularized generic one, "scripture" (or on the more predominantly Christian one, "Bible").

We proceed, as usual, empirically. Our attempt is to ascertain what the term Torah means—has meant—for those for whom it has been meaningful supremely. We say that the word applies to these or those books. Yet manifestly it does so by virtue of their being perceived as having a certain quality. Just as "scripture" has seemed to designate certain texts, yet our task is to ferret out the quality by virtue of which that attribute is legitimately given, that added dimension that—for some—renders that text scriptural, so here our task is to discern the special meaning that is at issue when the term Torah is used. The quality is not far to seek that Jews attribute to those matters that they have called Torah. (They would say, rather: the quality that they recognize as in fact underlying those matters. We might say: the operative quality that has been evinced in their lives lived in relation to them.) It is transcendent. The word *Torah* not merely connotes but primarily denotes that what is called this comes from God, and has been given for human enlightenment and fulfilment.

The word *Torah* is from a verb signifying[29] to instruct, to teach, to guide; and is so used in the Bible. With both verbal and nominal instances of it there[30], the subject is often human (parents' instructing their children, the teaching of sages, poets, priests, and others); in other cases it is divine. In mediæval usage, Maimonides's most famous work has a form of this root as the first word of its Hebrew title, usually translated "*Guide*" *(for the Perplexed)*[31]. The verbal noun, *torah*, could be rendered either "instructing" or, less dynamically, "instruction". In the Bible it sometimes is, and sometimes is not, used for a particular piece of objectivized instruction, in several cases then also in a plural; so that it is at times—but by no means persistently—translated "law(s)". In other instances it names an action. Thus as a category in Jewish religious thought, the word "Torah", meaning the divine Torah, may denote either the fact of God's mercifully guiding His people, or the guidance with which He has done so; or, eventually, the words in which that guidance is formulated; or again, the books in which those words are written. Those words and those books include, however, not only the content of the guidance but also the account—the reverberating affirmation—of His act of giving it.

In general the English word "Law" serves poorly to translate *Torah*. This is so particularly in modern times, when secularist and positivist views of law prevail, especially for societal matters, and when a polarity between, for instance, law and justice may be sensed as stark; let alone, a dichotomy between religion and state. There are as well several further reasons why it can be misleading.

Yet it does have one partial merit: it does make room for overtones to the material being referred to. "Law" is not the name for something that exists merely in libraries; or even primarily in libraries. Law is not contained in books. It lives, in society—even though in the case of literate groups one may have to look in books to find readily grasped indications of what that law is (has been), representing as it does a pattern of parameters of what is—or is deemed—normative practice in that group.

(Yet an argument can be mounted that for the Jewish case the term betrays a double misrendering: from Hebrew *torah* into Greek *nomos* and later from Greek *nomos* into English "law"—as two of perhaps the most consequential mistranslations in human history[32].)

It would not be far-fetched to say that "Torah" for Jews means revelation—whether this be taken as the term for a theological category, or for the content of revelation: the fact or the act of revealing, or what is revealed, or both. To the participant in the tradition these are hardly distinct. For observers from the outside, on the other hand, the situation is rather different. They can see what is perceived as revealed, hold it in their hands, or minds, study it historically and otherwise, compare it with other groups' scriptures or systems, and all, without a sense of divine provenance. Their perception of it is of a mundane object, or objective pattern, with the notion of divine involvement either dismissed or seen as at most a separate, added, "subjective" matter. They are perplexed, then, if the object is not delimited and specificable (after all, the orthodox modern Western secular ideology teaches that concepts are to refer to mundane things).

More elaborately still, it has been averred—and the suggestion is certainly not without serious plausibility—that "Torah" means "Judaism"[33]. I myself have contended that the modern-Western -*ism* formations recently coined to designate the various "religions" of the world do not stand up to scrutiny[34]; perhaps what is at stake here might be more effectively grasped if one substituted "Torah" to convey its most basic meaning. At least, one must recognize the fundamental reference to the intangibles.

All very well, one may retort, to entertain these grandiose accounts of the situation if one happens to be Jewish, or to believe in God. Otherwise, however—or even if one believes in God but happens not to recognize that He or She or It has through these channels of this particular people been speaking lovingly and demandingly to Jews over the centuries—what is one to make of these extravagant notions?

That question we defer for the moment, until we have considered also comparable but different instances of scripture in the lives of other groups around the world. Meanwhile our insistence is not on any particular interpretation of the facts, but on the facts themselves. Those facts, that situation, require comprehending, and explaining.

Outsiders have largely ignored or dismissed, as not of general human interest or serious intellectual concern, not only the Jewish interpretations, but also the day-to-day data that were being interpreted. At most, many have adopted the feeble nineteenth-century over-simplification of saying that Jews "believed" these things, as Muslims "believed" something else and similarly Hindus, Buddhists, Hottentots. The secularist "belief" theory is simplistic, and has many inadequacies; one is its supposing that the belief has caused the phenomena, without pondering the alternative hypothesis—much more plausible—that the experience underlay the belief. One must at least toy with the possibility that, for instance, the Jews' theories of their Torah, Muslims of their Qur'an, others of their divers scriptures, may have arisen, and have been sustained from one century to the next, and been held with both delight and conviction, because these theories made sense for them of what they knew to be happening—and knew to be precious—in their society and in their lives. Those of us who do not accept their theories are challenged to come up with a better explanation of those everyday facts: a more persuasive interpretation. It will, I would suggest, be one that is more comparative, universalisable.

We have been considering "Torah", and only indirectly either scripture or Bible. These three are not synonymous; nor indeed any two among them. Returning to scripture and the Bible, might we perhaps sum up in three propositions our investigation thus far:

1. The Bible—or: the Pentateuch—has been altogether central in Jewish religious life (considerably more so than, for instance, the Bible in Christian life);

2. The Bible has not been effectively important in Jewish religious life;

3. "Scripture" is not an appropriate category in the Jewish instance.

None of these propositions is valid. Yet neither is any one of them fully ridiculous. (I suggest this even though especially the second may appear, at first, quite outrageous.)

Let us consider each of these in turn. We do so even though any legitimate helpfulness that they might conceivably have comes from their being grasped jointly. Though none be valid singly, taking all three together may perhaps be seen to approach validity. We shall note the facts that support some plausibility of each. Once we have done that, we shall reject them, endeavouring to arrive rather at a more adequate interpretation of the situation.

The first, the centrality of the Bible, or at least of the Pentateuch, is a thesis easy to support. Indeed, it would be difficult to exaggerate in Jewish life a perceived primacy of the Bible, especially of its first five books. From time to time over the course of Jewish history there have been debates over other material widely regarded as sacred or authoritative in the legacy of the community: between Sadducees and Pharisees, between Karaites and the Rabbis, between Reform Judaism and other present-day movements, to cite examples at approximately thousand-year intervals. No group has ever disputed, however, the place of honour accorded to the revelation to Moses at Sinai; nor, by implication, to the recorded account of that. "From the formation of the Pentateuch onward, framers of various sorts of Judaism" (and we must note, in passing, that over the centuries there have indeed been various sorts, differing from one another quite significantly) "have had to take measure in particular of the Mosaic revelation and place themselves in relationship to it. Each version has found it necessary to lay claim in its own behalf to possess the sole valid interpretation of the Torah of Moses. All have alleged that they are the necessary and logical continuation of the revelation of Moses and the prophets" . . . "every sort of Judaism from the beginning to the present has had to make its peace with the Scriptures universally received as revealed by God to Moses at

Mount Sinai or to the prophets, or by the 'Holy Spirit' to the historians and chroniclers, psalmists and other writers."[35]

It is interesting to observe that within these few sentences, all taken from one paragraph of a recent Jewish critical scholarly work, the reference is in terms of four differing specifications of what is here at stake. The four are: first, the Mosaic revelation and the Torah of Moses, which may be taken as arguably identical; second, this revelation plus that of the prophets; third, these, from God, plus—in this case said to be from " the 'Holy Spirit' ", rather—the revelation to "the historians and chroniclers, psalmists and other writers"; and fourth, "the Scriptures". Illustrated here, casually— and the casualness is itself important—are some among the ambiguities on which we have already touched; or shall we say, some of the elasticity to which we have pointed. One could indeed say that a fifth possibility arises. For the first ("the Mosaic revelation", "the Torah of Moses") might be read as including the Oral along with the Written Torah[36]. In any case, the reference is to its content, rather than to its documentation. The next two successively add first one and then both of the other tiers, which together constitute the fourth entity here mentioned, the written Bible—although even in this last case, a plural is used, not a singular. Nor is the Bible explicitly mentioned.

However that may be, the basic point holds: that a scriptural corpus has for some two thousand years been an essential component in the Jewish worldview, or underlying it.

To be noted, however, before we proceed, is that our reference to "some two thousand years" nonetheless makes room for a time, which some would calculate as another thousand years or more, before the newer fact arose. The Jewish worldview presents itself as the outlook of a people dating from Abraham. The emergence of the Jews as a "people of a book", on the other hand, is, as we have noted, from a millennium or so later. (Even in the case of Moses, what is first set forth as allegedly in written form were "ten words" on two stone tablets, sacred objects[37] but not yet Scripture. That Moses wrote the books subsequently ascribed to his name is a much later idea.) The transition from worship of God centered in a temple to worship formed around a Bible was a gradual historical process that may roughly be seen as having begun with the destruction of the First Temple in the middle of the first millennium B.C., and as having been completed many centuries later, after the destruction of the Second Temple early in the first millennium A.D.[38].

The timing is not fortuitous. After this community's religious life could no longer have its focus on a temple and its ritual, its being centred on its scriptures became more compelling.

The "Biblical period" of Jewish history is often distinguished from a later "Rabbinic period". This is all right if by "Biblical" one means the period to which one or another of the Biblical writings ostensibly refers, or to which its being composed is ascribed by modern scholarship. If, however, we were to take it as indicating rather the period during which the Bible as known in recent centuries existed and was important, when the Jewish people were scriptural, revering that Bible as a sacred corpus, then the phrase "Biblical period" would designate the Rabbinic era and the centuries following it. In a strictly historical sense, the phase of Israel's development about which we read in the Bible was largely a pre-scriptural one. One reasonably might even call it pre-Biblical.

(In somewhat similar vein, although with less justification, some might wish to suggest that the Biblical period in Christian history begins with the Protestant Reformation.)

Certainly in those subsequent centuries the Bible has occupied pride of place in Jewish life. The Jewish movement became a Biblical movement after the period had long since come to an end that is today commonly called the Biblical period. Yet once this new development had happened, it would be difficult, as we have remarked, to exaggerate the centrality of that place. Its most powerful influence emerges in the reading of scripture in the synagogue service, which has both a weekly and a rich yearly dimension. We have already noted that the high point of each Sabbath service is the uncovering of the Torah scroll and its solemn recitation in Hebrew, followed at some periods by a reading in the current vernacular: in the old days, Greek or Aramaic; more recently, for instance English. Then both through mediæval and in modern times the sermon that follows normally relates some verse from that reading to the day-to-day lives of the congregation, keeping alive the contemporaneity of God's word.

Hardly less important is the constantly repeated annual cycle, organized in such a way that not merely is the Torah, in the sense of the first tier of the Biblical books, gone through each year, with the accompanying *Haftarot* or supplementing passages from the second tier, the Prophets (and on festival days, from one of "the [Five] Scrolls" from among "The Writings", the third tier). What the outside observer does well to recognize is that the lives of the congregation are hereby endued with a firm annual pattern, such that each year is lived with a structure that the Bible provides. It is not only that time is apprehended scripturally, so that a secularist's saying (thinking) that he or she will do such-and-such a thing "next July" or "before Christmas" has as counterpart the Jew's saying, thinking, feeling, that that will happen at the such-and-such season (even, in such-and-such week) in terms of the Biblical lectionary. Moreover this structuring of time has cosmic overtones. Or one might better say: certain cosmic overtones of our life are made available to Jews in these temporal forms. Religious systems symbolize and communicate transcendence and ultimacy sometimes most strikingly through plastic and visual artistry, or through sacred space, or the structuring of sound. Doubtless all groups have developed patterns of sacred time, also; but perhaps none so fully as have Jews. The concept of the week, with its culminating Sabbath as the sustaining and enriching element, is of course salient here. Also not to be ignored, however, in an understanding of the transcendent dimension of Jewish life and of the role of the Bible in fashioning and sustaining also this, is the year.

"The community effectively relives the myth of its Scripture each year", a modern scholar writes[39], noting how the annual lectionary and the seasonal festivals are co-ordinated. The new year begins each autumn with the creation of the world in Genesis; winter is related to the time of servitude in Egypt; with spring comes release from that oppression (pointed up in Passover); the summer is spent receiving the divine revelation at Sinai (marked in festival by Shavuot) and wandering in the desert (Sukkoth); the old year ends on the verge of entering the Promised Land[40]. (The actual story in the Bible of the conquest of Palestine is not in the Pentateuch, but at the beginning of the next book, Joshua—which in the Jewish pattern is the first of the next tier, the Prophets. In the formal Torah, the Promised Land lies still in the future.)

Unlike the Pentateuch, the supplementing readings from the Prophets (*Haftarot*) are arranged in the course of the year not sequentially but thematically, in relation to the annual cycle. Thus after the period commemorating the destruction of the First Temple in Jerusalem, passages of consolation are prescribed from Isaiah, in preparation for the season of Atonement and the High Holy Days of the early autumn. Then the cycle begins again.

Jews have differed from each other, of course, often drastically, in the realm of the facts in their individual life. The ordering, however, of those facts, whatever they severally might be, day by day, week by week, year by year, was given them by a scriptural pattern, proffered in liturgy. That pattern, being shared in common, gave order also to their life together, holding them in community.

The Bible was important, then, in this sense of providing form to and among persons whose living was of whatever varied content. We may note other matters attesting to its central importance in Jewish life. Apart from functional effectiveness, it has served as the most important Jewish sacred object. "Hasidic Jews dance with it, and even liberal Jews stand in its presence"[41]. Theologically, one may note a contrast with the Christian case, in that for Jews even Moses, however towering a figure, derives his significance from the fact that to him the Torah was revealed. For Christians, in reverse, even the New Testament, however central a scripture, derives its significance from the fact that it tells about Christ. (This holds for all Christians. In addition, for Roman Catholics the Bible derives its authority from the Church, which in turn is subordinate to Christ.) In the Jewish vision, Torah has been held to be pre-existent[42]; in the Christian, Christ has been. Jews participate in the divine mind, even the divine activity, and the more mystical have felt, in God Himself, through Torah; Christians, through Christ.

We have in our last chapter remarked on parallel comparisons or contrasts between the Islamic and Christian outlooks, with Qur'an in that case in a Christ-like position and Muhammad as significant derivatively. The Jewish and the Islamic patterns are much more similar to each other than either is to the Christian.

Torah in these cases has for some Jews had the full range and depth of meaning that we have seen the word at times to carry; for others, it has signified, at least basically, the Written and Oral Torah, including therefore the Bible.

Some of the mystics ascribed cosmic meaning not only to every jot and tittle of the text, as did the community at large, but also to the space in and around each letter[43]. (This is one way of indicating to us the transcendence that for them the text enshrined.) At another side, as it were, of the spectrum, it has been more than once remarked that throughout history "[t]he bulk of Jewish literature is in the form of commentary on Scripture"[44]. Again, "every manifestation of the Jewish mind, is in a very special sense interpretation of the Bible"[45].

In point of fact, it is misleading to take such remarks literally. Even the Mishnah and the Talmud[46], although traditionally taken as explicating the Bible, actually set forth a different and innovative outlook pertaining to a later age—though in the latter case skilfully linking or appearing to link new visions to the inherited texts. The literature and thought characterized in these statements as commentary have been original, not dependent. The writers and thinkers can today be seen to have evinced much ingenuity and artistry, and striking imaginative power, in casting whatever of significance they had to say in terms that correlated it with the Bible.

We shall return to these issues, in considering under our second proposition the suggestion that the Bible may in retrospect be seen to have been less important in practice than it has been in theory. First, however, we may press the opposite point: that they show how central a place the Bible has had in the ambience of Jewish life. Apart from general literature and thought, even in more narrowly religious matters the Rabbis themselves found scriptural passages purportedly justifying ritual practices and moral precepts that in fact were quite extra-Biblical[47]. These matters can be taken as indicating how important a role the Bible had come to play, and continued to play, in Jewish culture. Mediæval Jews took for granted the later elaborated accounts of Biblical stories, and read back into their sense of the Biblical text the embroidered details unknown there but amplified later in the Talmud[48]. This meant that those Jews lived in a world perceived with outlines given in scripture. They added their own data and substance, but always within that form and in relation to it.

The Bible was perceived as a unitary whole; at the same time, each part of it was held as having various levels of meaning—for some, four levels. (Christians shared or imitated this orientation in their mediæval involvement with their Bible.) These four were a straightforward or plain meaning, an allegorical, a homiletic, and a mystical. The Hebrew acronym for these four was *PARDES*. This term converges with the Hebrew form of the word for "paradise"—an idea that does not occur in their Bible[49]; but after the Persian period in their history it became for Jews, as presently also for Christians and then Muslims, a foundational element in their world-view. To live within the world of the Bible, as traditionally Jews have done, was to live, in a sense, in Paradise—or at least, to live in day-to-day relation with it. Less metaphorically, we may say that the richness of the scripture perceived as God's eternal self-communication to the nation and the world (the richness of His self-communication perceived as having its locus in or through scripture) signified something in Jewish life whose centrality and ramifications can hardly be over-estimated. We must recognize, too, that such richness, inexhaustible in principle as well as virtually in practice, and ever fresh, was perceived as inherent in it not as text but as scripture. Taken literally, some authorities were ready to affirm, it did not amount to much. We could write better stories ourselves, said one of the Rabbis[50]. But in each word of the Torah are "supernal truths and sublime mysteries"[51]. The Bible purveyed to Jews a capacity to live in relation to sublime matters. Or, recalling that for others this has been accomplished differently, we may say that the Bible realized for them our human capacity so to live, and gave it form.

What from the modern critical observer's viewpoint might seem among the most far-fetched of traditional expositions were those made in Haggadah, the homiletic interpretations of or sorties taking off from one or another Biblical passage, or in the Saturday sermons weaving contemporary messages based on or inspired by an often isolated text. Formally, Haggadah was deemed less basic than Halakhah, the authoritative "legal" injunctions derived—at least ostensibly—from scripture. In fact, however, it was the Haggadah and the sermons that gave Jewish life the shape within which the observance of the Halakhah precepts made sense. They "brought God into the home and made him a member of the family"[52].

Since it was the spiritual overtones of the Bible *as scripture* that provided the special quality that both made it so important in traditional Jewish life and make it the subject of our present inquiry, one might infer that in modern times it would be losing its central place. To some extent among modernized Jews that is indeed, and emphatically, the case[53]. It is not yet clear in what fashion, nor indeed whether, Jews in the future will be able to, or will, construct their living in forms related directly to the Bible. Yet it is certainly too early to suppose that it is no longer central in their spiritual—and mundane—affairs.

Our second proposition, "The Bible has not been particularly important in Jewish life", will strike Jewish readers as outrageous. Also to others, one would hope, who have read our preceding section it will seem at least bizarre. Nonetheless, we should consider certain grounds for our having thought it up, and for presenting it as a potentially helpful step on the way towards a fuller understanding.

Early this century the *Jewish Encyclopedia*—planned, written, and edited by Jews—was published in twelve volumes[54]. It constituted a major statement of Jewish intellectual life. It has no article "Bible".

(Also, it has none on "Tanakh", nor on "Scripture"[55].)

The outstanding mediæval Jewish philosopher, commentator, and jurisprudent Maimonides set forth his understanding of Jewish faith in his renowned "Thirteen Principles"[56]. These, although evoking controversy at first (though not on the matter that concerns us here), in due course became widely accepted. The formulation has been exceedingly influential in the community's life. Indeed, it has come to form the nearest thing to an established "creed" that the Jewish community has. Its thirteen principles were presently incorporated in slightly revised form into the standard liturgy; and are there today in the regular Morning Service in the Prayer Book[57]. They do not mention the Bible[58].

Correspondingly, a present-day work by a leading Rabbi of Britain on the *Principles of the Jewish Faith*[59], "an attempt to discuss what a modern Jew can believe", has one chapter expounding each of the thirteen principles; and again none of them is directly on the Bible.

Indirectly, yes indeed: the Bible is recognized as posing for modern Jews their chief difficulty in the realm of believing; and the problem is poignantly wrestled with. It would hardly be going too far to say that this work's two chapters on Torah are concerned basically to assure the reader that he or she may indeed subscribe to the notion of the Torah as divine and immutable even while recognizing, as a twentieth-century person must, that the Bible[60] is human and historically contingent.

In Rabbinic literature, the word Torah occurs, of course, repeatedly; along with this fact it must be noted that no other word for Bible or scripture is common there. (*Tanakh*, for instance, is not a Rabbinic term.)

An impresive recent Jewish work is entitled *The People of the Book*[61]. It portrays the Jewish religious movement traditionally as that of a community indeed book-oriented. The "Book" at issue is, however, not the Bible; it is the Talmud.

The Talmud is widely thought of as a commentary on the Bible. In fact, however, it is a commentary on the Mishnah[62].

At least, this is the case—indisputably so—if one is to think of it as a commentary at all, paying heed more to form than to substance. More realistic in modern historical awareness is to recognize it as an original production, explicitly continuous with what went before. Specifically, the Mishnah (early third century A.D.) with its provisions now revised and amplified is of continuing and normative import. (One may even find passages in the Talmud where one opinion set forth stated explicitly that "the Mishnah takes precedence over Scripture"[63], although admittedly this is unusual.)

The Mishnah, in its turn, has at times been thought of as a commentary on the Bible; but this simply is not the case. Even more than the Talmud, it is a strikingly original document. It is so in both form and content. "The Mishnah rarely cites a verse of Scripture, rarely alludes to Scripture as an entity, rarely links its own ideas with those of Scripture, and rarely appeals to what Scripture has said even by indirect or vague allusion"[64]. It presents a view of the world that is as innovative as that set forth in the New Testament. As certain modern Jewish scholars are recognizing and affirming, the Mishnah is to the Jews' Bible what the New Testament is to the Christians' Old Testament[65]. Or, one might say that insofar as the Bible has a place in the Mishnah it is one comparable to that of the Old Testament in the New: its heritage taken for granted, and from time to time isolated passages from it cited as corroborating its own new outlook. In both cases, rather than seeing these new works as commentaries on a preceding scripture, one might suggest rather that each of them in its own way presents as it were that preceding scripture, if at all, as a commentary on itself. The Mishnah and the movement growing from and with it led to the Jewish Bible's being read by Jews in a manner as idiosyncratic—

as creative?—as the way the counterpart Old Testament was henceforth read by Christians. In both cases these ancient Scriptures were now understood as elements within the worldview of the radically different time and situation and the strikingly novel religious vision now developed by the respective two communities—and were understood in each case as authenticating that new worldview[66]. Thus their authority was preserved, while their role and understanding had changed.

Even so, it was not Bible so much as Torah that was now the great concept in that religious life. In Rabbinic literature, as we have said, and in Jewish piety in general, there is no question but that the dominating concept has indeed been Torah. That this is not simply scripture is the result of two fundamental innovations in the post-Mishnah period. These strikingly differentiated the term from, enlarged it beyond, its earlier meanings; and especially from and beyond its limited referring specifically to the Pentateuch, or to the Bible.

Of these two transformations, one grew out of the introduction of a concept, noted above, of an additional ancient Torah, complementing the first. There is no question but that, in cases where within the Talmud our word does refer specifically to the Torah of Moses, it almost without exception intends to include, and was read as including, an Oral as well as the Written form of this. A while after it was written down, the Mishnah began to be given authority[67] by being dignified, indeed sacralized, with the name "Oral Torah". Noticeably later the enormously fruitful myth was fully developed and adopted—and presently was embedded in the Talmud as foundational—that the so-called Oral Torah had equal authority with the Written Torah.

These two forms of Torah are recognizable today as in content quite different and as coming out of social, political, intellectual, and spiritual contexts separated by over a thousand years. Jewish life came to be constructed, however, within the vision that the two are actually one, in that not only both originated with God as His integral intention for His people and His enduring bounty to them, but also both were presented to them through Moses at Sinai.

As remarked, the myth—in the best sense of that word—was that the two forms of this one Torah were of equal authority. In practice, although not in theory, the authority of the Oral form was greater, in the sense of more consequential. This was no doubt inevitable, since it was the newer one that rendered the earlier one, at the level both of theory and of practice, continuingly relevant to the new situations.

The other innovation went further, and was still more dynamic. The community came to assume, and operatively to feel, that in addition to the original double instruction, as given to, or through, Moses, as what was launched by God through him, was further the whole process of "Torah" in the sense of the on-going ever-contemporary activity of studying, discussing, and ever anew discovering and specifying what it ideally means for a community to be Jewish.

To the Mishnah, some fifty years or so after it was otherwise complete and had been published and legally enforced, a smallish addition was made, the *Pirqe Abot*. Except obliquely in this later increment, the Mishnah does not include the idea that what it propounds is "from Sinai", that it comes from God through Moses. As we have noted, that idea comes later[68]. The Mishnah's own view is different: namely, that the thinking of the rabbis constitutes the authoritative way to know God's will.

This too was incorporated into the Talmud. It is less explicit perhaps than the double-Torah-from-Sinai idea but if anything even more practically effective. As a modern Jewish scholar puts it: "one could rarely ask of Mishnah, what must I do according to Torah in case x; the believer needs have recourse to a living and breathing Torah, the rabbi. . . . [S]tudy, in the form of logical debate and rebuttal, [became] perceived as a means to transcendence. In such debates the rabbi shares in the experience of Moses 'Our Rabbi' on Sinai and even sees himself partaking of the mind of God himself"[69].

As it was later said: "What is Torah? It is: the interpretation of Torah"[70].

Moreover, the notion of *kitve qodesh* ("holy books"; the more precise rendering "books of holiness" could for some be more illuminating?)—one of the phrases that might be rendered as "scriptures"—came to mean not merely the Bible, certainly, and indeed not only it plus also the Mishnah, the Midrashim, the Talmud, and so on, and indeed not only these plus also the commentaries and the works of scholars on these other works, but even school-boy notes taken in a class studying the Talmud or discussing the thinking of these scholars[71]. The concept has been a cumulative one, and at times has been applied virtually to all books written in Hebrew. (Hebrew was—and is—called "the holy language"; better, "the language of holiness"[72].) What was holy, what was from God, was the process initiated through Moses and continuing from that day on, wherein God's love and concern and guidance were seen as enveloping and activating His people. That process included the Bible as one among its elements, but the process itself was primary. Also, it was continuing.

Certainly for many centuries, until the other day, Jews understood the Bible in the light of the Talmud and then of the commentaries. Among these last, major ones—Rashi, Radak (David Kimhi), Ramban ("Nachmanides")—were written in the first three centuries of the present millennium. These scholars and their fellows and successors represent the shift from Mesopotamia to Spain and Western Europe as the centre of Jewish intellectual and spiritual creativity[73]—which became the next home of that on-going process that we have mentioned. One might almost say, until quite recently Jews did not read the Bible except through the commentaries. Until well into the twentieth century, it was hardly ever published without one or other of them[74].

The Bible took its place as a component part of the worldview constructed in the Talmud and further developed by the on-going tradition resting on it.

To take one example: elaborations of the first seventy-five years of Abraham's life, about which nothing at all is said in the Bible, passed as well known to the man-and-woman-in-the-street: stories of the patriarch's smashing of his father's idols, for instance. Thus when the Bible does mention Abraham, it was to *that* familiar Abraham that the Jew automatically heard it as referring[75].

Not only new additions, however, were smuggled in; new and altogether revised understandings of the old were commonplace. In our previous section we quoted an authoritative Jewish writer's statement, "The bulk of Jewish literature is in the form of commentary on Scripture". In this present section, we must observe that the literature is here being said—carefully—to be "in the form of" commentary; and we must observe what amounts to the significant qualification immediately following this in the same sentence: "whether this form is always justified or not (often the pretense of commentary disguises a full-fledged original personal viewpoint)"[76]. As earlier remarked, the ingenuity, artistry, persistence, at times far-fetchedness, are impressive that Jewish preachers and others displayed in linking to the Bible whatever they had to say—whatever, that is, they deemed sufficiently serious and significant to deserve that link. (This has been altogether standard across the world in the use—indeed, the nature—of scriptures.) This fact we cited as evidence for the central importance of the Bible; but it may be invoked rather—better: at the same time—as showing its subsidiary role.

The statement should be qualified, however, by adding: . . . whatever they had to say in a consciously transcendent context, and linked to it. The sense of transcendence within which they lived and spoke continuingly sustained, and was sustained by, their having a scripture to which to link their therefore special perceptions.

Illustrative is the *Zohar*, that radiant "Book of Radiance" or ". . . Splendour"[77], which gradually became the chief literary expression of a new world-view, that of Qabbalah mystical movements in Jewish life, "a new religious attitude" unlike any that had preceded, and which "succeeded in establishing itself for three centuries, from about 1500 to 1800, as a source of doctrine and revelation equal in authority to the Bible and Talmud, and of the same canonical rank"[78]. Even the Zohar has the form of commentary on the Pentateuch[79].

We have pressed the point that neither the Talmud nor the Mishnah is even formally a commentary on the Bible. No doubt equally important is that, despite this fact, each has been thought of as such a commentary. Could we say that the Bible has not been important in Jewish life so much as has the idea of the Bible? Yet as we have seen, the language of their thought and writing shows that traditionally Jews have not in fact formed a major clear idea of it.

If we as observers today are for our purposes to form an idea of it, we must certainly note that for Jewish piety, the Bible is inexhaustibly rich. (The most sceptical of observers cannot but recognize that this has been an empirical historical fact.) They put it, in a renowned phrasing: "Turn it and turn it; for *all* is in it"[80]. Jews are iconoclast, vehemently rejecting "idols" and images. Yet for them the Written Torah has been what might be called the image of God's relation to them as a community.

In place of "image" here, some might prefer "icon", or "form".

One might toy with the formulation: "The Bible has not been

important in Jewish religious life except symbolically". Historically, this perhaps catches much of what has been afoot. Even it presently fails, however—perhaps chiefly because it is in danger of apparently under-estimating symbols. How else can anything on earth be important in religious life?

Our third proposition, that "scripture" is not the apt notion for the Jewish case, acquires what initial plausibility it might have from the failure of either of our first two propositions to be quite true—or quite useless. Might we solve our problem by reflecting on the possibility that in this instance—perhaps in all—the modern concept scripture does not fit?

There are several grounds for entertaining such an assessment. Before pondering them, however, we may note that to pose the question is to raise the fundamental concern of this book. If the concept does not fit, shall we drop the term "scripture", at least in the Jewish case, as irrelevant? That would seem a whit obstreperous. Or does it mean, rather, that to do justice to the Jewish situation we need not "the modern" concept scripture, but a substantial re-conception; a careful revision of our inherited understandings of what the word signifies? Such revising does seem in order, if one is not to ignore or to distort several facets of Jewish life that significantly pertain. We would profit more if, rather than being pushed to regard scripture as an inappropriate notion here, we could allow the Jewish material to help us move towards a more adequate conception, towards discerning more clearly the sort of affair to which it refers in human life, and what human beings have been in relation to it.

In the first instance, we may note a problem that we have previously met, and shall meet again, and that seems rather simple; yet it bears raising here once more because of some subtle implications. It is the difficulty arising from the etymology of "scripture", which term still tends to carry its original connotation of something written down: a text, and in our day even a bound volume. A Bible in Jewish life was given status as indeed a written document, back in the days when being preserved in writing was an added sign of dignity conferred on exceptionally prized materials. At that stage, as we have noted, it was "the books" (*siphre, sepharim*). Only later did it become "the holy books", to distinguish these prized ones from the by then gradually more common generic sort. "As it is written" (*ka-k-ketub*), however, continued as a phrase to designate a scriptural quotation. Yet a salient factor in elevating the texts to scriptural status and keeping them there over the centuries is witnessed in the alternative name *Miqra'*. This signifies what is read aloud and appropriated through hearing, rather than read by oneself silently and appropriated through the eyes. (Nowadays in English the verb "reading" unless qualified virtually never means "reading aloud"[81].) Furthermore, the term signifies, specifically, liturgical reading in the service. (We have noted that another form of the same word is the Arabic term *Qur'an*, and a Latin equivalent of it gives the Christian liturgical term "lesson" as read [*sic*: sc., read out loud] in the Sunday service.) It would be an error not to recognize the dominant role that the weekly reading aloud formally from the Torah scroll in the synagogue has played in giving the Bible its sanctity in Jewish life and keeping that renewed; and the dominant role of personalizing it inwardly in memory. This is paralleled in other communities also; some have thought of defining scripture in terms of use of its text in liturgy. A concept is hardly appropriate that does not incorporate centrally the ceremonial aura, and the extent to which it has meant people's having snatches from it, or phrases, verses, or even large sections, accompanying them as they went about their affairs. One could almost ask whether perhaps "scripture" is a name not for what is read so much as for the ceremonial reading of it, and for the process of personalizing it—as a cosmic relation; or of the complex formed by both the cause and the result of that process.

At the very least, we must recapture an awareness of how much personalism has been lost in the transition away from oral/aural language. (In fact, the word "language" has to a degree changed its meaning in modern culture.)

Another subtlety that obstructs the current concept scripture from serving for this material has also to do with modern pressure on us to have terms that refer each to a specific something, preferably delimited and concrete; and to think of scripture, if not as a text, at least as designating an independent matter—whereas in fact what we see here seems to be a facet of an elaborate and intertwining whole. Further, the way that we see it is in turn a facet of another intertwining whole: the modern world-outlook. We remarked above that the most important, most central, Jewish concept is "God". Yet it cannot be understood in isolation; it has been significant within a whole system of ideas, practices, values, symbols, and such, and of life, forming a pattern of which it is no doubt the keystone but not the totality—and not even the independent foundation. For theists, God is conceived, of course, as self-subsisting; the *idea* of God, on the other hand, is by non-theists misconceived if thought of so, as a separable item which can be considered by itself.

All words, all concepts, have meanings within some particular worldview. Modern culture has to revise its specific categories if it is to move towards comprehending other cultures—as today it must. This applies also, of course, to "scripture".

The story of the exodus from Egypt and of the reverberating revelation at Sinai were important in Jewish life before the Book of Exodus had become a scripture. (Americans can think of 1776 as an important date without canonizing the history books that tell them about it.) Nonetheless, the Book of Exodus as scripture, telling that story, has been exceedingly prized. This is partly because it has been apprehended by Jews not separately and not even simply in, as we have seen, intimate correlation with certain other texts. Rather, it has been one element in the total pattern of Jewish life, and gains its significance from the way that it participates in that pattern. Some might speak here of the pattern of Jewish *religious* life; and at the more personalist level, of its having been, and having to be recognized as, an integral component within the total spiritual awareness of the community and its diverse members and their response to that awareness. Yet its integration within the mundane aspects, also, of Jewish history it would be amiss to under-estimate. A concept of scripture is hardly appropriate that would extract it from that dynamic complex, of natural events and forces and of the lives of persons and groups; would extract it from the human situation to consider it discretely, in and of itself.

Today, our term "scripture" has become the name of an entity within the world (indeed, within *our* world). To use that sort of conception to attempt to understand people for whom it was not that—for whom we human beings are to be seen, rather, as items within *its* world—is to be prone to misconceiving.

Scripture, we have seen, hardly serves as a noun to name something exact in traditional Jewish life—and we repeatedly find, in human life generally. In all cases it comes closer to functioning as an adjective, indicating a quality felt in certain sets of words. Earlier, we propounded the position that scripture is something that people do. Should we now amend this to suggest that finally it is more of an adverb, relating rather to a way of their doing whatever it be that they do?

For it would be wrong to think of Jews—or indeed any other religious group—over the late ancient and the mediæval period as merchants or whatever who fell in love, married, had children, became ill, were successful financially or were in trouble, and such, and who in addition had in their lives an item that we call their scripture. Rather, Jews were persons who worked, fell ill, were successful or were victims, and so on, *in Jewish ways*. Their scripture may be discerned as a major component in the complex of which those ways were constituted.

There are further challenges to our concept, but we need not go on. We may close this sector by suggesting that the more closely one looks at the empirical historical facts the more one discovers that they point away from things to persons and from persons to their involvement with something beyond themselves, higher than they—or, better: to all of these in interaction. Our concept "scripture" is then shown to be misleading, insofar as it obstructs the required transition in our thinking.

To sum up. Until now, there have been three chief sorts of conception of scripture applied to the Jewish case: Jewish, Christian, and modern-secular-academic. The conclusion of our present investigation is that no one of the three is at all adequate to present-day observation. None comes near to satisfying intellectual rigour. None of them appropriately fits what we today know of the role historically of the Bible and of scripture in Jewish life. Modern Jews themselves are well aware that traditional Jewish interpretations require revision, perhaps radical, before they can serve even current Jewish perceptions; let alone, that in their traditional form they cannot serve outsiders' understanding nor academic analysis. Christian concepts of the Old Testament, traditional or recent, we began this chapter by noting briefly as not appropriate for the Jewish Bible; and traditional Christian notions of scripture generally were never meant to cover more than their own case. Further, the material at which we have been looking in this chapter indicates that the current generic notion of scripture, both in the academic world and in secular culture at large, does not describe what has in fact been going on in Jewish circles in this matter over the centuries.

Let us not abandon, however, the intellectual aspiration to apprehend in rational conceptual terms what has been the Jewish situation. Moreover, rather than abandoning a concept "scripture" altogether as an appropriate category for that aspiration, may we at least tentatively conclude not that the term "scripture" does not apply, but that the modern-secular conceptions for it do not apply, as our other inherited ones do not? May we not recognize that the intellectual world has yet to generate an adequate understanding? What would seem needed is to move beyond the current academic and other traditional interpretations, revising the concept, however radically, and hammering out a new form of it more adequate to what is today known of that instance, and in general with a deeper sense of what scripture has meant in human affairs. Before pursuing this task, however, we turn to other instances further from Western civilization, to discern how the situation may be there.

As we do so, we may perhaps feel that meanwhile the Jewish instance contributes significantly towards our task of constructing that new apprehension.

CHAPTER 6

THE HINDU INSTANCE

IN INDIA, IN THE FAR EAST, and elsewhere, humanity over many centuries has in profound yet diverse ways been involved in something sufficiently like what is scripture in the West to justify, it has seemed, that Western name. We have earlier observed that the West's recently growing awareness of the religious life of these other civilizations led it to certain changes of its own notions that have gone with the term—noting first its coming to designate something more pluralist than previously conceived, for a time at the cost of omitting the transcendence involved. Yet even in recognizing variety there is still a long way to go; especially variety in its more subtle and radical forms, and over time as well as over space. With regard to other dimensions of scriptural matters, Western learning about, and from, Asia has barely begun. A process of integrating what may be learned into a coherent concept for this human involvement is even more incipient.

The more the West knows about Asian scriptures and their role in Asian life in the past—and their potential role now and in the future, in world life—the closer it can gradually come to a valid interpretation both of its own scriptures and of our topic generally: to a valid meaning for the word. This is so also, however, in the other direction. Conceptual modification is itself requisite to grasping aright what other cultures have in fact been saying and doing, feeling and thinking. Subordinating Asian data to Western categories of thought, although natural enough during the early phases of learning, slows that learning, even cripples it.

India, as usual, illuminates our subject richly, in both ways. We might begin with Veda, widely seen in the West as the basic scripture of India. We shall presently contend that a wrestling with Veda is indeed necessary and has much to offer towards a fuller understanding of our topic. Further, we shall observe in passing how that Westerners' sense of Veda has often been in many ways significantly prejudiced ("skewed" would hardly be too strong a term) and seriously misleading. Since one of those many ways is in the widespread Western notion over the past century or so that this is where to begin, in any consideration of scripture in India, we here choose not to begin with it. We shall turn to it subsequently, after noting first other matters less widely familiar to outsiders that certainly deserve major attention in any inquiry into what Hindus have been doing scripturally. An important first step towards understanding scripture in India is to recognize that Veda is *not* where to begin.

It is not the purpose of this present volume to explore in depth Hindu, Buddhist, and other instances of our theme. Yet even the brief study that we do present will, we trust, serve our general aim, will raise new questions and open up new vistas, and contribute towards that eventual revision of the concept and deepening of discernment—discernment of scripture, and discernment of the human as illumined by our involvement with it.

The religious history of the world has been complex, variegated, diverse. It is so even in that relatively small sector of it constituting today's scene. It has been so not only of the whole but even in the case of each of the presumedly separate sections, such as the Christian or the Buddhist. In some of these sections, however, particularly the Christian and the Islamic, participants downplay the internal variety, having felt that their particular "religion" ought to be, is ideally, one—and accordingly have striven to make it so. They have thought in or towards uniform ways; at times they have acted to attain these. Also, some of their most central symbols they have in fact held in common: the theist concept "God"; and in the Christian case the figure of Christ; in the Muslim case a single scripture (and in the Christian, as we have seen, a Bible that comes relatively close to converging among the various parties); and so on. Hence they tend to be haunted by a strong sense of an at least theoretically coherent ideal, a formally systematic pattern, an in principle universalizable spiritual truth. Of the large religious movements on earth, probably the Islamic has even in practice diverged least far from being a system; and perhaps the Christian, for all its ever-changing multiformity, next. Over against these, one would be hard put to it, if one were looking for the most amorphous, to choose between the dynamic complex that we call Hindu, and the Buddhist movement. There is anyway no question but that the Hindu would be a serious contender—except that "polymorphic" would be a more perceptive adjective than "amorphous". The point that Westerners have most difficulty in appreciating, certainly in digesting, is that Hindus glory in variety. "That spiritual insight is not sharp that has not pricked the bubble of a unitary salvific pattern."

(One grounding for this is Hindus' profoundly humanist—or at least, personalist—sense of life, including spiritual life, which has contributed to their holding that religion is of course, and ought to be, as variegated as are personalities; and of course, as are groups.)

All of this is by introductory way of saying that there have been in the life of various Hindu groups large and small over the past couple of thousand years many texts (to use a Western term, on some of whose problems we have already touched in other chapters, and to which we will return), and many versions of most of those texts, that have played a scriptural role, and do so today and will do so tomorrow. That role in Hindu life and thought has been massive; and has been played in various ways. It may be seen as having approximated—yet only approximated: with varying degrees of closeness—to the role of scripture in the more familiar Western and Islamic cases. This too has varied at different times and amid differing groups, but the variety has not been joyfully recognized.

Among the most important large-scale candidates for a scripture category in India are the various Puranas. The ideal number eighteen has often been attributed to "major" ones amongst them—without universal agreement as to which eighteen these be (nor even, finally, as to what works are to be regarded as Purana at all). The Purana of the group concerned is included in each list, naturally, and of the remaining seventeen a half-dozen or so others standardly recur. Among these are the handful that have attracted the chief attention of Western students, recognizing their exceptional influence which went along with their wide and deep reception over a particularly long period of time, and extensive area, and among a statistically large number of people. One may note especially the Visnu Purana, which served as perhaps the principal verbal and conceptual source, and for a time principal channel and depository, of religious India's theism, with the enormously important Vaisnava (i.e., Vishnu-ite) orientation; the closely related Bhagavata Purana, similarly for Krishna; the Devi Mahatmya (not exactly a Purana[1], to the delight of those of us who are cheerful about India's spiritual exuberance) and later the Devi-Bhagavata Purana, for the transformative matter of perceiving the ultimate reality of the universe theistically as feminine.

It would be difficult to over-estimate, and misleading not to give major heed to, these scriptures' vast significance in the history of Indian life.

Sometimes included under the heading Puranas, at other times under a broadened heading of Puranas-and-Itihasas (as a literal English rendering for the latter term, "historical tales" is perhaps not too distorting; though it neglects the point that they are in verse), are two major works: the Mahabharata and the Ramayana. These are regularly paired in the West under a heading of The Indian Epics; in India they are perhaps more often considered not under an encompassing rubric but singly. The former is immensely long (roughly seven times the size of the *Iliad* and the *Odyssey* together), and touches on a correspondingly wide range of matters, presenting a broad (and immensely influential) picture of Indian culture. In return for being received by that culture scripturally, it has in turn given the culture dignity. It has helped preserve and nourish it, and has done much to inculcate its norms. Behind or over, in some fashion within, all the multifarious details of the poem looms a transcendent[2] ultimate, ever impinging on and infusing the human.

Among other forms of this impinging has been the reverberating concept of incarnations. This last, along with presentation of a cosmic dimension to the struggle on earth between good and evil, is characteristic particularly of the other of these two works, the much loved Ramayana[3]. (This work has been and continues today to be made alive and vivid for many millions annually in the great Ram-Lila festivals and performances—to which mediæval morality plays in Europe of yesteryear are remotely comparable[4].)

To say that the Puranas and these Epics[5] have been scripture in India is to affirm that in conscious relation to them Hindus have discerned their world and their life as what we may call mundane shot through with what we may call transcendent[6]. These scriptures enable outsiders to perceive the way in which they have done this— the distinctive way. Other human beings throughout the world have, of course, normally done the same; but in other, also quite distinctive, ways—ways again often patterned in their scriptures.

Included within most (not all) versions of the Mahabharata, yet even more often known, recited, read, memorized, commentated, cherished, and in recent times printed, as an independent work, is the Bhagavad Gita. In modern times it is sometimes said that this work has come closer than any other in the whole of Indian literature and thought to functioning formally as an instance of the imported concept "scripture". Its special status has, for a variety of discernible reasons, been consolidated especially in recent centuries. Yet the process began a millennium or so ago, when India's two greatest philosphers Sankara and presently Ramanuja each wrote a commentary on it, to be followed by several leading thinkers since.

(We remarked above[7] that for outside students, learning about the Gita means understanding how the lives of Hindus have been in part formed by their reading of it. At the present time, one might add to the scholar's task a consideration of the poem with a view to better understanding what is illumined about human life generally, and about modern history, by the new appeal of the Gita to growing numbers in the West.)

In India itself, somewhat counterpart to the northern Sanskritic items mentioned, may be noted from South India, in the Dravidian language Tamil, the highly influential devotional outpourings of personal theist experience of two groups of saints, the Alvars and the Nayanmars, in the latter half of the first millennium A.D. These celebrated the love and compassion of God and the intense joy and indeed the whole gamut of emotions of the worshipper, from despair to ecstasy. In the tenth and eleventh centuries these were brought together in formal collections, which have been cherished since in the South as in effect canonical scriptures. Particular poems came to be known in South India as "The Tamil Veda"[8].

In the North also, the influence of particularly the Alvars, through the Sanskrit writings—in prose—of some of their leading exponents, most powerfully Ramanuja, has been incalculable—on scriptural, sociological, linguistic, and other history.

Certain important movements, both Saiva (that is, oriented to

Siva ["Shiva"] as the pre-eminent High God) and Vaisnava (to Visnu ["Vishnu"]), in addition to their own various Puranas and such, cherished another group of works often called Agama[9] which have played a sacralized and sacralizing role in their history. These in some cases have been seen by participants as supreme and absolute—their words as higher than and prior to the gods, and God[10].

Almost all these works are in poetry, as are many further items that certainly must be included in our inquiry. Alongside the outstanding Sanskrit works, where that language itself lends an air of sanctity, there has been a wide and deep array of vernacular scriptures—it would be austere to begrudge them that name—where their language with its familiarity gives an accessibility and effectiveness that are highly consequential. These include such instances as collections of the devotional hymns of a wide range of particular socio-religious movements (especially mediæval *bhakti*); certain biographies of the persons around whose memory and teachings these movements have gathered; and much else. They are poetry not only in the substantive sense, but also formally, in verse. Their being in verse has helped, of course, in their being proclaimed, chanted, memorized, internalized. Their being in poetry has helped, too, in purveying the transcendent dimension. Poetry is a form of language that characteristically lifts us humans above the flatly mundane.

Other treatises (the name *Sastra* has regularly been used for a considerable sub-group among them), probably less influential yet by no means unimportant in past or present history nor for our purposes here, are sometimes in mixed verse and prose. Still others are fully in the latter. "Scriptural" not so much in the sense of devotional yet in that of authoritativeness and moral seriousness has been the Manu-sastra ("the law of Manu"[11]), the classical exposition of formalized moral—also ritual and other—conduct, normative or obligatory. (Included, not least, is the "caste system", which formally predates it but has been systematically preserved in part because of the status that this work has been accorded—and *vice versa*.) There is no concept in classical Sanskrit and allied Indian languages for the rather idiosyncratically Western notion "law"[12]. Westerners looking for a counterpart to this in India have normally turned to these "laws" [*dharma*] of Manu[13]. In the reverse direction, when Christian missionaries translated the Bible in India, they called it "Dharma-sastra", as if for them scripture were primarily a law-book—or at best a systematized moral or ritual code[14].

Writing came to India (from the Near East) after Indian civilization had got impressively under way; and even then it was not central to its culture, for some centuries. In due course, however, it was fairly fully appropriated. In religious matters, first by Buddhists but presently also by others, it was appropriated eventually in quite sacralized ways. The Epics and the first range of Puranas, originally recited before an audience (and the reciter honoured, revered), presently appeared (also) in the form of books (the later Puranas appeared from their start as books as well as recitations); and the book as a physical object could in some cases be seen explicitly as a form of God (or of Goddess[15]), and was worshipped (*puja*). (For "form", here, the terms *rupa* and *murti*—the latter being the usual word for statue or image also—are regularly used, including in the later Puranas themselves.) The efficacy (at times virtually magical, some would say; yet never wholly so) of reverently hearing the sacred words could now be supplemented by that of having a copy reverently in one's house; also, of copying it, of giving it as a present.

Of course, the claim that the devotee in seeing a copy of one of these books actually sees God (the highly visual orientation of Hindu piety[16]), presupposes that one looks with faith—personal involvement in the transcendence symbolized. As with a temple image, the outsider or tourist may see simply the book or the statue, not the divine that shines through.

The analogy is heightened by the recent addition to the holy places of Varanasi/Benares of a striking temple, otherwise bare, on whose shining white marble walls are beautifully inscribed the entire Ramayana[17].

These scriptures, and indeed others in the West and elsewhere that are more explicitly "books", have in fact—as we have earlier noted—been appropriated over the centuries into the lives of those enhanced by them chiefly through the ear. Yet in India as elsewhere, even for the majority who were illiterate the sense of sacredness of what is received and cherished could in some cases be made more solid by its having also a visible, tangible, form. Not surprisingly, bookishness as a dimension of scripture has increased notably since the advent of printing.

Nonetheless, the oral/aural dimension, originally predominant, and often formally ceremonial, has hardly ceased to be central.

We turn, then, to *veda*.

This term means basically "knowledge". It is fully cognate with the Greek and German words "to know" (*oida* and *wissen*), with Latin *video*, with English "wise", and "wit" (the root meaning of this last as a verb is still visible in, for instance, "to wit", "wittingly"). In India the word came quite early on to be used also—to some extent, especially—for transcendental knowledge[18], rendered accessible to humankind from ancient times in and through particular formulations of words. Accordingly, regarding the various Puranas and such it was affirmed that they were Veda. This view became widespread and has hardly ever been challenged.

The affirmation had already become established, however, in relation to certain other material, from a substantially earlier era in India and surviving among a quite limited circle. What came often to be affirmed of the works that we have been considering was, therefore, that they too were veda, or "Veda". The Puranas and the other scriptures saw themselves[19], and were seen[20], as continuous then with this older material, elaborating on it, and making its substance available in a new form. (More accurately, one should say that these saw themselves, and were seen, as making available through a new form awareness continuous with that made available earlier through the other material.) The newer works were set forth as giving the essence of (the)—otherwise elusive—Veda in intelligible form; also, in universally accessible form, outside that small closed circle: to everyone (even to women and children). Since the old form came presently to be known as fourfold ("the four Vedas"), the new regularly, and proudly, presented itself as a fifth Veda (or the fifth Veda).

Certainly the two forms were different, strikingly. Crucial, of course, is that the earlier one had, both in fierce theory and in strict practice, a severely limited audience—in principle, chiefly the small, yet of course uniquely influential, caste of Brahmins[21]; in practice, only certain ones among even these. For our purposes here, almost equally significant is that the Puranas and the many other later materials were, as we have observed, both heard and written; they were on occasion books. They are "scripture", therefore, in the literal sense of the word, which the earlier Veda was not: within its limited circle, this was received and transmitted only orally/aurally. This in itself might seem not finally to matter: to include both types is a required modification in the accepted sense of the Western concept more or less readily manageable. There is, however, still a good deal more to the lack of fit between Western concepts of scripture and what has been going on in India, in relation especially to the Rg-Veda.

Striking is that while the Puranas and all later Hindu works place considerable emphasis on verbal meaning, in the case of the early Veda the emphasis is primarily on sound. The sacred significance of the words is seen as lying in sound[22]. Thus once again it is the later group that is substantially more like scripture in the received Western sense, of revelation in conceptual form. Should we perhaps, for the early texts, think then in terms of music, rather than of poetry? Neither metaphor is right; yet the polarity between them might prove suggestive[23]. There has been a sense of sacrality, ultimacy, transcendence, of the *mantras*, as the particular phrases and sentences of these collections have been called[24]. This has to do with a central emphasis given in early times, and long nurtured, of a transcendent quality of sound: sounds as primordial elements finally constitutive of the universe, and constitutive especially of the (a?) relation between the ultimate and the human.

A small illustration of this as continued into later times is provided by the central Hindu symbol *Om*, representing for those who reverently utter or hear it all spiritual awareness to which they are capable of rising, and more. Yet it is not a lexical word and is without specific mundane reference[25]. A larger illustration is in the practice, and some of the theory, of Vedic recitation, which faithfully for three thousand years has preserved with "phonographic accuracy" the precise sounds, rhythms, intonations, pitch, modulations, of the ancient hymns and texts. One of the theories proffered to interpret what we might call the scriptural quality of "the Veda" as text is that this work was presented not as the words of some God, as theists incline to hold of their texts, but rather as self-existent and timeless. Those words have been conceived as eternally reverberating—somewhat in the fashion of the "music of the spheres"; as audible directly only to those uniquely gifted souls of ancient times, the *rsis*, who then recorded them (in their memories) and taught them to the élite of Brahmins to preserve. Thus to others of the privileged they have become indirectly audible, and continue so.

Often, this sort of view went along with a notion (and a widespread practice) that the verbal meaning[26] of the Veda is irrelevant—or even distracting[27]. We shall return to this.

Western understanding of all these matters has been complicated by the engaging fact that the Sanskrit term *veda* has in modern times been incorporated directly into English (and other Western languages), appearing there however as a concrete and even a proper noun, chiefly in three forms: "Veda", "the Veda", and "the Vedas". Most scholars and other writers who use these English words know (one must presume) what they intend by them in each case. Chiefly the tendency has been to designate certain early texts (so most English dictionaries). Yet even at that level a reader has to be constantly alert to discern (or to guess) which texts are in mind, in any given case (and to recognize that often—usually?—it is virtually impossible for a reader to be sure). This is so, apart from the further complicating fact that even in referring to specific texts the Westerner's meaning of the term almost always differs from Hindu usage —as we have adumbrated, and shall be elaborating in a moment. Sometimes—indeed, fairly often—English references are to texts in a distinctively early form of the Sanskrit language, which is accordingly called (in the West) Vedic. At other times, scholars include many more, and later, texts, making up "three Vedas" or "the three Vedas"; or still more, "(the) four Vedas". Most Western academics have resolutely refused[28] to go along with those many Indians (the overwhelming majority, doubtless) who call still later works "a (or the) fifth Veda". (This stubborn refusal is despite such facts as that this expression itself occurs within the recognized first four[29]. It is repeated regularly in the Puranas.)

The primary fact is that for many Indians the term *veda* denotes a transcendental knowledge or insight, spiritual awareness: one available no doubt to humankind in or through the texts concerned, yet knowledge rather than, or as well as, those texts. This appears, for instance, when it is said of later scriptural works not necessarily that they are a, or the, "fifth Veda" but simply that they are "veda". Here the word clearly is not a proper noun so much as an attributive epithet. It does not designate a text but characterizes it[30].

In any case, rather than "four" Vedas, the outside observer might well, regarding even the early texts, think in terms of sixteen; since there are traditionally four classes of text (Samhita, Brahmana, Aranyaka, and Upanisad) for each of the four orders of Veda (Rg-, Yajur-, Sama-, Atharva-). Even this elaboration over-simplifies, since there are two, or three (not altogether different) Yajur-Veda Samhitas; there are several more Brahmanas, for instance, than four; and many more Upanisads—a word that names not a corpus so much as an undelimited genre, with at least a hundred members, or even twice that, even though thirteen, sometimes fourteen, sometimes eighteen, "principal" Upanisads have regularly been recognized. When the English term "Veda" is used by modern Westerners there is a tendency for its meanings to fluctuate among one, or three, or four, or all sixteen, of this formal set.

It is my impression that the English adjective "Vedic" is even more likely than the noun to refer in a given Western author's mind to the Samhita(s) only, often only of the first one of the orders mentioned, or at times of the first three or perhaps the four. Both noun and adjective take on a pseudo-historical, almost antiquarian, verbal meaning signifying the chronologically earliest of the various components. (Our enumeration of the various sets mentioned above was in chronological order). Virtually never all four classes of all four orders are meant by the adjective. Even the noun is almost never used in the West in the true historical sense, of the on-going, cumulative Vedic legacy to and in Hindu culture, a legacy that has continued, and still continues, to evolve. (Some Upanisads, even, are relatively modern.) As we have suggested, exactly what *is* intended, in foreign usage, among the various possibilities one often cannot be sure.

As a general rule, one might suggest that "Veda" in English most often has meant "Rg-Veda", and that that in turn most often has meant "Rg-Veda Samhita"—the Rig Veda hymns.

In Indian usage also, the term *veda* in its basic meaning of transcendental knowledge has indeed been applied to these particular "texts", or utterances, although hardly ever without its primary reference united with this derivative one. To use the term in English as the name of certain books, without the simultaneous denotation of their cosmic import, is typical outside reductionism. The English meaning has regularly been restricted to these early works, to the total exclusion of the many later scriptures to which most[31] Hindus have normally also applied it (the Puranas, Epics, Gita, Agamas, Alvar hymns, sectarian poems, and so on). This is in addition to there being regularly a further restricting by Westerners to this-wordly, "objective", materials, to the total exclusion of all transcendence, even though the sole significance of those materials lies in the fact that their this-wordly objective material aspect has been subservient to that other.

More accurately, this is their sole significance except in our day for occasional historiographers (including comparative linguists) aiming at reconstructing the course of mundane events (or of language) in ancient times. Some readers might have wished to modify our above phrasing, conceding at most that their sole significance otherwise lies in the fact that their this-wordly aspect has for centuries been *perceived* as subservient to their transcendent. To say that, however, presupposes that the texts exist, and that people then have somehow imagined them to be cosmic. This, however—though established Western doctrine—is to reverse historical actualities. The texts were produced in the first place, and have been preserved generation by generation since, because of the human involvement beyond those texts as such. It is an error of perception to think that a "belief" that "the Vedas" were (are?) of spiritual worth has been something added on to the texts. The historical facts are the other way round. Human beings have, in India, added to their world-wide sense of a transcendent dimension to our life a conviction that this reality has been put within reach of some, at least, in and through particular forms of words. Spiritual truth has been made, has made itself, audible, learnable, appropriatable.

It is not that for traditional Hindus words—certain words—are veda, so much as that veda, lo and behold, is words.

Indeed, one should rather write, " . . . is words!" The exclamation mark should not be left out, so spectacular has this miracle been seen to be, so venerable, so precious.

Neither the general history of India, nor the particular usage of Indian languages, can be understood without grasping this.

Neither can humanity be understood without grasping this—our common humanity. To fail to apprehend the significance of these matters in India is to misunderstand what it means to be human.

It would be obtuse to under-estimate the continuing richness and continuingly consequential significance in India of the early Vedic legacy, especially in its narrowest sense of the Rg-Veda hymns: preserving the lively sense of a close and friendly two-way traffic between the human and the divine; and the lively sense of the holiness of truth, the truth of holiness. ("Truth" here includes, even emphasizes, being true; and being true to. It also includes "reality"[32].) The outsider's basic task is not to understand the objective verbal meaning of this text in the sense of the concrete references of its individual words—though one should note Indian philsophy's acute sensitivity to language that some see its sanctity as having launched. Rather, it is to recognize the power that it has had, in that sanctity, to convey. One must strive to understand that power, and to understand the multitude of developments over the course of history that it has helped inspire. One must come to intellectual terms with Hindus' tenacious clinging to it over three thousand years, their unrelenting resolve to preserve it intact and their unrelenting confidence that it is supremely worth the effort.

Some understanding of these matters, perhaps especially for modern times, may be facilitated by citing a sampling of some of its admonitions and hopes: "'Let the threads that bind us to divinity not be broken, let the sacred threads by which we weave the coloured web of our song remain intact. May we not lose track of the paths that run between the gods and men, nor fail in our contractual hospitality to the Immortal that has come as a guest in the mortal's house. May we not lose sight of the trace left behind by the bird in flight'"[33].

There is in addition much more to be wrestled with of a different sort less readily recognizable by Western scripturalists, before that understanding is near to being attained.

That only a small minority of Indians has heard, let alone studied, has known or in any fashion understood, these Veda texts, is a crucial fact. Yet even here caveats are to be entered. That minority is an enormously respected élite. Also the recognition, among a sizeable portion of the population, that a transcending wisdom does indeed exist on earth, even if in its fullness remote from themselves, has kept alive the awareness—or, is one bit of evidence that the awareness has among most persons persisted, here nurtured in part by this formal symbol—that we human beings live in a context greater, more splendid, than ourselves.

Nonetheless, we would repeat our earlier thesis. It is evident that for most Hindus at most times the effective scriptures in relation to which they have lived have been a range of other, later, works—Puranas, Epics, the Gita, Agamas, hagiographies, hymns, and so on—on which we have briefly touched. At some point—it is not clear when—a formal distinction arose and has become widely accepted between the two classes of texts: the early group was designated *sruti* ("heard"—sc. by the *rsis*, as noted above), and the later group was called *smrti* ("remembered"). (Like all attempts to systematize the data of the exuberant Hindu tradition, however, this one too over-simplifies. Things have not in fact been that straightforward: neither what is *sruti*, and certainly not what is *smrti*, has been fully clear. Nonetheless, the distinction has, once introduced, proven historically influential.) We may go beyond the final point made in our paragraph immediately above, with regard to the former group of texts' being recognized as transcendent from a distance, also by many that are precluded from knowing their content. One must note further regarding these latter—the generality of the population—their quiet yet explicit conviction that the scriptures in their hearts or hands were also *veda*, just as was the élite's. Moreover, to them their *smrti* scriptures were not an inferior substitute, *faute de mieux*. On the contrary, these people—rightly—held them to be more lucid than the arcane originals, more appropriate for their kind of life, their time, their group.

One is nowadays in a position to add nuances and to integrate some of the discrete observations that we have been making, by seeing them as developments within a long-range historical framework. The Western concept "Hinduism", as if it indicated some sort of cognizable entity, as well as conceptions of the unchanging East, has tended to obscure the very substantial differences in religious outlook in India in successive millennia, and even successive centuries. Characteristic of the culture, however, along with this, has been its genius never to repudiate earlier phases. Innovations there has been, many and major; but they have enriched a heritage and rendered it ever more complex, not supplanted it.

Both the innovation and the preservation matters are illustrated in the verbal realm in the three scriptural modes that we have noted: as sound, as verbal meaning, as book. A scholar has recently discerned and made explicit[34] an historical development here, of these three as successive phases of a long-range growth. One may add that even within the Veda itself, the great emphasis on sound, especially for the Rg-Veda hymns (*Samhita*), has persisted, yet the later portions of the Veda, namely the Upanisads, were more oriented to philosophic reflection, and during the mediæval period were richly mined to develop this. More recently, in late mediæval and most especially in modern times, the early hymns themselves have been studied with increasing attention to verbal meaning[35].

On the side of the Puranas and other later works where from the beginning verbal meaning predominated, nonetheless the significance of sound was not lost. Some preserved more than did others, in addition to their sense that they had a story to tell whose import was the primary point, a feeling also for the inherited significance of sound. This was encouraged by orality/aurality, and is evidenced in ceremonial chanting, ritual recitation, and much else. (There are counterpart phenomena in other religious traditions' orientations to their scriptures, of course. The same principle of the major importance of scriptural sound, in addition to and even distinct from verbal meaning, is illustrated, for example, in English-speaking Christendom in the resistance among some of the pious to modern translations of the Bible deviating from the familiar and much loved King James Authorised Version, with its stately phrasings and haunting cadences. Evidence from other traditions similarly is readily available.)

With regard to the later development of written books as a further form for scriptures, we have noted instances of this while noting also that what the West calls "the" Veda was emphatically not written down. This had and has to do with the Hindu personalist-humanist view of learning and of truth. (Truth is embodied not in words but in persons and in their living[36].) There is, however, more as well. For ancient Israel—followed by Islam—representation of the divine by Word was central, in due course giving us our concept "scripture". Representation by "graven images", on the other hand, was fiercely rejected. Most of humankind (certainly including India, at least from Buddhist days) has welcomed both. Recently it has been brilliantly observed that early India on the other hand "had proscriptions against their own kind of 'graven images,' namely, books. The written images of an alphabet, far from giving visual access to the sacred words of the Veda, were regarded as defilements of the holy sounds"[37]. This too can serve towards a new and enlarged conception today of scripture.

In the eighteenth century, European visitors to India found themselves wondering whether the Vedas really existed, since no one in India seemed ever to have seen or known a copy of these works; and were told by Brahmin teachers, "Veda is whatever pertains to religion; Veda is not books"[38]. In the nineteenth century, on the other hand, the West, in the heyday of its cultural imperialism, brought its different notion of scripture into India when the Oxford scholar Max Müller published a printed edition of the Rg-Veda, thus turning it for the first time into a book, both in fact and in theory[39]. This has affected not only Western conceptions of the work and attitudes to it, but also Hindu. The history of the Rg-Veda in Indian life has unwittingly been much more significantly modified as a result than has been recognized. And there is solid reason to suppose that it will stay modified: the place of the new Veda is now established.

The two transitions—from sound to verbal meaning; from verbal meaning to "image" on, for instance, paper—have occurred in differing degree. The shift from sound to verbal meaning went in many cases more than half way, except for many for the Rg-Veda, so that verbal meaning became paramount, even though usually without sounds becoming neglected. The later Hindu development, on the other hand, from mentally or spiritually apprehended word to written word, has on the whole gone decidedly less than half way: writing is something added, but never something that replaced.

In the matter of historical development, the Max Müller affair leads to a further observation. On the processes of Hindu orientations and practices in these matters, successive outside impingements have proven not insignificant: the rise of the Buddhist movement, the widespread establishment with deep cultural impact of the Islamic, and the arrival from Europe of the Christian and the modern-Western-secular. These movements, coming at roughly thousand-year intervals, had their own rather definite, and different, conceptions of scripture, which in each case was then to some degree less or more casually insinuated into or appropriated by indigenous developments. The history of every religious tradition around the world has been in part a function of the history of the others.

In addition to this matter, there is yet another dimension, quite different, that must be stressed: ritual use. Some scholars would tend towards actually defining scripture in terms of texts that are used in ritual. A more balanced view would see this as one element in the scriptural complex, one whose role and importance varies in differing instances, both between and within communities[40]. Certainly in India, most conspicuously perhaps with "the Veda" but also in other cases, such a role has varied from paramount on down. Unquestionably, the "meaning" of a scripture for some groups or persons has been, in varying part, its ritual meaning. Unquestionably, the student who wishes to understand a scripture must understand its ritual role in the life of those for whom it is scripture. Unquestionably, further, the issue of what ritual, in turn, means—to those for whom it is meaningful, and also to the observer—has proven a subtle and demanding one.

That issue, however, although involved with our concerns, is the topic for another study than this, by some other inquirer. It too is a part of the nature of being human. Steps towards elucidating it will help us to understand scripture better. May we not hope, also *vice versa*?

Since only recently has Western scholarship come to a recognition of the massive importance in Indian life of the later group of Hindu scriptures—more legitimately so-called—it is perhaps worth illustrating a little more amply what kind of thing has been involved. In our hastening survey above, after mentioning the Puranas and the Epics, we remarked almost in passing on other, less nation-wide, works that have a claim to be considered for inclusion in our category: devotional tales or hymns of particular socio-religious movements, biographies, "and much else". In closing, it is perhaps illuminating to elaborate briefly on one or two instances of such items, to suggest the sort of thing that has been going on. We may choose two, rather arbitrarily, from among scores that might be investigated.

One instance is provided by the Gaudiya Vaisnava movement, of Bengal, arising from the life and teaching of the sixteenth-century *bhakti* saint Chaitanya, whose impact was such that he has been perceived by his followers as an incarnation of Krishna or of both Krishna and his consort Radha. Moreover for them, being theists, Krishna is *parabrahman*, the Supreme Brahman, the Absolute Spirit (or even: beyond Brahman, in the sense that for these people the impersonal Ultimate of non-theists is a form in which Krishna appears to those non-theists). Accordingly, by this group the classical four-fold Veda, and as well the Epics (and especially then the Bhagavad Gita, "the essence of all the Upanisads"), and the Puranas (especially of course the beloved Bhagavatam), and all are deemed Krishna's word, with the group's theologians working out elaborately a theory for such perceptions and arguing carefully, for instance, the "Veda-ness" (*vedatva*) of these works[41] (illustrating once again the attributive force of that concept).

For our concerns, at least equally if not more interesting is practice. This movement has produced its own corpus of cherished works, both in verse and in prose, both in Sanskrit and in Bengali, including biographies of Chaitanya (produced from the sixteenth through the twentieth centuries), hymns, commentaries, devotional dramas, and much else. The Gaudiya Vaisnavas are a highly literate group as a whole, and love to write, certainly to read, and—especially, of course, illiterates among them, but not only they—to hear recited, and sung, these various works; and in the case of dramas, sometimes also to hear and to see, devotionally.

Once we come to think of scripture not as a particular sort of text but as something that people do—or that in their involvement is done to them—then one has to reflect carefully before deciding whether or not to include these text-related activities as scriptural.

The second of our two instances has to do with the poetry of and about another North Indian *bhakti* saint, a contemporary of Chaitanya, less renowned though recently receiving some increased attention: Ravidas. As with Chaitanya but on a smaller scale, a community has grown up around his memory, a community for whom he is the *guru* in not only the mundane sense but also the transcendent: he is revered virtually as divine (*sat-guru*, "the true guru", God)[42]. His utterances are cherished also, however, in other circles. Forty[43] of his poems are included in the Guru Granth Sahib, the decidedly formal scripture of the Sikhs. Other poems of Ravidas appear in collections ceremonially revered by another group, the Dadu Panth, collections that invite the notion scripture to characterize them for that group[44]. It is, however, the poems ascribed to him in the collection of his more immediate followers, the Guru Ravidas Granth, that will repay our particular attention.

Poems from this Ravidas volume are ceremonially chanted on a regular basis at, for instance, a new temple being built at his birthplace. In the closing line of each poem, as is the widespread custom[45], the guru's name is given indicating him as author. A Western scholar reporting on a recent visit to one of these sessions, in reference specifically to this point, notes that in the pronouncing and the community's hearing of the Ravidas name here, "the life and status of poet and audience are intimately involved. . . . In reciting the line, the community reaffirms its loyalty to its own ideals and consolidates its sense of identity by repeating words it understands as given to it rather than invented from within. The name Ravidās indicates that givenness"[46]. This response from and involvement of the audience, and their reverent devotion, along with the ritualized pattern of the proceedings conducted formally by a liturgist at fixed and regularly recurring times, would seem to suggest that one would be right in calling the activity scriptural.

Striking for our purposes here is the fact that the poems chanted turn out to be, in the critical eyes of modern scholars, not by but about Ravidas, and may well be fairly modern, with new ones perhaps continuing to be composed. The saint's praises are sung in these works, and heeding his commands is enjoined. His name's appearing as "signature" at the end of such poems signifies, as this careful report argues, primarily authority—rather than simply authorship. "If Ravidās is their author, they speak with the collective weight of the community's history before God"[47]. This observer goes on, however, to point out that the question of whether he actually wrote these poems does not in fact arise in the hearer's mind; it is rather the ascription of the works to him that serves the purpose.

(The ascription in the Bible of The Song of Songs to Solomon—or the Psalms, to David—provides a parallel.)

In conclusion, then, we note that so far as scripture in Hindu India is concerned, the question there as elsewhere is not primarily of texts so much as of persons. The texts chosen by various people at various times are no doubt striking. There is indeed significance in the choices that they have made and clung to, and these repay study, along with what individuals and groups have done with and to them, and what they have done with and to those people. A large variety of texts has been involved, and indeed of types of text. Some of them are ancient and persisting, widespread, highly renowned; even, now world-renowned. Others that have played a role in the lives of countless ordinary Hindus have been less prestigious, yet personally no less consequential. Varied also have been the theories hammered out by intellectual leaders to explain to those involved and to the world how and why it is that their particular scriptural-ized texts are as meaningful to them as they know—and as we can observe—that manifestly they are and have been, and to nurture the next generation in a capacity, and readiness, to find the treasures also for themselves. Some of these theories—on the whole those for the more renowned texts—have been sophisticated, subtle, grand; others, more homely. All can be interesting—yet to the sensitive student, subordinate to the living reality of the respective persons and groups.

The foundational fact about scripture in Hindu India is that most[48] Hindus at most times have, in one or another of hundreds of diverse forms, lived in a significantly scriptural relation to their fellows and the world around them, and to their personal destiny.

We have directed more attention to this point than to the con-comitant theories that, as noted in passing in the occasional aside, various groups have set forth in elucidation of their involvement. These theories, to repeat, have been many, among different groups and at different times. Several have been highly sophisticated. Many are decidedly interesting. For our purposes in this study they have the added interest that a large number of Westerners have tended to interpret scripture, or scripturalness, as something to be understood primarily or simply in terms of the particular theory that accom-panies it ("Scripture is the Word of God"; "scripture is any text that some group believes to be the word of a god" . . .). Our own view is that while participants' theories, once established, have certainly been influential in nurturing scriptural attitudes, and in helping to induce these in new generations, they have nonetheless been basi-cally derivative. In the historical situation, such theories, though secondary, are one interacting item among many. In the Hindu case we have noted two or three of the major ones: the thesis that the (Rg-)Veda is sounding eternally and self-subsistently, captured[49] for humanity on occasion by the *rsis*; the view that all scripture, and especially *this* scripture, is the word of Krishna, the supreme Lord; and so on.

There is the personalist-humanist notion, mentioned above in passing, which may be elaborated as holding that divinity is humanity perfected (or, *vice versa*, that humanity is divinity distorted by worldliness and Hindu counterparts to the Christian notion "sin"[50], and woefully obscured). Thus the holy saint who uttered what is now available to us lesser mortals as scripture had risen to a level—or penetrated to a depth—where he could and did know the truth (spiritual truth); therefore each of us can apprehend something, at least, of what he was (is) telling us if we have each a personal guru on his own way towards perfection to instruct us in its meaning, and its application to our particular lives. (We cannot be expected on our own, just by "studying" the text as a document, or with a teacher not himself spiritually advanced, to see the point[51].)

Another theory, which we have not previously mentioned, was that each of the various Puranas is an abbreviated version, for this degenerate age, of an original of one billion verses. Such a notion is surely a clear recognition of transcendence, reflecting a sense of the infinite beyond one's grasp, lying behind yet also in part within that to which one does here have access[52]. We might also mention the Saiva[53] philosophers, after the transition from sound to verbal meaning but holding on to (held on to by) the view that the actual words in given fixed form are ultimate: they wrestled with the issue of truth embodied in particular words, and were led to profound philosophic handling of questions of the relation between language and reality.

And so on. Theories illuminate what was in fact going on, in the society and its development, and in the hearts and minds of those involved. Maintaining our position that they have been, and indeed should be, derivative, we ourselves in our final chapter, after having looked briefly also at other instances, will be proffering suggestions towards forging a theory for scripture that might serve our own new situation today with its global awareness and its global concerns. That theory we will in principle as well as in fact endeavour to derive from the data before us; and even ideally it will of course only approximate to being apt for the current stage of historical development, to be superseded in its turn later as new stages are reached. It will learn from previous theories around the world; but chiefly, will learn from the actual scriptural situations of previous generations of various communities around the world, which those theories help to elucidate. Only as we understand better what has actually been going on shall we be able, partially, to hope for interpretive conceptions more apt for our time than inherited views have become.

May we perhaps, then, sum up thus what we have been able to understand of what has been going on in India. The Hindu situation in its diversity, its richness, its long development, would seem to lend itself to being understood most adequately, perhaps only, by recognizing as running through it all a persisting human sense of a transcendent reality and of that reality's having become accessible— humankind's having apprehended it, being able to apprehend it, having been enabled to apprehend it—through one or another, or through various, verbal forms.

It is the human awareness of transcendence that makes scripture intelligible—to those involved, certainly; but also to observers attempting to understand.

CHAPTER 7

THE BUDDHIST INSTANCE

THE BUDDHIST MOVEMENT has had a long and diffuse history, over many lands: in India, and then, moving outwards in ebullience, it was received and grandly developed in Sri Lanka to the south, Central Asia to the north, and eastwards to China, Korea, and Japan, as well as to South-East Asia; in recent times it has begun to grow in North America and Europe. In its elaborate, almost kaleidoscopic, process the human propensity to scriptural involvement has shown itself richly, and in many forms. Some of these have been such as to be more or less reminiscent of forms that we have noted in India—as is not surprising, for obvious historical as well as for other human reasons. (Historically, however, it would seem that on the whole Buddhist scriptural developments influenced later Hindu ones perhaps as much as *vice versa*.) Other Buddhist forms are more comparable to forms familiar in the West. This, again, is for generically human reasons. Yet it too is partly for historical reasons, though these are far less obvious than in the Indian case. Between the Buddhist world and Western civilization nineteenth- and twentieth-century interactions are less unexpected; but some from ancient times recently coming to light are quite remarkable, particularly historical interrelations and mutual influence between early Christian and early Buddhist scriptures. At some of these we shall be looking briefly[1]. Furthermore, some Buddhist scripturalizing forms reflect Chinese ones, as will become more evident in our next chapter, on China[2]. Others, on the other hand, are strikingly distinctive of this movement itself.

In the whole panorama, the first matter that strikes a comparativist observer is the stupendous quantities of Buddhist scriptures.

There are even a large number of distinct canons, if that word may reasonably serve: Pali, Chinese, Tibetan, Mongolian. . . . "Collections" would represent more closely the movement's own traditional concept (diverse sets of, for instance, "Three Baskets", and other classifications). As we shall see presently, in general no firm boundary can be drawn[3] between works that clearly and explicitly are to be called, in English, scriptures and those that, although perhaps in some ways more peripheral, may yet reasonably or arguably be perceived as also falling within such a category. In any case, of the former, formal, group the volume of material amounts altogether to a thousand and more times that of the Bible. To include the second, more ambiguous, group would swell this a great deal further. One may be confident that no one has ever read everything included in the Buddhist scriptural realm (or ever known all the languages needed to do so?); or ever wanted to[4]. Except for a relatively small minority of Buddhists, scripture has been seen as multiple[5].

The diversity is not only geographic, though that it is. From the "Southern Buddhists"—for well over a thousand years now chiefly Theravadin—the rest of the Buddhist world, Mahayana, differs primarily on the question of scriptures, the former recognizing a relatively closed canon, the latter having gone in for more open vastness. Even among the Mahayana, the Tibetan canon[6] does not at all co-incide with the Korean, nor the scriptures of the thirteen hundred years or so of Mahayana developments in India with those of the somewhat similar length of time in Japan. And so on. In addition to this geographic matter, however, the diversities have also an historical dimension. For characteristic of the Buddhist movement, over its whole twenty-five hundred years thus far, has been its surging exuberance. It was history's first great missionary movement (the four subsequent ones have been the Christian, the Islamic, the Marxist, and the Western-secular[7]); and it is still expanding. The Buddhist complex moved into and became a major component of more diverse civilizations than has any other outlook. Moreover, unlike the others mentioned, it has never sought to replace what it found, only to supplement and to enrich.

Nor has its dynamic been externalist only: in its inner life too it has ever been, and continues still today, in process, on the march. Although in some ways apparently answering to the modern Western notion of an "historical" religion, stemming from a specific "founder" at a particular time and place (like the Christian and the Islamic), yet it has had participants tending not to think of the truth as located primarily, or delivered once and for all, in a specific past. Thus in our special matter of scripture, for instance, as in other matters, it has gone on generating new scriptural works as the centuries have come and gone—as well as, like all other traditions, generating new attitudes to scriptures, new kinds of involvement with them: new meanings, one might say, for the term "scripture" for those who may choose to use it. Internally as well as geographically the Buddhist movement has been—and is today—a movement.

None of the great religious traditions on earth has failed to be continuingly creative, of course. Or one might say, none has become or remained great that has not continued to prove creative. Moreover, all—including the Buddhist—have stressed continuity. (This is a radically different matter from unchangingness. At issue is change without a rupture in on-going process: the new is different from, yet recognizedly continuous with, what has gone before; is elaborated or extrapolated from it.) However valid this observation be generically, nonetheless in much of Buddhist history, an observer can hardly fail to note, a sense of dynamic flow has been particularly strong: a sense that ultimate truth is timeless, and has at least as much to do with the present as with the past. The participants of all religious traditions have, of course, perceived their participation as putting them in touch with a contemporary reality. Yet the extent has varied to which they have conceived that reality as having become available to them by way of erstwhile historical events. The variation has obtained among individual persons and groups, certainly, but on large scale may be perceived among major traditions also. The matter might be better formulated by speaking of variation in the extent to which a sense of past historical happenings supplements or even underpins the sense of transcendent engagement with, or of, the human in the present moment of history.

One may say, then, that other traditions too have stressed, and have owed their vitality to, their relevance to extant situations over the centuries. Yet some have in addition insisted on a special relation to the temporal process in the past. Might one perhaps say, with obvious yet perhaps pardonable over-simplification, that in the Christian case, the good news has been that God did something in Christ, something unrepeatable which has changed forever the human condition—later ages' role being to respond; in the Jewish case, that God did something at Sinai, and in the Islamic case at Mecca and Madinah, which does not need repeating[8]; whereas in the Buddhist case, especially Mahayana, that even those oriented to the historical person on earth whom the West calls Buddha have seen him as one instance in a recurring series, or as a mundane (even, an almost negligible?[9]) counterpart to the cosmic reality, the true Buddha, that to them is alone of major importance, alone finally interesting; or as someone who said something that had been, was, is, and will continue to be true, or did or became something that it is subsequent persons' or generations' task and privilege to repeat— or at least, to hope to repeat, to move towards repeating.

Accordingly, growth in the Buddhist enterprise has been constant. Modern research finds that individual *sutra*s (sayings of Buddha) have developed over time[10]—to the point where a modern-Western editor, in search of the *Ur*-text of a given scripture, has to confess that "if one could reconstruct such a document . . . [r]emoving the conflations, the additions, the expansion of doctrinal themes, all for the sake of returning to a matrix from which" it all started, the results would be misleading for an understanding of Buddhist thought and teaching[11]. That is, they would be historically false. The fact is that in successive centuries Buddhists have had somewhat different versions of a given text serving as their scripture. Also, the important "Perfection of Wisdom" (or "Transcendent Insight[12]") *sutra*s (*Prajnaparamitasutra*s) comprise a family of versions, explicitly from "8,000 lines" and less (down to a single page[13]—or even to a single syllable[14]) to "25,000 lines" and more[15] (up to 100,000[16]).

In addition to this, new *sutra*s have been produced, in several cases after a number of centuries: in India[17], China[18], Tibet[19]. Also, certain texts that began as falling under some other rubric came in course of time to be called *sutra*[20]. Further, commentaries on established scriptures came in several instances to accompany or even to supersede the originals, not only sociologically in actual use in playing the primary scriptural role in the spiritual lives of a community but also at times also formally, by becoming explicitly included in a thereby enlarged canon and in ritual. Instances of all this abound[21].

The continuing liveliness of such elaboration is illustrated in Japan, where over the past eight centuries the largest of the sects has as it were recapitulated internally for its own group until today the kind of scriptural productivity and expansion that the Buddhist movement as a whole had been displaying already for more than twice that long[22]. It did so with firm assurance of continuity back not only to the Buddha that was Siddhartha Gautama in India but far beyond him to previous Buddhas on earth and the cosmic Buddha beyond time and space. The major sects there have taken the words of their founders as having in theory equal authority with Siddhartha's, and in practice greater authority.

In China, there have been in general successive editions of the canon—both before and after the days when China invented block printing (and paper) and applied it to this matter. (The first book ever printed anywhere on earth was, of course, in China and was— also of course?—a Buddhist *sutra*). And each new edition was larger than the last, included more texts[23]. In the Sung era, Buddhist monks reported to the emperor's court the doings and sayings of their particular master, in the hopes, or with the specific request, that these be included henceforth in the official Buddhist canon—which sometimes they were[24]. Later, growth had to do with the decision of financial sponsors, or of particular printers, and not only of imperial authorities or even Buddhist monks, deciding what to include in an edition of the scriptures; thus the collection reflected what was prized, or was generally expected to be there[25].

The manifest productivity in these developments has character- ized the Mahayana branch of the Buddhist movement, far and away the largest sector. Yet even the Theravadin or Southern group had in fact tacitly set the pattern—despite its ostensibly closed and in comparison rather small Pali canon, and its adhering to a theory of strictly limited "Word of Buddha" as scripture (*Buddhavacanam*: we shall be returning to this term to explore its force). For of this group's "Three Baskets" (*Tipitaka*) constituting that "canon", the *sutra* basket (*Sutta pitaka*) is but one. (It is, indeed, the largest. The smaller first one, *Vinaya pitaka*, comprises the rules of the monastic order.) Even that large second basket includes *sutra*s and passages that are presented as not exactly spoken by the Buddha but as approved by him either before or after being enunciated by one or another of his immediate followers, or else as spoken by someone certified by him as reliable. Indeed, in one of the *sutra*s in the canon the point is reached where it is asserted[26] that whatever doctrines lead to awakening are thereby *dharma*, and are the word of the Teacher[27]. (We shall presently see that the affirmation is less surprising the more one holds a transcending notion of *dharma*—seeing it as signifying the reality that the Buddha affirmed[28] rather than as simply what he taught—and of the meaning of "Buddha"[29].) Beyond this, the third of the Three Baskets, the *Abhidhammapitaka*, consists not of what Siddhartha Gautama had to say, but rather of later— though in present-day perspective still relatively early—philosophic explications of the true meaning of that teaching.

One might also, for comparative purposes, wish to note that within what purports to be the word of the Buddha an account occurs[30] of what an outsider would call his death, and Buddhists call his *parinirvana*, his ultimate passing over into nirvana—somewhat as in the Jewish and Christian case the "Five Books of Moses" include an account of the death of Moses. In the Buddhist case, this matter of accounts of the end of a leader's life is supplemented by accounts in the Pali Canon, voluminously, also of his many previous lives: the "Jataka tales". These exceedingly popular[31] stories relate virtuous incidents from those former lives, incidents whose virtues signified that the one that practised them over a succession of rebirths was a Bodhisattva on his way to rising eventually to the status of a (the) Buddha. (Of interest to the comparativist is that much in these beloved Jataka tales is Buddhistically adapted material derived historically from Indian lore shared with Hindus, and indeed shared with Indo-European lore linked also with Aesop's and Lafontaine's Fables in the West.)

Moreover, beyond the Tipitaka itself development in fact continued also among Theravadins[32]. The great Sinhalese commentator Buddhaghosa (fourth-fifth centuries A.D.—the tenth Buddhist century) stated that a work composed in the third century after Siddhartha Gautama's demise "became [*sic*] the word of the Buddha"[33]. Furthermore, in due course Buddhaghosa's own work, particularly his *magnum opus* "The Path of Purification" (*Visuddhimagga*)[34], itself came effectively to occupy a scriptural status for most Buddhists in Sri Lanka. (Should one qualify this by saying, rather, a *virtually* scriptural status? Is this different[35]?) Its role in their lives and thought amounted to a virtual neglect of a large part of the original Pali texts; and the later work came to be recognized as *Buddhavacanam*, Buddha word[36]. "Most Buddhists in Sri Lanka" here includes in practice the majority of monks[37]. In the fifteenth century A.D. (twentieth Buddhist century) this scholar's (this saint's) life was presented hagiographically in a way that recalls Siddhartha's own[38]. It is reported that in our own day Sri Lankans speaking English use the phrase "Bible study" for sessions at which the monks lead laity in study of Buddhaghosa's writing[39].

Another commentary, in Pali, on the outstanding Theravada canonical *sutra* the Dhammapada, has provided the material for a decisive vernacular Sinhalese work[40] embroidering the legend of Siddhartha's life and character. The supreme quality and venerability of Buddhahood has been nurtured by yet another vernacular work[41] which also has played a central role historically in Sri Lankan Buddhist piety, "creat[ing] a wondrous image of his unique and superhuman personality"[42].

Despite such considerations, one must again observe that Theravadins differ from the Mahayana movement in that conceptually they consciously revere a single fixed canon perceived as closed[43]. They attend the local temple or participate in religious festivals and hear the village priest expound a theme normally drawn from that canon but then elaborated from these "para-scriptural" works or illustrated from these non-canonical but thoroughly familiar and much-loved and richly embellished stories. Just as we noted that Jews have read about the Abraham of the Bible but perceived him as the Abraham of the Talmud, so for Theravada the secondary material has been practically consequential while the primary is theoretically paramount. One aspect of this is that in recent times—partly under direct Western influence, in part perhaps indirectly by way of Hindu India with its "back to the Veda" notion—there has been among the monks a resurgence of attention to the full Pali canon. This renewed interest is modifying traditional ways.

That that Theravada canon is definite and limited, a conceptually manageable entity as well as supremely esteemed, continues to be illustrated in modern times. In 1954 for a great occasion in Burma a monk was searched for and in due course one was found able to recite publicly the entire Tipitaka from memory[44]; while also in the nineteenth century a temple complex was erected in Mandalay where the canon was inscribed also in its entirety[45].

The Mahayana, on the other hand, to return to that majority movement of Buddhists, has developed not only practical involvement with but profound reverence for and conceptual elevation of other—later—writings, not subordinated even theoretically to what went before. We shall presently consider more directly the theories that Buddhists have at various times propounded to explain to themselves and to succeeding generations or alternative groups why their differing scriptures are of transcending worth. At the moment we may simply point out that the continuity that the historian observer notes, linking the innovations within an over-all process, has in some instances (not all) been called upon to undergird theoretically those very innovations. Later we shall remark on alternative justifications.

This continuity has been maintained by perceiving, in both practice and theory, new writing as having penetrated to new depths, and illuminated with new clarity, the meaning of some previous text. The result is that a new sect may arise, and the writings of its founder have in many cases then become scripturalized, perhaps to the neglect, though not to the disparagement nor repudiation, of earlier scriptures. Again, someone whom outsiders might characterize as a "reformer" in a given sect, giving its later development an innovative turn, is perceived similarly as having grasped and made accessible the true significance of the writings of that sect's founder, so that in turn the "reformer"'s writings also then come explicitly under a scriptural heading. An example of both of these is provided by the largest Buddhist community in present-day Japan, the True Pure Land (Jodo Shinshu)[46].

This feeling for continuity, attaching even to novelty, has led to, or been evidence of, the devotees' sense of being situated in a large context. Membership in the community of which the scripture is one symbolic form gives them the awareness of participating in a large contemporary reality here on earth far transcending their individual aloneness; the on-going tradition embodied for them also in the scripture and coming to them from a distant past gives the awareness of participating in a centuries-long process in which they are caught up; while primarily that scripture puts them in touch here and now with a timeless reality that along with enlarging their niche in both time and space also lifts them beyond both time and space to participate in eternity.

Moreover, Buddhists, no less than other major movements, indeed apparently more than most, have on occasion affirmed with force and clarity that the significant matter for spiritual life is far too intangible, too inexpressible, too deeply personal, too transforming, to be encapsulated in words, in texts, in material objects[47]. Scriptures, in this view, can be a distraction from truly spiritual life, an obstacle to genuine progress. This orientation was felt, cherished, developed, set forth, notably by the movement in China called Ch'an, Son in Korean, Zen in Japanese[48]. We can learn something important about scripture and about humanity by noting a resulting paradox. The story of this movement's leaders' affirming the antiscripturalist thesis, at times with dramatic vigour or even bizarre emphasis and always with manifest conviction, was retold by those impressed with it and impressed with those leaders: retold to their friends and children and to the populace at large. In some instances that retelling was in due course written down and revered and sacralized—and a new scripture was born. "The Platform Sutra" (of the Sixth Patriarch)—and even its title, with the word *sutra*—is an outstanding example of this[49]. The importance of this particular Sutra in Far Eastern history has been major.

(I like also the story from China of the monk who, haranguing his disciples, forbade them to take notes; we know about this because one of them disobeyed, and wrote it all up—whence one more illustrious, and sanctified, text[50]).

Jews and Christians have their parallels to this in the ironic case of Jeremiah and St. Paul[51].

(Some might be inclined to see Buddhist instances of subsequent works by identifiable historical persons being deemed to be "word of Buddha" as having their counterparts in comparable Jewish and Christian instances of works admittedly written by specific and named historical human beings—Moses, David, Luke, Paul . . .— being received as "word of God".)

On the question of translating scripture, the religious traditions of the world have differed. Jews like to teach their children Hebrew, so that the Bible may be read in its original ("holy") language. And among Muslims also—although theirs is a vast missionary movement—the practice has been widespread, from central Africa to Indonesia, of teaching children the Qur'an in Arabic even when the words may not be understood. In both cases translations, when provided, have been regarded as decidedly secondary, if not peripheral; as commentaries. The Christian movement, on the other hand, went in for translated scriptures from the beginning—the Gospels, even, were composed in Greek, a language foreign, certainly, to Jesus. For centuries the Latin Vulgate *was* the Bible of Western Christendom. For a few centuries scripture for the English-speaking world was the King James Authorised Version. In the Buddhist case, similarly, translating has been vigorous and effective (although scattered instances of over-riding veneration for an original have not been unknown).

The Buddhist movement arose in the first place with its striking use of the vernacular[52]—rather than the classical Sanskrit that was the recognized language of religious authority. The Mahayana emerges into historical view some centuries later as a movement centered on works in Sanskrit, by that time prevalent among a probably enlarged educated class. Translation of its *sutra*s into Chinese constituted over a few centuries one of history's most impressive translation enterprises. Subsequent renderings into Tibetan have also been major. Mongolian is a rather special case[53]. On the whole, Buddhists in their many cultures have had their scriptures in their own language. In our day, the missionary impulse as well as migration movements are resulting in massive new translation projects under way to make their scriptures available now in, especially, English. The recent pattern of Western orientalists' proffering in Western languages versions of individual Asian texts is being overtaken and will soon be quite overshadowed by Buddhist initiatives on a grand scale to present hundreds and presently thousands of volumes of Buddhist scriptures in the English language[54].

Over against these prevailing and in the past markedly successful moves, another facet of the human sense of sacred scripture is evinced in a few Buddhist instances where translating did not occur, or even was resisted. Early on in Central Asia a writer complains that his fellow countrymen prefer to have their Buddhist scriptures in a tongue that they do not understand, preserving thus its transcendence and holiness, although he himself disparages this view and is intent to offer them a translation in Khotanese[55]. Again, when a Tibetan king first brought the Buddhist tradition into his land it arrived in the form of scripture texts (he had asked for monks to come to teach, but they sent these rather). These texts he honoured, and built temples to house them; they were not studied but treated as mana-filled objects, in effect were worshipped. The next king, however, brought more texts, from China as well as from India, and some of these were translated into Tibetan—to be understood. In due course, Tibetan translation was vigorous and voluminous; further, a number of new scriptures in Tibetan, the teachings of later visionaries, were added[56]. Eventually the Tibetan canon was printed (in China) and became highly consequential.

Chinese *sutra*s were not traditionally translated in Japan[57], but were read in of course the Chinese characters shared by the two languages, and were recited with the ancient Chinese pronunciation. Some outstanding Japanese religious leaders, also, wrote some of their own works in Chinese, which were later chanted liturgically without being "understood" in the modern secular sense of that word. They were understood in another sense, of course, as awesome and symbolic—a sense of understanding scripture already noted and to which we shall be returning in due course. Japanese writings, however, of these and other religious figures were much more widely influential, becoming the primary scriptures of the communities concerned[58]. Although Buddhist scholars have throughout tended to be decidedly scholarly, in linguistic as in other matters, nonetheless we repeat our point that most Buddhists there as elsewhere have had their scriptures in their own language, whether original or as translated.

The supply has certainly been sufficient to make this quite feasible.

Given the vast quantity of texts, we turn next to the question of what it has meant in Buddhist life to be, if not confronted with, at least dimly or vividly aware of, an enormous range of scriptural material. There is no single or simple answer, of course. Yet certain points may be made, helping to elucidate the issue. Our first is historical, having to do with a long-range shift that can be discerned. Secondly, there is selectivity, and we do well to consider how it has worked both in practice and in theory. Finally, we shall look briefly once again at the matter of continuity.

Historically, there was a period of some centuries during which conflicting multiplicity posed a problem for intellectuals. That problem was stalwartly wrestled with. In due course it was for practical purposes solved. For well over a thousand years and more now the

Buddhist world has taken scriptural diversity in its stride. During the earlier period, there were two major sorts of issue: divergence between Theravada[59] and Mahayana (over not only new *sutra*s, but whether to have one collection or many), and perplexity within the latter group (over what to do about their many).

The Theravadins were by no means the only movement originally to issue from Siddhartha's life and preaching, nor the only one to cherish a collection of what became scriptural writings. After some centuries of multitudinous and complicated historical developments among the various groups, however, theirs proved eventually the most successful in becoming consolidated and established, lasting until today; and their set of scriptures eventually emerged as a clear and defined corpus, the so-called Pali canon[60]—again, the only one surviving from among these groups' collections[61]. Quite other streams from the same source but flowing in a distinctly other general direction presently came into view proffering *sutra*s of a seriously different sort. The more established group rejected these as spurious. They told those who were in danger of being, they felt, mis-led by them that these new *sutra*s were mere human poetry[62]. (This is a perception of scriptures not unusual among outsiders and skeptics[63]. We shall ourselves give heed in our concluding chapter to a relation among prose, poetry, and scripture.) The dispute surfaced also in China[64].

For the Southern Buddhists or Theravadins the conflict eventually went away—almost literally, as the Mahayana, their neighbours for a time in India, became presently separated from them by rather vast geographic distances, as a discrete East Asian movement. For the Mahayana itself the external conflict was presently dissolved by an outlook developed by them to deal with their internal problem: an acceptance of virtually total comprehensiveness along with a practice and theory of selection. They came to this solution only after a struggle; but once attained, it gave them lasting peace—and gave their various scriptures, lasting, and in fact growing, success.

Mahayana acceptance took the form not only of a theoretical recognition (not without nuance[65], as we shall see) of the validity of all Buddhist scriptures, early and late. Practically also it was evinced in, in fact, neither repudiating nor modifying the inherited texts. The Chinese canon, for instance, emphatically a Mahayana collection, even calls itself by a name, *San tsang*, in line with that of the

Pali Canon's, "The Three Baskets"[66]. It includes Chinese versions of the texts of that Theravadin grouping—as well as including, of course, in addition the much more extensive scriptures of the various divergent schools in China. The Korean canon of the late eleventh century A.D., explicitly "an extended canon", made a point of including a great many texts written by Chinese and Japanese scholars, as well as translated texts from India[67]. We have already remarked on the comprehensiveness of, for instance, the Japanese collections.

Individual persons' or groups' preference, or selectivity, has been the fundamental mediating factor between the plethora of scriptures and the piety of those persons or groups. It appears in many forms; both here, and across the world. In its objectivized form this is a question of a given community's specificity of scripture. Some traditions are perceived as prescribing quite clearly that a particular work, or that a designated collection, is absolute; others have been somewhat less precise; and still others, not precise at all, or the issue does not even arise. Individual Protestants, the most scripture-oriented group of Christians, have felt no qualms in personally having their own explicitly "favourite" verses, or even book, from among the many that constitute the Bible. (In fact, the less one has had such, the less scripturally involved one might seem to be.) A Muslim, on the other hand, has a single (much smaller) book and is likely to answer an outsider's questions as to which passages in the Qur'an seem to him the most beautiful or are his favourites by affirming disingenuously but sincerely, "It is all beautiful !" or "I love them all!"[68]. Yet in both these cases, Christian and Muslim, there is one boundaried definite corpus recognized by all. In the Hindu instance, as we have noted, there are recognized boundaries at one end, as it were, but not at the other. That the sacred works of other groups or communities as well as one's own should be recognized as holy[69] scriptures is also widely accepted among Hindus. In the Buddhist case, Theravada has gone in for a single delimited collection, while the Mahayana has chosen the route of a multitude of texts among which preference or selectivity is legitimated and exercised.

Before we comment on the legitimations provided, we shall take brief note of how the selectivity has operated. Yet before turning even to that, we should observe that fundamentally the many *sutras* and other writings that have dominated the Mahayana scene were and have been accepted because they were and have continued to be strikingly acceptable—to millions of persons and situations. They proved themselves. People were impressed, were won over, were inspired to sally forth to share them with others (their neighbours; or even at times on long and difficult missionary journeys across mountains and deserts to the rest of the known world); and those others in turn responded, with delight and reverence. In turn, of those others some at times crossed those mountains and deserts in the other direction, from China, Korea, Japan, Tibet, eager for more. The Buddhist missionary movement has been largely (not solely) a scriptural movement—and of more than one scripture.

The Christian movement during the latest quarter of its long history thus far has in its Protestant sector known the multiplicity of preferential denominationalism—although the selectivity that a Protestant exercises in choosing among denominations is not based on a choice among scriptures; perhaps among interpretations of the same Bible. The Buddhist movement over the most recent third of its even longer history has in its Japanese developments known the multiplicity of organized institutionalized sects, each with its own chosen scriptural tradition. In areas other than Japan the various Mahayana scriptural texts have attracted followers developing into what may be called schools, somewhat as Platonists and Aristotelians and pragmatists and others in the West cherish their own traditions without being organized into formal boundaried groupings[70]. In all these Buddhist cases (as traditionally in Protestant denominationalism) most people do not in fact exercise the choice available to them to go outside the sub-tradition in which they have grown up or to which they are chiefly exposed. Occasionally, however, persons do; and occasionally by new choices new traditions are wittingly or otherwise launched.

In China, to take an example, two types of selectivity may be mentioned. One is the choosing of a certain *sutra* or other text, or a few such, from among the many, for one's own or one's group's devotion, study, guidance, and ultimacy. The other is the effectively scriptural use of an anthology of passages culled from various recognized scriptures. Chinese "Daily recitation books" have been compiled, comprising selections of passages from various *sutra*s and ritual manuals, and these are recited both liturgically and privately. The earliest reportedly appeared at the beginning of the fifth century

A.D.; the historically most influential (*Chu-ching jih-sung*) dates from 1600; the one in most widespread use today was produced in modern times[71]. A modern scholar reports[72] that in a particular Chinese Buddhist convent in which she participated and lived, a few *sutra*s played a role in the lives of the nuns, while "heaps of other *sutra*s were locked up in closets, which were never opened" during her eighteen-month stay there. The anthologies of recitations were used morning and evening—with passages setting forth doctrine, constituting or prescribing ritual, and reminding the practitioner of requisite attitudes towards conduct and practice. It was these recitations that had the most formative impact in the lives of the nuns.

In Japan, we may take two quite differently illustrative examples: Shinran, and Nichiren—both thirteenth-century leaders, from whom two of the country's major sects have developed. Shinran, after much soul-searching and much disappointed exploring of diverse paths, finally came across and became enthusiastic about three interrelated *sutra*s and by the teachings of subsequent leaders in the tradition from them. He interpreted these in a striking new way, which won him a large and persisting following. This sect's "scriptures" (their own word, in their modern English-language editions[73]) comprise these three *sutra*s (Indian Mahayana, in translation); the teachings of seven "Patriarchs" or "Masters" (two or three each from India, China, and his own country); writings of Shinran himself; and certain writings of several subsequent leaders of the sect[74]. Similar is the case with Nichiren, who was an ardent nationalist disillusioned with all the then religious tendencies of his time and place, and who studied widely and presently came excitedly to the conclusion that the Lotus Sutra had the answers; that here in this one scripture was embodied eternal truth. He was not the first, by any means, in Japan or elsewhere, to single out this particular *sutra* for primary honouring. On the contrary, it has throughout Japanese history had an eminent place. He did read it with quite new eyes, however, and find in it major new outlooks. (As we have seen in previous chapters, a text hardly qualifies as scripture if it does not lend itself to, and indeed invite, new readings: of itself, of the world, of human life—the ever-new contemporary world, contemporary human life.) This *sutra*, along with some of Nichiren's own writings, and later compositions within the sect, have become basic scriptures of the group.

We have alluded earlier to the matter of continuity, to be linked here with the selectivity principle. Although each group or each generation may in fact, to outside observation, choose the writings that it finds of supreme worth, yet each perceives that writing as taking its rightful place in an unbroken great tradition going back historically usually to India to the beginnings of the whole movement on earth, and metaphysically (to use a Western concept) going back to the beginnings of time—so that it is conscious not of choosing, so much as of being privileged to have been introduced to the true meaning and essential core of the entire complex tradition.

(It could be challenging to speculate as to whether one might profitably draw parallels, or at least find comparabilities, between variety of scriptures in the Buddhist case and variety in, for instance, the Christian case among interpretations of an ostensibly single scripture. Another analogy might be the one that we have already raised, with the Protestant world's multi-denominationalism, which began with serious theoretical ["doctrinal"] divergences but for many has drifted into reasonably cheerful acceptance of diversity.)

We turn then to theories constructed as expressing these various Buddhist positions. Most Buddhists have for centuries now quietly gone about their religious affairs content to find their own particular scriptures precious and rewarding and content to know that there are many other scriptures prized by others, without bothering about such a situation or theorizing about it. Pluralism is culturally and spiritually an accepted context. This has been the case especially in China. In earlier times, on the other hand, as we have remarked, some intellectuals were challenged by diversity, and thought about it hard. Buddhist theories of scripture—to a consideration of these generally we shall come only later—have been many, sophisticated, and subtle, as had to be said similarly of Hindu counterparts in their different case. In the matter of selectivity we may at this point over-simplify by mentioning one idea that permeates many of the particular positions on our present issue: namely, the idea articulated in the concept *upaya*, or more elaborately *upaya-kausalya*.

This has traditionally been translated as "skill in means". Given the objective and mastering biases of modern culture, however, the words in that Western phrase seem to me to risk misleading. The original has to do rather with making available an effective avenue[75] along which someone may travel to arrive. It became a central Mahayana notion that the Buddha used or uses his great ability in this realm to provide all sorts and conditions of humankind with a variety of paths appropriate to the condition of each for attaining the goal that he in his infinite compassion wished, wishes, for all. A sect or school could justify its particular stand by calling on this concept to explain that the other *sutras*, the other sects, the other schools of Buddhist thought, or anyway those that seemed to differ seriously from, if not to contradict, their own, were authentic but at a lower level or more intermediate stage than theirs. According to this view, they could hold that the Buddha indeed proclaimed what a particular *sutra* reports him as saying, indeed taught what a given teaching propounds, but that this was intentionally circumscribed in accord with the limitations of those to whom at that point he was speaking (or to whom this record would subsequently appeal). It was perceived as adjusted down to meet their restricted capacities to understand or to respond. One's own *sutra* is the full truth, while alternative theses are evidence of the marvellous compassion and acumen of the Buddha in proffering to everyone a version of that truth suitable to that person's potential capacity.

A few went beyond this, to espouse a thesis more compelling, perhaps, to a modern-day comparativist: that all scriptures, all visions, all interpretations, are limited in this way, one's own[76] as well as others'; that every outlook held by human beings, even if of transcendent origin or divine inspiration, is contingent, is at best appropriate to the finite capacity—of human beings (including one-self), of eras, of groups—to rise towards truth or enlightenment.

One way that this vision was expressed was in a Mahayana notion, which indeed became somewhat current, of "Fingers Pointing to the Moon"[77]. This affirmed that no religious matter on earth is itself, or even touches, the reality at issue; it is, rather, a symbolic guide that may direct us to that reality—if we properly respond. The metaphor has become justly famous. One may hope—and strive—that in the modern world it may become more widespread, and more inwardly appropriated. It is no small attainment to ascribe religious diversity to human finitude in responding rather than to sheer human ineptitude—or than to astute accommodationism on the part of a Buddha or an initiating God or absolute.

At the very least, one may say that history is better understood when relativism is appreciative rather than disparaging. Relativism leads to nihilism except when recognized as approximation to something higher.

We turn next, from multiplicity, to another characteristic of the Buddhist scriptural case: textuality, tending at times towards bibliolatry. Variety of scriptures, or within a given scripture, is not of course unknown to any of the world's major religious movements; but we have suggested that it has characterized the Mahayana Buddhist instance in unusually generous measure. Similarly focus on a text as such, insofar as it may for instance be distinguished from the purport of what that text has to say, has been common to many scripturalist groups throughout history. The Buddhist movement has illustrated it, however, sufficiently often and with sufficient force to justify our taking special note of it here.

There have been instances of the usual matters wherein reciting a scripture, or copying it, or having it inscribed, or holding it in one's hands, is inherently an act of piety and merit; a person in preparation for copying it will cleanse him- or herself, wear proper clothes, sit in a prescribed position of reverence, and so on; the text as a physical or auditory object is sacralized, and in turn sanctifies. Scripture as talisman is world-wide. Popular stories were told about the often miraculous powers of a particular *sutra* not only for human beings but even for animals that heard it recited. The Mahayana has, however, gone much further than these fairly standard phenomena—to a point where at times an observer is tempted to feel not so much that the scripture is holy because of what it represents as that it is itself the (an?) ultimate source of holiness. At other times, an indication of this sort of outlook appears combined with other more customary attitudes.

The Mahayana movement first comes into historical view as a collection of groups each oriented to one or another particular scriptural work[78]. Its missionary movement, carrying Buddhist vision into northern and eastern Asia, took the form largely of preaching and proclaiming these various *sutra*s. The preacher of a given *sutra* was honoured and indeed virtually sanctified. A place with which it was associated became sacred. As one of many such texts affirmed, "a shrine is to be constructed"; elaborate—and joyous, celebrative—reverence is to be shown; and "worship is to be performed on whatever piece of ground this rehearsing of the Dharma [sc., this particular scriptural text] may be enunciated or exhibited or recited or chanted in unison or written out or, once written, may be set up in the form of a book, like a stupa[79]", because on such a piece of ground the Buddha is present wholly[80]. It is as if all Buddhas became enlightened through the teachings of this *sutra*[81]; and indeed in many another context a suggestion seems almost to surface that the Buddhas reverenced a particular scripture, rather than *vice versa*. Certainly the Buddhas are set forth in these scriptures as proclaiming that those—whether gods, human beings, demons, or whatever—who show due veneration to a given *sutra* and joyously accept it, or indeed delight in it, hearing even a single verse of it or single word, are destined to (eventual) total enlightenment[82]. Noteworthy for an outside observer is the number of Mahayana *sutra*s that devote a substantial portion of themselves to affirming their own ultimate worth, and salvific role.

The Pali scriptures are the record of enlightenment. The Mahayana ones tend to be presented as the cause of it.

Time and again in Buddhist history, turning points have come when someone discovered a for him new *sutra* and set out to tell his fellows how much it meant to him. Major new developments arose from such fresh encounters[83]. In an earlier chapter we noted that in the Islamic case, in contrast to for instance the Jewish and the Christian, it has been the scripture that has evoked the community. In the Buddhist instance, at the level of sub-communities within the whole, something of the sort may also be observed. (At this level of sub-community within a more general movement, one may reflect that the Protestant Reformation emerged in a scripturalist fashion potentially reminiscent of this.)

We have already noted that it was in the form of texts (at first, retained untranslated) that the Buddhist movement came to Tibet. In China, the first many centuries of Buddhist development took the form largely of translating Sanskrit texts and acquiring new ones from India as they were produced. In Korea, also, gathering and making available texts from China has been close to central. In

Japan, the "Buddhist Constantine"—Shotoku Taishi, the eighth-century emperor whose backing for the movement was decisive in establishing it there[84]—built temples, monasteries, and convents specifically to honour the Lotus Sutra, his own favourite among the new scriptures.

It would seem not unlikely that the move from oral/aural India to bibliophile China had something to do with Mahayana emphasis on the text, as did also later the major fact, already noted, that China invented both paper and printing, including printing from movable type—and was followed fairly quickly by both Korea and Japan in devoting this new art primarily to the printing and disseminating of (Buddhist) scriptures. The Far East has lived in "The Gutenberg Era" of McLuhan far longer than has the West. (And the West, longer than has India.) In China, calligraphy was an honoured art[85]. In addition to these matters bearing on our subject, one may note that still earlier in its development the Buddhist movement by entering Central Asia came into some contact with the Near Eastern scriptural tradition, at which we have previously looked; and there is some evidence that it got part at least of its predilection for books, and for casting its scriptures in the form of written books, from there. (There is some evidence also, as already remarked, that not only in form, but also in content, there may have been interaction—borrowing and influence in both directions—between this early Buddhist and that Near Eastern tradition, some scholars finding common motifs here and there among early Buddhist scriptures, the New Testament, and Jewish tales[86]).

Around the world, and also for Buddhists, a distinction between oral/aural and written dimensions of scripture can be tenuous, as we have observed. Most peoples (not all) have embraced the two jointly in their involvement with their scriptures. The modern West has quite recently tended to put more emphasis on the written (and on reading silently), and to some degree other cultures have now begun to evince this. What is needed for understanding historically is no doubt a re-capturing of a sense of the central importance of the other, but also, and perhaps even more firmly, a re-capturing of the sense of how interrelated the two have normally been, in cases where both have existed. Buddhists took more note of the written than did Hindus, as we have seen. Among Buddhists, the Mahayana took somewhat more note than the Theravada, probably; yet both have evinced both, and continue to do so. We shall be mentioning presently an insistence on the major point that spiritual truth to be significant has to be experienced, appropriated inwardly, known existentially. To memorize, to recite, even to hear, have always been more deeply personal ways of relating to the meaning of words than to look at them on the page. Along with, even despite, the plethora of written texts, the oral use of scripture by Buddhists has been and continues today to be central. Yet written texts have in several cases (for example, Tibet) preceded oral recitation, chanting, memorizing, and the like, historically; and they have their own aura. In modern times that construction of a pagoda in Mandalay with the entire Pali canon visibly inscribed was an impressive move; equally, that was a great occasion when a monk was able to be heard reciting at a major ceremony that entire canon from memory[87].

A special case of treatment, chiefly oral treatment, of scripture, and a highly important one, is its use in ritual, as we stressed in our Jewish chapter. Like other communities, Buddhists have made much of this. From one end of the Buddhist world to another the various scriptures have been pivotal in liturgical services, and their use in those services has been pivotal in the role of scripture in people's life. In the Tipitaka Pali Canon, the rules of the monastic order constitute as we have remarked the first Basket; and there is some evidence that the entire business of having a canonized scripture was a development out of the monks' ceremonial repetition fortnightly of a formal confession, now in that sector of it[88]. The services of the Pure Land Sect in Japan are devised in such a way as to include the Triple Sutra of that group, followed by unison recital of the heart of the founder's *magnum opus*, in un-understood Chinese, followed in turn by passages from writings in colloquial Japanese of the group's chief later leader. Thus "the whole of the tradition becomes available both at the level of symbolic meaning and power and at that of comprehension in colloquial terms"[89]. In between these two instances, widely separated in space and time, one may note that for the incipient Mahayana movement in India and Central Asia the book of scripture served as the central symbol in worship, the focus both physically and ideationally in each of its constituent sub-movements' spread and growth.

Alongside emphasis on the text itself as important (over against this, rather than alongside, a modern might almost say) has gone the emphasis on existential engagement. (Here again, ritual use pertains.) Siddhartha Gautama himself certainly stressed that persons must come themselves to recognize the truth, the reality, that is the point of it all. Shinran, the better part of two thousand years later, stressed that the decisive matter in his own life had been his "hearing" Amida's vow, through his reading of the pertinent texts, and vigorously disparaged those who read and study the scriptures without such "hearing"[90]. Kukai is one of those who stressed that the truth of scriptures or indeed of other works is a function of what the words do, to the reader[91]. We earlier remarked on the Platform Sutra, and its disparaging of scripture generally as virtually distracting from the spiritual life, yet itself presently scripturalized, and cherished because it taught that sort of thing: taught that it is not a text that is important, but one's own transformation. Nichiren, whom we have noted as excited about a particular *sutra*—the Lotus —and as effective in gathering others to turn to it, stressed that properly to read that scripture is not merely to read, nor even to understand, but to appropriate, to interiorize, to practise its precepts, to strive to realize (to make real, to actualize) its truth[92]. He was well aware that different readers find different things in a given scripture. Unlike some modern critics, he saw this as altogether right and proper, since one's ability to benefit from the reading is indeed a function of one's moral and spiritual personality brought to it[93]. (We have earlier noted St. Bernard's making a somewhat comparable point in relation to divergent interpretations of Christian scripture[94].)

Our concern in this book is not primarily with what the various scriptures say. This has been widely studied by modern scholarship, and the texts made fairly widely available in translation. Much more centrally, our engagement is with what scripture as such is—or does (has been; has done); with how it may best be conceived; with how one may understand it as the major factor in human history and personal life that demonstrably it has been. Thus far in this chapter, we have delineated some outline of what it is that, in the Buddhist case, is there to be understood. In conclusion, we must essay some general consideration of what in that case has been going on in this realm, hoping to infer theoretical points that might help to interpret the data and move us towards deeper understanding.

Among the historical data to be interpreted today are the interpretations that over the centuries major Buddhist intellectuals have themselves developed in their own attempts, within the movement, to understand and to make understandable. Their theories, of course, cannot be our theories. Yet by illuminating to us how matters appeared to those involved in them, they may contribute something to our grasping of what was afoot in these human-scriptural processes. They constitute one of the givens in the scriptural developments at which we are looking. Among the demands on any conception that we may formulate, one is that it must satisfactorily explain how it was that Buddhists thought and felt these ways about what they were doing and was being done to them, and for them, scripturally.

Buddhist theories of scripture, we have observed, have been subtle, sophisticated, and varied—far beyond anything that could be sketched in brief compass here[95]. (Moreover, they have of course often been tacit, evident more by implication than expressly.) On some of them and some of these implications we have already touched; for instance, in that matter of insistence on existential engagement. We shall develop briefly one already mentioned, and then note a couple of further positions set forth or implied, before proposing our own inferences. Specifically, we shall deal with three issues: the biblioclasm paradox, symbolism, and the "Buddha Word" concept.

We return, then, to that paradoxical matter of the minority whose distrust of verbalizing truth and especially of writing it and of reifying it led them to reject extant scriptures, their position later becoming scripturalized. This began, in a sense, with Siddhartha Gautama himself. He was honoured as Buddha in part because he—as most religious leaders around the world have been honoured in part because they—saw and publicly proclaimed the shallowness or downright inadequacy of the extant religious situation of their time insofar as or because it tended to reach no higher than a focus on the formal symbols of the inherited tradition, no longer calling primary attention to, and nurturing final reverence for and relation with, what those symbols symbolized, had originally symbolized; what they had been proffered to represent, to introduce us to, to lead us towards. The elevating metaphor that we have noted, of "fingers pointing to the moon", could be and was used to illustrate later this sort of common human failing. Buddhists came to speak of the human propensity to orient ourselves to those fingers, ignoring or forgetting the moon or even becoming unaware that it is there. In the instance of Siddhartha's own situation and with regard specifically to scripture, he and his immediate followers had been sceptical of their society's seemingly mechanical involvement with "the Vedas". This scepticism carried over into his own teaching about the contrasting need for existential involvement and personal experience of and engagement with the ultimate that liberates human beings from our thraldom in and to the world[96].

As with others of the world's religious leaders great and small, however, not only did Siddhartha's own teachings, with their emphasis on getting beyond mundane externals, in the course of time become cherished and revered because their insights proved indeed liberating. Also those teachings themselves became the focus of reverence and honour, and indeed the words in which they were recorded, and presently the books in which those words were written down, or even the sacred places where those books were lovingly enshrined, and the act of reciting or copying those books or visiting those places. (The situation is similar in spheres other than the scriptural which is our special interest. The person of the Buddha, and in due course representations of that person or relics of his body, and the places where these were enshrined, and so on, attracted to themselves attention because of his recognized greatness. Yet that greatness lay in his recognizing and affirming that attention is due, rather, to the eternal universal truth impinging directly on each one of us.) These tendencies in later developments are no doubt abundantly evinced in the course of Buddhist scripture history, and abundantly paralleled in the course of other sectors of human religious history. Yet we shall be arguing in a moment that however much they may stand in need of being superseded, they are nonetheless themselves evidence of a human sense, however dim or inchoate (yet often in fact vivid) of immanent transcendence. They are testimony to a no doubt narrow vision of the form in which the infinite impinges on our lives, yet to a persistent and sometimes powerful awareness that indeed it does so impinge (and that this particular form has been, and potentially is, a channel for it).

Indeed this process also, of paying attention not merely to eternal truth and human engagement with it but to the words in which are set forth that truth and the need and value of that engagement, began even before Siddhartha's life was over, and, we are told, with his endorsement. As he was approaching his earthly end, his disciples are said to have plaintively asked what they could do once he their teacher was no longer there to guide them. He is presented as replying, "The Ultimate Reality [*dhamma*97] and the moral norms [*vinaya*98] that I have pointed out and made known, let them, after I have gone, be Teacher for you"99. He may not have meant the "words" in which his teachings were verbalized—he was intuitively well aware of the difference between words and what they express. Yet this report, along with stories of a formal Council in which the community's leaders allegedly accepted an agreed text as definitely an accurate transcription of what he had taught, soon became the justification for the Pali scriptures that did indeed become a recognized repository of his teachings100. In fact, it is quite possible that both stories were produced in order to make that justification—that undergirding—available. The resplendent memory of the person who had discerned and lived the truth and proffered it to others was extended to later generations by way of this medium. The scripture was recognized as holy and good and true on the grounds that it was his—just as he was recognized as holy and good and true on the grounds of the scripture. (How else could subsequent ages recognize him to be so?).

Thus on the one hand the Buddhist movement has had from the start, and has developed lavishly, a scriptural component, even a scriptural focus. On the other hand, it has sustained, lurking in the wings, a strain of a certain restlessness with this. This latter was carried to an extreme by a few, who on occasion went so far as to affirm that Buddha taught nothing verbally; that throughout he maintained a total silence101. His principal message was this silence102. Or shall we say, it was his silent communication.

For we must recognize that such a feeling is not ultimately negative. Rather, it stems from the sense that there is something more, and that that something is supremely precious, is in danger of being left out; we are in danger of being distracted from it; however helpful, however apt, nonetheless anything finite is *ipso facto* other than that something more. Even the famous "emptiness" idea103, richly developed in several strands of the Mahayana, and linked in relation to our concerns to this position on scripture, has expressed a positive sensitivity to what lies beyond[104], discerned as essential in the Buddhist heritage.

Nonetheless, most Buddhists, as we have seen, rejected the rejection of scripture, while keeping its positive sense of a beyond. "In general, Buddhists saw the final truth to be beyond words"[105]— which could be said of most of us, perhaps (we shall return to the point in our concluding chapter). This stance included most of the theorists. The relation between truth or reality and its formulation in words is a teasing issue for all sensitive philosophers of language, and Buddhist thinkers have not failed to address it, subtly and acutely[106]: the relation even between knowledge—especially human knowledge—and words, let alone between wisdom[107] and words. Since their scriptures' role was to make available salvific knowledge—wisdom—the matter was the more tricky. Ordinary Buddhists did not fret about the trickiness, leaving that to the intellectuals; but they were quite conscious that their scriptures were indeed something different from ordinary wording, and treated them accordingly.

We have remarked that the apparently negative assertions of the minority have expressed a certain positive sensitivity. One might catch the flavour of this by contending that "emptiness", for instance, as a concept, has served for those who adopted it as a symbol (which is part of what makes it such a difficult religious conception for outsiders to grasp). We turn, then, to this notion "symbol", since one may equally or even more firmly recognize the symbolic quality, for those also on the other side of that particular issue, of the scriptures that they found good; those who found their scriptures far from empty.

Words, many of us would say, are symbolic. At the very least, they may and regularly do symbolize and not merely signify. Scriptural words, Buddhist as other religious history makes evident, have functioned symbolically. This is of prime import. Yet beyond this, each scripture has itself served for many as a symbol: each scripture as such, and not merely what it has had to say. For one thing, this explains why it has been often highly significant even for those who do not understand the language in which it is written[108]. Beyond also this, one of the facets of Buddhist developments in this realm has been the practice of taking a *sutra*'s title as substituting for (sc., as symbolizing) the entire *sutra*. More exactly, a person's uttering of the title is what is (can be) uplifting. We have noted that for Nichiren, his vehement and painful soul-searching and his quest for learning led him finally to discover the Lotus Sutra as "not only the perfect culmination of Buddhist truth, but the sole key to . . . salvation", and eventually, in "the white-heat of his faith and zeal . . . he simplified the whole practice of religion to . . . uttering the 'Sacred Title' of [this] Scripture". The title[109] prefixed by *Namu* ("honour to") "is, according to Nichiren, neither merely the title of the book, nor a mere [*sic!*] symbol, but an adequate embodiment of the whole truth revealed in that unique book"[110].

In this case, the title served as a symbol for the scripture (and what it signified); but in general, the scriptures themselves functioned symbolically—for a reality recognized as transcending them. In the Theravadin case, the tendency was for the historical Buddha and his teaching[111] to serve as the final symbols of transcendence, with the scriptures then perceived as logically secondary, derivative from and theoretically subordinate to these; although in practice in later ages, simply representing them. In the Mahayana, on the other hand, the scriptures more often themselves served as the highest this-world symbols[112], direct pointers to ultimacy. In both cases, here as elsewhere, an outsider's misapprehension as to the situation would be serious if he or she were to omit that ultimacy from consideration.

It is with this symbolic quality of transcendence that we conclude our investigation. The matter is illustrated by reference to an early Buddhist theory of scripture which could serve as a bridge to our own suggested interpretation. The Sanskrit term *Buddhavacanam* represented a central concept in the realm of Buddhists' sense of scripture, for some centuries. It has standardly been rendered in English as "the word of the Buddha"; but this could be seriously misleading. That *vacanam* means "word" is not in question (though what "word" means is no slight matter: one's notion of the significance in the cosmos of being human is at stake in one's conception of the significance in human life of our ability to speak, to each other and conceptually to ourselves; and to listen, to understand, to be in communication). More immediately, the problem has to do with whether *Buddha* is well translated as "the Buddha".

To most Westerners and other outsiders, this rendering suggests the historical figure Siddhartha Gautama, who lived in India twenty-five hundred years ago. To Buddhists, it designates primarily (and literally) a transcendent status. Certain Buddhists, chiefly the Theravadin group, see that status as indeed embodied in that historical figure; others, especially in the Mahayana movement, may not. (For some, the word may name hundreds of millions of celestial figures.) Even the former group are interested in the historical figure because, and only because, they perceive him as indeed this transcendent teacher, one whose Englightenment enabled him to be aware of eternal truth and rightness (*dharma*) and to communicate it then to them. (The word *Buddha* basically means "awake", "enlightened". It is an epithet, not a proper name.) Siddhartha Gautama has been called Buddha because he recognized eternal salvific truth (or: eternal salvific wisdom[113]) and made it available to them. Put more cautiously: he has been called Buddha by people who discern him as recognizing it and making it available to them. (The pattern is similar with the designation by some of Jesus as "Christ".) *Buddhavacanam*, then, might almost be translated as "salvific word". Certainly it means "enlightened (or: Enlightenment) word", or alternatively "word of him (or of one) that is Enlightened". For many Buddhists, a minimum would be "word of a Buddha"; a literary connection of their movement to Siddhartha could be seen as co-incidental, if not almost beside the point.

The movement arose in the first place and has continued for two and a half millennia and has spread over half the world because of this perception of transcendence. Outsiders must take pains to avoid the danger of a persistent reductionism, from which for a time many in our culture used not to be free. The danger is evident in the language that many among us have used, and in our conceptualizations and perceptions: a danger of thinking and speaking only of mundane matters in our moves to understand transcendent ones— or to understand human beings (which one could say amounts to the same thing, in the sense that the two involve each other). The mundane aspects of the movement are indeed important, and should certainly not be omitted. Yet even at the mundane level, historically they demonstrably have been and are secondary, derivative from the other. It is with a human perception of transcendence that we have here primarily to do. Not to give it pride of place in our understanding of the facts is to misunderstand those facts; to misrepresent, to distort.

Outsiders are condemned to see at best as two what Buddhists see as one. (Otherwise, we would not be outsiders.) For each religious community, the transcendent and the concrete converge in some particular point or pattern or person or ideas. We fail if we see only one. Even if we recognize that they are indeed two, mundane and transcendent, for those concerned—for Buddhists, in this case—nonetheless we somewhat fail if we forget that for them they are indeed not two, but one.

The meaning of words is at issue here. It is reductionist to hear in 'dharma' only Buddhist teaching, not "final truth and goodness"; in 'Buddha', only Siddhartha Gautama; in scriptures, only what they say. Also, it is misleading not to see that of the two steps that we must take, the second is the more important; is in some sense even primary.

The question of mundane alongside (not over against!) transcendent is not a matter of the historical as distinct from a timeless realm. On the contrary, what scriptural history presents to us is the involvement of the historical in the transcendent, the advent of the eternal into time. Even the most historicizing of the Buddhists, those who have held Siddhartha Gautama at a specific range of places and in a specific span of time as proclaiming a specific *dharma*, have seen that *dharma* as timeless. Whatever Siddhartha Gautama may have taught specifically, or the Canon may present him historically as teaching, and whatever one or another of the multitudinous Mahayana *sutra*s may present one or some among the celestial Buddhas in their millions as teaching specifically, yet an underlying message that all have conveyed is that transcendence is within our reach, and that it matters more than anything else in our life. This is the fundamental truth that Buddhists, if they did not know it already, have heard in their scriptures; and in any case that they have found set forth and nurtured as they went on then to perceive that transcendence (or the route to it) as of this or that specific shape[114].

Moreover, both Theravadin and almost all Mahayana Buddhists have contended not only that this transcendent reality became embodied in particular words at some point in the historical process, but further that it has again become historically actual, to some degree, and consequentially effective, to some extent, in their particular lives now, and the life of their families, their community. They have found, they report, their existence here on earth enlarged and given substance and worth by the reality beyond yet within history with which they have herein been put in touch.

Moderns may not agree with them on this point. Yet we must not fail to note, must not fail to try to understand, the hundreds of millions of Buddhists, including the most critically intelligent, testifying that in and through their scriptures—as related day by day to their own experience and intelligence and insight—this in fact is what has been going on.

CHAPTER 8

THE CLASSICS: CHINESE AND WESTERN

CHINESE CIVILIZATION over the past two or three thousand years and more has been dynamic and complex. In its course, its people have evinced both similarities with and differences from those of us in other civilizations—in other matters, and also in the affairs that primarily concern us in this study. It would be surprising, therefore, if in order to include them in our understanding we did not have to modify some of our preconceptions. One cannot look carefully into their participation in our total human involvement without becoming caught up in, and reflecting on, for instance the ideological conceptualizing that lies hidden in customary terminology. The challenge to re-think some of our categories can as usual prove markedly rewarding.

When Westerners, in the seventeenth century of the Christian era, began to get to know Chinese culture, they were introduced to the term *ching*, used by the Chinese to designate books that have held a special status in their life, of transcending worth. China had come to honour three major sets of books accorded this status. Westerners have regularly translated *ching* as "scripture" in those cases where it referred to Buddhist and Taoist works, as "classics" in the Confucian case. Thereby hangs an important tale; one with historical consequences within Western intellectual history, to some of which we shall presently return. The double standard continues in the West to this day; and continues important. For the moment, our concern is with the situation in China itself.

Both "scripture" and "classics" are Western terms, expressing ideas and categories of thought growing out of Western experience and the particular contours of Western cultural history. The experience and the history of other civilizations have of course been in significant ways different. It is requisite, now that we are all pushed towards endeavouring to understand humanity at large and to think less parochially, that we develop larger and more subtle ideas, and adjust our categories to become more inclusive and therefore more adequate. Moreover, in this instance as in many, one finds that the larger vision conduces to a more adequate, more accurate, understanding also of one's own situation. Our present study has been an attempt to explore, in the expanded human context, that Western concept "scripture" and the world-wide reality and experience to which today it is called upon to refer. It turns out that this involves a reconsideration also of the concept "Classics", and of the experience both of the Classical tradition in Chinese life and also of the Græco-Roman Classical tradition in Western life[1]. That reconsideration proves rewarding for a better understanding of scripture as well. First, however, specifically to China.

The Chinese Classical tradition, or "tradition of the literati", *Ju chiao*[2], has by outsiders been called Confucian[3]. Its carriers have been the *Ju chia*, which we may render as "the Classical school", or the Classicists. Those phases of this tradition's, these persons', on-going movement discernible over the past eight or so centuries have come to be dubbed in the West Neo-Confucian. The associated movements—of persons, groups, and ideas—have even been reified in the West as "Confucianism" and "Neo-Confucianism". This, even apart from the distorting connotations of all such "-ism" forms in general[4], has significant additional misleading qualities specifically for China[5]. Moreover, it becomes entangled with a further improper point. Although in China the figure of K'ung Fu-tzu, Confucius, has been profoundly cherished and even revered, as has that of Muhammad in the Islamic movement, nonetheless somewhat as the West has had to abandon its ethnocentric[6] impulse to speak of "Muhammadanism", similarly this Chinese tradition is to be recognized as having been focussed primarily, of course, on a transcendent vision; and at a close, yet emphatically secondary[7], level on the value of the books themselves—and then thirdly, on the person who called attention to the first two. For in those books they find that vision enshrined; through studying them they sense it as accessible also to themselves, centuries later. What they find in the books is seen as expressing it, nurturing it, giving it conceptual form. It has provided ways of thinking about, and talking to one other about, the highest truths, the highest human potentials and duties, that the tradition's participants could rise or aspire to perceiving.

Or, if not "the highest", at least some, major and decisive, among those highest. Certain persons or groups or ages in China have consciously recognized and appropriated for themselves no supplementary source for final wisdom. A great many others—their proportion varying from century to century; but normally a considerable majority—found inspiration and guidance for their living in all three of their culture's esteemed teachings: Confucian, Taoist, Buddhist. This is a point to which we shall be returning[8].

Our particular interest for the moment is the creative response in China, over the past twenty-five hundred years, and especially the important last twenty-two hundred, to what might be called this one tradition's central texts, those Chinese Classics, those *ching*[9]. Yet more accurately it is to be recognized as response to the world, by way of these texts and in terms of them. We would not only call attention to the inherent importance of this response—in Chinese and in global history—as well as to its significance for our specific concerns in this study. We would also explore its significance for our understanding of a counterpart, the Western Classical tradition: the legacy in Western civilization from Greece and Rome, as focussed also on—or by—an inherited corpus of literary texts. This will occupy us presently.

Within China, the interrelation among the differing sets of *ching* has been dynamic. As the centuries have come and gone the relation has varied, in particular, of the Confucian "Classics" to Buddhist and to Taoist "scriptures". There can be no question but that the development of these three traditions, and of the scriptures of each, has been historically intertwined; on occasion closely so, one would have to say. From century to century each has become what it has become in part because of its own past; in part because of new situations, and new persons arising; in part because of what had been or was happening with one or both of the other developments. On the other hand, the distinction among the three sets of *ching* has also, especially at certain periods, been marked; also among the status accorded each. On this last point, however, one may stress the fact that insofar as the term had somewhat differing connotations when used in reference to the three traditions, it comes closer to the Western notion of "scripture" in the Confucian case than in the other two. If one is going to translate *ching* as "scripture" at all, on most scores it is the Confucian *ching* that primarily deserve that epithet[10].

Admittedly, there have been certain phases in the long history when the loyal adherents of the Classical or literati tradition—although hardly those of the other two—have chosen to stress distance between the position derived through their *ching*, and the position of followers of other teachings, other *ching*: followers whom they perceived as uncouth[11]. At other times, these gentlemen[12] have consciously participated in the more standard attitude of Chinese culture as it has not only lived with, but indeed appreciated, religious and ideational pluralism—not merely as a social but also as a personal inward matter, long before the West consciously faced the issue[13]. That there should be diverse teachings, and that people might well find many of them persuasive and elevating, has seemed natural.

That such teachings should be enshrined in books, and that those books should be cherished as enormously precious and rewarding, have also seemed normal to most Chinese; and especially so to the literati of this bibliophile civilization. There can be no question, further, but that the Confucian Classics have for many Chinese at many periods been received scripturally. By this one means that their role in individual and corporate life, their reception, their esteem, their effect, have been strikingly comparable to counterparts in other recognizedly scriptural traditions around the world[14]. As with each of the others, their history has of course evinced to some degree also its own particular characteristics of treatment, and these can contribute to a fuller and deeper understanding of the fact of scripture in human life. Along with the others, it has evinced, certainly, instances of rigorous intellectual handling, together with many instances of deep existential involvement—the two regularly overlapping. Their study has commonly been a matter of wrestling with the texts in the attempt, or resolve, to learn *from* them—rather than in detached modern academic fashion to learn about them. One may note that those involved have customarily taken for granted that the meaning of a Classics text is always greater, even enormously greater, than our ability to apprehend it. They speak of awe in their relation to that text and to that transcending meaning. As a report of sages[15], the works are seen—and felt—as transcending the grasp of us ordinary human beings, as overflowing with a richness that it is a privilege to pursue and an unending but at each step rewarding task to approach. The more one explores—and lives one's life in accord therewith—the more gratifying one finds it to be, and at the same time the more one finds that there is yet to explore, with evidently still greater reward awaiting[16].

In many further ways these works' reception has been comparable to that of scripture. Persons in this tradition have memorized the texts, interiorized them, appropriated them, aspired to live (and indeed, to die) by what they have to impart. And they have felt it grandly worthwhile to do so.

Illustrative of our parenthetic addendum here on these works' potential significance also for one's dying, is a remark by one of those involved in taking them seriously: a thirteenth-century scholar-official (*Ju*), in prison facing death for refusing, on moral grounds, to offer allegiance to a usurping emperor. He derived his refusal from his study of the Classics. Referring to that study, it is recorded that he said: "The sun of those dead heroes has long since set; but their record is before me still. And, while the wind whistles under the eaves, I open my book and read; and lo! in their presence my heart glows with a borrowed fire"[17].

Further: in Chinese philosophy, for two thousand years new ideas have been expressed in terms not of explicit originality but of new interpetations of the ancient texts. New movements have taken the form of varying schools each with its particular way of understanding these. This has not stood in the way of the ideas' being often major, often brilliant, often novel indeed[18]. Innovation by way of a new reading of received texts reminds us forcefully of the scriptural scene throughout the world.

Another parallel with even the more conservative type of religious movement may be mentioned: that dominant positions—expressed as dominant interpretations—have at times seen themselves as to all intents and purposes orthodox, and have roundly criticized alternatives within the tradition (as well as outside) as in effect heretical[19].

Aside from such personal attitudes to the Classics, there has been no lack of conspicuous outer manifestations of reverence. These have standardly included temples, shrines, and ceremonial rites. Family-ancestor sacrifice rituals derive from one of the "Five Classics"; songs sung, or recited, at funerals, from another. There are "Confucian" temples throughout China, which have played no negligible part in the lives of the people. They are found (as have been these other characteristics that we have mentioned) also in Korea and Japan, and there of course also this tradition has been both honoured and highly influential. One might cite the case of the thousands of *sowon* set up (from mid-sixteenth-century) in the Yi period of Korea, in which the tablets [*sic*] of notable Classical scholars were enshrined and before them ceremonial rites were performed[20]. One might also cite the "Rites Controversy" of the Roman Catholic Church in the eighteenth century, when the Vatican officially pronounced against the Jesuit support of the Chinese Classical tradition, primarily on the grounds of the rites that were involved with it. The Jesuit position had been that this tradition could be seen as compatible with Christian faith, much as was the Classical tradition in Europe. The Church pondered the matter and forcefully decided that on the contrary, it was a "religious" tradition and therefore intolerable.

Western secularists, on the other hand, on reading the Jesuit accounts, preferred to see it as secular—and attractive[21]. By deeming it not religious, they could permit themselves to like it.

For, alongside such considerations as we have adduced, it is certainly not illegitimate to hold that these Confucian Classics are in significant ways comparable to the Western Classics. This is so especially in content. Yet there are other ways also in which they are comparable; such as that in their being prized, cosmological theories as to their provenance—though not absent—have regularly been implicit[22] only. Elaboration has not been felt particularly requisite of a sort that the West would recognize as metaphysical. Their impact on those who cherished them has at times been social and direct rather than social and via overt conceptualizings of an "other". Immanence has not been distinguished from, and not polarized over against, transcendence—nor *vice versa*.

The moral dimension, on the other hand, in this Chinese Classical tradition, has been pronounced—and morality of this kind is by no means positivist. Pervasive throughout the whole enterprise, and indeed foundational to its orientation, is a transcendentalizing view—conviction, assumption, goal: that some things that we human beings do are right, some are wrong, and that it matters. (The only reason that some Westerners have recognized theology as involving transcendence while failing to recognize morality as in essence doing so equally, is that many among them associate morality and ethics with their Classical tradition, theology with their Christian and Jewish one. This unconsciously continues for many even after the waning of the Classical.)

The fact is that the Confucian *ching*—the one other set of books in world history that the West has come to call "Classics" in a counterpart sense to its own—have in the course of the ages played a role in Chinese life indeed similar in some ways to the role played by the Græco-Roman Classics in Western life in the course of some of *its* ages, and indeed similar in other ways to that of the Bible.

Accordingly, we are not here wishing to contend that the "Confucian" books have in fact been scripture, rather than Classics. On the contrary, we are suggesting that it is naïve to insist that they should fit one or the other of these markedly Western concepts. Western thinkers have similarly never been able to answer satisfactorily the question as to whether "Confucianism is a religion or not", for the same reason: imagining that all the world must conform to one's own idiosyncratic categories[23]. Further, we are suggesting that the very ambiguity of the scripture/Classics matter in the China case may be helpful for the wider understanding of scripture required in our new situation—and understanding of the human. It can be helpful also for an understanding of the Western Classics, and their major role in the history of Western civilization and life.

Comparability of content, of subject matter, rather than of function, was one of the considerations that led European thinkers to perceive Chinese *ching* as "Classics" in the Confucian case, as "scripture" in the Buddhist and Taoist. This was before the West had begun to digest the point that the world's "scriptures" justify, if at all, being lumped together under a general rubric by no means because of similarity of content. Nor is there similarity of the particular metaphysical vision in which their status is framed—another matter underlying the Classics analogy. We now recognize that in both those regards, as in others, the diversity in our world, not similarity, has been stunning (as indeed to a lesser extent it turns out to be even in some instances within a single community's variegated scriptures[24]). As we have repeatedly seen, what makes any of the world's scriptures scripture is not only or even primarily what they have to say, nor the particular metaphysical constructs within which their admirers explain their revering, so much as the way that they are variously received by that particular group of persons for whom they serve as scripture. As we said in our opening chapter, "Scripture is a human activity".

(That activity regularly includes, no doubt, holding explicitly or taking quietly for granted some view of the universe that makes sense of the special status accorded, or perceived, for these works as scripture.)

Thus in this Chinese instance, our concern has been not primarily with the texts as such; rather, with the role that they have played in personal and social life. One finds that the Chinese Confucian texts and their reception have been comparable both to "scriptures" everywhere and to the particular case of the Western Classics. This is partly—we are suggesting—because these two are themselves in substantial ways comparable, and indeed form an overlapping category.

It is only in modern world perspective that this last becomes apparent; the two concepts "scripture" and "Classic" can today be seen somewhat to converge. For many centuries the West had good reason to distinguish the two in its own case, sharply. For what it called scripture and what it called its Classics are notably different—in content; in form; in treatment; in metaphysical assessment. "Scripture" had come down as signifying the Bible, from Palestine, with overtones from its having been seen as the Church, and Jews, regarded it; "The Classics" meant the literature cherished from the Græco-Roman legacy. Now, however, we all know that other things around the world that have perforce come to be recognized as "scriptures" also differ from the Bible—in content, in form, in treatment, in metaphysical assessment. We know even that the Bible itself at differing periods of Western history—and among differing sectors of the Christian Church—has, though less starkly, so differed, as has, strikingly, the West's knowledge of, respect for, reaction to, its own "Classics".

Let us turn, then, to the West: to those Græco-Roman Classics, and to their place historically in Western life.

Again, we do not insist that these Classics are, or have been, scripture. That is a question of how in the future our society will decide that the concept 'scripture' shall come to be construed. Meanwhile we are once more suggesting merely that in Western history they have functioned at times like some recognizedly scriptural counterparts.

A few years ago a Christian theologian advanced the suggestion that the writings collected in the Bible might be regarded as "the classics" of the Christian movement[25]. My view has long been, rather, that understanding is enhanced if the Græco-Roman Classics be recognized as in significant measure the scriptures of the Western idealist-rationalist-humanist movement. The Western Classical tradition can be seen as in another way a scriptural tradition, a special instance of this larger human propensity.

We today live in a post-scriptural age, it has been said—although that seems perhaps less obvious now than earlier in the twentieth century, so far as for instance Qur'an and Bible are concerned. Yet surely ours is indeed a post-Classical age, in the West. Young people do not have "a feel" for the Græco-Roman Classics as did earlier generations. It is difficult for moderns to imagine not merely the enthusiasm but the veneration for those Classics, and the inspiration that was derived through them. It is difficult for us to grasp not merely what delight many of the educated found in these treasures, but how they discovered or took for granted that in them they had an ideal for their own lives. We are not accustomed to expressions from major serious thinkers uttered in relation to the Classics like "transports of admiration . . . thrills of joy . . . divine enthusiasm" (Diderot[26]), "I cried with joy" (Vauvenargues[27]), "transport of shouting, weeping, frenzy" (Alfieri[28]), "I took fire" (Rousseau[29]), "intoxication" (Gibbon). These are snippets of much more elaborate exaltations[30]; the last, we might well quote here at greater length: ". . . Rome . . . I arrived in the beginning of October. My temper is not very susceptible of enthusiasm, and the enthusiasm which I do not feel I have ever scorned to affect. But at the distance of twenty five years I can neither forget nor express the strong emotions which agitated my mind as I first approached and entered the *eternal City*. After a sleepless night I trod with a lofty step the ruins of the

Forum; each memorable spot where Romulus *stood*, or Tully spoke, or Caesar fell was at once present to my eye; and several days of intoxication were lost or enjoyed before I could descend to a cool and minute investigation"[31].

Also, relatively few today take the Classics as their primary guide in facing the world and for coping with it[32].

Earlier, things were different. Horace has more than once been remarked as the most quoted author in the eighteenth century. He was cited in the British House of Commons more often than the Bible, and even at funerals more often than moderns can readily credit. The cultured had a sense of an erstwhile stupendous attainment, whose radiant literary attestation illumines the landscape, and proffers a process in which contemporary life is to participate, preserving it on the one hand, updating it on the other. (The analogy here with Confucian China is close.) Imitating and emulating were set forth as explicit ideals[33], involving later admirers not merely in admiring, and in enriching themselves by appropriating inwardly the inherited treasure, but in modelling their own lives and communities on that pattern and indeed carrying it further, to realize in their own time the excellences at which the Classics taught them to aim[34].

If "scripture" is nowadays to serve as a generic term, embracing under a single rubric the unending variety among cultures across the world, and within each culture among centuries—variety in the operative effectiveness, the conceptions held, and much else—then that rubric must be made large and dynamic and personalist enough to do justice to that variety. In that case, must we not recognize that the West's Classics and the part that they have played fall also under that rubric of scripture?

The truth of this has less to do with the nature of the various texts than with the tantalizing question of what it means to be human.

One facet of this is that human beings live in a double awareness: of the ideal and the actual, reality and appearance, the world as it might be, ought to be, and as it is. Throughout our world it has been the custom to conceive the former in arrestingly diverse ways: in terms of a time, a place, a realm, an ontological reality, a preexistent set of ideas, different from the latter. What the West has called scriptures have served (primarily?) to give that conception form for many millions of persons in many cultures and centuries. What it has called its Classics have so served for its humanist tradition.

We are by no means the first to draw a parallel between the two[35]. The modern French humanist Gusdorf, for example, writes: "Just as the Jews were molded by the sacred writings of the Torah and Talmud and the Muslims and other Oriental peoples by their own sacred texts, Europeans have discovered their spiritual identity and the secret of their humanist calling through the masterpieces of ancient culture"[36]; or again, "Greek and Roman antiquity took its place as a second sacred history, not obliterating the Bible but sometimes overshadowing it"[37]. It was here that these groups' apprehension of transcendence was given form, by being expressed in the values[38] of Truth, Beauty, and Justice or the Good; and that faith in these ideals was inculcated and nurtured. We may say that in these they perceived a transcendent order, and responded, less or more positively—responded with what it is certainly not unreasonable to call faith, one particular form of faith[39].

(The West used to speak of a distinction between reason and faith. Modern awareness may recognize, rather, two species: faith in reason, and faith in God.)

Foundational was their rationalism and humanism, which they found ideally set forth in their Classical heritage: in its art, specifically sculpture and architecture, but primarily in its writings. From the Greeks and Romans they learned to perceive the universe as rational, and to perceive humanity, alone among living beings, as privileged to participate in that rationality. Reason—*logos*[40]—was perceived by the Greeks as a pre-existent cosmic reality, to some degree become incarnate, we might say, in the human. Later Western Classicists perceived it as having become incarnate in exemplary fashion in Greece and Rome, inspiring them to rise to emulating this, to developing their own human potentiality to participate, to making rational their own lives and works, and their communities. To live rationally, they saw, is to live well, individually and socially. (The word "well" here is to be understood in all seriousness.) The collapse of the Classical philosophic tradition in the West has resulted in a massive shift in recent times in the concept of reason. It moved away trom referring to something above us: something demanding and rewarding, which it is our privilege and task to serve

(and which to serve is final freedom); something that may salvifi-
cally adjudicate between or among us if we disagree or conflict with
one another yet agree on recognizing rationality's authority. Reason
has come to designate instead something at our service. It has
become seen as relating to means and no longer to ends; as something ensuring at best merely that whatever we severally opt, or
happen, to pursue—our own discrete "interests" or random goals
or whatever—we may be helped instrumentally to attain. We use
it for our purposes, rather than fashioning our purposes so as to rise
towards it.

Humanism, similarly. As we noted also in the "Confucian" case,
the ideal of the human set forth and cherished was a transcendent,
not a merely empirical, notion[41]. In this outlook, each of us can,
should, must, strive to become more fully human than we yet are.
Being truly [sic] human is immanent within us yet transcends our
present approximation to it.

Awareness of and active response to the ideal were nurtured
through the honoured writings—and, not least, through the
honouring of them. Idealism, another fundamental Classical contribution to Western civilization's thinking and feeling, was a form in
which their sense of transcendence was articulated—a form comparable to the idea of God in theist patterns, and to other articulations
around the world.

Familiarity with the phenomena of the role of scripture elsewhere in human history thus enables one to recognize and to appreciate several facets of the history of the Classical tradition in the
cultural development of the West. I do not wish to over-state
the case. The Western Classical tradition has been a quieter one
than those often called religious. Moreover, there have been persons, groups, moments, eras, that have ignored it, or taken it relatively lightly; or have taken it relatively seriously but as a delight,
not as a guide. Yet at other times and for other persons and groups
(drawn, normally, from an educated élite) it has had an importance
that one does well not to neglect; and that shows affinities with
scripture that it is rewarding not to overlook.

In fact these affinities are many. Several are close.

As with scripture, honouring the Classics in the West has played
different roles at different times. At certain stages, they have served
as support and justification for innovative tendencies. Those striv-

ing against the status quo have been inspired and their convictions given strength by their appropriation of this tradition; and their dreams of a brave new world waiting to be realized have been formed in its terms. A conspicuous instance was, of course, the European Renascence ("Renaissance"[42]). A more combative one emerged a few centuries later, with the *philosophes* and to no inconsiderable degree with the American and French Revolutions. At other times, in contrast, upholding the Classics has served as a conservative force. This may mean sustaining one's own traditional convictions against pressures to adapt to others', perceived as "new-fangled" ones. Socially, it may mean simply sustaining the current scene against insouciance and disarray. Or it may be more contentious, competing against active champions of rising alternative social proposals. Examples of both have been recurrent. Of the second type the most recent[43] is within living memory of many today, when non-conformists, aspiring to modernize, have perceived Classicists—who also have perceived themselves—as guardians of an older order now under fire.

(On the other hand, a rather different use of the term from ours here must be noted. "Romanticism", in pitting itself in the nineteenth century against what it called "Classicism", was itself substantially inspired by the Classics—just as, often, rebels against the Church [not merely a Luther, but even circuitously a Marx[44]] have been inspired by Biblical teachings. "It is painful to hear such a poet as Shelley described as 'romantic' . . . when 'romantic' is taken to mean 'turning away from Greek and Latin literary tradition'; for very few great English poets have loved Greco-Roman literature more deeply or understood it better"[45].)

As with scripture, changes have involved not only such large-scale attitudes and roles as these relations to social change, but also differing readings of particulars. The series of ways in which Homer, for instance, has at various times been read, is certainly instructive[46]. Interpretations of Plato and Aristotle over the centuries would provide a more obvious and complex illustration, of course. Yet neither Æschylus nor Cicero would be exempt.

As with scripture, dynamism has been in evidence in relation not only to general outlook. We may note again that oscillating between on the one hand preserving what has been traditional, and on the other replacing what is established and has become traditional with a new and perhaps subversive programme inspired by a vision of antiquity. There have been not only specific interpretations of individual writers or passages or ideas. There has been, further, a matter of selective (however unconscious) emphasis among the varied parts of the tradition, which as with scripture is sufficiently rich and diverse to provide devotees with substantial choice. Alexander Pope found in Horace, and offered to his readers via his own poetry, an idyllic vision of the quiet countryside[47], as a counterpoise to, or escape from, the wrong-headedness of the life of commercial busy-ness in London; others, of course—in, for instance, Aristotle's writings—found grounds, and patterns, for plunging wholeheartedly and with wisdom into the political activities of a national capital. And so on.

As with scripture, except in both cases in some recent academic moods, the Classics have been treasured not for the light that they throw on a distant past so much as for their relevance to the contemporary present-day. "The advocates of any Classicist movement whatever are invariably interested in their own culture rather than in the culture of the model; and in themselves more than in their heroes"[48].

As with scripture, devotees of the Classics so familiarized themselves, from childhood, with the texts and held them as so integral a part of themselves that this emerged not only in overt citation—which in the eighteenth century, for instance, abounded on both sides of the Atlantic[49]—but in addition, "their writings swarm with invisible quotations"[50]. The ubiquity of this latter phenomenon, often unconscious[51], in countless religious communities with regard to scripture has lately been stressed. "The major Christian thinkers—and the major thinkers of the Muslim, Indian, Jewish, and other scriptural traditions—have been characterized by the . . . capacity to (or rather the *incapacity not* to) 'speak scripture' when they write or utter any words at all"[52].

As with scripture, a symbolic role has been centrally important. Our study thus far would suggest that scripture's role in human life, to be seen perceptively, requires an active appreciation of the power and function of symbols in both individual and corporate living. Here also the role of the Græco-Roman Classics in the history of the West is best or only understood with a similar appreciation of the symbolic. Might one not say, that same appreciation? At stake is our ability not in understanding symbols, so much, as in understanding ourselves as human[53].

And so on. In these and other ways one is struck by a convergence between how the Classics have been received during certain phases of Western history, and the reception of scriptures around the world[54]. So evident, in fact, are such overlappings once noted that the issue for us might seem to become: how is one to explain the point that the parallels have not been more widely recognized all along. (They have been noticed, but not widely[55].) Actually, however, the explanation is quite straightforward historically. First is the manifest point that only in modern times has a global perspective come to the fore, so that the comparability of these two Western complexes emerges as one instance among others of the new comparability along with almost unnerving diversity between any two of the world's great spiritual traditions. The outlooks recognized in the modern West as "religious" differ among themselves, we now know, more drastically than has been supposed (and than superficially is still presumed—for instance by imagining that they give varying answers to the same questions, rather than highlighting differing ones). Their similarities and their differences, both, are turning out to be at a much more basic level than was thought, and both to be surprising.

Alongside and over against significant convergence between the Classics and the Bible as factors in Western people's lives, certainly divergences too have been stark: quite imposing enough to clarify Westerners' long-standing tendency to bifurcate the two. (Even today the suggestion that, although admittedly disparate, they are yet comparable may meet substantial resistance.) For both Christians and humanists in the recent West have operated in their thinking not only with two deeply embedded categories in their outlook that separate the legacy from Palestine and the legacy from Greece and Rome, firmly envisaged as two matters distinct in kind. They also, in the one case—the Palestinian—have been inheritors, or observers, of a tradition that has included an almost fierce sense of exclusivism, of incomparability and uniqueness. Both Christians and Jews are strictly trained to offer resistance to any sense of comparability, to suppress any awareness that just as Chinese have been presented as accustomed, in the inept Western phrasing, to "belong to three religions at the same time"[56], similarly they themselves have been brought up to participate, often loyally, cheerfully, gratefully, in two of the "great spiritual traditions of humankind"[57], of which the Western legacy from Greece and Rome is one. The secular West has generated[58] the idiosyncratic concept "religion" to designate one side of its culture's dual involvement. In recent centuries it has extended it to characterize various others of the world's cultural traditions, even though most of these in fact indiscriminately evince affinities with *both* sides of the Western experience[59].

No other civilization has marked off some particular area of life as distinct from the rest, as something special that the modern West dubs "religion". There is pressure for Christians and Jews not to be caught recognizing any other spiritual orientation as admissible; lately there has been equal pressure for secularists not to be caught accepting their own position as in any way "religious". As we now all firmly know, from unconscious pressures it is exceptionally difficult to free oneself.

One way to overcome the difficulty is to become aware of the development that has produced it.

We said above that the West used to have good reason to polarize its two traditions. As remarked, they were manifestly different. We might have gone further, noting that at some stages they have been in bitter conflict, notably in eighteenth century and notably in France (*écrasez l'infâme!*), and reaching another climax in the late nineteenth. Indeed to some degree that phase continues almost into the present, particularly on the academic scene. The unconscious outlook of many educated Westerners in recent times has largely been shaped by it. Late-nineteenth-early-twentieth-century strife took the overt form of a science-religion wrangle. Science, however, ("value-free") provides no basis for moral assessment; nor even, in the end, for assessment of truth other than mundane practical effectiveness. Accordingly its champions have on the whole taken their stand on humanist bases, calling on the Greek value of Truth, if not also Good. (One of the ways in which the Classical tradition in the West maintained its force for a time after the waning of the Christian-Jewish, especially among intellectuals, was by its integration of knowledge and value. In the latter twentieth century, when the Classical too has waned in the West, liberal thought tends to find itself rather floundering in the realm of morality. Fortunately, in science and the ir-"religious" populace at large, the Classical outlook has, in an implicit rather than overt fashion, continued effective[60].

One of the peculiarities arising from this has been that, as we suggested above in passing with regard to (in contrast with) the Chinese Classical tradition, many Westerners have perceived "morality" and "religion" as two different things. For this group, morality—or at least, ethics—has been associated with the legacy from Greece and Rome, while "religion" has in modern times become their name for what was inherited from Palestine. Virtually no other people on earth has shared this idiosyncracy. To think of morality and religion as distinct is rare: Western, and indeed modern Western.

One of the grounds on which the West has based its feeling of a polarity has been its tendency to think in terms of a focus in the two instances either on this world or on an Other World, and to feel that this distinction is crucial. This perception has been advanced chiefly by secularists; but it both grossly underestimates the central concern of transcendentalists for the life of us human beings on this planet, and also on the other hand sorely neglects the transcendence immanent in effective humanisms[61].

We are not contending that the differences among the various traditions are unimportant, are not deep, have not been consequential. At times they have been strident. We are simply saying that those differences do not constitute grounds for holding them to belong to different categories.

We suggested above that neither scriptures nor the Classics can be understood in their role in human affairs without an appreciation of their symbolic function over the centuries. If this be true of the role of each, it is even more true of the differences so conspicuous among and between the world's recognizedly scriptural traditions; and of the divergence betwen the West's scriptural and Classical. Also, that the relation between these Western two was for a time one of conflict is hardly a reason for concluding that they represent different species of tradition. Shared symbols are about the most powerful factor in binding a group together; divergent symbols are about the most powerful force in generating conflict between groups. The late twentieth century is no time to underestimate potential clash of disparate scripturally-inspired orientations to the world.

Besides, the phenomenon of conflict between those Western traditions is easily exaggerated; and of late, it has been. Things were by no means always so. Rather, the cultural history of the West has developed over the centuries with the two usually in harmony, sometimes juxtaposed, sometimes in clashing discord; and more often fused than is nowadays readily appreciated. For the Middle Ages, it would be an understatement to say that the two were on friendly terms. Rather, they were happily married, with a St. Thomas Aquinas as the perhaps today best known among the multitudinous offspring of the union—and on the Jewish side, Maimonides. The Church Fathers were Classicists[62]. Until very recently, schooling for the Western world has standardly been both Christian and Classical. Mediæval Church schools taught Classical alongside Christian authors, almost indiscriminately[63]. Not only were the universities of Europe established as Christian institutions; so more recently in the United States was Harvard, as its first, in the eighteenth century, and also right through the nineteenth almost all American colleges were set up by the Church, with normally a clergyman as president. In the early modern era, after the Greek authors were added to the Latin as additional authoritative models, the Jesuit order was—by far—continental Europe's most effective teacher of the Classics. (To the import with regard to China of this last point we shall presently be returning.)

In the English-speaking world several Protestant thinkers led in the Christian-Classicist amalgam. Noteworthy, for instance, is Richard Bentley, Regius Professor of Divinity at Cambridge and Royal Librarian around the turn of the seventeenth-eighteenth centuries, at once both a leading Churchman and a major Classics scholar. He *inter alia* made the important discovery of the letter *digamma* in pre-Attic Greek, and also proposed a parallel between Homer and Moses as names given, he suggested, in each case as a pious fiction as author for a coalescence of diverse older materials. (It is perhaps not irrelevant to add that when this suggestion was taken up and elaborated in Germany a little later[64], it was dubbed "Homeric atheism".) Another characteristic of the development illustrated by Bentley is his including in the amalgam of Christian and Classical loyalties the newest forms of science, in a quiet and seemingly effortless integrating that to a modern today cannot but be striking[65].

Presently, especially on the continent, there came a significant falling apart of Christian and Classicist. The deists and the *philosophes* in particular were attacking the former and, one may again say, establishing an amalgam with a sector of the latter and science. Nonetheless, a great many Westerners—probably the majority?—have lived, consciously or not, in terms of both traditions; and continue so. Western civilization is founded squarely on both. Certainly in the phase preceding that overt falling apart, yet once the duality had become strong, the leading promoters of the broader synthesis were explicit Christians—notably the Jesuits, as we have remarked. This brings us back to China, and the special correlation between the Chinese Classics and the Western—a correlation that turns out to owe much to the adventitious historical contingency of the timing of their first contact.

There has been an ebb and flow of the dynamic interplay in the West between the Classical and the Christian, and a not quite so fluid yet by no means fixed interplay in China between its Classical and the Buddhist and Taoist (and among these three). It so happens that the two distant civilizations met seriously at a moment in both developments that led in our particular realm to specific results. Had the first serious Christian missionaries arrived in China several hundred years earlier than in fact the Jesuits did (end of the sixteenth century), or a couple of centuries or more later (as the Protestants did), things would have turned out differently. So far as China is concerned, we have already noted[66] that the pre-T'ang and T'ang synthesis (*san chiao ho i*—"three teachings unite as one") was worked out and widely accepted during the first millennium A.D. This phrase was still current when the Jesuits arrived and has remained so into the twentieth century, and among a great many Chinese the worldview that it expressed continued and has persisted. Nonetheless by the middle of the second millennium A.D. many among the Classicists (*Ju chia*) had in practice switched to an outlook in which they saw their own tradition as right and those practising the other two as wrong.

At that time, on the latter point—the wrongness of Buddhists and Taoists—Christians were sadly quick to agree, given their firm exclusivism. (In the late twentieth century, in contrast, many Christian thinkers are finding Buddhists the most congenial of any of the world's communities outside their own borders[67].) On the other hand, as we have just observed, at that time innumerable Classicist-scientific types in the West were Christians, taking for granted firmly and unselfconsciously that of course being Christian in no way signified excluding or compromising the Classicist tradition. Some of them also joined the Jesuits, who were an order "distinguishing themselves in scientific research as well as in their voyages to the new worlds"[68]. One such, Matteo Ricci, an acutely intelligent person, led the Roman Catholic mission into China (from 1592). Over against the usual interpretation, there is on the evidence reason to speculate that in his personal inner temperament the Classical and scientific components were in fact primary, the Christian element less major. Yet even if this was not in fact the case, at least in his overt activities this was apparent[69].

In the eighteenth century the situation in Europe changed. Conflict between the rationalist Enlightenment and the Christian tradition had begun[70]. Yet on one matter convergence continued: neither Christians nor the anti-religious folk could allow themselves to be attracted to a Chinese "religion". Both groups, however, did find attractive what they read in the Jesuit reports on the Confucians. The *philosophes* were excited to discover "philosophers"[71] running the government in China; Christian Classicists were at liberty to take an interest in another "Classical" tradition. In the twentieth century, on the other hand, Western scholarship has increasingly moved towards recognizing the "religious" quality of that tradition[72]—and secularists, towards a lack of interest in a Classical legacy from the past (with philosophers no less than others quite unengaged by remote ancient wisdom).

We venture to predict that it may not be long before certainly the "Confucian" Classics, and presently also the Græco-Roman, become acknowledged also in the West as having in their own way functioned as scriptures. However that may be, meanwhile both of them can be helpful in our understanding of what it means for a work to be scripture, and what it means for human beings to be involved with a work scripturally. Or might it not be better to say: . . . what it means—has meant, can mean—for us human beings to be involved with our lives, with our neighbours, with the universe, in scripturally-linked ways[73]?

CHAPTER 9

BRIEF
FURTHER CONSIDERATIONS

OUR STUDY HAS BEEN of various ways in which different groups of people have developed a mode of living and of perceiving that has involved something that looks like what the West knows as scripture. One could go on and on with this, since such involvement has long since been almost universally human—and ubiquitously diverse. Yet we do not pursue it further, even though several of the instances that we have not yet noted are markedly engaging, and instructive. The Sikh community, for example, at a certain point in its relatively short history thus far decided to move on from its tradition of living leaders (*Gurus*) for the community and to adopt in its stead a new pattern of authority[1]. Retaining those great men's revered memory and indeed perpetuating it, the group chose explicitly to organize their life henceforth, after the death of the tenth *Guru*, in terms, rather, of an authoritative collection of recognized writings—the cherished teachings chiefly of those earlier leaders, along with pieces from a few other "saints"[2]. This collection they have called, in personalizing fashion, the Guru Granth Sahib (the "Honourable Book" guru)[3].

One may deem it delinquent for us not to plumb the role of this sacred collection in the corporate life and personal piety of this remarkable community. Among overt and observable aspects of the special treatment accorded it are the little shrines or separate rooms that in recent times many Sikhs have come to maintain in their homes, wherein the scripture is decoratively and reverently housed. An outsider can hardly but be struck by the devotion and engagement evinced in Sikhs' turning to these, regularly opening them each day and worshipping God before them. Similarly in group services, reading from the Guru Granth Sahib is of course central[4]. The temples as well as the household cabinets are called *gurdwara*, "access to the Gurus". The scripture's close-to-supreme place in Sikh life is reminiscent of the Near Eastern scriptural tradition, even though of course analogies also with Hindu patterns are discernible—aside from the basic uniqueness of the Sikh orientation, which can be quite special. One recent Western scholar goes so far as to say: ". . . the Sikhs [became] a people of the book to an extent and in a manner which is not found in any other religion"[5].

In the Shinto tradition of Japan, on the other hand, at first blush it might seem that a scriptural component has, in contrast, occupied a remarkably smaller place than in most religious outlooks. Some would even raise a question as to whether the Shinto is not the one major movement in the world over the past many centuries to be scriptureless. Although this is a teasing notion deserving investigation in depth, certainly arguments could be raised against it of various sorts. Part of its problem stems from the modern-Western tendency to perceive religious matters in terms of discrete "religions" or—more sensitively—of religious traditions, but not in terms of the actual life and faith of persons and societies. This "misplaced concreteness" can everywhere be misleading; yet Japanese history[6] is distorted more than most by any attempt to sort out as independent variables there (or even as interdependent yet presumably distinct conceivables) various religious entities such as "Shinto", "Buddhism", and the like that elsewhere have been thought of as having each a life of its own. The world's religious history is a matter of the life of human beings—with the abstractions that we concoct derivative and at best secondary. Given the fact that in Japan, Buddhist scriptures, and for some, also Confucian and Taoist, have played an integral role, it is probably the case that most Japanese at most times over the past thousand years have in fact treated or at least recognized some body or piece of literature as scripture, and that their lives have been significantly shaped by their doing so. What may be called "Shinto" has usually related to those lives as one (varying) coloration among others (—no doubt, at many times an important one). (In this study we, for instance, have followed this Western cultural outlook on religious matters by treating Japanese Buddhist life as a subtopic in our Buddhist chapter, rather than presenting it as a subsector of a chapter on Japan. That was acceptable for appreciating Buddhist matters, but the alternative would be more helpful for understanding Japan.)

Moreover, even within what passes as more strictly "Shinto", there has been the far from negligible concept of *kotodama*, the spiritual power of words. This has shown itself (especially before modern times, but still today) less strongly with regard to the two or three notable texts that have been handed down such as the N*ihongi*, the *Kojiki*, the *Manyoshu*, than in the traditional rather fixed[7] "prayers" (*norito*) recited to a particular *kami* or sacred spirit, in individual devotions and also often publicly by a priest before a group congregated at the relevant shrine. In recent times, the 1890 imperial "Rescript on Education", and the 1937 *Kokutai no Hongi* ("Fundamentals of the Japanese Essence"), were at a certain stage formally treated with ritualized reverence[8]. Altogether the issue is a highly complex one.

Yet whatever one makes of such arguments, one should not dismiss that interesting challenge posed in Shinto considerations to any theory of scripture.

Another area that would repay close study is the Jain situation. It would illustrate diversity, as have other instances, though of course again in its own way[9]. More striking for our purposes is that it would illustrate the extent to which modern Western scholarly studies of Jain scripture have developed by unconsciously imposing Western patterns and categories, without adjusting these to the actual Jain case. This of course worked to the serious detriment of genuine outside understanding. Beyond that, Jain self-understanding was affected as well, such a study would show—illustrating the revealing degree to which modern Western studies and ideas with their foreign presuppositions began surreptitiously to influence, in fact, the recent development of Jain ideas and practice in this realm[10]. The pattern is not altogether absent also in some other instances, as we have had occasion to observe.

Nonetheless, engrossing though it would be to explore the Sikh, the Shinto, the Jain, and other instances, we do not pursue them. This is not only because to do so would prolong unduly this already lengthy study. Besides, our aim has not been to provide a descriptive account of world history's scriptural situation! Rather, we seek to proffer representative material illustrating salient parts of it, sufficiently revealing to enable us to deepen our understanding of the place of scripture in human life: to move towards not only an increased understanding of scripture as such but an increased understanding also of humanity, as evinced in his and her long, and varied, involvement with it. What has thus far been set forth must almost suffice, tentatively, for that purpose. We omit, therefore, not only these numerically smaller groups, but also much of a massively important and luxuriant component of the whole: much of China—except insofar as we have dealt cursorily with its Buddhist strand, and have touched on that one further facet of its life that is crucial for an element of the total human picture, its Classics. The rich development of the Taoist scriptural tradition, on the other hand, as well as the elaborate evolution over the centuries even of the Buddhist and the Confucian, and the multitudinous ways in which the outlook on the world of successive Chinese generations has been variously formed in terms of them, we omit; as we omit too the ever-changing interplay among the three.

We may turn briefly, however, in the matter of historical interplay, to that same question on a larger scale, in Asia and world-wide. In an earlier chapter, we considered the emergence of scriptural form and of conceptualization of scripture for the Western world. We shall not attempt a similar study of the Eastern developments, although that would prove comparably suggestive and coherent. Moreover, not only have the diverse strands of the over-all scripture history of Asia been interconnected among themselves. In addition, one finds here and there occasional yet quite significant contact and mutual influences between the Western and the Asian developments, even in pre-modern times. On both points we have already, in our Hindu and Buddhist sections, as well as in our Chinese, noted some facets of this complex history; we may here make a few further hurried observations, of matters that may illuminate in new ways our general inquiry.

In early India the major emphasis on the spoken and heard word emerged and was seriously developed before writing was introduced into the sub-continent from the Near East. In all civilizations human beings have put emphasis on the sounds that for human beings symbolize ideas, and objects in the world; and on our capacity through speech to relate to each other in community and communion and to relate to the world around us, and to think. The particular form of this, however, was distinctive to India. There the emphasis was, as we saw, also on sounds that as such symbolize for at least those particular human beings the universe, reality as a whole, including its transcendence and its infinity. Since spoken language, even in our present day, is more intimate and personal than written or machine-processed, this involvement spiritually with the oral/aural dimension is of interest to us wherever it has remained strong, as it has in India even more than elsewhere. In our quick survey of the course of Western scriptural evolutions we left open a question as to whether the primacy of the oral, recitation, memorizing, chanting aspects of scriptural life in Iran—Zarathushtrian and other, obviously related to the situation in India—may also have influenced the course of scriptural developments in the more westerly traditions, whose original conceptual orientation had involved the primacy of a written document, though in practice this was presently lavishly supplemented.

Influence in the other direction is clear. This came in the Hindu case with the advent of writing, introduced as we have said from the Near East, not from China where it had been invented perhaps[11] independently and was given central importance. Later Hindu developments were, we saw, influenced by Buddhist; as later Buddhist developments were, we also saw, influenced by Hindu. Of central importance to the whole process is that the Buddhist movement, in its passage through Central Asia, picked up a major Near Eastern book-orientation, which it passed back to its community in India as well as carrying it forward in its further expansion into China and then Japan. I have not studied, from this particular point of view, the developing situation in South-East Asia, both Buddhist and Hindu for a time; it would be illuminating to have that input. In any case, it is manifest that the Buddhist movement on entering China, that "land of bibliophiles", soon took on to a discernible degree the imprint of that outlook on this matter, as well as contributing to its further development. The central position of books in Chinese culture shaped the emergence of that country's "Classical tradition" (and even its Taoist) as text-oriented; and the place of scriptural texts in Chinese Buddhist life, and then Japanese, was by no means unaffected by this—as well as *vice versa*.

Some centuries later, to return to India, we have noted the seventeenth-century emergence, within the developing Sikh community, of the Guru Granth Sahib as indicating a decidedly formal scripture, more formal than previously standard in that country. This scripture's form, status, role in practice, and metaphysical interpretation in theory, have approximated more closely to Western counterparts, including especially the Qur'an, than have any other within India. This came after the Islamic movement had settled down, following a period of violent aggression in India, to some centuries of a pervasive and collaborative cultural presence—culminating in the brilliance of the Mughul empire. Those scholars who see Islamic influence historically behind the formalism of this new Sikh scripture's emergence and development are able to make a telling case[12]. It is not apparent how far this influence affected also the process, on which we briefly touched, of Hindu groups' turning in these centuries much more than previously, and in some cases for the first time, to perceiving as *books* what one may call their scriptures but that had previously not been felt as in that format. In any case, it has been demonstrated that a shared formalizing transition was going on at this time among all three of the Muslim, Hindu, and Sikh communities[13]. (The interaction between Islamic and Hindu in India in mediæval times has been only incipiently investigated; but that that interaction proved consequential in the religious history of the two communities is becoming increasingly evident to those familiar with both traditions.)

At about that time, the introduction into the West from China of printing, and specifically the printing of scripture, was obviously of major import for our particular concerns. In China and Korea, then Japan, the use of printing for the Buddhist "canon" was central for centuries; the Gutenberg Bible and its many successors enlarged this ramifying matter also for Christendom. (Both Christians and Jews were affected. Following China's lead, the West's first printed book was the Bible. The Muslim world, in contrast, adopted printing for the Qur'an only belatedly—preserving it for other kinds of book only for a considerable while, and quite formally[14].)

Careful investigation into the history of scripture as a world process will probably conclude that it had three seemingly independent origins: in Indo-European Central Asia (and carried then with the Indo-European invasions into India); in the Semitic (and Egyptian) Near East (concerning which we have taken a preliminary look in an earlier chapter above); and in China. Relatively soon the three began occasionally to interact, as well as to ramify grandly in internal differentation; and today that world process is moving into a phase where it is gradually becoming, or is about to become, one complex. As with other intertwining and converging developments in which we human beings around the world are participants, it will gradually become a self-conscious process.

We may note one instance, hardly as yet self-conscious, of the wider development. The irresistibly expansive upsurge of the West, both secular and religious, has manifestly been affecting the religious development of the rest of the world—for good or ill. The nineteenth-century Christian missionary movement, it is now clear, was much less important and consequential in its avowed aim, of making converts from the other religious communities to the Christian, than it was in the unintended and largely unnoticed yet deep ways in which Western Christian forms and attitudes generated new developments within those other communities. (These came partly in movements of reaction against what was by some regarded as the onslaught.) This is a large topic, not to be explored here; but specifically in the scriptural realm, we might note three developments exemplifying a much wider trend: the emergence in India of an active Society for the Printing and Distribution of the Bhagavad Gita, financed by voluntary contributions from interested faithful; in Japan the novel tendency at the turn of the century for the Jodo Shinshu movement to have its scriptures now bound in soft leather covers overlapping inner gilt-edged India-paper pages[15]; a recent development whereby copies of a book of selections of Buddhist scriptures are being placed in American hotel rooms, in a well-financed counterpart to the Gideon project. These are external manifestations of a matter more subtle and going much deeper. There are many others[16].

Still more recently, novelty in various affairs including scripture, its reception, its understanding, has been introduced in the Buddhist case by the incipient but by now quite significant expansion of the Buddhist movement to the West, both by migration and by conversion, followed by the emergence of a generation of Buddhists who know only Western languages, and therefore think in Western conceptual categories different from those current in earlier phases of their spiritual tradition.

That some of these Buddhists are the wives, husbands, sons,

daughters, colleagues, neighbours, of Christians and Jews with other scriptures and other conceptions of scripture is beginning to affect also these latter. This happens in ways that begin to induce among them an outlook carrying far further and going well beyond the enlarged horizon already attained when Asian scriptures had become known to Westerners as impersonal texts from afar.

In these and a multitude of other ways we are entering a new situation; not least, in awareness.

In all, then, one may see that an intertwining of Western and Eastern developments of scriptural forms and concepts has been long-standing in some scattered ways, and recently has been increasing in major fashion. This is in addition to the fact that within the diverse Asian traditions themselves, developments of the scriptural forms and concepts have had over the past three thousand years their own intertwining history. This has yet to be carefully explored but manifestly it has been substantial.

We are drawing attention to these points, though without elaboration, in order to suggest an important recognition: that the various scriptures of the world, while as texts they are seen as diverse, and the lines between them have at times been felt as sharp, nonetheless constitute strands in a world complex. That complex is entering today a new phase in its on-going history, one in which not only are the various strands increasingly intertwined, but in which also all human beings are increasingly—and corporately—involved. Moreover, our awareness of all this is increasing swiftly: self-consciousness grows, and can become increasingly determinative. In our opening chapter above we contended that scripture is a human activity; the point has been corroborated, we trust, by what we have seen in subsequent chapters. Today that human activity is increasingly becoming shared. Particularly in the West and the Islamic realm, each group has been brought up to think of its scripture as very much its own, discrete from any others of which it might be aware. Yet the group's attitude and understanding of its own works, constituting them as scripture, are now being formed by generations that increasingly share an ambience worldwide, especially intellectual but also practical; and that increasingly share knowledge, even in the religious realm. Alert young people see themselves as heirs of the spiritual history of the widened world. Many in the West read the Gita, or the Lotus Sutra, with at least as much interest as the Bible, and at times with a greater sense of reward.

Intellectuals who think about the scripture of their own community and wrestle with the challenge of working out what the next stage shall or should or may well be in its ever-developing history, are participating in a collective process across the world. Their fellows are thinking and wrestling with the same sort of issue in other communities. Some will so participate unwittingly. Others will be more discerning: aware at least of the global problem; aware also to some extent of proposed solutions in other groups; and beginning to recognize that effective solutions will bear the marks of today's interrelated world.

The various scriptures of humankind have differed among themselves, each distinct. One may suppose that this will largely continue. On the other hand, as we have seen, boundaries have been less clear between the processes in which each has been involved, in interaction in each case with successive generations of people themselves interacting with ever-changing life situations. Such boundaries have been at times surprisingly permeable. This situation will not merely continue; obviously it is developing fast.

Another boundary erected in the specifically Western conceptual tradition also becomes a good deal less firm in the light of enlarged modern awareness of history and more reflective observation. This is the line delimiting what has been explicitly called scripture from all other writings. To the surprise of those accustomed to thinking in Western ways, that boundary has been less clear than was traditionally presumed—even in the West; let alone, elsewhere in the human community. One significant matter relevant here is the fairly widespread pairing of materials, with two authoritative bodies of writings of which one is considered loftier in theory, in cosmic status, even while in practice the other may be also decidedly consequential—and at times equally, if not actually more, authoritative. One thinks of the Bible and Talmud[17] in the Jewish case, the Qur'an and Sunnah[18] in the Islamic, the *sruti/smrti* pair[19] in the Hindu[20]. It is noticeable that in the innovating modern period there have arisen reformist, not to say radical, movements that would eliminate the second of the pair and in novel historicizing mood "go back to" the other: "Back to the Vedas!"[21]; the comparable[22] minority *Ahl-i-Qur'an* movement in what is now Pakistan; and so on. (The Protestant Reformation might be seen as setting some sort of precedent for this in its replacing of the Church's scripture-and-tradition pair with a *sola scriptura* proposal.) This is over and above the widespread scripture/commentary phenomenon; in that matter also the distinction has been drawn less sharply in some cases than in others. For instance, whether, or how far, Hindus' commentaries are to be called "scripture" is a Western-language question that Hindus have of course not asked, and that Western scholars have not answered[23].

In these paired instances the "secondary" work that has functioned as religiously important, at times just as unquestionedly decisive as the "higher" one, has often been recognized traditionally in an inclusive theory of some sort. (An obvious example would be the oral Torah supplementing the written Torah—though both are now written—for Jews.) History has evinced another type of book-like material that has in fact functioned as authoritative and has had outstanding esteem, without comparable backing in theory alongside its more explicit counterpart. An example might be the Anglican/Episcopalian Book of Common Prayer. In England, most of those who have known the Psalms at all—and loved them—have known and loved them from this setting, rather than from the Bible: it is the Prayer Book version that, in snatches or more fully, they recognize and in many cases have by heart. One may go futher, and note that for Anglicans generally around the world the book itself is treated with exceptional honour, carried with reverence, presented to and received by adolescents as a precious symbol, and so on.

Among Christians, Anglicans thus approximate more closely than do the Reformed Churches and other Protestants to those many religious movements around the world in which patterns of the service are spiritually more important than patterns of ideas. In their case, a written form for that pattern can seem as important as written scripture. In other civilizations, they can *be* the written scripture[24].

Comparable phenomena are fairly common in some other cultures. Often those cultures do not work within conceptual categories, embedded in their languages, that separate these two matters clearly. They have then no immediate basis to resist appreciating the scripture-like quality of the role of such works (some would say, that quality of the works themselves) in the life of those involved. For the West, or in Western languages, one might suggest a term such as "para-scripture" for these items. This would seem reasonable certainly for Talmud, Sunnah, *smrti*—though in this last case our own presentation has suggested that it is *smrti* that historically deserves pride of observed place.

Once it has been recognized that the meaning of the concept "scripture" is not cosmically given in any one culture's traditional understanding, but has to be explored in the light of our new knowledge and broadened horizons, still further data offer themselves for possible consideration. We made bold to ponder the role in Western history of the Græco-Roman Classics, but one is pushed to go on to thinking about that other class—undefined, and not delimited—of works that in Western culture are called "classics" in a different (yet not altogether unlike) sense[25]. These are more modern writings, including some virtually contemporary, that have come to be, or are seen as deserving to be, widely honoured: particular writers, particular poems or essays, and so on, reckoned as standing out from their fellows: Racine, Goethe, Milton, *Finnegan's Wake*, the *Imitatio Christi*. (A Chinese term for such works in that culture is *ku-tien*.) The West in early modern times slowly adopted the rather obscure late-Latin term *classicus* for this modern reference[26]; it was a while later that "Græco-Roman Antiquity as a whole was declared 'classical'"[27].

Any school or school system (and any parent) has to select, from an unmanageable range available, what it shall teach, in literature as in other subjects. This is another way of saying that any society chooses what it deems most worth passing on to the next generation; put another way, each generation grows up being informed as to what is regarded as valuable. Just as one is told that a work is scripture before one reads it, so most people are told that a given work is valuable, is a classic, before turning to it. Its reputation leads to its being noticed; if this is general, and continues over time, it becomes a classic.

We are not here contending that these other works that we have been mentioning "are" scripture, or should be so considered. Rather, we are urging that the line between what is scripture and what is not, between what should be so considered and what should not be, is tenuous. That it is so has become evident since the world situation has come into view. That line, drawn in the imagination of a not yet well-informed West, has been imposed on a large array of material that in historical fact it does not fit. Once again, a conception has yet to be forged adequate to interpret to ourselves now the important realm that it purports to cover.

Neither are we contending that the works that subsequent ages have treasured owe their sole validity to that treasuring. It is later generations that make certain works scripture, make certain works classics; yet the suggestion is not that any old bit of writing could equally serve this purpose, no special merit attaching to the original, only to its later use. (One relatively rare instance where this has been the case, some would be inclined to say, has been The Song of Songs; some would find other examples. Many today would hold that certain specific passages in otherwise justly venerated books were not worth preserving in the first place and still mar the whole.) Most scripture, certainly, and most classics, well deserve special status; yet that is by no means the whole story. Without question it is a highly interesting and significant fact that at a particular time and place a Confucius said the wise things that he did, or that a Shakespeare wrote the plays that he wrote, or an Amos enunciated the passion for social justice with which he was endowed. We can all be proud that one among us once reached such levels. Nonetheless, still more interesting, more significant, historically vastly more consequential, is that once those things had been said, those plays written, that passion expressed in ringing verse, thereafter huge numbers of much more ordinary men and women have risen to recognizing the wisdom, the profundity, the value also for the rest of us that such persons attained; and have chosen, striven, rejoiced, to try to plumb it, and to appropriate it. Pivotal also is that in turn we too may—should?—respond.

That millions of us have had the potentiality to appreciate the power, the poetry, the insights encapsulated in their words speaks well for us, not merely for them. If an illuminating part of the answer to the searching question of what it means to be human is that occasionally rare heights are attained, or are vouchsafed, an even more illuminating, even more decisive, part of the answer is that we human beings can and often do recognize greatness when we see it, can and do recognize that some rare heights are above us yet not totally out of our reach if we stretch and grope our way upwards by way of the paths that they have constructed; that we must cherish what they have shown, pass it on to our children with the injunction that here is something that they do well to heed. Only if they find that we were right and that they too are indeed rewarded by such heeding, do they in turn pass it on to the next generation and in due course Shakespeare becomes great, the Confucian Classics become sacred, the book of Amos becomes canonized.

Examples in other cultures come to mind. Rumi's *Masnavi* for Persian-reading Sufis would be one. National epics, also—such as the Irish, and many another—form a special class for our interests. Illustrative is the *Shah-nameh* in Persian. Highly consequential in practice is in Poland the national epic poem *Pan Tadeusz*, playing a role in national life whose centrality, power, and quasi-sacredness it would be difficult to exaggerate. In our own day, history's first Polish pope, on his first public appearance back in his native land, naturally quoted from it in his formal address. An in some ways quasi-scriptural quality of the U.S. constitution in the sensibilities of many Americans has more than once been remarked. Also the role of any national anthem in its particular country bears reflecting upon, with its capacity to stir emotions and to symbolize commitments—and to receive more than profane status. (Interesting in passing is that no one *reads* national anthems. They are for ritual use, not for the study; and for the group[28], not the individual. Also interesting is that to study the U.S. constitution without taking seriously how it has been interpreted since it was first written, would be not merely uncouth but misleading.)

Some movements become institutionalized. This has happened conspicuously in the case of the Christian Church, far beyond anything known in other "religious" instances. It has happened in the case of the Western classics (both Græco-Roman and modern such as Shakespeare) in universities and school systems. Thereby the honouring of particular works is ensured; though too it may be prolonged beyond a point where people's response statistically perhaps warrants it. (Whether that be the people's failure, is another question.) Even institutional backing, in any case, will not preserve the esteem indefinitely, without the appreciation. Referring to the Græco-Roman, we earlier noted that today most people in the West live in a post-Classical age. In China, the Confucian Classics' preservation and status were ensured for over two thousand years by the education pattern and state support, and by the temples, the rituals, and family enactments. There too in the twentieth century both these types of support waned; whether the cherishing in people's hearts will persist, or perhaps be rekindled, is a great question in and concerning modern China.

With regard to Shakespeare in the English-speaking world, I find it interesting in our present context that in modern anglophone culture one is permitted to disparage Tennyson, to say that one does not find Pope appealing, that one deems James Joyce tedious or contrived . . . ; but one is not allowed to say that one thinks ill of Shakespeare. As with scripture traditionally, one does not judge the true classics; one is judged by them[29].

There is another body of material that has already begun to expand Western understandings of "scripture", despite the seeming verbal paradox[30]: the "oral scripture" of non-literate societies[31]. Anthropologists have reported that in the individual and corporate life of such societies the role played by the stories, moral instructions, poems, lore and all in formalized patterns of wording handed down from generation to generation and venerated, oft-repeated ceremonially by the group, standardly interiorized by the members, bears far too many resemblances to what such observers have known in their own societies as scripture not to be recognized as such. They have long since given up any feeling that the anomaly of calling it "scripture" when it is oral rather than written is outweighed by what would be the absurdity of *not* calling it "scripture" when it is so patently the same sort of affair.

This Western category has inherited specific characteristics from its specific Western use; but one's understanding has to be enlarged—not to say, refashioned; also, enriched—to accommodate matters that differ in specifics but converge in general.

Moreover, it is beginning to be recognized also in the West that, as we have already had more than one occasion to remark, even "written" scriptures have in historical fact served most people at most times orally/aurally. Here again the world scene turns out to be more coherent than we have been led to suppose. All of us participate in a process more common than has traditionally been recognized by any of us. Furthermore, even when scripture is seen as, is understood to be, explicitly written, it is an error to suppose that this means written *rather than* oral[32].

Still another body of material of which a study such as ours could profitably take note are new emergents in our realm[33]; but we do not take time to develop this point even minimally.

In this chapter we have mentioned a few matters that seem to warrant being brought into our discussion, rounding it out; but we have not elaborated them. Some Christians might feel that among the materials that we have ventured to include, some, whatever passing interest might be idly elicited by speculation regarding potential analogies, are so markedly less elevated in esteem than the Bible that it is tendentious, even absurd, to think of encompassing them within the same category. One problem with this kind of objection is that there are recognized scriptures—most notably Qur'an; Veda; Torah—given a higher metaphysical status than the Bible. If one were to insist with rigour on a single level of conceptual loftiness to demarcate the scope of our term, one would find oneself pushed into leaving the Christian Bible out of consideration of what truly constitutes the class of scriptures in our world. This would seem a whit ironic. The fact is that once we have agreed to apply the word "scripture" in the case of others' practices and orientations, and not only our own—or for that matter, in the case of other centuries than our most recent—we find ourselves having to conceive it in a number of novel ways, based on empirical observation and widened human experience, and recognizing a variety of phenomena in diverse times and cultures that the concept nowadays inescapably covers (or that our society has decided that it is to cover). Others are not "inescapably" harboured under the term, but show teasing similarities. We are suggesting not that they are surely scripture; rather, that the question of whether or not any deserve to be considered under the rubric cannot be pre-judged, and that pondering that question may prove illuminating. If nothing else, our study would seem to suggest that we do not yet fully understand just what this scripture matter actually is, and has been, in human affairs.

A possible title for this chapter would have been "What we are leaving out", to confirm a point already stressed: that our study is not intended as a comprehensive catalogue of scripture throughout the world, but is proffered as an introductory essay indicating possible new ways of approach to the topic, and adducing evidence suggesting the richness that awaits. Fascinating though each of the

unexplored instances of our theme could prove, and highly rewarding though it could be to relate them to each other and to the
developing of a new global view—and however necessary that enterprise will eventually become for generating a genuine understanding in this realm—nonetheless at this point we draw our investigation to a close, turning in conclusion to reflecting on what we have
seen, and pondering what inferences may be discerned as perhaps
emerging.

CHAPTER 10

CONCLUSION:
SCRIPTURE AND
THE HUMAN CONDITION

OUR STUDY HAS LOOKED at the complex process of human involvement with what has been called scripture. This process shows itself as world-wide; as almost (though significantly not quite) history-long; with impressive diversities; and with never-ceasing developments, intermeshing in unexpected patterns. One is faced then with that question: what are we to make of it all? What emerges from the present-day deepened awareness of this dimension of our human scene? To what does the evidence point?

We return to a remark set forth in our opening chapter, and implicit in our treatment throughout: that our aspiration is not to proffer a resolution to this issue so much as to engage others in thinking afresh about it. Our goal is that this study of ours may be received as some contribution to moving ahead on the problem. This final chapter will constitute a conclusion to the book; it is not meant as a conclusion to the topic! Our primary hope is to encourage some, at least, among intellectuals, theologians, scholars, responsible leaders, to address the issues that arise.

If to characterize the whole panorama there be one suggestion that may be offered with a fair degree of confidence, it is this: that probably no one on earth today quite knows what scripture "is", or why; understands the special status that human beings have discerned in the materials so treated; grasps what has been going on in human life in this realm (and as ramifying consequence, in countless realms). Yet surely one may feel that we cannot afford to let that unsatisfactory situation continue; time and energy must go into advancing towards greater understanding. Scripture has played too important a part in human life for its role to be ignored. Furthermore, it shows signs of once again becoming too important here and there in our own day for that role not to be authentically apprehended. For individuals or societies, either scripture's continuing to be accepted as before, or playing its part in creatively, or destructively, new ways, or lapsing, are possibilities each far too important for the next steps of its elaborate historical development not to be carefully thought out.

Or is this indeed so? Does it really matter? Scripture has been a major factor in human life in the past, no doubt; but has its time not come and gone? In the maelstrom of our beleaguered world's problems today, does it deserve this much attention? We shall be arguing presently that the true issue is not scripture itself. Rather, what is requisite is an *understanding* of scripture, and of the place in human life that it has filled when and where it has been important—for the light that may shed on those other manifold problems. Modern culture is in trouble. A heightened discernment of our past is needed, and a truer understanding of ourselves as human; both may be helped by new insight in this particular realm.

To the diversity among—and within—the world's scriptures our present study has given prolonged heed. Also, to interentanglements among what have been perceived traditionally as disparate elements in the whole it has called attention. Further, it has stressed the enrichment of life that scripture has at times often mediated. There is one matter, mentioned here and there, on which we have not dwelt, and yet it too is integral to a just appreciation of humanity's involvement in this affair. It has at times been, continues to be, threatens again to become, of massive importance. This is the appalling harm that from time to time scriptures have wrought, the suffering that on occasion they have not only condoned but instigated. It would be misleading to under-estimate this; and inept to try to forge a modern theory not giving also this glaring fact its due weight.

The devil can cite scripture for his purpose, we were reminded long ago[1]. Gullible devout folk follow. The pious, certainly, can at times cite it with equal damage while fooling themselves, and alas some others, that it is for God's purpose. Historical instances abound. Scripture served as the chief moral justification for slavery among those who resisted proposals to abolish that institution; and indeed as sanctifying many an oppressive *status quo* against move-ments for justice[2]. There is the fearsome extent to which scripture has served in outrageous wars to make both sides self-righteous, and all the more fierce. Again, it has served the degradation of women[3]. Many further instances could be cited, from the past and from the present day. Another: the mighty force of a scripture's binding a community together has worked to make sharp, and often relent-less, divergence between communities. Especially in the case of the Western triad—Jewish, Christian, Islamic—the scripture-based dis-paragement of those deemed outsiders has been, and continues to be, disastrous.

Any intelligent conception of scripture (of one's own, of others', or in general) must make room for both the positive and the nega-tive aspects. A general theory must account not only for variety, for persistence, for effectiveness, and the rest, but also for the darker aspects.

For that general theory, in all its comprehensiveness, where are we to look? More modestly, where are we to look even for contribu-tions to it?

The scholarly world has scarcely begun to come up with a per-suasive interpretation about the full panoply of what here confronts us all. In fact, it has in the past devoted remarkably little thought to the matter, preferring usually to investigate individual trees while hardly noticing neighbouring ones or the woods that they together constitute. To such scholars one owes knowledge of facts; theories they have rarely attempted. That would seem a task for the new phase. Encouragingly, there are substantial signs that this is appear-ing on the agenda[4]. Interestingly, some of the more striking studies of Western scripture from academia recently have been by scholars in other "disciplines" than those focussing on religion[5].

In the past, theories of scriptures have come from within one or another of the various major worldviews, and in each case has been a subordinate, derivative part of that general outlook on the uni-verse. All these have something to contribute to modern under-standing, though patently none is in any way adequate. Each was constructed not on the basis of a familiarity—let alone, a serious discernment or appreciation—of the whole field, but from the par-ticular premises of the worldview in question. Each has its strengths, of course; and each, we can now see all too painfully, has its limitations. We may glance briefly at religious movements, for their traditional position on our concern, and at the Western secular worldview. We shall note the strengths in each case that may help in forging an interpretation more apt for the present-day, and consider the evident limitations.

Most religious communities living scripturally have indeed produced over the centuries theories, for their members to explain—to themselves, to each other, to their children—how it is that their scriptures are so important and mean so much to them. The formulations have served also to nurture and to strengthen a continuing involvement. At the present time, at least for thoughtful and knowledgeable people, these theories from earlier eras are no longer calculated to serve either of these purposes: neither the informative nor the corroborative. They no longer give scripture a clear firm place within the total awareness of those concerned, no longer integrate its role into the coherent living of its devotees. Commitment proceeds more from momentum than from renewal.

Nonetheless, obviously the sensitivity to at least their own situation can be crucial in contributing to the modern inquirer a sense of what has been involved. Although no one of the traditional conceptions is adequate for us today, all must be comprehended, to impart a fundamental understanding of the role that scriptures can play and have been playing in human life. Without these clues to illuminate what was going on in the hearts and minds behind the conceptualizing, without the basic spiritual substance behind these religious forms, one could hardly begin today to appreciate the global situation.

Hindus and Buddhists have not, classically, generated careful theories regarding other people's scriptures as such, or scripture in general. Yet both groups have outlooks that in practice make room for these; in the former case, generous room. Hindu traditions in general are the world's most sophisticated in dealing with pluralism; and the community has differed from some others, especially in the West, in having gone far towards both appreciating, and explaining metaphysically the value of, non-Hindus' scripture. These understandings, as well as the Buddhist suggestions on dealing with their own Buddhist movement's internal pluralism of scriptures, can be of substantial service to any of us in the modern world thinking about scriptural multiplicity. (Of the Western instances, some of the Sufis in the Islamic case and of philosophically-minded mystics in the Jewish and Christian have also generated theories that are helpful and relevant to today's pluralist issue.)

The strengths of the Western secular tradition have been equally foundational for our current enterprise. Like the religious movements, it has luxuriantly enriched the cultures and lives of those whom it has served. In particular, one must emphasize the movement's profound impetus and imperative, stemming from its Græco-Roman classical legacy (that is, from before its recent negative phase), to know and to understand: that movement's insatiable drive rationally to inquire, to learn, to understand the world around it. Clearly, this present study, like all modern scholarly inquiry, takes its place within that movement.

Also, obviously, our study builds on one of the results of that drive: namely, the cardinal novelty of the human intellectual and spiritual condition today that emerges from humanity's drastically expanded knowledge in general but in particular, knowledge of the human historical process, world-wide. An important strength of modernity is a development indebted both to the Enlightenment and to secularism on the one hand, and to the Biblical outlook on the other[6]. This is the copious development from the nineteenth century of historical awareness, and the resulting historicist consciousness. In due course it may well be recognized that this development is, finally, as profound and enriching a matter intellectually and spiritually as the development of science. Not least significant in this will be—incipiently is—its contribution to the growth of critical self-consciousness for us all, and for all our worldviews. Again, clearly this present study rests firmly on an assumption that an understanding of scripture must in significant part grow out of this orientation to the matter.

A new conception of scripture for our day will be continuous with and will extrapolate from what has gone before, in the discrete traditions both religious and secular. Despite this, it will be critical of all, and must move well beyond them, to supersede. None has yet been revised sufficiently to be abreast of the new situations in which we humans keep finding ourselves—these days, with increasing rapidity; nor even of our new knowledge. We turn, then, to note the major limitations inherent in each.

So far as the religious traditions are concerned, there are two decisive deficiencies in most of these inherited interpretations. One is that they have tended to clarify, even to aim at clarifying, the particular scripture of the group concerned but without an intellectual (or theological) elucidation of other scriptures' role throughout the world—or even perhaps of their own at differing times and among differing sectors of their community. They have proffered little or no elucidation of humanity's involvement with scripture in its noticeably many forms.

The other problem is that inherited interpretations have tended to explain, even to aim at explaining, the heights to which at times their own community's involvement with its scriptures at its best raises its participants but without giving an account of the sorry depths into which also at times it leads them to fall.

Such ambiguity, the course of history shows, has been inherent in all scripture. Yet the indisputable facts seem to have been noticeable in the case of other people much more than in one's own. (In this way the two matters that we have noted, pluralism and negativities, are interrelated.) In addition to the regrettable record from of old of such external disparagement, decrying other people's faults, the fact that on occasion other groups' scriptures have been and continue to be a cause for distress has become of late for the Western world even a daily newspaper item. Christians and Jews deplore Muslim and Hindu "Fundamentalists", and each other's. Secularists are zealous in deploring all such movements. Christian theologians, however, and their counterparts elsewhere, have wrestled relatively little with the parallel problem in their own case. A Christian tendency would seem to be to ascribe especially Muslim aberrations, for instance, to the Qur'an, but corresponding Christian aberrations to the failings of the actual persons involved in them. Our own suggestion, of course, is that in all cases, good and bad, at stake is the varying relation between human beings and their scriptures—better: the relation between human beings and the cosmos, as mediated by their scriptures. It might be affirmed that we have to do simply with human living in its scriptural context. Simple, however, the matter has rarely been; and indeed in principle it is not. One could be tempted to say of scripture, as has been said of religion as a whole: that it raises people "not . . . above the human level; only to it"[7].

We must revert to the observation above that theories of scripture propounded within separate communities in the past have on the whole served only to clarify each its own instance; and we added that each community aimed at little more than this. The latter remark requires some reconsideration, since although substantially valid, particularly for Western movements, formally it fails to do justice to the full situation. For in fact, in the process of underwriting its own idiosyncratic view of the world, each group has, admittedly, on occasion taken just enough notice of others' scriptures to bolster still further its own outlook. We may note the Christian, the Muslim, and the secularist instances. (We have already remarked on the rather contrasting Hindu.)

The Christian Church, emerging out of the Jewish movement, inherited the latter's nascent scriptural tradition and participated in it, and indeed presently incorporated these Jewish scriptures into its eventual own, as an "Old Testament". In this sense, one might say that the Church has given great honour to what of late a few now call "the Hebrew Bible". As we observed above in our Judaica chapter, however, its treatment of the works concerned has diverged so substantially from the Jewish, that as we noted it has the same texts, but not the same scripture. Christians have a sorry record, so far as concerns appreciating, even understanding, the role of the Jewish Bible in the life of post-first-century Jews: its scriptural role. And when, some centuries after the rise of the Christian movement the Islamic also arose, with a new scripture, the Church did not fail to notice its existence and to proffer a theory to explain it: namely, that it was the work of the Devil.

Muslims similarly have taken note of Christian and Jewish scriptures, which they recognize but see their own as superseding. (The Islamic enterprise was spared, until modern times[8], the shock of a *subsequent* religious community's arriving on the scene, a shock with which the Christian Church, when confronted by Islam, was in effect unable to come to terms.) Islamic theology worked out a theory[9] about these earlier scriptures with which the Qur'an was explicitly continuous. When it later met other instances of sacred books, in Iran, India, and elsewhere, relatively few Muslim thinkers were willing to acknowledge them as scriptures in the Islamic sense of the term[10].

We turn to the secularist movement in modern times. Without a scripture of its own, it has nevertheless had comprehensive theories of the world around it that in passing have tacitly offered interpretations for the various scriptures of alternate outlooks on that world. To these interpretations we must give extended attention, since the secular worldview has coloured so deeply the whole of modern culture.

As we have suggested, secularism has been one of the mighty movements of the human spirit. Like those that it calls "religious", it has much to its credit. Also, like those others, being human it has served its participants in limited, finite, ways. Some of those ways worked for its adherents better in the past, during periods of expansive upsurge and seemingly independent effectiveness, than now, when it is beginning conspicuously to flounder. Like the others, in today's cosmopolitan world it must genuinely come to terms with alternative finite worldviews. Like the others, it is not yet pluralist, self-critically recognizing that its interpretation of the universe is one ideology among many, relative rather than absolute. It will have to enlarge its vision—in its case, chiefly its understanding of what it means to be human; just as the Jewish, Christian, Muslim movements require a modified and enlarged understanding of God and His/Her/Its activities, as well as of multiform humanity. The secular and the religious will both have to recognize that vital revisions are in order in some of their apparently central inherited theories (in both cases not of scripture only; also more broadly).

The analogy with the other Western instances is close. Christian and Islamic views of other people's scriptures have in the past been based on, respectively, Christian and Islamic ideas, not on a careful assessment of the actual scriptural life of other people. Similarly, secularist theories of other people's scriptures begin from and are calculated to confirm secularism's own basic and prior postulates—and especially, its rejection of transcendence. As we have observed, it has taken meticulous academic interest in the various texts, but given relatively little attention to their role *as scripture* in the lives of those whom they have so served. Those concerned have loudly complained at their scriptures' being misunderstood[11]. (Also, just as in the other Western instances, secularists have noticed negative scriptural consequences among other communities more readily than positive. Furthermore, they have noticed them more readily than the negative consequences of the lack of anything in their own movement to play the role of providing scripture's positive contributions[12].)

Certainly secularists have, as we have noted, taken the trouble to learn a great deal about, but have taken comparatively little on themselves to learn from, the cultural life of other civilizations. Indeed, like the exclusivist religious groups, it has hardly felt that these other movements of the human spirit on earth are something that one's own movement can, or must, learn *from*. It is curious that those erstwhile exclusivist religious groups seem currently to be showing perhaps more signs than are leaders of secular thought in the West of beginning, however gropingly, to turn the corner of opening themselves and their on-going traditions to learning from their erstwhile "rivals". Most secularists still think that non-secularist vews of reality ("religious", they call them) are simply wrong, their own being obviously right.

Enlightenment secularism as an intellectual movement in the West got under way with a debunking of Christianity. The Church, meanwhile, was equally disparaging of non-Christian religious movements. As contact with the peoples and cultures of Asia became gradually established, these two Western movements, at loggerheads at home, joined forces abroad to deprecate all exotic religious traditions: as benighted or at the very least as simply false. This has softened among both groups in more recent times. In fact they are no longer quite so markedly two groups, as secularist presuppositions have permeated the thinking of virtually all Westerners and of many outside the West, partly because of the dazzling success of the natural sciences and their close ties with secularism. Despite the softening, and in line with the *rapprochement*, the underlying assumptions of the secularist outlook—not only its "irreligiousness", but the general mind-set—have continued to colour an exceedingly wide range of Western interpretations of the world, including those done by academic scholarship. This has been apparent also in Biblical studies, Vedic, Qur'anic, and so on. (There has been rather little sense of learning from, as well as about, such things!) We are ready now, surely, to move beyond this, towards an enhanced realization of what new discernments have been made possible by what has been attained thus far; and indeed made imperative. Fortunately, this is beginning to happen.

At the outset we remarked that one of the West's initial responses to becoming in modern times seriously aware of the panorama of other cultures' sacred books was a new de-transcendentalized meaning for the plural term "scriptures", in contrast with a previous transcendent sense of its own Bible as a unique scripture[13]. For many the de-transcendentalizing has persisted; to it we shall return presently. First, our concern here is to note that it amounted also to a de-personalizing step: it involved a virtual losing sight of the human involvement. This penchant to focus on things, detached from the human dimension which constitutes their significance, and even, as here in the case of scripture, constitutes their essential quality, has taken place also in regard to multitudinous other matters. Indeed such de-personalizing, such impersonalism, has become something of a hallmark of modern culture. Several thinkers have begun to recognize that it is time to correct this aberration. Scripture, we have been seeing, can be understood only in relation to a community of persons. We shall presently suggest that this human component, when taken seriously, raises in new form the question of transcendence (and the immanence that is involved with it[14]). No doubt, we are heir to a shift in meaning of the term "scripture" from its specifying something originally celestial to its characterizing various matters on this earth. Yet this need not, and must not, lead to under-estimating them. We shall ask whether recognizing scripture as human rules out, or instead frankly poses in a different form, the issue of transcendent significance.

The matter has been related to a recently dominant fallacy, that of subject-object polarity[15]. This heresy has gone far to divide up our world into lonely individualisms on the one hand and impersonal objects on the other—the kind of world in which modern secular culture has forced a distressingly large number of moderns to live[16]. Much of what is fundamental to human life is omitted from this desperately narrow theory, this mistaken categorizing. Community is one example of what gets lost: our participation, as persons, in groups that transcend us as individuals—groups ranging from two persons in love, all the way to the whole of humanity—and their participation in us. The on-going process of history is another example: our participation in the movement over the centuries from our predecessors in the past (whether of family, nation, language, stream of ideas, or other) to our successors in a future still to come, perhaps long after we individually die. Art, too, is an example—by which what might look like objects to philistines are transformed for those more authentically human into something immensely grander. Sunsets are a further example, and flowers and the natural world generally—much of whose truth is omitted if we perceive them in merely objective ways. Language is an example: it is not an object, nor is it simply subjective, but vastly richer and more decisive than either. And so on, and on, for a multitude of matters that make each of us more than subject, and our environment more than object.

To be victim of some notion that the only alternative to an objective view of anything is a subjective view, is grossly to misunderstand humankind. It drastically falsifies what it means for us to be persons.

It is impossible adequately to understand persons objectively, as if they were objects; and it is misleading to understand persons "subjectively", as if they were merely subjects and we were isolated from them. Just as objectivity is a way of dealing intellectually with objects, so we must adopt a better, more rational way of intellectualizing about persons—and indeed about the universe as a whole[17]. (For such a way some might suggest "personalist" as perhaps a suitable name[18]?)

For to fall into objective-subjective dualism is to accept a less close approximation to the truth, not only of ourselves and our fellow human beings but also of the world around us, which we are trying to understand, than could be ours[19]. Both objectivity and subjectivity are derivative, almost arbitrarily, from a prior and far richer reality. The relation between each of us and the rest of us, and the rest of the environment, is not secondary but constitutive[20]. (By appropriating this truth inwardly we do not diminish our own individual quality but greatly enhance it[21]. Nor do we diminish our capacity for science, but significantly supplement it, or indeed enlarge it.)

The understanding of scripture provides a telling example of the object-subject split and of current moves towards healing it. There was a time when Western scholarship on the world's scriptures approached each as an object—a text—and held, in line with current ideology's orthodoxy, the virtually unchallengeable conviction that objectivity is the best way to understand anything, the only correct way. This either ignored the human involvement in them, and therefore their scriptural quality, or thought to explain (to dismiss?) it by calling in the contemporary West's concept of "believing". This notion in its modern form—that "believing" is what religious people basically do—secularism had introduced as a way of reducing religion in general to a subjective concept in (other) people's minds. We have elsewhere examined the distortions that this has produced in general[22]. With regard to our particular concern here, it may be seen as one more instance of beginning from an established theory and clinging to it, rather than revising one's theory in the light of the observable facts. The notion was set forth that it was because some group of people "believed" that one or another of certain texts was of superhuman origin, or the like, that those people treated it scripturally, and that in turn it affected them as it has demonstrably done. Having thus seemingly explained those facts, one then could, and often did, dismiss them as neither greatly interesting nor seriously significant, and many accordingly turned their attention away from the people involved and their on-going involvement—the subsequent history—to look at the texts themselves, unencumbered by the imagined scriptural quality. This way of dealing with the matter accords with the fundamental secular ideological conviction that transcendence is an illusion; that "objective" (that is, objectively perceived) things constitute reality, these other—human—matters being a "subjective" response (among the credulous) to material things. It does not, however, and apart from that, accord with the historical fact that whatever various cultures have believed about their scriptures has in each case followed from, not generated, their respect for the texts.

More recent attitudes, marking a major advance, have recognized that the human involvement has gone beyond mere gullibility, and requires serious attention. The development of "the history of interpretation", and an emphasis on hermeneutics, have been two important steps along the way towards a rehumanizing, repersonalizing. Both have tended, however, to orient themselves to interpretation of texts, understanding of texts, rather than the scripturalist's focus on interpreting (on understanding) the universe and human life—with the texts as mediating, and in effect secondary.

Scriptures are not texts!

Among significant newer advances has been the work of the late literary critic Northrop Frye[23] with regard to the massive role of the Bible in the course of Western civilization, its centrality in European culture. His presentations speak of the West's involvement in it partly in terms of imagination[24]. This has proven effective with fellow academics and with secular intellectuals, including even those who may be so deeply influenced by (so firmly imprisoned within?) the dogmas of a recent phase of modern culture as to presume—as taught—that there is nothing in the universe higher than the empirical human (or even, finally, than oneself?). When such persons are confronted with the manifest historical reality that most human beings at most times, including those whom they admire, have in fact been vividly aware of something higher, and have striven or delighted to live in relation to it, or in this case have taken seriously the Bible (and we might add, in other cases the Qur'an or the Lotus Sutra or the humanist classics or the concept of Truth), they are ready to interpret this as indicating simply that we are endowed with imagination able to reach beyond itself and beyond the empirical world round about us.

That we are so endowed is of course so. Nonetheless, to recognize it settles nothing—except arbitrarily, for those who gratuitously think of imagination as a form of hallucination.

Frye himself does not explicitly raise the issue[25]. Certainly he does not close it. (His thesis in effect is that the imaginative function of this particular scripture must be taken with great seriousness—as with all literature. He does not deal with other scriptures, but it is clear that the approach could apply universally.)

There arises, however, for any who like to think of themselves as rational, a haunting question as to whether it be rational to imagine; rational to strive and to delight, in relation to imagination's work. Are we intelligent, or dupes, in exercising such imagination, and taking it seriously? Crucially: is there a role for *critical* imagination, so that it makes sense to aspire—and to struggle—to being more right tomorrow in relation to what we imagine than we were yesterday[26]?

(The notion of imagination at work in scriptural and other more-than-prosaic matters has the advantage of leaving room also for wrongness, moral and intellectual. Not only is it vulnerable to error. We human beings can and at times do exercise imagination towards evil, can and do use imagination to become more wicked than we could otherwise be—as well as at times attaining through it greater heights than we would otherwise know.)

Reason, especially with a capital "R", is one form in which imagination has envisaged the "higher". (The concept "reason" is a product of human imagination. As conceived especially in the Western classical tradition[27], reason is neither objective nor subjective, which is one ground for its outstanding importance.) Other such forms are Truth, Beauty, Good. "God" is another such form. In India there are thousands more[28]. If the transcending reality be genuinely higher, broader, grander—perhaps infinitely so?—and certainly beyond not only our immediate but also our theoretical grasp, then the diversity in human awareness in this realm, and in formulations of that awareness in particular imaginative patterns, is less surprising than it might otherwise seem.

It may be that Coleridge, for instance, did well in choosing the English word "imagination" to name this distinctive and central capacity of human living. Others prefer alternative concepts. (Coleridge himself certainly saw imagination not disparagingly, but as philosophically virtually supreme: as humanity's prime avenue to metaphysical truth[29].) If, of course, there be no reality corresponding to our best imagining, or discerning, then it does not matter whether the well-nigh ubiquitous human sense of a loftier dimension of our life is, or is not, "true" or "right" or "noble" or reasonable or worth cultivating—or ridiculous. Indeed, it does not finally mean anything to pass such evaluative judgements. Such predicates are themselves elements contributed by that imaginative or discerning awareness of some transcending reality by which we can be judged; or by which we can ourselves judge how we ought to live, or think, how we do well to live, to think. There is no positivist reason why it would be good or right or rational to be a positivist[30].

However the issue be decided finally, we repeat our point that it has been a major step forward to move beyond objectification (which objectivity, as often, became or generated): treating as objects matters that are in fact deeply personal, are essentially human. And once the human is at issue, the question of transcendence is not far behind.

Before addressing that question, however, we turn first to what might seem a more mundane, more manageable, matter, though actually it is an integrally human and therefore ultimately unfathomable one, rather: namely, language. Scriptures represent the fact that most religious movements have found language to be a form of expression that serves them well; sometimes, centrally[31]. At first, I myself thought that a study of scripture such as this present one should begin, naturally, with a consideration of language. The further the investigation of scripture proceeded, however, the more evident it became that the problem was, rather, the other way around: one should perhaps better end with it. No theory of language is complete that does not include, and serve to elucidate, scripture; include and elucidate the prodigiously wide-ranging and highly special part that it has played in human affairs. For many people at many times and places, one could almost say, scripture has been the most significant form of language that they have known. One might conclude that a study of scripture illuminates language more than *vice versa*.

One elevates—deepens, broadens—the human, and the fact of humanity's being linguistic—the human capacity to relate to reality by thinking, and to our fellow humans by speaking—once one has recognized what these involve in the rich scriptural field.

Certain linguistic philosophers for a time strove to set aside all instances of language other than those that deal prosaically with tangible objects. They even at times itched to legislate that any other use of language is illegitimate. Linguistic science generally has focussed primarily on prose, paying relatively little heed even to poetry and its luxuriant place in our being human, let alone to scripture and its historically even more central place.

In the matter of language, and this emphasis on its use as prose, certainly one must note that in addition to its relation to us as human beings, there is indeed a question of its relation to reality. Yet even this should be more accurately, and more humanly, put: of its relating us to reality, and *vice versa*. The answer given to this will vary with one's conception both of reality itself and of the relation of humanity to it. If one conceives of reality as primarily, or exclusively, material and our relation to it as primarily one, say, of knowledge and control, especially technical knowledge enabling us to dominate it and to use it for our own purposes whatever these may be, then one's philosophy of language will be of a certain sort. If one be an intellectual dedicated to a pure attempt to know and to understand, one will envisage language as primarily an instrument for articulating an approximation to truth (Truth). Insofar, on the other hand, as one thinks of the universe primarily in aesthetic terms, and of our relation to it as primarily one of appreciation, then a different orientation obtains. If, again, humankind's chief business, or privilege, here on earth is to attain, or to accept, transformation, liberation, salvation, sanctification, then in mediating between reality and us (reality perceived now as including but also going beyond concrete tangibles, in awesome and holy ways) the role of language takes on a still different hue. Similar considerations apply if our relation to reality is felt in primarily moral terms.

Further, I have spoken of "our" relation to the universe. If one thinks or feels in less pluralist fashion, of "my" relation to it, then the outlook is still further affected. Moreover, even if "our", then it makes a difference whether that "our" refers to "my circumscribed group"—national, ethnic, ideological, religious, whatever—or to "us all", throughout the world and through time.

At stake in each of these issues and in various combinations among them is one's view of humanity, of oneself, of one's neighbour, and of the world. Even the outside observer's attempt to understand scripture, accordingly, becomes existentially demanding! For participants, the multi-dimensional human involvement with language has served to elaborate their participation almost, it might seem, without limit—even while they are forming their awareness of humanity and of reality largely in terms of that very participation.

In our introductory chapter we remarked that the human activity of scripture has been more significant than many others—than art, for instance. Art is another element in human life, like scripture, by which we transcend (are enabled to transcend) the immediate dimensions of our environment and that also cannot be understood objectively, by being considered apart from the persons and groups involved, on the one hand, and apart from the higher levels of the universe and of the self, on the other, between which it has served to mediate. As we noted then, these two—scripture and art—have been closely intertwined at many points through human history. Far Eastern, Indian, Near Eastern, Western, and other art—in many forms: architecture, painting, music, and other—would be fatuously depleted if one removed from it what was scripturally derived or inspired.

What engages us now is a relation to be observed between scripture and one particular form of art: namely, poetry. The place of language—that profound, intimate, and mysterious quality of our being human—may be illumined if one ponders the suggestion that we human beings seem to have been involved in *three principal modes of language: prose, poetry, and scripture*[32].

Some might be tempted to dissent, objecting that scriptures are written in either prose or poetry. This does not mean, however, that it can be subsumed under the other two; just as poetry cannot be perceived as a form of prose simply because all poetry presupposes prose and in effect makes use of it[33]. In most Western languages the word "prose" or its counterpart has come to designate separately that use of language from which the added element is missing that poetry, using essentially the same form but going beyond it, contributes. The mode of language apparent in what we call prose is not rejected or negated in what we call poetry; it is elevated, rather, and sublimated. Similarly scripture incorporates the other two modes, but in subsuming instances of them it enhances those modes into something noticeably other. We are referring, of course, to a text read by persons and received as scripture. It is possible for that same text to be treated unscripturally by other persons; for them it is no longer scripture, and they see in it only prose or poetry. This is in some ways comparable to a reader who insensitively treats a piece of poetry as if it were merely language in prose[34]. (The line, "My love is like a red red rose"[35] is, formally, prose; but substantially, it is not *merely* prose; to treat it as if it were is to render it untrue, and is an insult to both the person who wrote it and to his love—and unconsciously, to oneself.)

In this connection one may recall our noting Muslims, Buddhists, and others having occasion to complain of outside skeptics disparagingly assessing their scriptures as merely poetry. (Some of the Greeks, on the other hand, perceived poetry as "inspired"— almost suggesting that they saw poetry as on its way, as it were, towards what is scriptural.)

We turn then to transcendence. This, of course, is at the heart of involvement with scripture; though it impinges also on language at large—especially, one might say, on poetry; and on literature at large, and the role of language in great fiction. It impinges most especially on the matter of truth. A certain sector of modern Western culture has moved lately to link truth closely or totally to language[36], and somewhat insouciantly to suppose then further that it has to do primarily (or only) with prose[37]. Yet even were one to grant the former point (which is relatively recent, and certainly debatable), it is by no means obvious (except to those already converted) that prose can always proffer truth more reliably than can poetry[38]. It is an error to imagine that truth[39] and falsity—or approximations to the former, which is all that finite human beings may hope for—lie in sentences, statements, or even propositions[40] (or for that matter, in poems as such). All these are a function, rather, of what these mean to persons.

Reality transcends us, and we do well to be constantly mindful of this fact even while we may marvel at the richness, yet finitude, of human capacity to apprehend it. Each of us at best has a reach that exceeds our grasp; a partial vision of immediate, let alone of ultimate, truth. This is the case at every level: it applies to scientific truth, in prose; it applies to poetry; it applies to scripture. Many (by no means all) religious people used to think otherwise (some, insensitive to pluralism, synchronic and diachronic, apparently still do). They supposed that religious truth as they knew it—formulated in language whether of scripture, of doctrine, or whatever—was exempt from this general rule, of the inherently limited nature of language, and human use of, involvement with, language. (Their view, though no longer tenable, remains significant for our understanding—of them, and of scripture for them.) Science-oriented people, similarly, used to think that scientific "truths", in somewhat the same fashion, were not vulnerable—particularly before the days of historical consciousness also in this realm. Christians and Jews familiar with the way in which "historical criticism" of the Bible led to its no longer being considered true, by many, may be amused—or sobered, indeed saddened—to observe a counterpart in science. For present-day historical criticism of the development of science has in turn not only led many to recognize that what appear at any given time as truths in that realm are all subject to being presently superseded—including the current ones; it has led some leaders of thought in the area to come close to suggesting that there is no such thing as truth at all pertaining to science[41] (or to anything else?).

A lively sense of approximation, especially when linked with personalism, obviates these difficulties. In addition, it is helpful to recognize that while reality always transcends our apprehending of it, also our apprehending transcends our ability to express it in words. Again, we may, and should, marvel at the capacity of human beings to formulate in language our awareness of truth, and yet we must ever remember that that language succeeds often very well, yet never perfectly, in conveying even our best awareness. Truth transcends us; but even our finite grasp of truth transcends language.

It is possible also to perceive our relation to truth as more personalist, even, than the term "aware" implies; more intimate. The poet Yeats speaks of arriving, evidently after effort and search, at expressing such a perception in words (while implying that words are not in fact the proper locale), when he writes: "I have found what I wanted—to put it all in a phrase, I say, 'Man can embody the truth, but he cannot know it' "[42].

Apart from these considerations, in turn a hearer or reader may at times get from a sentence a closer approximation to truth and reality than its formulator grasped. This may perhaps be particularly the case with poetry and with scripture. In the case of scripture this seems historically to have been exceptionally important—as we saw, as one instance, with The Song of Songs.

It has to do, one may readily suppose, with the surpassingly lofty realm with which people are able at best to be put into some kind of imperfect touch through their scriptural involvements—and with the widely varying capacity of individuals, groups, eras, to attain such touch. Obviously, one may feel, languages are inadequate to the ambitious venture that communities take on in their scriptural involvement. We today with our knowledge of both the historical fluidity and the pluralism of languages may recognize more decisively than any earlier era that it is no easy task to couch in words even an approximation to eternal verities. And one should hardly expect such words in any case to have an unfailingly constant effect in inducing a response in multifarious readers.

This present study was undertaken originally to inquire into what we spoke of, in our introductory chapter, as the surprising worldwide fact of scriptural involvement, and the diversity of its forms: the human activity of treating this or that text or texts as scripture. At the outset we thought in terms of endeavouring to understand, and if possible to help make intelligible, what seemed to be legitimately described as people's separating out some piece of literature from all others and "elevating" it to a special, yet puzzling, status. As the investigation progressed it grew clear that the concept of elevating was seriously inadequate. For the movement turns out to have been from above down, not from below up.

(To phrase the point this way is to continue to use the spatial metaphor, which is itself faulty, and can for some prove quite misleading. Should we speak rather of larger, greater, richer, more basic, more encompassing, . . . ? The transcendent is not necessarily "above" us, however often that metaphor may have been used, but within us and all around us, suffusing the world. Language and other symbolic forms can communicate it in a community, sometimes and to some extent among some persons, but not with precision and not "literally".)

What has been going on here is not that persons and groups have raised a form of language to serve transcendent functions, so much as the other way around[43]. The scriptural phenomena begin with people's awareness of involvement in transcendence; and persist so also. That awareness has then been somehow *reduced* to speech or writing, has been brought down to earth and given accessible form in words. It is impossible, we suggest, to understand the world's scriptures without such a perception.

Scripture is not differentiated from other forms of literature, then, so much as distinguishable from—however closely integrated with—other forms of a people's symbolizing of the transcendent within and among and around them.

Many in Western religious groups have been inhibited from seeing this by their inherited thesis that matters have proceeded in this way only in their own case. Many secularists have been inhibited from it by *their* recent thesis that the purported transcendence involved just is not there. (Some, more guardedly, would say rather that whether it be there or not, we are not allowed to include it in explaining—or understanding?—anything; at least, not publicly. Human perception of transcendence is and has been, however, a highly consequential historical fact.) To us it seems evident that all inherited ideologies stand in need of significant development and revision in the light of today's new situation, especially today's pluralism—pluralism of worldviews on the one hand, and the apparent pluralism of floundering. We must all move forward if we are to do justice to each other and to the facts; or are to cope with our own new problems. In the meantime, while we await that happier day, each of these limited groups could agree with the above proposal by speaking not of people's awareness of transcendence as underlying their scriptural involvement, but of their *sense* of transcendence. (Some would prefer "their presumption of transcendence". In due course, as they get to know the persons involved better, and understand the history better, this disdainful attitude will give way to respect and appreciation[44].)

For peoples have found their scriptures good; have found that these proved themselves good. We might say, supremely good. For indeed those involved, *engagés*, have consistently reported that their scriptures—and this is indeed those scriptures' *raison d'être*—open up a window, or constitute that window, to a world of ultimate reality and truth and goodness. Over against the mundane world of sorrow, of self-interest and its loneliness, of injustice and failure, scriptures have played a role of enabling human beings to be aware of and indeed to live in relation to the other dimension of reality that characterizes our humanity by being somehow near and within our life yet also somehow far from it. Theists have explained what has been going on in their engagement by saying that those scriptures are the word of God. Non-theists have of course used other phrasing. Yet all have reported that by seeing something actual as scripture, they have been in touch with, to use Greek terms, the ideal.

Our own contention is that once one's focus for scripture has shifted from the texts to the people whose relation to them constitutes them as scripture—from objects to the human—the issue of transcendence soon re-asserts itself. For human beings live their lives—and most have been firmly aware that we do so—in what may be called a double environment: mundane and transcendent, finite and absolute, or however they be named. What the relation is between the two has been variously perceived, to put it mildly. Whether the two be continuous, overlapping, or discrete; the same environment diversely perceived; in conflict or complementary; both real or one (or both?) imaginary; superficial and more profound aspects or dimensions of the one world; material and spiritual; and so on and on, are issues that characterize our human pluralism, and that it would be both distracting and ironic to think of settling finitely, humanly. (Various disparate groups used to hold that it had been settled—and not only for them—transcendently, divinely, for instance in their particular scriptures; but this was back in the pre-pluralist phase.)

This double involvement of the human is found, as we have reiterated, in all those matters that lift us, we say, out of ourselves. A better way of saying it is that at a certain moment they lift us above our former, lower, selves and bring us nearer to our true selves (to use humanist phrasing), to God (to use theist; and there are several other vocabularies). These matters include our appreciation of art; our membership in a community; love, and marriage; science, and our intellectual understanding of the universe, and of human history; any approximation to truth, any pursuit of justice, any serving of those in need; courage; a recognition of beauty in nature. Such matters constitute the lower reaches of the mountain on whose slopes we all live and whose peak is, according to theists, God; according to classicists, Truth, Beauty, Goodness; according to Buddhists, supreme enlightenment; and so on.

Even those reluctant to agree must recognize that scripture has owed its existence among those whose lives are involved with it to the fact that these persons and groups have seen things so. For the skeptics too, to *understand* scripture and its participants is to come to a genuine existential comprehension of some such view of the world; and to appreciate scripture is to appreciate this orientation.

In the course of our survey we have observed actively at work in repeated cases this sense of the transcending nature of what is involved in and through scripture. Always implicit, this is often also explicit[45]; and not seldom, stressed. Nichiren is representative of scripturalists of many diverse communities, not only the Buddhist, when he speaks of the truths that saints perceive in scripture as "inexhaustible"[46]. It is altogether standard to feel, and to say, that this finite work held in the hand, or mind, enshrines much more than overtly appears. Buddhists, Jews, Muslims, and others concur in locating ultimate truth and reality in every letter, every stroke of the pen[47]. The Zohar speaks of the narratives that the Torah tells as being the outer garment, which one must move beyond by attending to the body behind the garment, and indeed beyond that to its soul, and even this last as transcended in its super-soul[48]. Similarly Bonaventura, "while he respects the literal sense and seeks the intention of the scriptural writer . . . insists that to stop with that and ignore the spiritual senses of scripture is to ignore 'the tree of life' for the fateful 'tree of knowledge,' and for the sake of the Law to destroy what Christ has done"[49]. (One could imagine, in reading this, that it is almost as if he were chiding modern readers focussing on the text rather than on its role for the devout; or were chiding outsiders reading it as if it were merely prose or poetry rather than discerning its being scripture; or were chiding academics seeking to know but not pushing on to understand; or were reproaching any observer who is being pedestrian rather than seeing the point.) Beyond the sacred page, devotees have standardly held, and beyond its written word, stands, as the popular Christian hymn puts it, "the Lord, the Living Word"[50].

Yet is it not merely that readers are to move up from the immediate to a loftier level (or out to a wider, or down to a deeper). Supplementing, and indeed undergirding, this has been a sense of movement rather in the other direction: that scripture begins on high, and has found its way down to us, or such. The Qur'an that Muslims revere is originally on a heavenly tablet[51], from before the beginning of time. In fact, the standard way of referring to it is that it "came down"—or rather, was sent down[52]. The Zohar speaks of the Torah as primordially without division into words, and only later unfolding into its verbal form[53]. Veda, as we have seen, has been sounding from all eternity; the *rsis* captured some part of it. And so on.

Thus in the accepted approach the overt meaning of the words of the text not only is transcended by far in the loftier, deeper, more inner realms of what is inherently present in or through the scripture, but also is seen as derivative from them—and even, perhaps, as superseded by them. This last sometimes takes the form of neglecting or even rejecting those lower levels or narrower or shallower ranges of more immediate significance, as a way of better holding on to the higher, wider, deeper. Resistance in Turkey earlier this century to the public reciting, proclaiming, of the Qur'an in Turkish translation, or in Central Asia a couple of millennia ago the resistance to a rendering of the Buddhist *dharma* into Khotanese, or the sense that the sounds, rather than the meaning, of the Rig-Veda are its essential ultimate significance, or the remark to me once of a nun that she had grown up in a family in which a copy of the Bible on the coffee-table in her family's living room was "always treated with utmost reverence; but it never occurred to any of us to open it and read it"—all these are indications of a deep sense of the holy associated with scripture, where the sense of holiness, transcendence, is more important than any concrete detail that it may offer.

The more general practice, however, has been to see the two as concurrent: the transcendence in or through the concrete.

Even so, the two have *become* concurrent; the transcendence is primary, the mundane is derived.

A curious, and rather disastrous, instance of the opposite extreme, with very little humility, and hence with (or because of?) little sense of genuine transcendence, is seen in that modern aberration called "Fundamentalism". This treats the scripture in one's hand almost as if it determined what is absolute, rather than *vice versa*. It arose fairly recently—nineteenth century in the West, twentieth century in Asia—as a reaction against modern secularism at large and its potential human vacuity, and specifically against a reducing of scripture to something much less than it had been in more congenial times. It has produced in many parts of the world its own novel movements, of desperately circumscribed outlook. Their chief significance for our study is perhaps simply their illustrating the high price that participants in a given scriptural tradition, and unfortunately then also the rest of us, may have to pay if a more adequate understanding of scripture for our day is not achieved[54].

Our survey has revealed the stark diversity of the role that scripture has played in human life; and we have stressed that diversity explicitly. So varied have been the various texts that have served as scripture, and so multi-dimensional has been the treatment that a people—or differing people—have given even a single scripture, that a serious question might be posed as to whether it be finally legitimate to retain the concept at all, as a generic to cover the vast field. The term "scripture" was, after all, Western, naming not a basic human category but constituting a Western one. It was recently summoned into service to interpret data from the rest of the world that at first blush appeared roughly similar; but these have proven on inquiry to be considerably less similar than had been imagined. (Past instances of understanding one's own inherited scripture are also turning out on inquiry to have been less similar, too.) The term was imposed on other cultures hastily—in retrospect one could almost say: arbitrarily. Now that we know something of how variegated a collection the various instances have turned out to be, is it reasonable to continue to call the whole motley grouping by a single name[55]?

The diversity is because humanity has been and is diverse; more so than was realized when the categories of Western thinking were generated—"scripture" among them. Every civilization's categories require re-thinking today, certainly. No doubt one must choose the best available, yet recognizing that even that will require revision. Even confining oneself to Western categories, a different one might have seemed to some a better concept for interpreting to oneself what has been going on: "revelation"[56], for instance, or *logos*, Word[57]. Comparable to this last is the Islamic theological doctrine that *kalam* is one of the attributes, or characteristics (*sifah*), of God. *Kalam* is "speech", or "speaking" (in some contexts it is rendered as "word"); and Muslims call the Qur'an, the *kalam* of God[58]. The treatises affirm first that a characteristic of God is that He speaks, and only secondly then that the Qur'an is what He says. They go on to affirm that (therefore) that scripture is eternal, pre-existent, much as the Christians have said that Christ is. Herein they may be discerned as saying, among other things, that God is the kind of God Who from all eternity has something to say to humankind. Others may differ as to what He has said and where He has said it—and one may differ on whether "He" is the right word, and on whether "God" is; and on whether one might rather say that human beings are that kind of creature to whom the universe has something to say, and are in a limited way somewhat capable of discerning it. Yet the basic idea can in any case be perceived as significant (and widely ramifying). Using non-theist language, one might see in this an affirmation that the universe is intelligible, and with cosmic ideal patterns for humans to emulate, as in the Greek faith of Western culture; and, as we saw in The Song of Songs, that it presses on us to be understood, and that its ideals attract.

The basic issue, however, is that the inherited conceptual categories of no one tradition, religious or secular, no one civilization, are adequate for comprehending, for doing justice to, the new awareness that today is available to us. For this purpose we must either construct new categories, or carefully modify old ones.

Since this present work is being written and read in the English language, the limitations and biases built into that language thus far have to be wrestled with, its categories and presuppositions. Although English is not well suited, no other language is better suited to our modern purposes; and in any case we English-speaking people are one of the groups that certainly must learn to think with new conceptions more nearly adequate to our modern condition, and must hammer out a vocabulary with which to do so.

It seems, then, perhaps defensible that this presents itself as a book about "scripture". Yet it must be recognized that calling it that could be part of the very problem that it ostensibly is trying to solve. *There is no ontology of scripture.* The concept has no metaphysical, nor logical, reference; there is nothing that scripture finally "is". Our study, we trust, has made this clear—despite its title, and theme. It has recognized, and we hope has made apparent, that at issue is not the texts of scripture that are to be understood and about which a theory is to be sought, but the dynamic human involvement with them. That engagement has constituted an historical process, still continuing; often a number of seemingly separate processes, rather, though these are beginning to be perceptible as interrelated and converging, as strands of the whole. Scripture has been, as we have said from the start, a human activity; it has been also a human propensity, and potentiality. There is no ontology of scripture; just as, at a lower level, there is no ontology of art, nor of language, nor of other things that we human beings do, and are. Rather than existing independently of us, all are subsections of the ontology of our being persons.

Recalling our suggestion from an earlier chapter, should one speculate that all these matters with which persons and communities of persons are involved, along with scripture, might be more truly apprehended if conceived not as nouns but as some sort of adverb, a mode of our relating to the world?

Whether "scripture" be a viable category is therefore a matter finally of no great moment. At our particular phase in history, the term serves a practical purpose. It should not, as a term, be taken too seriously. Yet what it has been used loosely to characterize has been very serious indeed. That to which the concept effectively or cavalierly refers is an important clue both to the human, and to the universe.

For, once we undertake with modern awareness to try to understand scripture—which means, to understand the historical process of scripture past and present—that becomes the real issue: how to understand ourselves and our fellows as human beings, and how to understand the world—the cosmos—in which we live. Significant progress in wrestling with scripture means moving towards a new and enhanced discernment in these broader realms. Our traditional notions of the matter, both religious and secular, patently require revision once we recognize more perceptively what actually has been going on in the scriptural realm. Our inherited conceptions of the human in relation to the world must for our day be enlarged. This, of course, is already clear on many other grounds. What we have in scripture is one more clue to help us wrestle with the puzzle.

Our study has focussed on scripture, but as remarked we do not wish to suggest that it is a central issue in the welter of the world's present problems. Rather, it can serve as one clue to what is, indeed, a central issue. The effort to understand what the West has come to call "religion" is a broader matter, to which reflection on scripture can be thought of as subordinate, but also can be thought of as perhaps a helpful route towards struggling with it. Yet understanding "religion" too is important fundamentally—some would say, only?—as a clue to understanding humanity and the world.

In our opening chapter we noted the movement whereby our term "scripture", from having designated a single instance—one's own: Bible, Qur'an, or whatever—shifted to covering, rather, all instances around the world; and we noted further the de-transcendentalizing shift that accompanied this. That downwards or narrowing shift was virtually inevitable at the time, given the then regnant intellectual climate, and given the shallowness, of course, of appreciation by outsiders at first encounter. Manifestly now, a century or so later, substantial further movement is in order. It is imperative to carrry our conceptions forward to embrace the depth, as well as the breadth, of our new awareness. Any intelligent informed person is able now to recognize the mundane, contingent, historical flavour and relativity of his or her own scriptural text, in those cases where some text still functions as significantly scripture for that person. (For many, the mundane historicity and obvious relativity of their text—which has turned out very far from inerrant!—has meant that they personally became unable any longer to be scripturally involved: whether regretfully, or insouciantly uninterested, or firmly alienated.) At the same time any intelligent informed person, whether with a scripture of his or her own or having rejected any personal involvement in such things, is able to recognize ways in which all the world's scriptures have in empirical fact, *inter alia*, mediated transcendence in observable finite ways to the finite persons and groups and ages involved.

With the lack of a common scripture or of something counterpart to play its role, modern secular culture is in danger of finding itself without a shared vocabulary to enable it corporately to live well, or even to talk and think about doing so, or its members to encourage each other to aim so. The deficiency is hardly made up by the comic strips or sports pages, the commercialized television programmes, the cunning advertising presentations, that largely prevail as the common lore in society.

The de-transcendentalizing has indeed become a central issue.

Also in our opening chapter we said that scripture, one can nowadays observe, is a bilateral term, naming a relation between two matters: an *engagement*, we have since called it, in this case of humans with a text. We may by now make the further refinement, to do justice to what we have observed throughout: that it is best characterized as, rather, trilateral[59]: referring to a relation—an *engagement*—among humans, the transcendent, and a text.

When one asks, then, what are we to make of such a relation, one answer, in the language of us modern intellectuals, and repeatedly suggested in the course of this inquiry, is to affirm that scripture has functioned symbolically. It has served as a channel for something beyond itself. One cannot understand any symbol simply by studying that symbol. Nothing is "objectively" a symbol, and its meaning does not lie in itself. It lies in the hearts, minds, lives of those persons and groups for whom it is symbolic (and not in those of other persons and groups, their neighbours—or perhaps their children—for whom it is not symbolic. This double fact keeps history from being dull!). It is a big step forward for us, if we are to understand the meaning of the term "scripture", to recognize it as inescapably designating a certain sort of symbol. This, among other advantages, takes care of the variety of texts, the variety of readings, the constant historical change, the human *engagement*, the possibilities of harm. If it does not take care of, at least it makes room for, the latent or manifest power.

Unanswered, however, is the teasing question, symbol of what? And unelucidated is the power. Those of us working on the concept symbol over recent decades have come to feel that the term is indeed helpful but not yet adequate: not quite clear and firm enough to bear the great weight of all that it is proffered to carry[60]. To Christians—but only a minority of others—one might propose a further step: that of calling scripture, and the various scriptures of the world, "sacrament"[61]. Such wording might serve as the trilateral term that is needed: the notion bespeaks divine initiative, and human involvement, plus the empirical object that mediates. In other cultures, specific traditional terms are similarly available[62]. Yet no generally received intellectualist vocabulary seems yet to have been constructed.

In our Buddhist chapter we referred to one of the theories advanced in that community at a couple of points in its historical development as a way of explaining the variety of scriptures extant in the Buddhist movement itself, and clearly fruitful there. The ironic suggestion was that in fact the Buddha had said nothing at all; yet that the encompassing range of his compassion and the effectiveness of his wisdom (or of the Buddha-nature of each of us working within us) resulted in all sorts and conditions of people wherever they might be in their diversity being supplied with scriptures appropriate to their particular capacities and pointing them to the enlightenment that he himself embodied and wished for others. One might wonder whether any theists today, confronted with our still vaster diversity of scriptures throughout the world and the diversity of readings of those scriptures over the centuries, might find themselves emulating these Buddhist theorists by speculating that God has in fact remained (verbally) silent, yet has set up the human situation in such a way that diverse peoples in diverse conditions would have scriptures capable of letting Him/Her/It enter their lives and capable of guiding them to Him/Her/It and to spiritual richness. Or again, one might wonder how many humanists, similarly, might using their own vocabulary take a cue from these Buddhists and theorize that the universe is in fact mute yet cosmically there are ideals appropriate to our being truly human, and human nature has within it a quality historically manifested in an almost universal propensity among us human beings to have scriptures and to find in them inspiration and nurture to sense and to pursue those ideals, or the highest approximations to them of which we are severally capable. (Such ideals Feuerbach cheerfully took for granted, but he did not adequately explain how we come to be endued with them[63].)

Again, some might resort to theist vocabulary to reflect on the situation that our contemporary knowledge of world history sets before us, and therein consider it "from God's point of view"; if so, might they not then see God using scriptures more or less successfully in the divine on-going endeavour to salvage human beings from sin and despair and to invite us to higher realms, of truth and love?

In such a case, one would certainly have to say "more or less successfully" in order to make room for the less successful: those repeated times when scripture has in fact served as a symbol for starkly limited vision, or for nastiness. Should religious leaders not accept then the responsibility in this realm for aiming at (or praying for the grace for) seeing to it that scripture function sacramentally and well henceforth? And should secular intellectuals not accept the responsibility for clarifying what has been going on; of making clear to us human beings what we have been doing in this matter; of making rationally intelligible the process in which most of humanity has been and much of it continues to be involved, with results that have been prodigious, and for reasons that have thus far eluded us?

Neverthess, over against all this it would not do to appear to be suggesting that the endeavour to understand scripture necessarily leads to an aspiration to resuscitate it. We have throughout insisted on the fundamental historicity of this matter; and there are some who see persuasive reason to consider whether our present phase of historical development may not mean that the age of scripture is coming to an end. For those who take the transcendence dimension seriously, the question is not what can we do to salvage scripture in our day so that it may once again, though in modern ways, serve the purposes that at its best it has served so notably for many centuries. It has been, after all, but one component along with many others in what for the rest of the world has been its civilizations and cultures, and what the West has called its spiritual traditions. It has been one until now standard element, yet only one, in the complex patterns in and by which human beings have lived. Our study has dealt with it because it seems illustrative of, yet perhaps is not essential to, the richness of human life. The basic question is not about scripture, but is about us.

Scripture's role in the past poses a challenge for the future: how may we hear the voice of the universe, however finitely, and find ways to think it, and to talk to one another about it, and to be motivated to order our life so that we may live in tune with it, and find the courage and delight to do so ourselves and find encouragement also from one another.

NOTES

1. Introduction:
Presenting the Issues

1. In "modernity" I include, here and throughout, its current phase. Certain parts of this some people have taken to calling "post-modern". Has anyone with new ideas since the early Stone Age not been "post-modern" in this new sense of moving beyond what in his or her recent past had been perceived as modern? Furthermore, the "post-modern" concept is intolerably provincial, dismissing the recent history of all cultures other than the West's.

2. I use a capital initial for the word "Fundamentalism", here and throughout this study, to indicate that it is a proper name, presumptuously adopted for itself by a particular movement arising in the United States in the late nineteenth century. For others to dignify it by treating the word as a generic is to acquiesce in that particular movement's dubious claim that what it elected (or concocted) to emphasize are in fact the fundamentals of the tradition concerned. To see love and justice and humility as more fundamental Christian matters than Biblical inerrancy and the Virgin Birth is to adopt a different assessment, both of the universe and of Church history. Journalists' and others' transferring the term to characterize certain present-day Islamic, Sikh, Hindu, and other movements can be attributed to an anti-religious bias (or an insensitivity to language).

3. Robert Walter Stevenson, "Historical Change in Scriptural Interpretation: a comparative study of classical and contemporary commentaries on the Bhagavadgītā", 1975; Jane K. Smith, "An Historical and Semantic Study of the Term 'Islām' as seen in a sequence of Qur'ān Commentaries", 1970, subsequently published under the same title (Missoula, Montana: Scholars Press, 1975—Harvard Dissertations in Religion, number 1; there the author's name is given as Jane I. Smith); William E. Deal, "Ascetics, Aristo-

243

crats, and the Lotus Sutra: the construction of the Buddhist universe in eleventh-century Japan", 1988.

4. *The Sacred Books of the East, translated by various oriental scholars, and edited by* F. Max Müller (Oxford: Clarendon Press, 49 voll., 1879–1894; vol. 50, *A General Index . . . , compiled by* M. Winternitz, 1910). A second edition (ibid.) began to appear in 1898. About half the volumes of the series were republished in New York, 1897 ff., by various publishers, and again in mid-twentieth-century. Parts of the series (the China volumes, the Buddhist, *Sacred Books of the Jains,* etc.) were republished as distinct sets; substantial selections from among the lot appeared also in shorter series. The entire fifty volumes have been republished more recently (Delhi: Motilal Banarsi-dass, 1962–1967), and are still in print. It is interesting to note that when Müller's "friends first submitted to the Delegates of the University Press at Oxford [his] plan of publishing . . . all the Sacred Books of the East", one of the delegates, the substantial scholar and prominent clergyman E. B. Pusey "strongly supported [the] plan, only stipulating that the Old and New Testaments should not be included"; Müller tried to persuade him otherwise, arguing for his own wish, "very near to my heart", that "these two, the most important Sacred Books of the East" should indeed be in the set, but "[in] vain. . . . I had to give up [that] wish . . . in order to save the rest", yet almost half a century later, shortly before his death, he was still hoping that "the gap thus left" would eventually be filled and the two Testaments "find their proper place in [the] collection"—Müller, *Auld Lang Syne—second series: My Indian Friends* (London and Bombay: Longmans, Green, 1899), p. 87.

5. Also, "the Bible[s] of the world". Some examples: *The Bible of the World,* Robert O. Ballou et al., edd. (New York: Viking, and Toronto, London: Macmillan, 1939—a long sequence, 1944 ff., of "condensed" paperback reprints [same publishers] followed, with the revised title *World Bible); The Bible of Mankind,* Mirza Ahmad Sohrab, ed. (New York: Universal, 1939).

6. Yet one must note also the Hebrew term *miqrâ'* as another Jewish designation for their scripture, which denotes not a *written* form but a (liturgically) oral; we return to it presently.

7. William A. Graham, *Beyond the Written Word: oral aspects of scripture in the history of religion* (Cambridge, New York, &c: Cambridge University Press, 1987). A more compressed presentation of the thesis is available in the same author's chapter "Scripture as Spoken Word", in Miriam Lever-ing, ed., *Rethinking Scripture: essays from a comparative perspective* (Albany, NY: State University of New York Press, 1989), pp. 129–169.

8. The word *qur'ān* served to designate at first, in the Qur'ān itself and later, a reciting of a scriptural passage, and only subsequently came to designate, with the definite article, the scripture as a whole. On this see Graham, " 'An Arabic Reciting': Qur'ān as Spoken Book", constituting Part

III (sc. chapp. 7, 8, 9; pp. 79–115) of his 1987 work mentioned in our note 7 immediately above; cf. some of his earlier articles (listed in that work's bibliography, p. 259) setting this forth in technical detail. Later in this chapter, more fully in chapter 3 below, and in passing in other chapters regarding specific instances, we observe the historical processes by which only gradually do what we know today as the various scriptures of the world come to be perceived and conceived as units, and finally by outsiders as objects.

9. The orality of this scripture in Muslim life until today, which for long was in the Islamic world taken for granted, in the Western world ignored, has of late begun to be a focus of scholarship. See, for instance, in addition to the Graham items listed in our note 8 immediately above: Labib as-Said, *The Recited Koran: a history of the first recorded version, translated and adapted by* Bernard Weiss, M. A. Rauf, and Morroe Berger (Princeton: Darwin Press, 1975)—this is an adaptation and abridgement of an Arabic work: Labīb al-Saʿīd, *al-Jamʿ al-ṣawtī al-awwal li-l-Qurʾān al-Karīm, aw al-muṣḥaf al-murattal* . . . (Cairo: Dār al-Kātib al-ʿArabī [1967]); Frederick M. Denny, "The *ADAB* of Qurʾan Recitation: text and context", in [A. H. Johns, ed.,] *International Congress for the Study of The Qurʾan . . . May 1980* (Canberra: Australian National University, [n.d.]), pp. 143–160; also, Denny, "Exegesis and Recitation: their development as classical forms of Qurʾānic piety", in Frank E. Reynolds and Theodore M. Ludwig, edd., *Transitions and Transformations in the History of Religions: essays in honor of Joseph M. Kitagawa* (Leiden: Brill, 1980—Studies in the History of Religions [Supplements to *Numen*], M. Heerma van Voss et al., edd., vol. XXXIX), pp. [91]–123.

10. Cf. above, at our note 6.

11. Saturday, in the Seventh-Day Adventist case.

12. See, for instance, Graham, opp. citt. (our note 7 above), on the extent to which even written texts have been treated orally/aurally by those reading them; let alone, by those hearing them read. There is the further matter of persons or groups for whom scripture has been conceived as oral/aural on earth, written in heaven.

13. The first great translation project in human history was the rendering in Mesopotamia ca. 2000 B.C. of Sumerian sacred texts into Akkadian. A couple of millenia later the next were the translating of the Jewish scriptures into Greek, and the large-scale turning from Sanskrit into Chinese of Buddhist scriptures. These movements affected the history of the world much more profoundly than any other translations have done; and in general scriptures have played a larger role in translating in the course of history than has any other genre. In addition to the Buddhist (which continued with translations into Tibetan, Korean, Japanese, and more), the Christian movement has been enthusiastic in this matter, and in fact the Church actually began with its Gospels already a translation out of

the language of Jesus and his disciples. In the twentieth century the two most massive translating projects have been those of the foundational writings of the Marxist movement into a large number of new languages, and the rendering of the Bible into a much larger number (approaching two thousand). See our next note 14 just below on the missionary aspect.

14. The Buddhist and the Christian are salient examples of translating movements that have been missionary, and it would seem evident that in each case the two aspects have been related. Also, during the one phase of its history—the Hellenistic—when the Jewish movement was missionary, it did translate its scriptures into Greek, though this was primarily for internal community purposes. The Islamic movement, however, equally missionary, has been one of those for whom translating the scriptures has on the whole (until recent times) been either rejected or seen as questionable.

15. An Indian friend of mine, an exceptionally penetrating intellectual, once remarked in my hearing at a public gathering: "Being a Hindu, I am not a victim of the notion that history is going anywhere". In the early years of the twentieth century, most Western intellectuals and Western religious persons both would have found such a stance remote, even pitiable; at the end of the century, it may seem to many to make much sense. Today the Bhagavad Gītā's anti-pragmatist morality can be recognized in the West as not so odd as once it may have seemed ("Seek justice though the heavens fall" has itself been one sort of Western counterpart?).

16. Certainly not to contrast with it. In my usage it contrasts with "mundane"; or as here, with "positive" or "positivist". Transcendence can be known only through immanence; yet is known as transcending that immanence. For my sense of the term, which is crucial for the argument of this study, see my 1988 Ingersoll Lecture at Harvard, "Transcendence", published in *Harvard Divinity Bulletin*, 18/3 (Fall 1988): 10–15; republished as "Thoughts on Transcendence" in *Zeitschrift für Religions- und Geistesgeschichte*, 42 (1990): [32]–49.

17. Shortly before Gutenberg, but only shortly before, one-volume Bibles in manuscript form had become common—as we observe more fully in our chap. 3 below, note 28. On the mediæval situation generally and the gradual developments within it, see that chapter, at p. 53 with its notes (25–29). With the advent of printing, a new conception emerged as to what is a "book". It was only then that the various Christian Churches for the first time formally defined, gave explicit shape to, their Bible—saw it as a unit with demarcated boundaries, and formalized what specific "books" [*sic*—the previous sense] make up its contents: made it a scripture, one might almost say, in the modern sense. Had this been previously attained, they would presumably not have diverged among themselves in their then series of first formal canonizations (as indicated at the end of this paragraph in our text, and through its next paragraph, with the next two notes, 18 and 19, below).

18. The notion "canon", in Greek and then Latin (the word is originally

from the Semitic Near East, and ultimately from the earlier Sumerian, or perhaps even Dravidian), involved one or other, or in Christian usage often both, of two ideas: of a measuring rod, standard, or norm; and of a list, or catalogue. Along with such a list of what we would call scriptural writings, one may mention also lists of various other authoritative matters: for instance, in Roman law, of jurists recognized as carrying weight; in the Church, of early Christian writers recognized as "the Church Fathers"; of persons formally recognized as saints; again, of rules and regulations recognized as Church laws; and so on. On this matter generally, see for instance Ernst Robert Curtius, *Europäische Literatur und lateinisches Mittelalter* (Bern: Francke, 1948), pp. 259–263. (There is an English version: Curtius, *European Literature and the Latin Middle Ages*, Willard R. Trask, trans.— New York: Pantheon for Bollingen, 1953; Bollingen series XXXVI—where this section is pp. 256–260.) On canons of scripture world-wide, see also the recent article of Gerald T. Sheppard, "CANON" in *The Encyclopedia of Religion* (New York: Macmillan, and London: Collier Macmillan, 16 voll., 1987, Mircea Eliade, gen. ed.), 3:62–69. On the canonization specifically of the Christian New Testament, see our chap. 3 below, note 18.

19. Luther omitted the Apocrypha formally from, but included them (with few exceptions) as an appendix in, his German translation of the Bible, discriminating them from the other books as good but not authoritative, not "Holy Scripture". The Council of Trent in response defined for the Roman Church for the first time what parts constitute its Bible, decreeing that most, though not all, of the now challenged "apocrypha" were indeed fully canonical, even the few exceptions being published in the Vulgate since that time as an Appendix. For the Anglican Church, whose position followed one of its Thirty-Nine Articles (in their final form, 1571), see our next note 20 just below.

20. "The Archbishop of CANTERBURY . . . in 1615, directed public notice to be given that no *Bibles* were to be bound up and sold without the *Apocrypha* on pain of a whole year's imprisonment"—"The *Records* of The Worshipful Company of Stationers. By Charles Robert Rivington, Clerk of the Company", in Edward Arber, ed., *A Transcript of the Registers of the Company of Stationers of London: 1554–1640 A.D.* (5 voll., London & Birmingham: privately printed, 1875–1894), vol. V, p. xlix. For the subsequent two centuries, see *Historical Catalogue of the Printed Editions of Holy Scripture in the Library of The British and Foreign Bible Society*, compiled by T. H. Darlow and H. F. Moule ([London, 1903] New York: Kraus Reprint Corporation, 2 voll., 1963), vol. I—English. Note especially the "Explanatory Notes", p. [xiv], tenth para. ("From 1535 to 1800 . . . "), and the "Note" on p. 316, second para. ("It is also to be understood . . . "). On the Apocrypha more generally cf. our chap. 3 below, note 25.

21. I owe this trenchant observation to my former student the late Dr. Kendall Folkert.

22. Except in the new doctoral programme in The Study of Religion at Harvard. (Even there it is chosen only exceptionally.)

23. Brevard Childs ([London: SCM] and Philadelphia: Fortress Press, 1979).

24. To them we return briefly in our concluding chapter.

2: A Particular Example, to Illustrate

1. On this see Levering, "Scripture and its Reception: a Buddhist case", in Miriam Levering, ed., *Rethinking Scripture* (op. cit., our chap. 1 above, note 7), pp. 58–101.

2. See any of the several biographies of Gandhi; also, his autobiography. This last was written in the 1920's in Gujarati and published serially in an Ahmedabad weekly, *Navajīvan*. The instalments were later collected and published in book form, which went through many editions, and were translated, with Gandhi's involvement, into English by Mahadev Desai, appearing first also serially, in *Young India*, and later in book form as *The Story of My Experiments with Truth* (Ahmedabad: Navajivan, 1927; a second vol., trans. by him and Pyarelal Nair, ibid., 1929; one vol. edn., ibid., 1940, and many subsequent reprints; Washington, D.C.: Public Affairs Press, [1948], 1960; [London : Phœnix, 1949]). The later editions in India bore the new title *An Autobiography; or, The Story* . . . , and in the West the title *Gandhi's Autobiography*, with the earlier wording as now sub-title (without "*or*"). Furthermore, an anthology of Gandhi's comments on the Bhagavad Gītā, his favourite scripture, has been published as *Gita the Mother: M. K. Gandhi*, Jag Parvesh Chander, ed., (Lahore: Free India Publications, n.d. [sc., early 1940's]). I have not seen his *Gita—My Mother*, Anand T. Hingorani, ed. [Bombay: Pearl, 1965]. In the 1920's also Gandhi translated the Gītā into Gujarati from English (he did not know Sanskrit). Translations of his "Introduction" to this Gujarati version were later published in Hindi, Bengali, Marathi, and in due course English.

3. Mani "is perhaps the first person in human history ever to have written a scripture consciously". See my *The Meaning and End of Religion* (New York: Macmillan, 1962, 1963; Minneapolis: Fortress Press, 1991), pp. 92–98; the quotation just given is from p. 95. On Manichee scripture see more specifically in our next chapter here, pp. 51–52, with its notes 19, 20.

4. These various statements are corroborated by material in the following. (i) Fridericus Stegmüller, ed., *Repertorium Biblicum Medii Aevi*, Matriti: Instituto Francisco Suárez—Consejo Superior de Investigaciones Científicas, "1940" (actually, 1950?) ff., where the entries for "Osculetur me . . . " cover virtually sixteen pages from vol. 11 (1980), p. 166. (ii) The indexes (sc., voll. 218–221, [1863?–1879?]) to J.-P. Migne, ed., *Patrologiæ Cursus Completus . . . series Latina . . .* (Paris: Garnier Fratres, 217 voll., 1844–[1864?]—the

individual voll. of this great set were many times reprinted, making precision of original dates elusive; even the printed catalogues of the Bibliothèque Nationale, the British Library, and the Library of Congress disagree)—of these indexes, that on titles (vol. 218, 1887 reprint) lists *Canticum Canticorum* at coll. 676 ff.; that on scripture (vol. 219, 1879 reprint) gives references for this work at col. 92; that on scripture sermons (although that modern English word is admittedly a somewhat free rendering of the Latin *sermones*—cf. our note 18 below) (vol. 221, 1890 reprint: coll. 19 ff.) gives the entries for it at col. 22 (cf. for Psalms at 19–21f. and the Gospels at 23 f.–25f.). (iii) Jean Leclercq, *L'Amour des lettres et le désir de Dieu: initiation aux auteurs monastiques du moyen âge* (Paris: Éditions du Cerf, 1957), chap. 5, "Les lettres sacrées", and especially pp. 83–86. (Note: here and throughout our study, where in a given note a cross-reference is given to another note, the words "below" and "above" without further specification refer to notes within the same chapter; references to notes in a different chapter specify that other chapter explicitly. When referring not to another note but to a passage in the body of our text, the same principle applies.)

5. Quoted in the Mishnāh, in the order *Ṭohºrôt* (*Ṭºhorôt*, etc.), tractate *Yādayim* 3: 5: *Ên kol hā-'olām kullô kºda'y ka-y-yôm she-n-nîttan bô Shîr ha-sh-Shîrîm lº-Yisrā'ēl, she-k-kol ha-k-kºtûbîm qōdesh wº-Shîr ha-sh-Shîrîm qōdesh q ºdoshîm.* Hebrew text, with trans. and notes, in *Mishnāyôt* (*bº-shishshāh kºrākîm, û-kerek shºbî'î mûṣāp) . . . / Mishnayoth: in six volumes, and supplementary volume VII,* Philip Blackman [ed. and trans.] (London: Mishna Press [L. M. Schoenfeld], '711–'716/1951–1956; New York: Judaica Press, without the sub-titles, '724/1963, 1964), vol. 6, p. 764. (My translation. I have followed Jewish scholars in presenting *kºtûbîm* here as signifying the Hagiographa, since I suppose that that represents how the sentence was widely heard during the centuries that concern us here, when this word served in part as a mediæval Jewish technical term for those books. Some might speculate, however, whether Rabbi 'Aqîbâ himself when he made the statement may not be imagined as conceivably saying "all scripture" is holy. . . .) Rabbi 'Aqîbâ is furthermore quoted as saying: "If the Tôrāh had not been given, The Song of Songs would have sufficed to guide the world"—Hebrew text in S. Schechter, "Agadath Shir Hashirim" in *Jewish Quarterly Review,* 6 (1893–94): 672–697 and 7 (1894–1895): 145–163 and 729–754; this statement is on 6:674 (my trans.).

6. Until recently, Rashi's commentary in the original Hebrew was included in the margin of most printed Hebrew versions of the Jewish Bible. Recently, for The Song separately: *Rashî, Mºgillat Shîr ha-sh-Shîrîm, 'im Pêrûsh . . . Rashî . . . û-Pêrûsh Ahºbat qºdûmîm . . .* (Bºnê Bº rāq: Y. Pîsher [sc. Jacob Fisher (Fischer?)], [1979]). It is available also, along with an English translation, in *Ha-m-Mºgillôt [*] 'im Pêrûsh Rashi, mºturgāmîm [*] shûrāh bº-shûrāh: Eṣtēr, Shîr ha-sh-Shîrîm, Rût / The Megilloth and Rashi's commentary with linear translation: Esther, The Song of Songs, Ruth,* Avraham

Schwartz and Yisroel Schwartz, transs. [and edd.] (New York: Hebrew
Linear Classics, 1983), pp. 57–149. Something of the flavour of Rashî's
interpretation, along with indications of a number of collateral Rabbinic
positions on The Song—and of these we have cited some in what follows—
is available for English-speaking readers also in the small and somewhat
informal work *Shir haShirim—Song of Songs: An Allegorical Translation based
upon Rashi with a commentary anthologized from Talmudic, Midrashic and Rabbinic Sources. Commentary compiled by Rabbi Meir Zlotowitz. Allegorical translation, and overview, by Rabbi Nosson Scherman* (New York: Mesorah Publications, 1977. ArtScroll Tanach Series: a traditional commentary on the Books
of the Bible). [* Note: An asterisk in a transliteration here and throughout
our study indicates a short vowel that in an unpointed Hebrew text has
been written with scriptio plena. Thus in this case the text has *m-g-y-l-w-t*.]

7. *Sermones super Cantica Canticorum*, published as volumes 1–2 in
S. Bernardi, *Opera*, J. Leclercq et al., edd. (Romae: Editiones Cistercienses,
1957 ff.–in process). The most recent English translation is: Bernard of
Clairvaux, *On The Song of Songs*, Kilian Walsh (voll. 1–3) and Irene M.
Edmonds (voll. 3–4), transs. (Spencer, Mass. [vol.1] and Kalamazoo, Mich-
igan [voll. 2–3–4]; also London and Oxford: Mowbray [vol. 2]: Cistercian
Publications, 4 voll., 1971–1980—Cistercian Fathers Series, nos. 4, 7, 31,
40). In what follows, all references to Bernard are to these editions.

8. The work that I have chiefly consulted here is Ibn 'Aqnîn, *Inkishâf
al-Asrâr wa-Ẓuhûr al-Anwâr*. The text in the original Arabic is available
only, so far as I have been able to ascertain, in Hebrew characters: with the
Hebrew title *R. Yôsēp ben Yᵉhûdāh ben Yaᶜaqôb ibn 'Aqnîn, Hitgallût ha-ṣ-Ṣôdôt
wa-Hôpā'at ha-m-Mᵉ'ôrôt: Pêrûsh Shîr ha-sh-Shîrîm—mᵉqôrô hā-ᶜarābî, 'ārak
higgîyāh wᵉ-targēm bᵉ-çêrûp heᶜārôt* Abrāhām Shᵉlômôh Halqîn (Yᵉrûshālayim:
Mᵉqîçê Nirdāmîm, '724) and the Latin title *Josephi b. Judah b. Jacob ibn
'Aḵnîn, Divulgatio Mysteriorum Luminumque Apparentia: Commentarius in
Canticum Canticorum—textum arabicum emendavit, versione Hebraica et notis
instruxit* A. S. Halkin (Hierosolymis: Societas Mekize Nirdamim, MCM-
LXIV). Another significant commentary is that of Ibn Ezra. It was appar-
ently issued in three successive and fairly differing versions; I have seen the
following edition of the first, giving Hebrew text, English translation, and
notes: *Pêrûsh Shîr ha-sh-Shîrîm (mahᵃdûrâ rî'shônâh) lᵉ-Rabbî Abrāhām ben
Mᵉ'îr ibn 'Ezrâ ha-ṣ-Ṣᵉpārādî*, Hênrî Yôhānan Mātî'ûṣ, ed. and trans. / *Abraham ibn Ezra's Commentary on the Canticles, after the first recension*, H. J.
Mathews, ed. and trans. (London: Trübner—the Hebrew title-page says
Oxford: Clarendon Press—, 1874); I have, however, followed secondary
sources for him and others for a fuller picture. Among these, I may note
that before bringing out his edition Halkin published an introductory essay
on his author, placing him in the general context of Muslim and especially
Jewish philosophic thinking and Jewish Song exegesis of the time: "Ibn
'Aḵnîn's Commentary on The Song of Songs", in *Alexander Marx Jubilee*

Volume: on the occasion of his seventieth birthday—English section, Saul Lieberman, ed. (New York: The Jewish Theological Seminary of America, 1950), pp. 389–424.

9. Song 1:2. The verse numbering of The Song differs in the Vulgate in the first chapter, though not in the others, from that found in the standard Hebrew text, in the Septuagint, and in the King James Authorised Version with its successors in English. In this case, for instance, our "opening verse" is 1:2 (1:1 being the book's title and the ascription to Solomon), whereas in the Vulgate it is 1:1 (since the ascription has been included rather in the preceding Prologue to the three books of Solomon, and the title is not enumerated as a verse). In our treatment throughout this present chapter we indicate any such divergences when they pertain to references that we have occasion to give. The practice of having Biblical books appear with discriminated chapters and verses, however, became established only in relatively late times; the mediæval thinkers with whom we are here concerned were not involved with such matters. More significant are instances of divergence between the actual readings of the Vulgate Latin text and the Hebrew; of these there is one in this particular verse. The written Hebrew consonantal text in early centuries was unpointed (sc., vowels were omitted); the word (phrase) *d-d-y-k* here was therefore ambivalent. The Masoretes, followed by Reformation translators, and modern scholars, read it as *dōdêka* ("your [*masc.*] love"), so that mediæval Jews and Protestants have had that as their scripture here; and this is the translation that I have offered above. The Septuagint translators, on the other hand, (*mastoi sou*), and also Jerome in the Vulgate (*ubera tua*), evidently read the Hebrew differently, as *daddêka* ("your [*masc.*] breasts"), with that interpretation serving then the Greek-speaking majority of Jews for a few centuries, and mediæval Christians, as *their* scripture. (It would be possible also to read the Hebrew characters as *daddayik*, "your [*fem.*] breasts"—the Greek and Latin leave that point undifferentiated; but so far as concerns us in this chapter, Bernard, like most, certainly reads the Vulgate as referring here to the breasts of the Bridegroom.) The divergence does not affect our presentation in what follows regarding Bernard, since we build no argument on his reading of this particular verse; it does come into our reference to Origen's reading of the Septuagint version of it, our note 61 below. I have throughout used the Privilegierte Württembergische Bibelanstalt ednn. of the Hebrew Bible (1937), of the Septuagint (n.d. [sc. 1935]), and of the Vulgate (1969). Unless otherwise indicated, references to Biblical book, chapter, and verse are to the standard Protestant versions, such as the King James Authorised, the Revised Standard, etc.

10. Song 8:14.

11. "You should realize, my brother, that you will find great diversities in exegesis of the Song of Songs. They diverge because, indeed, the Song of Songs is like locks whose keys have been lost"—(my translation) from the

commentary attributed to Ṣā 'adyāh Gā'ôn, the great mediæval scholar (and poet) who translated the Jewish Bible into Arabic; as quoted in Hebrew (without reference) in Eprayim '[E]. Ûrbak, "Derāshôt Ḥ'z'l [sc., ḥᵒkomênû zikrōnām li-bᵉrākāh] û-pêrûshê Ôrîgênêṣ lᵉ-Shîr ha-sh-Shîrîm . . .", in Tarbîç, Yᵉrûshālayim, vol. 30 no. 2, 1960, pp. [148]–170, p. [148], footnote 2 (which also adduces evidence that this simile, but relating to the Bible in general, goes back many centuries in Jewish lore). This version is quoted also, in English, again without reference, and in a translation worded slightly differently, by Marvin H. Pope, Song of Songs: a new translation with introduction and commentary (Garden City, N.Y.: Doubleday, 1977—The Anchor Bible), p. 89. The (an) Arabic original of this work has recently been published; it (and the editor's Hebrew translation) differ substantially from this version, the reference to diversities being less explicit and the key of the lock (two singulars) having in this case been "destroyed" (talifa)—Yôṣēp ben Dāwid Qâpaḥ, ed., Ḥāmēsh Mᵉgillôt [*]. . . 'im pêrûshîm 'attîqîm ha-y-yôç ᵉ'îm lᵉ'ôr pa'am rî'shônāh 'al-pî kitᵉbê yād bᵉ-çêrûp mᵉbô'ôt he'ārôt wᵉ-he'ārôt (Yᵉrûshālayim: Hôçᵉ'at hā-Agûdāh lᵉ-Haççālat Ginzê Têmān, '722 [1962]), p. 26.

12. So marked is this that one may perhaps correlate the modern skeptical sociologist Durkheim's thinking to derive religion as such, as a universal human phenomenon, from the fact of human beings' membership in a society, with his being from a Jewish background. He took community for granted, as a given. He lived at a time after faith had formally waned for many European intellectuals, but before the point had become dolefully apparent how once faith has weakened a sense of community can then—or therein—become lost, leaving in its place society as but a congeries of separated, competing, lonely individuals. Faith and spiritual sensitivity turn out to be a foundation rather than merely a superstructure of community. Put another way, the capacity of human beings to relate to one another as jointly participants in what may then be called community rather than as solitary individuals in separation (alienation) from one another, is one aspect of our perception of immanent transcendence; of what we mean by "faith".

13. Gerson D. Cohen, "The Rabbinic Heritage", in Leo W. Schwarz, ed., Great Ages and Ideas of the Jewish People (New York: The Modern Library, 1956), p. 181.

14. Nosson Scherman in Zlotowitz, Shir . . . (op. cit. above, our note 6), p. xxi.

15. As I have previously indicated (see note page 11), it is my practice to use the three pronouns Him/Her/It to refer to God, over against those moderns who confine themselves to the first two, or those traditionalists who fasten on one. Yet in representing eras or groups with a less transcending perception, I tend throughout this study to use the one that seems most faithfully to portray the outlook of the particular person or group being

considered. It can be seen as a somewhat alluring question, however, whether the Hebrew pronoun *Hû* used for God, unfailingly translated into English as masculine, harbours in this case just a whiff, perhaps—given the transcendence involved—of what in English would or might be a neuter ("It"). (Hebrew and other Semitic languages are among the many on earth—French being another—that do not distinguish "it" from "him" and "her".) It is, of course, of significance, and not only of interest, that mediæval Jews spoke of the *shakînah* of God, which is feminine. Perhaps I should have written "serving Him/Her/It" above after all?

16. *b^e-gālûthāh û-b^e'alm^enûtāh—b^e'alm^enût ḥayyût*—Rashi on Song 1:2 and 1:4 (Vulgate 1:1 and 1:3); Schwartz edn. (op. cit., our note 6 above), pp. 58, 60. The idea here picks up the Midrash on Psalm 68:6 (in Protestant Bibles, 68:5), para. 3, which in turn calls on Lamentations 5:3 and Jeremiah 51:5—see *Midrash T^ehillîm ha-m-m^ekûnneh Shôḥar Ṭôb*, edn. of "Vîlnâ: hā-Almānāh û-hā-Aḥîm Rām", 1890 (this date is on the Cyrillic verso of the half-title of *Ḥēleq / sēfer Sh^elîshî*; sc. on f. [165] verso = p. [330]) ([reprinted], Y^erûshālayim, '726 [sc.=1965–1966], 5 parts, with continuous pagination), f. 158 verso = p. 316. English: *The Midrash on Psalms: translated from the Hebrew and Aramaic* by William G. Braude (New Haven: Yale University Press, 2 vol., 1959—Yale Judaica Series, ed. Leon Nemoy, vol. xiii), vol. 1, p. 539. (Note: here and throughout my study I give the pagination—foliation?—of Hebrew and Aramaic books, where the original does so, according to the folio designated by the Hebrew alphabet-number, with "recto" and "verso" [note that "recto" here indicates paradoxically the left-hand side of a double page spread] and along with it the page-number in what the West calls "Arabic" numerals, in either case in square brackets in references where the numbering does not overtly occur on the specific page that is being cited.)

17. I use the word "fellow" not in its new colloquial or slang meaning of male, to which feminists would rightly object, but in its literal and prime meaning, of male or female associate (so both the *Oxford Concise* and *Webster's New Collegiate* dictionaries, currently).

18. To translate mediæval Latin *sermones* into modern English as "sermons" is to take certain liberties. Yet I have here and there allowed myself to follow the usual practice in doing so. Certainly there is a question as to whether the texts that we have were ever intended to be preached or were, rather, literary compositions to be read. On this point see Jean Leclercq, "Introduction" to vol. 2 of the Cistercian edition mentioned in our note 7 above; pp. vii–xxx. In any case, the works are certainly homiletic in spirit.

19. For instance, Sermon 82:ii/2 (Latin, 2:293; Eng., 4:172–173). At many places throughout his work he makes the same point, basic to his whole presentation: that the human soul is originally and essentially divine, but has become overlaid.

20. Sermon 83:i/1 (Latin, 2:298; Eng., 4:180)—the full roster of woes to

which he here depicts the human soul as subject, is long, vivid, impassioned.

21. Ibid. (298–299; 181).

22. This wording is from M. Corneille Halflants, "Introduction" to vol. 1 of the Eng. translation, p. xiii; I do not find (or, having found, have misplaced) Bernard's own wording, but the idea rings true enough—although one must admit that his sense of the convergence of the human soul both potentially and essentially with God is repeatedly set forth without any qualification's being mentioned.

23. Sermon 74:i/2 (Latin, 2:240, *mysterium*; Eng., 4 p. 86). Cf. also 74:i/1 (ibid.; Latin, *mirabilia super me* and *sacramentum;* in English, these are not unreasonably rendered as "mysteries beyond me" and "mystery"); and *passim.* He uses esp. the word *mysterium* regularly; and indeed his sense of transcendence is almost overwhelming: his awareness of the degree to which God and the reality that confronts us all transcend not only our apprehension, but almost our ability to stand before them. Cf. further below, our note 35.

24. Song 3:1. We stated above that his sermons are commentary on the work only into the second chapter; this instance is not an exception, his citing it coming incidentally (Latin, 2:318; Eng., 4:213) in the course of his elaborating (Sermon 86:i/2) on an earlier passage.

25. Sermon 86 (Latin, 2:317–320; Eng., 4:[211]–215).

26. Matthew 6:6; Bernard, ibid., i/2 (Latin, 2:318; Eng., 4:213)

27. Bernard, ibid.

28. Song 2:16.

29. Sermon 71:i/1 (Latin, 2:214; Eng., 4:48).

30. "It is . . . of fundamental importance that justice should not only be done, but should manifestly and undoubtedly be seen to be done"—Lord Hewart, in *Rex v. Sussex Justices*, 1923, as cited in *The Oxford Dictionary of Quotations* (Oxford, New York, &c: Oxford University Press [1941], 3rd edn. [1979], 2nd corrected imp. 1980), p. 250, no. 20.

31. Bernard's citing of this verse (sermon 71:i/2), as in the great preponderance of similar cases with him, is not explicit. In the English translations (e.g., the Cistercian, vol. 4, p. 49, where this verse is given as ". . . will always intend what is good, not only before God but also in the sight of men") it is not obvious; at least, not to Protestants. Romans 12:17 in the King James Authorised Version reads, "Provide things honest in the sight of all men", and in the Revised Standard Version, "take thought for what is noble in the sight of all". In the Latin, however (vol. 2, p. 215), his phrasing is virtually word-for-word directly from the Vulgate.

32. Bernard, ibid.

33. Sermon 62:iii/5 (Latin, 2:158; Eng., 3:156).

34. This point is amply illustrated on almost every page of the Cistercian edition of the Latin that we have been citing, which gives references

for Biblical quotations or allusions at the foot of each page between the text and the critical apparatus. Bernard's lavish quoting from the Bible in this way exemplifies something that is widely observable over the centuries and throughout the world: that the speaking and writing of many of the devout tends to be shot through with scriptural phrases and snippets and allusions. (Cf the quotation given below, our chap. 8, p. 189, at its note 52.)

35. Cf. above, at our note 23. A further example, chosen more or less at random, is Sermon 67:i/ 1 (Latin, 2:188; Eng., 4:4), where the attribute of mystery is applied twice in a few sentences, in this case to the words of the Bride. For Bernard, one of the virtues of reading scriptures is indeed the humbling experience of finding our "intellectual powers overcome" (ibid.) by the sheer profundity of the message with which we are confronted.

36. Sermon 67:i/2 (Latin, 2:189; Eng., 4:5).

37. Sermon 67:ii/1 (Latin and Eng., ibid.).

38. Sermon 73:iii/7 (Latin, 2:237; Eng., 4:81. The Latin that is here rendered as "I do not dissent" is *non contendo;* I would myself tend to translate this with a somewhat more confrontational term, such as "I do not object").

39. Sermon 73:iii/9 (Latin, 2:239; Eng., 4:83).

40. Pope, *Song* (op. cit., our note 11 above), p. 105.

41. For instance, his *De Anima*, III, chap. 5/430 a 10–25. I have used the edition of the Greek text in R. D. Hicks, ed. and trans., Aristotle, *De Anima* ([London: Cambridge University Press, 1907] Amsterdam: Hakkert, 1965), where this passage is pp. 134, 136. (There is an English translation on facing pages—not altogether lucid; the text is known as somewhat obscure, and Hicks's long note, pp. 498–510, helps to elucidate.) Further, one may note another phrase of Aristotle, *nous thyrathen*, alluding to a comparable idea. It he explicitly characterizes as *theios*—divine. See, for instance, his *De Generatione Animalorum*, II, chap. 3/736 b 27–29. Here I have used the edition of the Greek text of A. L. Peck, ed. and trans. (Cambridge, Mass.: Harvard University Press, and London: Heinemann, [1943], rev. edn., 1953—Loeb Classical Library), p. 170, with English trans. on facing page; Peck here translates *nous* as "Reason" (p. 171), not "intellect".

42. This remark might seem to conflict with the title, and the content, of our fourth chapter, below, on the Qur'ān; but we differentiate between scripture and text.

43. This is a statement that I composed and circulated some years ago to a class of students in an introductory history-of-religion course.

44. Our note 8 above.

45. On this point, of "text" as an inappropriate concept for scriptures, see the paragraph in our text that follows here, and cf. our chap. 1 above, pp. 18–19; and further, our concluding chap. below.

46. Op. cit., our note 11 above.

47. Spinoza ". . .der als erster den Gedanken der Geschichtlichkeit der Bibel

in voller Schärfe erfaßt, und der ihn in nüchterner Schärfe und Sachlichkeit durchgefürt hat"—Ernst Cassirer, *Die Philosophie der Aufklärung* (Tübingen: J.C.B. Mohr [Paul Siebeck], 1932), p. 248. In the English trans., Ernst Cassirer, *The Philosophy of the Enlightenment*, Fritz C. A. Koelln and James P. Pettegrove, transs., ([Princeton: Princeton University Press, 1951], Boston: Beacon, 1962), p. 185.

48. So even the Encyclopaedia Judaica (Jerusalem: Macmillan, and Keter; voll. 2–16, 1971, vol. 1 [introduction and index], 1972), the article BIBLE, vol. 4, col. 849.

49. Text on margin of intermittent pages in *Ḥāmēsh Mᶜgillôt* [*]: *Shîr ha-sh-Shîrîm, Rût, Qōhelet . . . Miqrâ, Targûm, Tapṣîr (ᶜᵃrābît), ʿim pērûshîm . . . wa-. . . wa-. . .*, Shim'ûn ben Shᵉmû'ēl Najjâr ([Hertseliyah]: [n.pub.]., 5730 [sc.= 1969–1970]), pp. 1–82. English version: *'The Targum to the Song of Songs.': translated from the Aramaic by* Hermann Gollancz (London: Luzac, 1909). See also Raphael Loewe, "Apologetic Motifs in the Targum to the Song of Songs" in Alexander Altmann, ed., *Biblical Motifs: origins and transformations* (Cambridge, Mass.: Harvard University Press, 1966—Philip W. Lown Institute of Advanced Judaic Studies, Brandeis University: Studies and Texts: vol. III), pp. 159–196; also, Francis Landy, *Paradoxes of Paradise: identity and difference in The Song of Songs* (Sheffield: Almond Press, 1983). Of additional interest is Schechter, "Agadath Shir Hashirim" (op. cit., our note 5 above). Cf. also the English version of *Midrash Rabbah . . . Song of Songs*, Maurice Simon, trans., published along with *Esther* (but separately paginated) as vol. 9 of the series (13 voll. in 10) H. Freedman and Maurice Simon, edd., *Midrash Rabbah: translated into English with notes, glossary and indices* (London: Soncino Press, [1939], 1961). By and large, Rashî's sense of the work as portraying God's love for Israel goes back through the Talmûd to the Talmûd's sources, his sense of its representing Israel's history is in line with the Targûm and Midrash Rabbah.

50. Origen produced two studies of The Song of Songs, of which one was a formal commentary and the other a series of sermons that together could also be considered such but is standardly called, rather, his "Homilies" on the work. Both were in Greek, but have not survived in that language except for a few fragments. It was in both cases, however, the Latin version of parts of them (by Rufinus and Jerome respectively—the former, at least, done in an "extremely free" manner) that was highly influential in later Western thought. Both works are now conveniently available—Latin text with French translation on facing pages—in *Origène, Commentaire sur le Cantique des Cantiques: texte de la version latine de Rufin, introduction, traduction et notes, par Luc Brésard, o.c.s.o., et Henri Crouzel, s.j., avec la collaboration de Marcel Borret, s.j.* (Paris: Éditions du Cerf, 2 tomes, 1991–92), and *Origène, Homélies sur le Cantique des Cantiques: introduction, traduction et notes de Dom O. Rousseau, O.S.B.* (Paris: Éditions du Cerf, 1954). Both constitute volumes in the series "Sources chrétiennes", nos. 375–376 and no. 37,

respectively. (In the 1954 instance this series carries the further notation "H. de Lubac, J. Daniélou, dirr.; C. Mondésert, sec. dir."; almost four decades later in the Commentary these personal names are replaced with ref. to "l'Institut des Sources Chrétiennes".) An English version of both: *Origen, The Song of Songs: commentary and homilies, translated and annotated by* R. P. Lawson (Westminster, Md.: Newman Press, and London: Longmans, Green, 1957—Johannes Quasten, Joseph C. Plumpe, edd., Ancient Christian Writers: The Works of the Fathers in Translation, no. 26).

51. "The question of meaning was split up in two tenses: 'What *did* it mean?' and 'What *does* it mean?'"—Krister Stendahl, in his article BIBLICAL THEOLOGY, CONTEMPORARY, in *The Interpreter's Dictionary of the Bible: an illustrated encyclopedia*, George Arthur Buttrick, ed. (New York / Nashville, Tenn.: Abingdon, 4 voll., 1962), vol. 1, p. 419. "What it meant and what it means" is the title of a section of the article: pp. 418, 419–420. The full article is pp. 418–432.

52. Because consideration went on for centuries both on the issue in general as to what scripture-like works should constitute together a canonized Bible, and on the debates specifically on whether The Song should be considered to be in the running at all for being treated scripturally, the final clause of this sentence in our text is admittedly vague. On the former issue see our chapter 1 above and our chapter 3 below; on the latter, it is generally recognized that The Song was one of the last books to be widely admitted into scriptural status by either the Jewish community or the Christian Church.

53. Pope had already noted certain possible links with India, the point having been raised shortly before by Chaim Rabin, "The Song of Songs and Tamil Poetry", *[SR] Studies in Religion / Sciences religieuses*, 3 (1973–1974): [205]–219. It has since been developed by Peter C. Craigie, "Biblical and Tamil Poetry: some further reflections", ibid. 8 (1979): [169]–175, and more fully by Abraham Mariaselvam, *The Song of Songs and Ancient Tamil Love Poems: poetry and symbolism* (Roma: Pontificio Istituto Biblico, 1988—Analecta Biblica, Investigationes Scientificae in Res Biblicas, no. 118)

54. The Tôsēptâ tractate Sanhēdrîn 12: 10 reports Rabbi ʿAqîbâ deprecating the practice. The report of his doing so has by modern scholars been cited almost as often, it might almost seem, as his earlier-quoted extolling of the work (above, our note 5). Hebrew text: *Tôsēptâ: ʿal-pî kitʿbê yād ʿErpûrṭ û-Wiyennāh . . . mē-ēt* Mōsheh Shᵉmûʾēl Çûqermândel, *ʿim "Tashlûm Tôsēptâ"; mē-ēt* Shāʾûl Lîbermān (Yᵉrûshālayim: Wâhᵉrmān, ʿ730 / *Tosephta: based on the Erfurt and Vienna Codices, with parallels and variants, by* M. S. Zuckermandel, *with "Supplement to the Tosephta"* [1881]; *new edn., with additional notes and corrections,* Saul Liebermann, ed. (Jerusalem: Wahrmann, 1970), p. 433. The Hebrew that I have translated by the term "taverns" above is *bêt ha-m-mishtaʾôt*, which some prefer to render as "banquet hall"—a reading of the Rabbi's remark that makes the point at issue that much the

more revealing, if indeed this sacrilegious treatment of The Song was current even in such more formal settings. The word is from the verb *shatâ* (Aramaic; Hebrew, *shatāb*) "to drink". "Banquet" is used in both English translations: Herbert Danby, *Tractate Sanhedrin: Mishnah and* Tosefta—*the judicial procedure of the Jews as codified towards the end of the second century* A.D., *translated from the Hebrew with brief annotations* (London: Society for Promoting Christian Knowledge, and New York: Macmillan, 1919), p. 121; and Jacob Neusner, *The Tosefta: translated from the Hebrew* (New York: Ktav, 1977–1981, several voll.), Fourth Division, *Neziqin (The Order of Damages)*, p. 237.

55. It has become somewhat customary in certain academic circles to avoid the designations "B.C." and "A.D." in dating, by resorting to the neologisms "B.C.E." and "C.E." respectively. This is either intolerably provincial, or ambiguous, or both. Usually the abbreviations are interpreted as standing for "Before the Common Era" and "Common Era", which is based on the idea that the latter time-period is common to both Jews and Christians. It is not common, however, to Buddhists and Hindus, nor to Jews and Confucians, nor to most other groups on earth; and it simply will not do. This problem may be evaded by insinuating that the "C" stands for "Christian", but this seems an ingenuous afterthought, too opaque to be effective, and too insensitive to be acceptable. Some might settle for "B.Xn.E." and "Xn.E", but this is still insensitive, having the highly dubious implication that the era in question has been significantly Christian, which is problematic for the West and certainly not appropriate for the history of the rest of the world. To refer to an event in mediæval China as falling within a Christian era is hardly apt. The notion that our world since 1 A.D. may be said to have been going through a Christian era, or that the present age on earth is a Christian one, either is laughable or elicits tears. It is the calendar that has been Christian, not the era that its dates note. "B.C." is intellectually more or less precise for the period before Christ; those ill at ease with the "D" of A.D. might settle for "A.C." for the subsequent era. The problem of the import of the term "Christ" is not a theological difficulty for Hindus, Muslims, and many others, just as non-Buddhists do not balk at referring to Siddhartha Gautama as Buddha or non-Hindus to early Sanskrit priestly hymns as Veda; yet it tends to be unacceptable to those Jews sensitive to its received (but surely erroneous) equivalence to "Messiah" (both terms have etymologically to do with "anointing", but for perhaps nineteen centuries have had little else in common). This difficulty could be avoided by "B.J." and "A.J." (although 25 A.D. was not in fact "after Jesus"); it seems unlikely that this will prevail. "M.I.C." for "modern international calendar" could be proposed. This would solve much of the problem—it is the calendar that is to be characterized—but how to designate B.C. dates? To sum up, then, I propose to continue to use "B.C." and "A.D." until the issue is satisfactorily resolved. I do so not because I am insensitive to the problems (I have never

suggested that religious diversity does not pose a major predicament for our today's world!) but for the moment *faute de mieux*. I invite others to put their minds to the matter.

56. Cf. note 52 above.

57. Christian and Jewish Bible commentators were more aware of each other and of each other's views in the early centuries of the Church than in mediæval and early modern times; as of course they have again become in recent centuries. We have mentioned in passing Origen, whose interpretation of The Song laid the foundation for later Christian exegesis, launching the tradition in which also Bernard wrote. Origen was in touch with Rabbinic contemporaries, and there were open disputes between representatives of the two groups on their divergent positions on many matters, especially Biblical interpretation, and explicitly The Song. See, for instance, Reuven Kimelman, "Rabbi Yoḥanan and Origen on The Song of Songs: a third-century Jewish-Christian disputation", in *The Harvard Theological Review*, 73 (1980): [567]–595; and the Hebrew article mentioned above in our note 11, of which also an English translation appeared later: Ephraim E. Urbach, "The Homiletical Interpretations of the Sages and the Expositions of Origen on Canticles, and the Jewish-Christian Disputation", in Joseph Heinemann and Dov Noy, edd., *Studies in Aggadah and Folk-Literature* (Jerusalem: Magnes Press, The Hebrew University, on behalf of the Institute of Jewish Studies, 1971—Scripta Hierosolymitana, vol. XXII), pp. [247] ff. In the Middle Ages Rashî's Biblical commentaries in general became known to some Christian exegetes and were, indeed, influential—particularly with Andrew of St. Victor and Nicholas of Lyra, who knew Hebrew though not Greek; but this was barely the case, apparently, specifically on The Song. One interestingly Christianized Latin translation or paraphrase of Rashî's commentary on this work was made in the thirteenth century, but seems to have been inconsequential at the time; a manuscript has in recent times come to light and been discussed in scholarly circles, and has now been published: *Secundum Salomonem: a thirteenth century Latin commentary on the Song of Solomon, edited with an introduction by* Sarah Kamin [and] Avrom Saltman (Ramat Gan, Bar-Ilan University Press, 1989).

58. Pope, *Song of Songs* . . . (op. cit. above, our note 11); e.g., p. 131.

59. Zlotowitz, *Shir* . . . (op. cit., our note 6 above), pp. 71–72.

60. Rashî on, e.g., Song 2:4 (Schwartz edn. [op. cit., our note 6 above]), p. 73.

61. Interestingly comparable to this is Origen's interpretation of wine— in Song 1:2 [Vulgate 1:1]—the teachings inherited from of old, through "the Law and the Prophets". See his Commentary, Book 1 §2, and specifically its para. 8 (opp. citt. above, our note 50: Latin, vol. 1, pp. [190]–204, spec. p. 196; French, vol. 1, pp. [189]–205, spec. p. 197; English, pp. 62–70, spec. p. 65). Typically, however, he is reading this passage (in the wording cited in our note 9 above) as saying that this wine—for him, virtually the

Old Testament—is good, but what we receive from Christ is better; while Rashî, commenting on "wine" in a different verse, speaks of its delights, as we go on in our text to cite, as superlative. In somewhat similar fashion, but in this case more convergently, the two breasts of the Bride are likened by Jewish readers to the Written and the Oral Torah, and by Christians to the Old and New Testaments—on the former, see Kimelman, "Rabbi Yoḥanan . . . (op. cit., our note 57 above), p. 578; on the latter, see below, note 64.

62. Song 1:13 (Vulgate, 1:12)

63. Rashî *ad loc*; Schwartz edn. (op. cit., our note 6 above), p. 69. His reading follows a Talmudic interpretation of this matter: *Yoma* 54a of the Babylonian Talmud—Zlotowitz, *Shir* (op. cit., in that same note), p. 90; Pope, *Song* . . . (op. cit., our note 11 above), p. 352.

64. Pope, *Song* . . .. loc. cit. (our immediately preceding note just above). For the Jewish counterpart, of the Written and Oral Torah, cf. our note 61 above.

65. Pope, *Song* . . . loc. cit. (our two immediately preceding notes just above). In passing, one may note that in mediæval as in various other cultures a woman's breasts were regularly thought of in relation to maternity and nourishment of an infant, rather than, in the recent West's style, in relation primarily to sexual attractiveness to men. The former sense runs through much of the pre-modern commentaries both Jewish and Christian. In addition to instances from and before Origen through Rashî and Bernard one may mention an eighteenth-century Jewish example: Rabbi Dob Ber treats the breasts in this verse as signifying such nourishment, "as an allusion to scholars who 'nourish' others by instructing them in Torah. He renders: 'If I provide spiritual nourishment for others, God will cause His presence to '*dwell*' upon me'"—Zlotowitz, *Shir* . . . (op. cit., our note 6 above), pp. 90–91.

66. Although at times Bernard stresses that love among human beings is the acme of moral attainment and of conformity to God's will for us, at other times he sets up in order three types of love (*caritas*). The first is corporeal or sensual (*carnalis*). The second we might call intellectual and practical, moral: acting in a loving way by an act of will—reason's submissiveness to God, he calls it. This (which the derived English word "charity" has moved towards meaning), he says, though strong, is dry (*sicca, sed fortis*; the Cistercian English version that we have normally been citing has "emotionless but strong"). Finally, there is love seasoned with *sapientia*, a term usually and rightly translated "wisdom" but with Bernard the literal sense of "tasting" is not lost (*gustat, et sapit*): the connotation is always of experience, an experiential participation both with the loved one and also, indeed especially, in the divine. In this analysis, the first is evil; the second deserves a reward; the third *is* a reward.—Sermon 50, esp. ii/4 (Latin, 2:80; Eng., 3:32–33; but i/4 [ibid.] is also important).

67. For him, dichotomously, and following St. Paul, spirituality means

war against the flesh. By the spirit, one mortifies the deeds of the flesh, crucifies the flesh with its defects, its lusts, its melancholy contradictions, and lives again. Sermon 72:iii/8–9 (Latin: 2:230–231; Eng., 4:70–71.)

68. The passage to which we have just referred is, more fully, an example of the sort that may elicit pity from some among us (from others perhaps admiration for his courage as he faced his racking distress). He speaks there of the flesh ceaselessly striving against the spirit, and sees death as a divine mercy, "whereby the elect of God . . . may not long be wearied by the strife and trouble which holds them captive to the law of sin which is in their members. For it is with anguish of mind that they suffer the shame . . . and the bitterness of their struggle . . ."—ibid., our immediately preceding note, 67 above.

3. Scripture as Form and Concept: Historical Background

1. "*Islam . . . Vor allem . . . ist eine rechte Buchreligion*"—G. van der Leeuw, *Phänomenologie der Religion* (Tübingen: J.C.B. Mohr [Paul Siebeck], 1933), p. 415. I have quoted from the English translation: G. van der Leeuw, *Religion in Essence & Manifestation: a study in phenomenology*, trans. by J. E. Turner (London: Allen & Unwin, 1938), p. 438. The remark, with the term *rechte*, comes in the course of his certainly valid contention that the place of the Qur'ān in Muslim life is more pivotal than is that of the Bible in either Jewish or Christian; yet one could well translate *vor allem* here as "above all", affirming that its place in Muslim life is more crucial than is anything else religiously in that life.

2. This idea had been touched on in passing in classical Islamic times. It was first put forth in the West, apparently, by Nathan Söderblom. Unaware of this, I independently recognized the analogy; and I have come increasingly to discern its force and its importance. See my "Some Similarities and Some Differences between Christianity and Islam: an essay in comparative religion", first published in James Kritzeck and R. Bayly Winder, edd., *The World of Islam: studies in honour of Philip K. Hitti* (London: Macmillan, and New York: St. Martin's Press, 1959), pp. 47–59 (esp. p. 52), and several times reprinted, most recently in my *On Understanding Islam* (The Hague, Paris, New York: Mouton, 1981; Berlin & New York: deGruyter, 1984; Delhi: Idarah-i Adabiyat-i Delli, 1985) pp. 233–246; a Muslim translation of this article into Urdu was published in 1964, and some present-day Muslim thinkers have published acceptance of the analogy.

3. This parallel is that observed between the facts of the Christian historical situation and those of the Islamic historical situation. At a doctrinal level, orthodox Islamic thought and feeling would reject such a comparison vigorously; as also, unreflectively, standard Western thought has in effect done. Doctrinally, using the categories of their own thought to interpret in

its terms other religious movements' outlooks—as all ideologies have traditionally done, and the secular one still does—Muslims have held that Jesus Christ was a "prophet" (like Muḥammad) who "brought the *Injīl*" (sc. the Gospel ["... the Evangel"]) conceived as a revealed book from Heaven (like the Qur'ān)—a position that, although historically inaccurate, comes theologically somewhat closer to accurate appreciation of Christians' faith than Christians' understanding of the Islamic position has done. Regarding Christians' having done something comparable in making both the word "gospel", in "the four Gospels", and the phrase "new testament", into names of books, see our note 18 below, and cf. also our chap. 7 below, its note 51.

4. The various attributes (*ṣifāt*) of God recognized by Muslims were conceptualized in Islamic theology as related to God in ways that are nowadays reminiscent of the relation envisaged in traditional Christian theology among the three Persons of the Trinity. (The statement that we have quoted regarding the Qur'ān, "... not He and not other than He", could surely be applied nicely to the Son and the Holy Spirit in relation to God the Father.) Also, the relation between empirical copies or concrete human recitings of the Qur'ān, on earth, and the timeless Word (*kalām*) of God were articulated by Muslim theologians in ways that lend themselves to comparison with Christian theological wrestling with the relation between the human and the divine natures of Christ, or between the historical figure of Jesus of Nazareth and the eternal (pre-existent; anhistorical) Word, Logos. The phrase cited in our text (*hiya lā huwa wa-lā ghayruhu*) goes back at least to the *Waṣīyat Abī Ḥanīfah* (probably early third Islamic century, ninth cent. A.D.), and remained standard. For a full discussion of many aspects and elaborations of the doctrine by various recognized later thinkers, see for instance *Sharḥ ... al-Taftāzānī 'alá al-'Aqā'id al-Nasafīyah* (Cairo: Dār Iḥyā' al-Kutub al- 'Arabīyah—'Īsá al-Bābī al-Ḥalabī), n.d. [sc. 1335 h./ 1916]), pp. 70f. We touch on a Jewish parallel to this matter, with regard to God and the Tôrāh, in our Judaica chapter, its note 11.

5. On Sikh scripture, cf. the opening paragraphs of our chap. 9 below. As observed there (cf. that chap.'s note 5), most scholars tend to think of the Sikh movement historically in relation to the Hindu, probably because it has been studied chiefly by Indologists, although those equally familiar with the Islamic can hardly fail to see the continuities also, or even more noticeably, there—esp. in the scripture matter.

6. Other examples also are noted in our chap. 9 below, at its note 33.

7. *A Catalogue of the Provincial Capitals of Ērānshahr (Pahlavi text, version and commentary)* by J. Markwart; ed. by G. Messina (Roma: Pontificio Istituto Biblico, 1931—Analecta Orientalia 3), p. 9. See also the remarks on this section on that work's pp. 28–29, where *inter alia* the alternative is mentioned of his having written rather on twelve thousand cowhides, another widespread view. (The word in classical Sanskrit for "book" [*pustaka*] is not of Sanskrit origin but is a loan-word from the Persian term for

"hide". As we shall see in a later chapter, India even less than Iran had specifically *written* scriptures before contact with the Islamic movement.)

8. This position was set forth influentially by François Nau, "La dernière rédaction de l'Avesta", being chap. III (pp. 192–199) of his article "La transmission de l'Avesta et l'époque probable de sa dernière rédaction", *Revue de l'histoire des religions*, xcv (1927): 149–199.

9. The "some form" of book emerged apparently during the reign of Khusrau (Khosro, Xosrau, Chosroes, &c) Anūshīrvān (A.D. 531–579), probably as a court initiative. The consolidating of a canon (oral) is probably somewhat earlier than this; and there is some evidence for a scattered writing down of passages from that still predominantly oral-recitation tradition also from before Khusrau's time. Yet the elevating of such writings into a form that may reasonably be called a book may be even later: it is on this point that my word "incipiently" in the text above is based. Widengren, who pushes an early writing of texts at least as strongly as do other scholars, nonetheless says that this next step occurred presumably after the Islamic movement had arrived: "When the Arabs conquered Iran . . . it was only then that they [the Zarathushtrians] started thinking of Avesta as a *Book*", containing a divine revelation received by Zarathushtra (p. 52 of Widengren, "Holy Book . . .", op. cit. infra within this note). On this whole matter for Iran the most recent summary is "The written Avesta" in Mary Boyce, *Zoroastrians: their religious beliefs and practices* (London, Boston &c: Routledge & Kegan Paul, 1979), pp. 134–136. For earlier statements, see Geo Widengren, "Holy Book and Holy Tradition in Iran: the problem of the Sassanid Avesta", in F. F. Bruce and E. G. Rupp, edd., *Holy Book and Holy Tradition: international colloquium held in the Faculty of Theology, University of Manchester* (Manchester: Manchester University Press, and Grand Rapids, Michigan: Eerdmans, 1968), pp. 36–53; Richard N. Frye, *The Heritage of Persia* (Cleveland and New York: World Publishing Company, 1963), p. 213; H. W. Bailey, *Zoroastrian Problems in the Ninth-Century Books: Ratanbai Katrak Lectures* (Oxford: Clarendon [1943], 1971), pp. 168–170. It is clear to all concerned that the oral tradition took precedence over the written throughout this period and beyond; also it is widely recognized that when the Muslims conquered Iran, they did not forthwith perceive the Zarathushtrians as a community possessing a holy book. This aspect of the matter is taken up again later in our text.

10. Arthur Jeffery, *The Foreign Vocabulary of the Qur'ān* (Baroda: Oriental Institute, 1938), pp. 233–234; with the references there cited. More recently and fully: John Bowman, "Holy Scriptures, Lectionaries and the Qur'an", in *International Congress for the Study of the Qur'an . . .* (op. cit., our chap. 1 above, note 9), pp. 29–37.

11. An example: the use of the Syriac term *retnâ*, sometimes accompanied with disparaging adjectives. See, for a Christian instance, Paul Bedjan, ed., *Histoire de Mar-Jabalaha, de trois autres patriarches, d'un prêtre et de deux*

laïques, nestoriens (Paris, Leipzig: Harrassowitz, 1895), p. 240, line 5. The same word was used in Zarathushtrian references in Jewish Aramaic: e.g., *TB Sotah* 22a, cited in Saul Lieberman, *Hellenism in Jewish Palestine: studies in the literary transmission, beliefs and manners of Palestine in the I century B.C.E.—IV century C.E.* (New York: Jewish Theological Seminary of America, 5722–1962—Texts and Studies, vol. XVIII; Stroock Publication Fund), p. 88, where this author translates "The magian mumbles and understands not what he says".

12. Widengren, "Holy Book . . ." (above, our note 9), pp. 45–47.

13. See the material in our note 9 above.

14. On this point cf. remarks in our chap. 1 above, and see the powerful exposition of duality in the Islām section of Graham, *Beyond the Written Word* (op. cit. at note 7 of that chap.), giving attention primarily to his p. 80.

15. Various scholars take differing positions on just when the work, which was in process for untold years, was "brought to closure".

16. Again, dating is in dispute. About 400 A.D. seems to be favoured.

17. In the academies, discussion was always based on oral texts. If there was a problem regarding a particular passage, the Rabbis called on the *tannâ*, a professional memorizer who functioned the way published books do for us today. His memorized version was authoritative; written texts, in contrast, were but notes to aid beginners, and were quite private and without authority. See Lieberman, "The Publication of the *Mishnah*", in his *Hellenism* . . . (op. cit., our note 11 above), pp. 83–99, esp. p. 88. See also Birger Gerhardsson, *Memory and Manuscript: oral tradition and written transmission in Rabbinic Judaism and early Christianity* (Uppsala [Acta Seminarii Neotestamentici Upsaliensis, XXII]; Lund: C. W. K. Gleerup; and Copenhagen: Ejnar Munksgaard; 1961), trans. (from the [unpublished?] Swedish) by Eric J. Sharpe; esp. "The Transmission of the Oral Torah", chap. 6, pp. [71]–78. (It may be noted, in passing, that while Gerhardsson's book has been criticized for its interpretations on the Christian side, now superseded, evidently it remains recognized as excellent on Judaic matters.) For long, the Tôrāh in writing was what is today the Pentateuch; the Oral Tôrāh was at that stage indeed oral. In my observations above regarding an "Iranian" predilection for oral/aural "Scripture", Semitic for written, as possible influence on or continuity with later Islamic, I admitted unclarity as to historical connections in this matter; and I admit further unclarity as to possible continuities between Jewish "Oral Tôrāh" and Muslim oral Qur'ān, and indeed as to possible comparable continuity between Iranian (Mesopotamian?) practice and Jewish developments. More comparativist historical work is requisite here.

18. The Greek phrase so translated (*hē kainē diathēkē*) designated originally a new divine dispensation: "This cup is the new testament in my blood . . ."—Luke 22:20, King James version (cf. the Revised Standard

version, ". . . new covenant . . ."). It reproduces the central Jewish concept *bᵉrît*, which recurs a couple of hundred times in the "Old Testament" and continues paramount in Jewish life today (cf. also Jer. 31: 31, *bᵉrît ḥᵃdāshāh*, "new covenant"). For a discussion of the historical process by which the phrase changed its meaning to become the name of a collection of texts, see W. C. van Unnik, "Ἡ καινὴ διαθήκη—a problem in the early history of the canon" [*Studia Patristica*, 1 (1961): 212–227], in *Sparsa Collecta: the collected essays of W. C. van Unnik* (3 voll., Leiden: E. J. Brill, 1973–1983— Supplements to *Novum Testamentum*, 29–31), vol. 1 (1980): [157]–171; and cf. also our chap. 7 below, its note 51. For the general process of a canonizing of a New Testament as a scripture—in significant part, of course, as *the* scripture—of the Church, see, for instance, chapters 5, 6, 7 of Hans Freiherr von Campenhausen, *Die Enstehung der christlichen Bibel* (Tübingen: J. C. B. Mohr [Paul Siebeck], 1968—Gerhard Ebeling, ed., Beiträge zur historischen Theologie, 39)—English trans. by J. A. Baker: von Campenhausen, *The Formation of the Christian Bible* (London: A. and C. Black, and Philadelphia: Fortress, 1972); and Werner Georg Kümmel, "Die Entstehung des Kanons des Neuen Testaments," being 2er Teil of his *Einleitung in das Neue Testament* (Heidelberg: Quelle & Meyer, 1973—which is formally a revised 17th ed. of a 19th century Feine-Behm work of the same title), esp. §§35–36, pp. [420]–444; in the English translation, by Howard Clark Kee: Kümmel, *Introduction to the New Testament* (Nashville and New York: Abingdon, 1975), pp. 475–503. And see below; e.g., p. 54. More recently, in summary: Helmut Köster, *Einführung in das Neue Testament: im Rahmen der Religionsgeschichte und Kulturgeschichte der hellenistischen und römischen Zeit* (Philadelphia: Fortress, and Berlin, New York: de Gruyter, 1980), §7: 1(b): "Der neutestamentliche Kanon", pp. 433–440, and Eng. trans. (by the author), Helmut Koester, *Introduction to the New Testament:* vol. 2, *History and Literature of Early Christianity* (Berlin and New York: de Gruyter, 1982), §7: 1(b): "The Canon of the New Testament", pp. 5–12). See also Brevard S. Childs, "The Canon as an Historical and Theological Problem", being chap. 2 of his *The New Testament as Canon: an introduction* (Philadelphia: Fortress, 1985), pp. [16]–33; as its title indicates, this chapter correlates theological and historical issues. A handy collection of some significant source material (Greek and Latin, with English translations, on facing pages) for those wishing to see the gradual consolidating of a Biblical corpus, are Part II, "History of The New Testament Books", and Part III, "Canon", pp. 39–126, of Daniel J. Theron, *Evidence of Tradition: selected source material for the study of the history of the early Church—introduction and canon of the New Testament* (London: Bowes & Bowes, 1957). It may be observed (cf. note 18 of our chap. 1 above) that the Church's process of canonizing scripture, extending over a number of centuries, developed along with other comparable processes: those by which it came to a formal selection of certain from among its many revered figures to be recognized as "saints"—that one was actually called "canonizing"; to a formal selection from among its many rules and regulations to be recognized as "canon" law; and similarly, to a formal selection from among its many theologians to be recognized as Church "Fathers" (here, it was affirmed *inter alia* that to qualify, a thinker had to have been dead for a considerable while, which was a way of saying that this canon—although in this case that actual term was not much used—was closed).

19. Introductory presentations are available in sectors of general works on the Manichees, such as Geo Widengren, *Mani und der Manichäismus* (Stuttgart: Kohlhammer, [n.d.; sc.,1961]—Die Wissenschaftliche Taschenbuchreihe, Fritz Ernst, ed., 57: Urban-bücher), with an English version *Mani and Manichaeism* (London: Weidenfeld and Nicolson, and New York &c: Holt, Rinehart and Winston, 1965—History of Religion series, E. O. James, gen. ed.), chap. 5, esp. its §2, "Der Kanon", pp. 79–83, Eng. pp. 76–81 (which lists and describes the seven items); and Henri-Charles Puech, *Le Manichéisme: son fondateur – sa doctrine* (Paris: Civilisation du Sud, S. A. E. P., 1949—Musée Guimet, Bibliothèque de Diffusion, tome LVI), pp. 66–68, with the notes thereto, pp. 149–150. Specifically on Manichee scriptures see Albert Henrichs, "Literary Criticism of the Cologne Mani Codex" in Bentley Layton, ed., *The Rediscovery of Gnosticism: proceedings of the international conference on Gnosticism at Yale—New Haven, Connecticut, March 28–31, 1978* (Leiden: E. J. Brill, 1980–1981, 2 voll.—M. Heerma van Voss, E. J. Sharpe, R.J.Z. Werblowsky, edd., Studies in the History of Religions—Supplements to *Numen*, XLI), 2:[724]–733; G. Haloun and W. B. Henning, "The Manichaean Canon," being Part ii, pp. 204–212, of their "The Compendium of the Doctrines and Styles of the Teaching of Mani, The Buddha of Light", in *Asia Major*, new series/vol. III (1953), pp. [180]–212; and Carl Schmidt und H. J. Polotsky, "Ein Mani-Fund in Ägypten: Originalschriften des Mani und seiner Schüler—mit einem Beitrag von . . . H. Ibscher", *Sonderausgabe aus den Sitzungsberichten der preussischen Akademie der Wissenschaften—Phil.-Hist. Klasse, 1933*, I (Berlin: Akademie der Wissenschaften/de Gruyter, 1933).

20. The remarks are quoted in translation from an unpublished manuscript in the Berlin State Museum, in Johannes Leipoldt und Siegfried Morenz, *Heilige Schriften: Betrachtungen zur Religionsgeschichte der antiken Mittelmeerwelt* (Leipzig: Harrassowitz, 1953), p. 7. The implication that the passage is apocryphal comes in Haloun and Henning, "Manichaean Canon" (op. cit., our preceding note—no. 19—just above), p. 211.

21. See L. Wittgenstein, *Lectures & Conversations on Aesthetics, Psychology and Religious Belief*, Cyril Barrett, ed. (Oxford: Blackwell, and Berkeley and Los Angeles: University of California Press, [1966], 1967, 1970), noting especially the Preface, pp. [vii]–[viii]. The opening paragraph of that Preface, displaying our modern sense of a book as not merely composed by but carefully proof-read by its author, reads: "The first thing to be said about

this book is that nothing contained herein was written by Wittgenstein himself. The notes published here are not Wittgenstein's own lecture notes but notes taken down by students, which he neither saw nor checked. It is even doubtful if he would have approved of their publication, at least in their present form. Since, however, they deal with topics only briefly touched upon in his other published writings, and since for some time they have been circulating privately, it was thought best to publish them in a form approved by their authors." These "authors" of the notes are dutifully listed on the title-page, in a sub-title: "compiled from notes taken by Yorick Smythies, Rush Rhees and James Taylor". (All of Wittgenstein's now available works were published after his death by his disciples, except only the *Tractatus*, 1921, 1922; the posthumous *Investigations* he had vacillatingly intended, on and off, to publish, yet not, it would seem, in just the form in which the work eventually appeared. See Ludwig Wittgenstein, *Philosophische Untersuchungen/Philsophical Investigations*, translated by G. E. M. Anscombe (Anscombe and R. Rhees, edd.), (Oxford: Basil Blackwell, 1953)—noting especially the Vorwort/Preface-Foreword, pp. ix–x^c.)

22. There is some question, however, whether it be apt to call these notions "Mandæan" this early. Perhaps. The community that cherished them and that goes by that Aramaic term for "Gnostic" (i.e., the Aramaic equivalent of that Greek term) coalesces in the next century—the fifth—or so as a distinct identifiable and self-conscious group—doing so perhaps in part as a result of these Gnostic scriptural writings, these traditions that became written, became scriptures? See my *Meaning and End of Religion* (op. cit., our chap. 2 above, note 3), pp. 283f., 285f.

23. The Mandæan texts on this are found in the *Book of John* and the *Ginzā*. See *Das Johannesbuch der Mandäer: Einleitung, Übersetzung, Kommentar*, Mark Lidzbarski, ed. & trans. (Giessen: Töpelmann, 1915), texts, pp. 137, 242; German, pp. 134 , 222; and *Ginzā: der Schatz oder das grosse Buch der Mandäer, übersetzt und erklärt von* Mark Lidzbarski (Göttingen: Vandenhoeck & Ruprecht; and Leipzig: J. C. Hinrichs, 1925), Book III, §68—p. 65; cf. the perception of these texts in Geo Widengren, *The Ascension of the Apostle and the Heavenly Book (King and Saviour III)* (Uppsala: Lundequistska; and Leipzig/Wiesbaden: Harrassowitz, 1950—Uppsala Universitets Årsskrift / Acta Universitatis Upsaliensis, 1950: 7), his chapter 4, "Mandaean Literature" (pp. [59]–76) in general, and pp. 74–75 in particular. (Note his negative statement on p. 71.)

24. In the Jewish case, Wisdom Literature, later largely included in both the Jewish and the Christian Bibles, had long since affirmed Wisdom (Hebrew, *ḥokmāh*) to be pre-existent; and had come to equate Tôrāh with it. The Near Eastern concept "Wisdom", developed thus in Israel, goes back to third-millenium-B.C. Egypt, and had become a major motif throughout the area. In the Hellenistic period, and espcially of course once the Bible was translated into Greek and became prevalent in that form, it was

correlated and by some identified with the Greek philosophic concept *sophia*. We come to Jewish consolidating of scripture (which on the whole was earlier than other groups') later in this chapter; and we return to its larger implications for Jewish life in our chapter 5 below. For an engaging recent discussion specifically of this Wisdom-Tôrāh matter, in its early phases and then especially of its later profuse elaboration, see Barbara A. Holdrege, "Torah and Creation", in her article "The Bride of Israel: the ontological status of scripture in the Rabbinic and Kabbalistic traditions", pp. 188–213 in Levering, ed., *Rethinking Scripture* (op. cit. above, our chap. 1 note 7).

25. So far as the resulting New Testament is concerned, Jerome's work provided only the four Gospels, as his revisions—in the light of the Greek—of earlier Latin translations; probably no other New Testament books were from his hand. In the case of the Old Testament, Jerome, who lived part of his life in Palestine and knew Hebrew, adopted for those Christian Scriptures the then innovative discrimination between the books in the Greek Septuagint that were also in the Hebrew canon and the several others that were original in Greek, or had been recognized as scripture only in the Greek. He coined the word "apocrypha" for these latter. The distinction hardly took hold, however, until many centuries later, after the Reformation (cf. above, our chap. 1, p. 13, with its notes 19, 20). Most editions of the Vulgate do not use the term. With regard to Jerome and the Old Testament, only books from the Hebrew were from his hand; the Latin versions of the others that became included (except the Greek parts of Daniel and Esther, and the Aramaic of Tobit and Judith) were by other translators—mostly the already circulating Old Latin versions.

26. "The first unambiguous reference to a collection of Biblical books within one cover occurs in the work of Cassiodorus (*Institutes*, I. xii. 3)", who died ca. 580; "the oldest known MS. containing the whole Vulgate is the Codex Amiatinus" at about the end of the seventh century. These quotations are from the article "Vulgate" in *The Oxford Dictionary of the Christian Church*, 2nd edn., F. L. Cross and E. A. Livingstone, edd. (London &c: Oxford University Press, 1974).

27. It was within a week of the ninth century when Alcuin finally produced a standardized text and offered it to Charles the Great at his coronation, who then pushed acceptance of this. It was not attained quickly. "Corrupt" copies, and mixed copies with partly old-Latin and partly Vulgate readings, remained current, even within his realm; let alone, outside it. Cf. also our next two notes, nos. 28 and 29, immediately below.

28. It was "the early thirteenth century" before one-volume Bibles became common, according to the careful scholars Richard H. Rouse and Mary A. Rouse: "*Statim Invenire*: schools, preachers, and new attitudes to the page", in Robert L. Benson and Giles Constable, with Carol D. Lanham, edd., *Renaissance and Renewal in the Twelfth Century* (Cambridge, Mass.: Harvard University Press, 1982), pp. [201]–225, at p. 221—"The Bible"

[should we not rather say, 'what we call the Bible'?] " . . . in the twelfth century had invariably been in multiple volumes" (ibid.) (— though cf. our note 26 above, re the Codex Amiatinus).

29. Extant mediæval manuscripts of the Vulgate differ not only in text. They differ also to some degree as to what books, especially of the New Testament, are included or excluded. In some cases, pseudo-Paul's letter to the Laodicæans, III Corinthians, and such are to be found. In more instances, books now in the canon were not there. In fact, interest in a formal "canon" concept waned after Augustine, and revived only from the twelfth century (cf. also our immediately preceding note no. 28 above). On certain aspects of the general situation, see, for instance, Kümmel, *Introduction* . . . (op. cit., our note 18 above), who nevertheless seems to hold that, despite these admitted variations, "really" the extent of the New Testament was fixed "from the beginning of the fifth century on" for the Latin Church (p. 443; Eng., p. 501), while noting that for the Greek Church and the Oriental Churches the situation for the New Testament was formally different, and even in the Western Church was so in practice also. The Gelasian Decree, variously attributed to Pope Damasus in the late fourth century, to Pope Gelasius at the end of the fifth, and to an unknown sixth-century hand, is relevant to the whole development but perhaps not as authoritatively as once it seemed.

30. See, for instance, Hans Freiherr von Campenhausen, "Das Alte Testament als Bibel der Kirche, vom Ausgang des Urchristentums bis zur Entstehung des Neuen Testaments", in his *Aus der Frühzeit des Christentums: Studien zur Kirchensgeschichte des ersten und zweiten Jahrhunderts* (Tübingen: J. C. B. Mohr [Paul Siebeck], 1963), pp. [152]–196. Also: Albert C. Sundberg, Jr., *The Old Testament of the Early Church* (Cambridge: Harvard University Press, and London: Oxford University Press, 1964— Harvard Theological Studies, xx). Sidney Jellicoe, *The Septuagint and Modern Study* (Oxford: Clarendon, 1968), as the title indicates, is primarily a presentation of recent wrestling with the many problems concerning the text that have attracted academic attention; and is biliographically rich. To the Septuagint generally, we return below.

31. . . . *war ein solches nicht einmal als Vorstellung vorhanden*—von Campenhausen, *Entstehung* . . ., (op. cit., our note 18 above), German, p. 193; Eng., p. 165. Cf. also other studies mentioned in that note. It is generally recognized today that the "Muratorian canon" was misnamed a canon.

32. Modern study begins with Harnack. The recent work of R. Joseph Hoffmann, *Marcion: On the Restitution of Christianity—an essay on the development of radical Paulinist theology in the second century* (Chico, California: Scholars Press, 1984; American Academy of Religion, Academy series, Carl A. Raschke, ed.), although not dealing primarily with the question of canon, has a full bibliography. The thesis is now widely accepted among scholars

that the emergence of a canonized New Testament was the Church's response to Marcion's initiative in proffering a specifically Christian Scripture. See, for instance, "Die Entstehung des Neuen Testaments", chap. 5 in von Campenhausen, *Entstehung* . . . (op. cit., our note 18 above), esp. pp. [173]–201, Eng. pp. 147–172; and "Der neutestamentliche Kanon", §7: 1(b) in Köster, *Einführung* . . . (op. cit., also our note 18 above), pp. 433–440; cf. also §12:3(c), pp. 767–773; English, 2:5–12, 328–334. Although I have just averred that this view is "widely accepted among scholars", yet it is not unanimous; see for instance Childs, *The New Testament as Canon* (op. cit., also our note 18 above), p. 19, with his references.

33. The Śrī Gurū Granth Ṣāḥib includes primarily the hymns and sayings of the Sikh Gurus, but also a relatively small percentage of other passages by the "Bhagats" (Panjabi; cf. Sanskrit *bhakta*) of a slightly earlier time or not formally members of what has subsequently coalesced into the Sikh community.

34. The relative force of the two Testaments, for Christian faith, has been a subtle and involuted matter. The Old began as solely authoritative, and remained for long as more authoritative; the two were in principle equal for many centuries; the extent to which the New supplements, interprets, re-interprets, or supersedes the Old defies neat or agreeable formulation.

35. See, for instance, the Lieberman chapter "Publication . . ." (op. cit., our note 17 above). See also Jacob Neusner's Richard Lectures at Virginia, summarizing his long work on the Mishnāh up to 1981: *Ancient Israel after Catastrophe: the religious world view of the Mishnah* (Charlottesville: University Press of Virginia, 1983); for his writings since that, see the several references in our chapter 5. See also that chapter generally for substantial discussion on the Mishnāh.

36. *Corpus Hermeticum*, A. D. Nock, ed., A.-J. Festugière, trans. (Paris: "Les Belles Lettres", 2 voll., 1945; 2nd edn., 1960; voll. 3, 4, *Fragments: extraits de Stobée*, Festugière, ed. & trans., 1954; vol. 4 adds also *Fragments divers*, Nock, ed., Festugière, trans.—Collection des Universités de France: Association Guillaume Budé). A good introduction is Festugière, *Hermétisme et mystique païenne* (Paris: Aubier—Montaigne, 1967).

37. An excellent recent summary for Greek developments, with full bibliography, is Zeph Stewart in his "Astrologia e magia", in Ranuccio Bianchi Bandinelli, dir., Luigi Moretti et al., redd., *Storia e Civiltà dei Greci* (Milano: Bompiani, 10 tomes in 5 voll., 1977–1979), vol. 4 (tome 8), pp. [598]–605.

38. For the entire movement, an excellent survey, with good bibliography, was the major article "Astrology" by "D.E.P."—sc. the Indologist and widely erudite historian of science David Pingree (cf. our next note) in the Macropædia, vol. 2, pp. 219–223 of The New Encyclopædia Britannica, 15th edn. (first version, 1974). In more recent versions of the

Britannica, the same 15th edn., this has been reduced to or replaced by a lesser section "Astrology" in the Macropædia article "Occultism": in the 1986 printing, vol. 25, pp. 80–84 (one may cf. the Micropædia article "Astrology", ibid., vol. 1, pp. 654–655).

39. The most consequential of these in the second century that is known was made ca. 150 A.D. at Ujjain by one Yavaneśvara from an Alexandrian text, but it has since been lost although a widely influential third-century verse-rendering of its material, the *Yavanajātaka*, has recently been published with English translation and extensive commentary: David Pingree, ed. and trans., *The Yavanajātaka of Sphujidhvaja* (Cambridge, Mass. and London: Harvard University Press, 2 voll., 1978; Harvard Oriental Series, Daniel H. H. Ingalls, ed., vol. 48). The opening pages of the introduction to this work (I: 3–6) and pointedly the "Index of Authorities cited: I. Greek and Latin" (II: 466–471) tell the story. For a somewhat earlier and more general account, see the same writer's article "Astronomy and Astrology in India and Iran", *Isis*, 54 (1963): 229–246.

40. Known also as the *Apotelesmatika*. The text has been critically edited as volume III: 1 of *Claudii Ptolemaei Opera quae exstant omnia*, F. Boll and Æ. Boer, edd. ([1940], revised edn., Leipzig: Teubner, 1957). An earlier edition of the text, with English translation on facing pages, is available as *Ptolemy: Tetrabiblos*, F. E. Robbins, ed. and trans. (London: Heinemann, and Cambridge, Mass.: Harvard University Press, 1940, fourth impr., 1964).

41. *Hephaestionis Thebani Apotelesmaticorum: libri tres, epitomae quattuor*, David Pingree, ed. (Leipzig: Teubner, 2 voll.—Bibliotheca Scriptorum Graecorum et Romanorum Teubneriana: Akademie der Wissenschaften der DDR, Zentralinstitut für alte Geschichte und Archäologie, 1973–1974).

42. For "considerably" later, see the important article of Jack N. Lightstone, "The Formation of the Biblical Canon in Judaism of Late Antiquity: prolegomenon to a general reassessment", in *[SR] Studies in Religion / Sciences religieuses*, 8 (1979): [135]–142. Even earlier writers, however, whom he convincingly criticizes, are agreed on our "later". See, for example, Sid Z. Leiman, *The Canonization of Hebrew Scripture: the Talmudic and Midrashic evidence* (Hamden, Conn.: Archon, 1976—Transactions, the Connecticut Academy of Arts and Sciences, vol. 47); specifically on the question of Javneh see pp. 120–124; and Jack P. Lewis, "What Do We Mean By Jabneh?" in Sid Z. Leiman, ed., *The Canon and Masorah of the Hebrew Bible: an introductory reader* (New York: Ktav, 1974—The Library of Biblical Studies, Harry M. Orlinsky, ed.), pp. [125]–132 (sc. 254–261). These two agree that in this matter Javneh decided nothing.

43. For a sampling of the very large and growing literature on this matter, see the Lightstone item and the two Leiman works referenced in our preceding note no. 42 just above (noting, in the Leiman-edited collection, esp. the articles of Zeitlin and Freedman; over against the latter, on "The Law and the Prophets", which argues for an early date for the canon-

izing of these two classes of texts, see the unpublished Swanson dissertation noted at p. 49 in the Childs bibliography—about to be mentioned—and the Sundberg item in our note 30 above); also Brevard S. Childs, "The Problem of the Canon", being chapter 2 of his *Introduction to the Old Testament* . . . (op. cit., our chap. 1 above, p. 15 with its note 23), pp. [46]–68, and its extensive bibliography (pp. [46]–49), noting also that work's chapp. 3, 4, pp. [69]–106. Moreover, with a somewhat diverging orientation, methodological rather than (as well as) historical, see James A. Sanders, *Torah and Canon* (Philadelphia: Fortress, 1972); *Canon and Community: a guide to canonical criticism* (ibid., 1984); and *From Sacred Story to Sacred Text: canon as paradigm* (ibid, 1987).

44. Thus we leave aside also, for others, the careful or full telling of Iranian developments; of those from Ancient Egypt; of the ceremonialized reciting in neo-Babylonian festivals of ancient epics; and other Mesopotamian matters. For properly establishing the context with which we are here concerned, no doubt these should be included. On the Iranian, cf. the bibliography listed in our note 9 above, where we touched on some of the later phases of these; I have not much investigated the pre-written phases. To one aspect of a particular use of writing in that land we return presently, in our discussion of the writing component in scripture generally. Ancient Egypt, also, is an area that I have not much explored. Relevant are the following: Leipoldt und Morenz, *Heilige Schriften* . . . (op. cit., our note 20 above); also Johannes Leipoldt, "Zur Geschichte der Auslegung", and Siegfried Morenz, "Entstehung und Wesen der Buchreligion", both in *Theologische Literaturzeitung*, 75 (1950): 229–234 and 709–716; further, C. J. Bleeker, "Religious Tradition and Sacred Books in Ancient Egypt", in Bruce & Rupp, *Holy Book* . . . (op. cit., our note 9 above), pp. 20–35. Regarding Mesopotamia, it has been suggested that one should investigate classicizing tendencies in Ashurbanipal's library. The translation process from Sumerian into Akkadian, with its of course inescapable selectivity, might be compared to the later Alexandrian canonizing of Hebrew texts? (Cf. our p. 58 below.) One scholar speaks of "long process of canonization" of Sumerian literature—William W. Hallo, p. 194 in his "Toward a History of Sumerian Literature", in *Sumerological Studies in Honor of Thorkild Jacobsen on his seventieth birthday* . . . (Chicago and London: University of Chicago Press, 1974—The Oriental Institute of the University of Chicago: Assyriological Studies, no. 20), pp.181–203; see esp. 194–201 for this author's explicit though somewhat guarded use of the terms "canon" and "canonization". W. G. Lambert, in his "Ancestors, Authors, and Canonicity", *Journal of Cuneiform Studies*, 11 (1957): 1–14, 112, had opined that "The . . . word 'canon' is unfortunate" (p. 9) in this matter; Hallo replied, e.g., in his "New Viewpoints on Cuneiform Literature", *Israel Exploration Journal* 12 (1962): 13–26, esp. 23, 26. Note, further, the section on Mesopotamian "Belles-Lettres . . ." in William W. Hallo and William Kelly Simpson, *The Ancient*

Near East: a history, John Morton Blum, gen. ed. (New York, etc.: Harcourt Brace Jovanovich, 1971), pp. 163–169. See especially the reference to the cultic reciting, in the neo-Babylonian New Year's festival, of Enūma Elish (they spell it *emūma eliš*), the "epic of creation", p. 166. Acknowledgement of a "process of canonization" of "classical literary texts", not necessarily "religious", in Mesopotamia in the latter 2nd millenium B.C. is proffered also in the Encylopaedia Judaica (1971–1972) article "Bible", vol. 4, col. 818–819.

45. What is more, of these very poets a large number of plays had been extant and are listed in the Alexandrian catalogues but were not included in the corpus as selected and preserved—and consequently those have been totally lost; they are not part of what have become in the West the Greek Classics. Curtius, *Europäische Literatur . . .* (op. cit., our chap. 1 above, note 18), German, p. 252, Eng., p. 249. Is it significant that in each case the number of plays selected was seven?

46. On this general matter see, among other sources, the following. Albin Lesky, "Die Überlieferung der griechischen Literatur", being Chapter I of his *Geschichte der griechischen Literatur* (Bern, München: Francke, [1957/1958] rev. edn. 1963), pp. [15]–20—cf. the English translation of the revised edition: "The transmission of Greek literature," in his *A History of Greek Literature*, trans. James Willis and Cornelis de Heer (London: Methuen, 1966), pp. 1–6. Rudolf Pfeiffer, *History of Classical Scholarship* (Oxford: Clarendon Press, 2 voll., 1968–1976)—see especially vol. I: *From the Beginings to the End of the Hellenistic Age*, chiefly Part Two, "The Hellenistic Age", pp. [87] ff.; particularly its chap. 5, "Alexandrian Scholarship at its Height . . .", pp. [171]–209, esp. p. 203 to the end. (See also, in his vol. II: *From 1300 to 1850*, p. 84, a discussion of the first use, at the Renascence, of the terms *classicus, classici.*) "G.P.G." (sc. Georges Paul Gusdorf), "The Hellenistic Period", p. 1172–1173 in his article "Humanistic Scholarship, History of" in the New Encyclopædia Britannica, 15th edn., 1974, Macropædia, 8: 1170–1179 (this entire article has been dropped from more recent printings of the 15th edn.). Ernst Robert Curtius, "Klassik", being chapter 14 of his *Europäische Literatur . . .* (op. cit., our chap. 1 above, note 18), pp. 251–274; English, "Classicism", pp. 247–272 (cf. also his chap. 16; "Das Buch als Symbol", pp. 304–351; "The Book as Symbol", pp. 302–347).

47. This Greek term was in current use among Hellenistic Jews, the equivalent to their earlier term *sôpᵉrîm, sōpᵉrîm*, in Hebrew, originally "people who know how to write" and used in the Old Testament (where it too is rendered as "scribes" in the King James Authorised and other English versions) for recording secretaries, and later for this class of religious leaders teaching and interpreting the (sc. written) Tôrāh.

48. A good deal has been written on this matter, without necessarily using the concept "scripture". One interesting example is the first lecture of James Adam's 1904–1906 Gifford Lectures, posthumously published as his

The Religious Teachers of Greece (Edinburgh: T. & T. Clark, 1908), perhaps especially a passage pp. 7–16.

49. Aristotle's "writings" that have come down to us exercising an incalculable impact on Western civilization became writings only after his death, as spoken lectures posthumously published by his pupils; the books that he wrote have all been lost (with one possible exception recently discovered).

50. We have spoken basically of the Greek classics. The Latin Classics, equally or even more important in certain phases of Western civilization into modern times, were consolidated somewhat later, beginning largely and deliberately under Augustus in a process that also then should be noted as a Roman component characterizing that phase in the general Mediterranean and Middle Eastern scripturalizing process that we are noting.

51. The notion of the miracle was subsequently embellished, but is based on a work known as the "Letter of Aristeas to Philocrates". This has been published, with a careful Introduction, as *Aristeas to Philocrates (Letter of Aristeas)*, Moses Hadas, ed. and trans. (New York: Harper & Brothers, 1951, for The Dropsie College—Solomon Zeitlin, ed.-in-chief, Jewish Apocryphal Literature). The exact date of this letter within the second century is still under discussion; Hadas opted for ca. 130 B.C. (p. 54). Cf. E. Bickermann, "Zur Datierung des Pseudo-Aristeas", *Zeitschrift für die neutestamentliche Wissenschaft und die Kunde der älteren Kirche*, 29 (1930): 280–298.

52. Cf. our note 44 above, for the comparable issue in translating from Sumerian into Akkadian.

53. For modern scholarly positions on the Septuagint and matters treated in the above paragraph in our text and the one preceding it, see Jellicoe, *The Septuagint* . . . (op. cit., our note 30 above) and the other works there mentioned.

54. And even then, not fully. See our note 25 above and its reff. to our chap. 1, for a continuing place in even Protestant usage for the Septuagint-derived parts of the Bible, the "Apocrypha". Reformation Bibles in modern vernaculars, however, such as the King James Authorised version, translated those parts of the Bible that were originally Hebrew from Hebrew, no longer from Septuagint Greek.

55. See, for instance, Lesky, *Geschichte*, and vol. 1 of Rudolf Pfeiffer, *History* . . . (opp. citt. above, our note 46).

56. On this development see especially Jean Pépin, *Mythe et allégorie: les origines grecques et les contestations judéo-chrétiennes* ([1958], nouvelle édn., Paris: Études augustiniennes, 1976).

57. Geo Widengren, *The Ascension of the Apostle* . . . (op. cit., our note 23 above); and his *Muḥammad, the Apostle of God, and his Ascension (King and Saviour V)* (Uppsala: Lundequistska, and Wiesbaden: Harrassowitz, 1955—Uppsala Universitets Årsskrift 1955: 1). This material brings into focus matters that were adumbrated in some of this author's earlier Swedish

work, *Religionens Värld: religionsfenomenologiska studier och översikter* (Stockholm: Svenska Kyrkans Diakonistyrels, 1945) and were developed by him later in his revised German translation of the second edition (1953) of that Swedish work: *Religionsphänomenologie* (Berlin: de Gruyter, 1969).

58. En-me-dur-an-ki, a legendary Sumerian king from before The Flood. The text, in (transcribed) Akkadian with French trans. on opposite pages, is given in, e.g., Paul Dhorme, *Choix de textes religieux assyro-babyloniens: transcription, traduction, commentaire* (Paris: Victor Lecoffre / J. Gabalda, 1907—Études Bibliques), pp. [140]–147; some of the relevant opening section is cited by Widengren, *Ascension* . . . (op. cit., our note 23 above), pp. [7]–8. The quotation that we have given above is of verse 8 (Dhorme, pp. [140]–141), repeated twice as verses 14 and 16 (pp. 142–143).

59. So the usual view. Driver and Miles, in a footnote, doubt that the relationship between the god and the laws is quite so clear, though relationship clearly there is: the diorite stele mentioned in the latter part of the sentence in our presentation has at its top an engraving of the god, with Hammurabi reverently before him and the text of the laws engraved around the stone below. See G. R. Driver and John C. Miles, edd., *The Babylonian Laws*, edited with translation and commentary, vol. 1, "Legal Commentary" (Oxford: Clarendon, 1952), p. 28, and its fn. 4.

60. Also, sun-god; *shamash* is the Semitic word for the sun. Both he and Adad were oracle-givers, to whom requests for oracles were addressed.

61. In modern English the colloquial phrase "cut in stone" is still used, to signify metaphorically what is enduring rather than transient: timeless—though the transcendent dimension of the phrase has been almost entirely lost.

62. Qur'ān 85:22, etc.

63. Exodus 24:12, etc. (The term rendered "tablets" in the Akkadian text that we have quoted is, on the other hand, not a Semitic word at all but a loan-word [*duppi*] from Sumerian.)

64. E. Theodore Mullen, Jr., *The Divine Council in Canaanite and Early Hebrew Literature* (Chico, California: Scholars Press, 1980—Harvard Semitic Museum: Harvard Semitic Monographs, Frank Moore Cross, Jr., ed., no. 24). (Note: The title of this book on the outside cover differs from that given here, which is from the title-page: it reads, rather, *The Assembly of the Gods*.) Echoes of the "tablets of destiny" idea in Jewish apocalyptic literature and in the Qumrān materials is (sc., had been) noted in, for instance, John J. Collins, *The Apocalyptic Vision of the Book of Daniel* (n.p. [sc., Chico, California and Cambridge, Massachusetts]: Scholars Press, for Harvard Semitic Museum, 1977—Harvard Semitic Monographs, Frank Moore Cross, Jr., ed., no. 16), p. 80, with notes p. 91. One must note, of course, that apart from any link specifically with scripture, or with the Near East, imagery is widespread and persistent throughout the religious history of the world of an ascension of a special human being to heavenly spheres and on

returning reporting to his or her fellow humans the vision had there or (some of) the knowledge gained there—from shamans to others of many types.

65. Codified, but not yet as a book, in today's sense of the word; it remained an oral text for some time. Cf. our note 17 above. Throughout this paragraph, our delineation over-simplifies by telescoping somewhat the wide-ranging transition from book form to written book form, on which we have touched above more than once. The nineteenth-century view of Scripture with which I grew up was particularly reified, as was typical of several aspects of Western nineteenth-century religious thought generally perhaps.

66. See David Diringer, *The Alphabet: a key to the history of mankind* ([London: Hutchinson, 1948], third ed., *completely revised with the collaboration of* Reinhold Regensburger (2 voll., London: Hutchinson, and New York: Funk & Wagnalls, 1968). Despite the book's title, in fact Part I (pp. 15–141 of vol. 1) of this third edn. deals explicitly with non-alphabetic writing, the cuneiform and the hieroglyphic of Mesopotamia and Egypt, and the various others.

67. Diringer, ibid., vol. 1, esp. pp. 159f.

68. II Kings 22 and 23. Some modern scholars put the date as 622, rather.

69. Of modern scholarship I have followed largely E. W. Nicholson, *Deuteronomy and Tradition* (Oxford: Blackwell, and Philadelphia: Fortress, 1967).

70. For a situating of the Josiah-Deuteronomy "reform" in a broader geographic context and a linking of it with the then contemporary situation in Egypt and esp. Assyria, see William Foxwell Albright, *From the Stone Age to Christianity: monotheism and the historical process* (Baltimore: Johns Hopkins, and London: Oxford, [1940] 2nd ed. 1946), pp. 241–244.

71. "Behistun" is the traditional Western name; the present-day village near which it stands is in modern Persian Bīsitūn or Bīsutūn or Bīsotūn. See [L. W. King and R. C. Thompson, with prefatory remarks by E. A. Wallis Budge and Mr. King], *The Sculptures and Inscription of Darius the Great on the Rock of Behistûn in Persia: a new collation of the Persian, Susian, and Babylonian texts, with English translations, etc.; with illustrations* (London: The British Museum, 1907). In addition to the texts, this gives a good and illustrated description of the monument. A more recent edition and translation of the Old Persian text are found in Roland G. Kent, *Old Persian: grammar—texts—lexicon* ([1950], second edition, New Haven, Connecticut: American Oriental Society, 1953), pp. 116–134. A more accessible brief account is available in, for instance, A. T. Olmstead, *History of the Persian Empire (Achaemenid period)* (Chicago: University of Chicago Press, 1948), pp. 116–118.

72. The blessing and curse are to be found on lines 72–80 of the fourth column—in Kent, *Old Persian* . . . (op. cit., preceding note, 71, just above), text, pp. 129–130; translation, p. 132, §§66–67.

73. Cf. Revelation 22:18-19. Coming as this does at the end not only of the Book of Revelation, but of the Western Christian Bible, this passage has often been read as applying to the Bible generally. A similar motif is common among inscriptions of the Græco-Roman world, especially of tombstones; though here the curse is often on those who disturb the tomb, rather than on those who disturb the writing as such. Some such inscriptions may ante-date Darius, although the majority are later. I do note that this type of curse is evidently considerably more common among Greek tombstones in Asia Minor than in Greece itself. See Richmond Lattimore, *Themes in Greek and Latin Epitaphs* (Urbana: University of Illinois Press, 1942—Illinois Studies in Language and Literature, vol. XXVIII, nos. 1–2), esp. pp. 106–126 (cf. on Christian inscriptions, pp. 306–309). (At a more general level, not referring specifically to a written text, cf. also such passages as Deuteronomy 4:2 and 12:32. One may note also W. C. van Unnik, "De la règle Μήτε προσθεῖναι μήτε 'αφελεῖν dans l'histoire du canon", [*Vigiliae Christianae*, 3 (1949): 1–36], in his *Sparsa Collecta* . . . (op. cit., our note 18 above), 2: [123]–156.)

74. See Willard Gurdon Oxtoby, *Some Inscriptions of the Safaitic Bedouin* (New Haven, Conn.: American Oriental Society, 1968—American Oriental Series, Ernest Bender, ed., vol. 50); esp. p. 17.

75. Cf. our chap. 2 above, note 47.

4. The True Meaning of Scripture: The Qur'ān as an Example

1. In other chapters I give documentation for the particular data on which my presentation, interpretation, and argument are based, so that specialists in the field concerned knowing more than I do in each case may assess the validity. In the Islamic case here, my thesis has grown out of half an adult life of academic study, much greater familiarity with the languages involved, years of living in Muslim lands, and having Muslims as good friends. Accordingly, here I give references only for direct quotations, plus notes of general rather than specialist purport.

2. I owe to my former colleague Krister Stendahl the original of this aphorism, which he tells me is current in Swedish in the form "theology is . . . ". One may compare the remark of the nineteenth-century American philosopher of religion Charles Carroll Everett: "religion is poetry believed in" (although his meaning for "believe" here is not manifest, his era being in the midst of the transition from that term's old sense of giving loyalty to a recognized truth, taking it seriously to heart and life, to its modern sense of imagining to be true. One may readily suppose that he had the older meaning in mind, since his sentence goes on to say: "when poetry is true, it is truer than anything beside"). This is taken from C. C. Everett, *Poetry, Comedy, and Duty* (Boston and New York: Houghton, Mifflin—Cambridge:

Riverside Press, 1890), p. 44. My taking the liberty of speaking here of "religion" rather than "theology" has to do with my sense that poetry also lies not in the poem itself but in a human involvement in it, discernment of it. Poetry is a human quality, finding expression in overt forms; it too is a human activity.

3. On the Western academic treatment of the Bible so, not as scripture but as any other book, cf. above, our chap. 1; and we return to the issue in our concluding chapter.

4. In my "Some Similarities and Some Differences . . ." (op. cit., our chap. 3 above, note 2), pp. 56–58 (1959), 244–245 (1981, 1985) .

5. Some would say: the ability of truth and goodness to get themselves discerned? Theists might say, God's success has been strikingly varied in enabling humans to discern. (A certain kind of exclusivist might say, His—they would select only the masculine pronoun—choosing to enable those in religious traditions other than their own to discern, has been particularized, or "strikingly limited"?)

6. Surah 17:1. A night journey is explicit in that verse; there can be a question as to whether an ascent to heaven is mentioned, but certainly most Muslims have seen and heard it so. It is this "ascension" that Widengren links scripturally to ancient Mesopotamian motifs, and that we noted in our chap. 3 above, at pp. 59–60. Such an ascension-to-heaven motif, quite apart from scripturality, has been common throughout much of the religious life of the world.

7. Besides, mediævals—Western, Islamic, and many others—took dreams seriously. Interesting, also, is the sensitive comment of a modern scholar, on the interpretation that the "ascension took place in spirit; it is a question of a vision that occurred during the Prophet's sleep. In a sense it was Heaven that visited Muḥammad"—J. E. Bencheikh, in the article MIʿRĀDJ in *The Encyclopaedia of Islam, new edition* (Leiden: Brill, and London: Luzac, several volumes and Supplements; in process, 1960–), 7: 101. This article (7: 97–105) (1990), in several sections and by various hands (B. Schrieke et al.) gives a careful summary of much of the discussion, with extensive bibliographies.

8. A thesis of Dante's crucial dependence on Islamic sources for one of Western civilization's greatest poems was first set forth carefully and with rich documentation in a study by the Catholic priest and leading Arabic scholar Miguel Asín Palacios. See his *La escatología musulmana en la Divina Comedia, seguida de la Historia y crítica de una polémica* (Madrid, Granada: Escuelas de estudios árabes de Madrid y Granada, 1943; tercera edición, Madrid, 1961, Instituto Hispano Árabe de Cultura). As the title indicates, this is a combination of two items: (i) a republication, with minimal change, of his earlier book (Madrid, 1919, with the first seven words of the 1943 title), and (ii) a republication of a journal article (1924, under its last six words) in which he had set forth a balanced and informative year-by-year

outline of the debate elicited by the first item—the outline is here updated to carry the story beyond its original five-year coverage, to 1943—and his careful answers to significant objections that had been raised. The original work had attracted wide and agitated attention in Europe and stirred vigorous controversy, its conclusions seeming startling to all and threatening to some, its arguments proving at once or soon convincing to many—probably a majority of literary critics, Dante scholars, and orientalists—but eliciting also zealous resistance from some, especially patriotic Italian Danteists. Today, virtually all concerned accept the thesis that he had propounded, and had underwritten with elaborate evidence. On the background of the matter, see also the *Encyclopaedia of Islam* article MI'RĀDJ in our immediately preceding note, no. 7, above.

9. The construction of our previous chapter turns out to be an exhibit of this; we recall our insistence that it was but a first step—followed by the attempt in this chapter to understand its eventual outcome.

10. The standard Western move of (Christian, Jewish, secularist) scholars has been to stress political, economic, and other merely mundane factors in these conversions, hardly pausing to consider *religious* and intellectual grounds for (particularly Christians') becoming Muslim. Indeed, there has often been an underlying (or overt!) presumption that conversions were, must have been, insincere. Although all religious history, Christian and other, evinces instances of such, to make it a blanket judgement is to insult also those millions of Christians and Jews who made the move.

11. This paragraph is taken from my "The Study of Religion and the Study of the Bible", *Journal of the American Academy of Religion*, 39 (1971): 133.

12. For an instance of the quite parallel development in Western academic study of the Indian Veda last century and a discerning comment on it by a sympathetic yet penetrating modern Indian philosopher, see the remarks of J. L. Mehta on F. Max Müller in our chap. 6 below, p. 136.

13. I have enjoyed showing my students an entrancing book illustrating the mood: *Error's Chains: How Forged and Broken—a complete, graphic, and comparative history of the many strange beliefs, superstitious practices, domestic peculiarities, . . . of mankind throughout the world, . . . by* Frank S. Dobbins, *assisted by Hon.* S. Wells Williams *and* Isaac Hall, *the whole profusely illustrated . . .* (New York: Standard Publishing House, 1883). It presents, in close to 800 pages, "The odd and the curious, the enchanting and the revolting . . . factors of heathen devotion" (from the second sentence of the Preface, p. v). Beyond this general self-righteousness, in the special case of Islam the West inherited from a thousand years earlier an antagonism of which few recognize the persistence (until today) or the depth. Of India and China the West became aware only after it was no longer afraid of anybody; by the Islamic world—with which alone it shared a common frontier—it had at times been cowed, and over several centuries remained threatened. The

siege of Vienna was lifted only in 1683; and the memory of the Crusades (largely now unconscious or subconscious on the Western side) is still an important factor in world politics in the late twentieth century. Recent Western fear and bitterness expressed in anti-Communism were relatively mild, and strikingly short-lived, in comparison with centuries of mediæval anti-Islamic perceptions and emotions. On the terror evoked in mediæval Europe, and the grotesque portrayal of Muhammad in particular—as a Satanic figure replete with horns, and morally abominable—see illuminating recent studies such as Norman Daniel, *Islam and the West: the making of an image* (Edinburgh: the University Press, 1960); R. W. Southern, *Western Views of Islam in the Middle Ages* (Cambridge, Mass.: Harvard University Press, 1962); and Kenneth M. Setton, *Western Hostility to Islam: and prophecies of Turkish Doom* (Philadelphia: American Philosophical Society—Memoirs, vol. 201, 1992). In this connection, it is important to recognize how Western academic and even Christian missionary studies, both in the Islamic and in other cases, whatever their earlier phases, have in recent times themselves contributed immeasurably to gradually increasing Western appreciation of non-Western religious movements, including the Islamic.

14. In this connection it is interesting to notice a century's shift in dictionary meanings for "Buddhism", from the 1888 six-word definition "The religious system founded by Buddha" in the first edn. of the Oxford English Dictionary to "a religion of eastern and central Asia growing out of the teaching of Gautama Buddha . . ." (Webster's, ninth edn. of their *New Collegiate Dictionary*), 1989—although even the latter, while its "growing out of" metaphor is commendable, is still too reified and too doctrinal for my taste (it goes on to define that "teaching" in eighteen words), underplaying the living complexity of religious, as of all human, life. After another while (but one may hope—and presume?—not another century), still further improvement will see "a religion" here superseded by "a religious movement" (and "teaching", by something more integrated; the impact and then the embroidered memory of Siddhārtha's total personality on his immediate followers, and of its embroidered image on later ones, and the community dimension throughout, were surely not negligible). For "Hinduism"—a rather absurd noun—which among other things had no "founder", this Western mind-set focussing on beginnings fastened instead, as we shall observe in our chapter 6 below, on "the Veda", the earliest "texts" of the movement, with equally distorting results.

15. Yet if the hearer's feelings are hurt by a remark, or votes alienated, or an article or book is misunderstood, the speaker or writer is not fully exonerated by having "meant no harm" (as feminists these days are stressing), nor by having meant something different (as politicians know well, and authors eventually learn).

16. The concluding two lines of his "Ars Poetica". Archibald MacLeish,

Streets in the Moon (Boston and New York: Houghton Mifflin—Cambridge: The Riverside Press, 1926), p. 38.

17. In the natural sciences, on the other hand, in contradistinction from most human discourse, statements aim at impersonalism, it would seem. Even here, however, fortunately it is not fully reached. To some people, "e=mc²" means little or nothing; to physicists it has come to mean more and more, as further work has continued apace and its richness further uncovered. It means more today than it did to Einstein, certainly (although in subtle ways also, less).

18. For a challenge of the traditional but facile view that the Qur'ān— and by implication, then, we may say: any scripture or indeed any remark or any piece of music or other human construct—is *either* the word of God *or* that of a human being, but not both, see my "Is the Qur'an the Word of God?", chap. 2 of my *Questions of Religious Truth* (New York: Scribner's, and London: Gollancz, 1967), reprinted in Willard G. Oxtoby, ed., *Religious Diversity* (New York and London: Harper & Row, 1976), pp. 23–40, and in my *On Understanding Islam* (op. cit. above, chap. 3, note 2), pp. 283–300.

19. Those of us that speak English may say that *fenêtre* in French means "window". Less illegitimate would be to say that *fenêtre* in French means what "window" means in English—but still more exactly, more personally: that French-speakers mean by *fenêtre* what English-speakers mean by "window". Only this last mode does justice to the truth that meaning is first and last a human matter. It is always people who mean, or to whom something means something; not words. The meaning of *fenêtre* does not in the final analysis lie in the word; it lies (has always lain) in the minds and hearts of people who speak and understand French—and *nowhere else*. We return to this issue in our concluding chapter below.

20. *Man qara'a al-Qur'ān fa-ka-innamā shāfahanī wa-shāfahtuhu.* This Ḥadīth Qudsī is recorded in Badī'u-z-Zamān Furūzānfar, *Aḥādīth mathnawī* (Tehran, [1327 (sc., *hijrī*=1909)], 1341[=1922–1923]³), p. 17, citing *Kunūz al-Ḥaqā'iq*, p. 132. My translation.

21. The Christian doctrine of the Holy Spirit would make this a rich theological interpretation of the whole world's scriptural history.

22. A classical humanist might resist this thesis on the grounds that it could seem nihilist—as advocating "anything goes". Such a humanist might accept the suggestion that this constitutes indeed the actual meaning of the Qur'an as scripture—or any other instance of the *genre*; but balk at recognizing it as its *true* meaning (as in our chapter heading). In such a view people should recognize as truly scripture only what is indeed true and good. A response would be that classical humanism (as we shall revert to considering in our chapter 8 below) involves a faith in humanity—recognized as higher ideally than actually—such that, accepting the view just

noted, it would hold that hundreds of millions of persons (including the group's most intelligent) over a long series of centuries would cherish as transcendingly good and true only a scripture that was, or in a way that was, to some degree related to that ideal dimension of being human that classical humanism consists in sensing. This idealist postulate can be seen as some sort of classical-humanist counterpart to a theist doctrine of the Holy Spirit's activity within human history, illumining, and to some extent constraining, the *actual* human from within. To this point too we shall return in our concluding chapter. In the meantime, we may note, and indeed emphasize, our contention in an earlier paragraph here that the actual meaning that the scripture or any part of it has had for persons who treat it scripturally has *ipso facto* included, elicited, nurtured, a (*lege*, this?) transcendent facet. One may also argue, on the basis of observation, that all major scriptures manifestly have in fact included (have purveyed) matters that are good and true, as well as—admittedly—others that are not. In both connections I would feel that all that can be required of a scripture, or any other use of words, is not that it be true in an absolute sense—that is a position that the pluralist modern world is compelled to move beyond; but that it elicit an approximation to truth, preferably the closest approximation of which the persons concerned are capable. It is immoral to interpret scripture in a way less true than it might be—but also, inept to have a general theory of scripture, one's own or others', less true than one might rise to.

5. The Bible in Jewish Life?

1. Although it has long since passed, there was a time when the Hebrew term for "covenant", *bᵉrît*, and specifically the phrase "book of the covenant", *sēper ha-b-bᵉrît*, were in fact used by Jews on occasion—even if it not be clear how frequently—with reference to their nascent scriptures. For the phrase, cf. Exodus 24:7, II Kings 23:2, 21. Jews in Hellenistic times sometimes used as counterpart the Greek word *diathēkē* as in Ecclesiasticus ("[The Wisdom of Jesus ben] Sira[ch]") 24:23 (in the Septuagint; in the Vulgate this verse is 24:32) and I Maccabees 1:57 (Vulgate, 1:60). Christians also then used this Greek term for the "covenant" idea, and it lies behind their Latin and Latin-derived term "Testament". In more recent ages, the concepts *bᵉrît* and "covenant" have continued central in Jewish outlook, but without specific relation to a book or books. In the Christian case, the opposite movement has occurred: "testament", originally referring to what Jews called *bᵉrît*, has dropped that connotation and become fixed as referring to scripture. (The remark in our text here, "as we have previously noted", refers to chapter 3 above, p. 51 and its note 18.) Note that the word "testament" occurs thirteen times in the King James Authorised Version of the Bible, translating *diathēkē* from the Greek (but never *bᵉrît* from

the Hebrew); most notably in the then ritualized phrase "this cup is the new testament in my blood" (Luke 22:20 and I Corinthians 11:25; cf. Matthew 26:28 and Mark 14:24). It is everywhere replaced in the Revised Standard Version: eleven times by "covenant", twice (in a single context, Hebrews 9:16 and 17) by "will" (as in "last will and testament"). For the early history and pre-history of the Jewish concept one may refer to two articles of George E. Mendenhall, "Ancient Oriental and Biblical Law" and "Covenant Forms in Israelite Tradition", in *The Biblical Archaeologist*, 17 (1954): 2:26–46 and 3:50–76 respectively; these were subsequently issued together as a pamphlet under the title *Law and Covenant in Israel and the Ancient Near East* (Pittsburgh, Penna.: Presbyterian Board of Colportage, 1955).

2. This would be automatically true for those whose sensitivity to the transcendence in their environment is lively—sensitivity to the presence of God, to use theist vocabulary. Moreover, it has been standard for Jews in later ages to hold that God was speaking through Moses not only to the Israelites of that day but also and decidedly to their descendants. (This was explicit in the understanding of the passage in Deuteronomy 29, verses 13–14 in the Hebrew, 14–15 in English versions.) The immediacy is further formalized in the commentaries. See, for example, Rashî on Deuteronomy 6:6, which immediately follows the *shᵉmaʿ*. The Biblical verse reads, "And these words, which I command thee this day . . .". Explicating this last phrase, Rashî indicates that "this day" [*ha-y-yôm*] is to be read as signifying the day that the commands are being heard or read, rather than a day in the past when they were first being given. They are constantly re-iterated afresh. Thus the commandments, he explicitly remarks, are to be treated not as ancient but as new, fresh (*hᵃdāshāh*); the situation is likened to a scene conjured up of crowds hurrying out into the streets to hear the latest royal proclamation. I have used the following edition, of Hebrew text with English translation: Abraham ben Isaiah and Benjamin Sharfman, edd., *Ḥᵃmishshāh Ḥûmᵉshê Tôrāh, ʿim Pêrûsh Rashî bi-kᵉtāb mᵉrubbāʿ* [*] *û-mᵉnuqqād* [*] *mᵉturgām* [*] *angᵉlît lᵉ-pî shûrāh / The Pentateuch and Rashi's Commentary: a linear translation into English* (Brooklyn, N.Y.: S. S. & R. Publishing Co., 5 voll., 1949), vol. 5, *Sēper Dᵉbārîm / Deuteronomy*, p. 65. Rashî here is following (virtually word-for-word, including even the by-his-day rare Hellenist loan-word *dᵉyôṭagmâ*, "a public edict"; Greek *diatagma*), the early Midrash on Deuteronomy from the Tannaitic period called *Ṣiprê*—as indeed I get the impression that virtually all other commentators on this verse had and have done over the centuries (and still do today: e.g., Hertz, *Pentateuch and Haftorahs*—op. cit. below, our note 16, 1960 edn. p. 771). For the text: *Ṣiprê ʿal-Sēper Dᵉbārîm, ʿim ḥillûpê girṣâʾôt wᵉ-heʿārôt . . . mēʾēt Ēlîʿazar Aryēʾ Pînqelsṭayʾn, bᵉ-Hishtammᵉshût ʿiz ᵉbônô she-li-*Ḥayyîm Shâʾûl Hārāʾôwîṭç (New York: Bêt ha-m-Midrash li-r-Rabbānîm bᵉ-ʾAmērîqāh, ʾ729 [sc.=1968–1969]). An English version: *Sifre to Deuteronomy: an analytical*

translation, Jacob Neusner, trans. (Atlanta, Georgia: Scholars Press, 2 voll.: vol. 1, 1987; vol. 2, n.d. [sc. 1987 or 1988]—Brown Judaic Studies, Jacob Neusner, ed., nos. 98, 101), vol. 1, p. 91.

3. Ultimately the word "Bible" derives from the Jewish use of *ha-ṣ-ṣᵉpārîm*, "the Books", in Hebrew, and its counterpart used for a time by Greek-speaking Jews in the Hellenistic period, *ta Biblia*. Later this was elaborated into "the Holy Books": in Greek, *ta hagia Biblia*, or *hay hierai biblioi*, both of which are found in Jewish Greek writing, although they never became as current there as among Christians; they were supplemented also by *hai hierai graphai* ("the holy writings") which it is my impression became rather more common. This shift from "the Books" to "the Holy Books"—evident also a little later in Hebrew (*kitᵉbê ha-q-qōdesh*)— is considered below later in this chapter.

4. (*Tanak*, according to the transliteration system that I use in this book, which for Hebrew and Aramaic reproduces the consonants as written, and therefore for the *bᵉgadkᵉpat* letters neglects what in a pointed text would be an absence of *dagesh lene*.) English versions published by the Jewish Publication Society regularly bore the title *The Holy Scriptures* in editions prior to 1985; since that date, the new term has appeared on a new version, whose title-page reads: *Tanakh: a new translation of The Holy Scriptures, according to the traditional Hebrew text* (Philadelphia, New York, Jerusalem: The Jewish Publication Society 5746 · 1985). (The word *Tanakh* of the title is written both in roman and in Hebrew script. Also, on the facing page, the names of its three components are written out in full both in roman and in Hebrew script.) Reading the Bible in English began among Jews in a substantial way in the eighteenth century, for a time using chiefly the King James Authorised Version or, presently, Jewish modifications of it, later producing Jewish translations. See also the section Anglo-Jewish Versions (vol 4, coll. 871–872) in the article Bible of the *Encylopaedia Judaica* (1971–1972). I have not been able to find any instance of *Tanakh* rather than *Bible* as title in English before 1985, but I am of course not in a position to affirm that it did not occur.

5. Or Christians, if they distribute the various "books" of their Old Testament into groups at all, do so differently. Their usual groupings are: the Historical books (of these a sub-set are the first five, the "five books of Moses", called the Pentateuch in scholarly circles in recent times), the Psalms, the Wisdom writings, and the Prophets. These divisions are hardly household words among most Christians, however, except the second (and to a lesser extent, the fourth).

6. This is in the Protestant Bible. The Roman Catholic Old Testament ends with II Maccabees (although the Jewish Septuagint that it translates did not).

7. And indeed by different centuries. One of many illustrative examples of recent studies of instances of the fact as regards the Bible is Jack P.

Lewis, *A Study of the Interpretation of Noah and the Flood in Jewish and Christian Literature* (Leiden: Brill, 1968). Another is Daniel Jeremy Silver, *Images of Moses* (New York: Basic Books, 1982).

8. One illustrative example is studied with thoroughness in Adolf Posnanski, *Schiloh: ein Beitrag zur Geschichte der Messiaslehre*, Erster Teil: *Die Auslegung von Genesis 49, 10 im Altertume bis zu Ende des Mittelalters* (Leipzig: J. C. Hinrichs, 1904).

9. An example was supplied by *The Fifty-third Chapter of Isaiah according to the Jewish Interpreters / Pêrûshê Hinnēh Yaskîl 'Abdî 'al-pî Ḥakemê Yisrā'ēl* . . ., vol. I: *Texts* [sc. in Hebrew, Greek, Aramaic, Arabic, Latin, Spanish, French], *edited from printed books and mss. by* Ad. [sc. Adolf] Neubauer; vol II: *Translations* [in English], *by* S. R. Driver and Ad. Neubauer, *with an introduction to the translations by* Rev. E. B. Pusey (Oxford and London: James Parker [sc., Oxford University Press]; Leipzig: T. O. Weigel; 1876–1877). Both volumes have been reprinted in Harry M. Orlinsky, ed., The Library of Biblical Studies (New York: Ktav, 1969; and with title-page bearing the modified title *The "Suffering Servant" of Isaiah, according to the Jewish interpreters*, the second volume was reprinted separately, New York: Hermon Press, 1969).

10. In general the history of the on-going political role of the story is rather vibrantly told in Michael Walzer, *Exodus and Revolution* (New York: Basic Books, 1985).

11. Or more carefully, in negative form: that they are *ên* . . . *ellâ*, "not different", "not other"—the Zōhar. (Cf. the Islamic counterpart: our chap. 3 above, note 4.) I have used the following edition: "Shim'ôn ben Yôḥa'î" [reputed second-century author; actually, in its present form at least, probably by Moses de León (Mōsheh ben Shēm Ṭôb) d. 1305], *Sēper ha-z-Zōhar 'al Ḥᵃmishshāh Ḥûmshê Tôrāh* . . ., Rᵉ'ûben b. Mōsheh Margōliyôt, ed. (Yᵉrûshālayim: Môṣad hā-Rāb Qûq, 3 voll., '724/1964, re-issued '730/[sc. 1970]; one could say 4 voll., since a fresh title-page—vol. 3: f. [116 recto]/p. [231]—introduces another, *Sēper Bᵉ-Midbar-Dᵉbārîm*, although that "volume", in the traditional pattern [established from the first printed edition, Mantua, 1558–1560], is printed and bound with the third in continuous pagination; to both, reff. here and subsequently are given as "vol. 3:" plus the relevant folio and page numbers). This statement is found at vol. 2: f. 60 recto / p. [119] and again f. 60 verso / p. 120. More positively, though this time indirectly: "the Tôrāh is . . . the Name of God Himself . . . [and] He and His Name are one"—vol. 2: f. 90 verso / p. 180. (That "He and His name are one" had already been re-iterated: cf. vol. 2: f. 86 recto / p. [171], vol. 2: f. 87 recto / p. [173]). English translation: *The Zohar. Translated by* Harry Sperling, Maurice Simon, *and* (voll. 3,4) Paul P. Levertoff (London: Soncino, 5 voll., 1931–1934), vol. 3, pp. 188 (bis), 278, 261, 264. In the matter of the relation between God and His Self-communication to humankind, once again (cf. our chap. 3 above, note 4 also) one notes that

parallels are not too far-fetched between these Jewish (and Islamic) perceptions and Christian trinitarian doctrines that God the Creator—the Father—and God as revealed on earth—the Son—are (along with God as Holy Spirit) "one God".

12. On a conception of a wedding, with the Tôrāh seen either as the marriage contract for the permanent union of God and Israel, or alternatively as a bride given to Israel by her father, God, see the important article of Barbara A. Holdrege, "The Bride of Israel . . . " (op. cit., our chap. 3 above, note 24), pp. 180–261, esp. pp. 184–185. Also, Holdrege, *Torah and Veda* (Albany: State University of New York Press), forthcoming.

13. This English term "Pentateuch", one of whose Greek elements means "five", falls on outsiders' ears as a whit recondite; it is slightly less uncongenial to Jews because of their re-iterated and explicit sense of there being indeed five books, together making up a distinct and precise entity. The Hebrew phrase *Ḥᵃmishshāh Ḥûmshê Tôrāh* ("the five fifths of Torah": sc., the five books of the Pentateuch) is established. In English, for example, in the *Encyclopaedia Judaica* (1971–1972) the article TORAH, READING OF, begins: "The practice of reading the Pentateuch (Torah) . . .". On the other hand, one may note that its main article TORAH deals rather with the concept in our fourth sense below, as extra-scriptural; while the article BIBLE is a quite different one (in it too the word "Pentateuch" occurs—as in our note 17 below). Of the first two articles mentioned here (15: 1246–1255 and 1235–1246) the authors are, respectively, "I.J.", sc. Immanuel Jakobovits, and "W.H.", sc. Warren Harvey; the complex BIBLE article, 78 pp. in all, is by many hands.

14. And, as we note in our next paragraph, on festival days also from the "Five Scrolls".

15. See Jacob Mann, *The Bible as Read and Preached in the Old Synagogue: a study in the cycles of the readings from Torah and Prophets, as well as from Psalms, and in the structure of the Midrashic homilies* (Cincinnati, Ohio: vol. I published by the author, 1940; vol. II—which is by Mann and Isaiah Sonne, both posthumously—Victor E. Reichert, ed., Cincinnati, Ohio: Hebrew Union College / Jewish Institute of Religion, 1966), vol. 1, p. 23.

16. At the beginning of printing in Europe, nine instances already from the fifteenth century are listed in Herbert C. Zafren, "Bible Editions, Bible Study and the Early History of Hebrew Printing", *Eretz-Israel: archaeological, historical and geographical studies* (Jerusalem: Israel Exploration Society, with Hebrew Union College / Jewish Institute of Religion, 16 (1982): [240]–251. A recent example is Yôsēp ṣᵊbî H'erç [ed. and trans.], *Ḥᵃmishshāh Ḥûmshê Tôrāh, 'im hā-Hapṭārôt* [or: *Hapṭorôt*] . . . *'im pêrûsh qāçēr* . . . / J. H. Hertz, ed., *The Pentateuch and Haftorahs: Hebrew text, English translation, and commentary* (some voll., . . . *with commentary*) (London: Oxford University Press, 5689–5696/1929–1936, 5 voll. A "new" one-vol. edn. [London: Soncino, 1937] replaced the King James Authorised Version of the English

Pentateuch with a twentieth-century New York Jewish one; a "second" edn., enlarged and revised, again in one volume, London: Soncino, '720—1960).

17. The great article BIBLE in the *Encyclopaedia Judaica*, already mentioned (note 13 above) includes the following remark: "In discussing the Bible among the Jews it is essential to make a sharp distinction between their preoccupation with the Pentateuch and with the other sections of the Bible. . . . The Pentateuch was regarded as the main authoritative source for the *halakhah*, and verses from the prophets and the Hagiographa were regarded merely as giving secondary support to it" (col. 917). (This section of the article is by "L.I.R."—sc. Louis Isaac Rabinowitz.)

18. See Zafren, "Bible Editions . . ." article (op. cit., our note 16 above), which lists editions for the first sixty years. The first six, 1469–1476?, all commentaries, five on the Pentateuch and one on the Book of Daniel, are given on p. 247. Also, in early printing in general, he observes, "editions of commentaries on the Pentateuch outnumber all commentaries on other books by at least five to one" (p. 241).

19. It seems an interesting point, although I am not sure how far it may be significant, that the Hebrew word rendered "tradition", *Qabbālāh*, means what is received, while the corresponding Christian term, *traditio* and its cognates, means what is handed on: designating in the one case the act of receiving from the past, in the other case the action in the past of extrapolating onwards (one's tradition is what one's predecesssors have passed down).

20. ". . . the prophets and the Hagiographa . . . were called 'Kabbalah' (tradition) and it was laid down that 'no inference may be drawn concerning statements of the Pentateuch from statements found in the Kabbalah'"—Rabinowitz, ("Bible", op. cit., our note 17 above), col. 917, the maxim cited being referred to Hag. 10b.

21. "For many centuries, study of the Pentateuch and the Talmud meant, in essence, study of R[ashi]'s commentaries"—from the concluding sentence of the article RASHI in *The Encyclopedia of the Jewish Religion*, R. J. Zwi Werblowsky and Geoffrey Wigoder, edd. (New York &c: Holt, Rinehart and Winston, 1965), p. 322.

22. An illustrative example, interesting for its opening disclaimer: "May no one say to you, the Psalms are not Tôrāh. Indeed they *are* Tôrāh, and the Prophets too are certainly Tôrāh as well . . ."—from the Midrash on Psalms (my translation). The passage is from *Midrash T*ᵉ*hillîm* (opp. citt., our chap. 2 above, note 16), Hebrew, f. 172 verso = p. 344; Eng., vol. 2, p. [22]. The commentary here is on Psalm 78, verse 1: "Give ear, O my people, to my teaching". The word "teaching", here, renders into English *tôrāh* in the original, as is of course normal in the Bible. Another example: Zōhar 3:86b, where Rabbî Shim'ûn is reported as being found "absorbed in the study of the Torah [*but read rather "the study of Tôrāh"*?]. He was

meditating aloud upon" a certain verse that is thereupon quoted, which is in fact also from the Psalms (Ps. 102: verse 1 [Hebrew] = Psalm 102, heading that precedes verse 1 [English])—*Zōhar* (opp. citt., our note 11 above), vol. 2, f. 86 verso/p. 172 (the Aramaic for "Tôrāh", used here, is *Ôrîyatâ*, Aramaic form from the same root); Eng., vol. 3, p. 262. Furthermore, a curious passage in Maimonides would seem to support the matter also, although I am not clear as to whether it does so only in part. In the *Mishneh Tôrāh* he writes: *Dibrê qabbālāh bi-keᵗlal tôrāh she-b-bi-keᵗtāb hēn û-pêrûshān bi-keᵗlal tôrāh she-b-beᵗ-'al-peh—Mishneh Tôrāh*, Book 1, chap. 1, §12. Hebrew text and English translation in Mōsheh Ḥayyam Ḥayyamzô'hn / Moses Hyamson, ed., *Mishneh Tôrāh, li-Rabbēnû Mōsheh beᵗ-Rabbî Maymôn: ṣeper rî'shôn, weᵗ-hû' ṣeper ha-m-maddā'* . . . /*The Mishneh Torah by Maimonides, Book I* . . . (New York: [n.pub.; sc. Bloch], 1937; with modified title-pages, Yeᵗrûshālayim: Qiryāh Neᵗ'emānāh/Jerusalem: Boys Town, '722/1962), f. 58a/ p. 58a. I should be inclined to take this as meaning (surely, as having meant when it was written) that the whole of the Bible as traditionally received constitutes the Written Tôrāh, while interpretations thereof are Oral Tôrāh. It is clear from the predicate that the later mystics' "Qabbālāh" is not here at issue (cf. our note 20 above). For many, however, the word has come to connote, in this usage, specifically the second of the three sectors of the Bible, rather than it and the third together. Hyamson, for instance, translates *Dibrê qabbālāh* here as "the words of the Prophets"—which in the context seems oddly circumscribed? The most recent Rabbinic rendering compromises, translating also as indeed 'the "words of the prophetic tradition"', yet footnoting this as meaning (sc., as meaning here) "the remainder of the Bible—i.e., the works of the prophets and the holy writings": *Rambam, Mishneh Tôrāh: turgēm* [*] *meᵗḥuddāsh leᵗ-angeᵗlît 'im meᵗqôrôt weᵗ-he'ārôt*, Ēlîyāhû Tūger / *Maimonides: Mishneh Torah, a new translation with commentary and notes by* Eliyahu Touger [et al.] (Yeᵗrûshālayim, Niyû Yârq: Mâzeᵗnayim / New York, Jerusalem: Moznaim, several [unnumbered] volumes, in process, '746/1986–), vol. *Hilkôt Dē'ôt, Hilkôt Talmûd Tôrāh*, Hebrew, p. 175; Eng., p. 174.

23. One may mention also the somewhat parallel but finalized somewhat later "Tosefta".

24. Cf. our chapter 3 above, note 17. Cf. also: even the Talmûd was "to the end of the gaonic period . . . for the most part . . . recited from memory" and "only on rare occasions read", and even after 1000 A.D. there was uncertainty as to its "authentic" version—Hermann L. Strack, *Introduction to the Talmud and Midrash* ([Philadelphia: Jewish Publication Society of America, 1931], New York: Meridian Books and the Jewish Publication Society, 1959 and many subsequent reprints, esp. as "A Temple Book", New York: Atheneum, 1969ff.), p. 77. [Note: normally one is hesitant to cite merely, or to rely on, a translation; but this posthumous English version in effect constitutes [see 1959 edn., p. v] a new—sixth—edition, since

it incorporates revisions planned by the author before his death, beyond the already substantially revised fifth edition of the German, *Einleitung in Talmud und Midraš* (München: C. H. Beck [Oskar Beck], 1921), where the corresponding passages are found on p. 78. The first edn. appeared in 1887, with the simpler title and older spelling *Einleitung in den Thalmud* ([Leipzig: J. C. Hinrichs)], which was itself an offprint from Strack's article in the *Real-Encyklopädie für protestantische Theologie und Kirche*, 2nd edn. (Leipzig: J. C. Hinrichs)., vol. 18.

25. Cited in Jacob Neusner, *The Oral Torah: the sacred books of Judaism, an introduction* (San Francisco &c: Harper & Row, 1986), p. xiii, and again pp. 178 (without a comma after "Moses") and 182.

26. Neusner, *The Oral Torah* . . . (op. cit. in our preceding note immediately above no. 25), p. [vii].

27. So the (unattributed) *Micropædia* article TOSAFOT in the 1986 *Encyclopædia Britannica* (11: 862).

28. See, for instance, Jonathan Rosenbaum, "Judaism: Torah and Tradition", in Frederick M. Denny & Rodney L. Taylor, edd., *The Holy Book in Comparative Perspective* (Columbia, South Carolina: The University of South Carolina Press, 1985—Studies in Comparative Religion, ed. Frederick M. Denny), pp. 10–35. See our further discussion on the wide inclusiveness of the "holy books (*kitᵉbê qōdesh*)" concept towards the end of this chapter.

29. In the Hiph'îl form. In the Qal it signifies "to throw", "to shoot" (an arrow). This derivation is the generally accepted view; certain scholars recently have disputed it and have proposed alternative etymologies.

30. Again, in the Hiph'îl form.

31. Maimonides wrote this work in Arabic, under the title *Dalālat al-Ḥā'irîn*, a phrase whose words were (and are) without sacred connotations, in either standard Arabic or Judæo-Arabic; it was translated into Hebrew, however, as *Môreh* [sic] *Nᵉbûkîm*. It is perhaps legitimate also to note that to his great halakhic work (written in Hebrew) he gave as title the maybe slightly ambiguous wording *Mishneh Tôrāh* ("copy of the Tôrāh"? "deputy-Tôrāh"?).

32. The issue was forcefully raised early this century by Solomon Schechter—see S. Schechter, *Some Aspects of Rabbinic Theology* (London: Adam and Charles Black; New York &c: Macmillan; Melbourne: Oxford University Press, 1909; many times reprinted, with recent editions omitting "Some" from the wording of the title). The matter continues to be canvassed. For recent discussions summarizing later treatments and giving bibliography see Peter Richardson, Stephen Westerholm, et al., *Law in Religious Communities in the Roman Period: the debate over Torah and Nomos in post-Biblical Judaism and early Christianity* (n.p. [sc., Waterloo, Ontario]: Wilfrid Laurier University Press for the Canadian Corporation for Studies in Religion/Corporation canadienne des sciences religieuses, 1991—Studies in Christianity and Judaism/Études sur le christianisme et le judaïsme, no. 4).

33. An example can be found in Jacob Neusner, *Judaism and Scripture: the evidence of Leviticus Rabbah* (Chicago and London: University of Chicago Press, 1986—Chicago Studies in the History of Judaism, Jacob Neusner, ed.), p. xii : " 'Judaism,' that is, in their mythic language, 'the Torah'". Or again, in his *The Oral Torah* (op. cit. above, our note 25): "The religion that the world calls 'Judaism' calls itself 'Torah.'" (p. xiii); and elsewhere.

34. My *Meaning and End* . . . (op. cit., our chap. 2 above, note 3).

35. Jacob Neusner, *Judaism: The Evidence of the Mishnah* (Chicago and London: University of Chicago Press, 1981), p. 167.

36. In other words, in this phrasing the Mishnāh and the Talmûds could conceivably be understood as being referred to; and for most Jewish readers (yet not for all) this would be highly probable, at least subconsciously.

37. For which, according to Deuteronomy 10:1–5, the Ark of the Covenant was built by Moses; and that Ark then became a (for a time, the) sacred tangible symbol of Israel's life. Arks of this kind were evidently traditional tribal items—in a few instances counterparts have survived in Arabia into modern times: for photographs of something in Bedouin life today that is surely comparable see Plates V, VI in Kritzeck and Winder, edd., *The World of Islam* (op. cit., our chap. 3 above, note 2) facing pp. 195, 197, and the article of Jibra'il Jabbur, "Abu-al-Duhūr, the Ruwalah *'Utfah*", ibid., pp. 195–198. A parallel is drawn between, on the one hand, the Hebrews' reputed enshrining thus of these tablets "written by the finger of God", and, on the other, a chapter-heading in the Egyptian Book of the Dead affirming that that particular chapter was found written by the god Thoth himself on a stone at a shrine of that god, by R. de Vaux, *Les institutions de l'Ancien Testament* (Paris: Éditions du Cerf, 2 voll., 1958–1960), vol. II: *institutions militaires, institutions religieuses*, p. 132; in the English version, Roland de Vaux, *Ancient Israel: its life and institutions, translated by* John McHugh ([London: Darton, Longman & Todd, 1961], New York &c: McGraw-Hill, n.d. [sc., 1961]; reprinted, 1965), p. 301.

38. Already in Second-Temple times a practice is attested whereby priests from various localities were sent on a rotating basis to Jerusalem to take part in the rituals there and while they were absent those left behind read relevant passages from scripture; and generally a process evidently developed in due course that for participation in rites a substitute came to be a formal recitation of the description of those rites. For early roots of this see, e.g., passages in the Mishnāh, such as the tractate *Ta'ănît* of the order *Mô'ēd*, 4:2—in the Blackman edn. (op. cit., our chap. 2 above, note 5—2nd, New York, edn.), vol. II, p. 428. Again, one may trace an historical transition wherein the word *d-r-sh* gradually over some centuries moved from naming the act of consulting a seer or prophet as to God's will, to naming rather the act of consulting scripture for that purpose. (We might say: this latter came to mean consulting the report of seers and prophets

received from the past). It became in due course the standard word for Biblical exegesis. Thus, for the earlier usage: "when a man went to inquire [*d-r-sh*] of God, he said, 'Come, and let us go to the seer'" (I Samuel 9:9); and when Josiah found the book of instruction (book of *tôrāh*, "of the Law") in the Temple (cf. our chap. 3 above, pp. 62–63), he had recourse to a seer, and inquired [*d-r-sh*] of the Lord through her as to whether it was to be taken seriously (II Kings 22:13, 18). Later, on the other hand, this word, especially in the form *midrash*, became the standard term for what some might call textual interpretation; although in this case too, since it referred to scriptural interpretation—and scriptures are not simply texts!—the sense of seeking something concerning oneself, of consulting, continued to be involved (and the modern talk of "hermenutics" is therein inadequate). The verb is the normal Biblical word for looking for, going in search of, inquiring expectantly—as with God's asking of human beings, in the famous verse of Micah: "What doth the Lord require [*d-r-sh*] of thee, but to do justly . . ." (Micah 6:8).

39. Frederick Greenspahn, in an unpublished essay (presented in my post-doctoral seminar at Harvard, 1984).

40. "Ends" is a problematic term here; for at the same service (Simḥat Tôrāh) at which the reading of the Pentateuch is completed, the book of Genesis is again begun—so that the process of reading from the Tôrāh never concludes, liturgically.

41. Greenspahn, as in our note 39 above.

42. In the part of the Bible known in Christian circles as "Wisdom literature"—which comes to some extent from Hellenistic times but the Wisdom aspect of it is now seen as having had its chief sources in Ancient Near Eastern cultures—Wisdom (*Ḥokmāh*) is presented as pre-existent. This would seem to be the source of the later view that Tôrāh is so. Indeed, God is said to have taken counsel with Tôrāh when eventually He set about to create the world (e.g., Proverbs 3:19.) In later Hellenistic time the concept converged among Greek-speaking Jews with Greek *sophia* (the word was translated so in the Septuagint). Cf. our chap. 3 above, note 24.

43. See, for instance, Gershom Scholem, *Zur Kabbala und ihrer Symbolik* (Zürich: Rhein, 1960), p. 111. In the English version, Gershom G. Scholem, *On the Kabbalah and its Symbolism*, Ralph Manheim, trans. (New York: Schocken Books, 1965), this passage is p. 82.

44. This instance is from Moshe Greenberg, "On Sharing the Scriptures", in Frank Moore Cross et al., edd., *Magnalia Dei, the Mighty Acts of God: essays on the Bible and archaeology in memory of G. Ernest Wright* (New York: Doubleday, 1976), p. 462. Another example: "The bulk of postbiblical Hebrew and Jewish literature is in fact interpretation of the Bible"— Erwin I. J. Rosenthal, "The Study of the Bible in Medieval Judaism", in *The Cambridge History of the Bible* (Cambridge and New York: Cambridge University Press, 3 voll., 1963–1970), vol. 2, p. 253. Both this statement and the

one that follows in our text (cf. our immediately following note no. 45, just below) would in my view be improved—made more accurate—by a substituting of some other term for "interpretation"; or adding a qualifying word such as "ostensibly interpretation" or Greenberg's " 'in the form of' interpretation"; or, in line with our present study more generally, by reading "interpretation of the Bible perceived as scripture".

45. Rosenthal, "Study of the Bible . . ." (op. cit., our immediately preceding note, no. 44, just above), p. 257.

46. There are two Talmûds, as we have noted; but the singular, with in English the definite article, is, unless otherwise explicitly or implicitly indicated, regularly used (also by us in this study) as a generic referring to their merged place in Jewish life. Jews are well aware that there are two; but normally interact with but one or the other.

47. Two examples: the procedure for lighting Ḥanukkāh candles, even though the Ḥanukkāh festival was introduced into Jewish life considerably after the close of the canon; and the principle, later of well-known importance, of keeping milk and meat things separated in food preparation, which has no Biblical precedent. The scriptural passage utilized to underwrite the latter was the precept "Thou shalt not seethe a kid in its mother's milk" (Exodus 23:19), originally relating, it seems, to a religious ritual of a neighbouring non-Jewish people, which to critical modern Jews seems intrinsically irrelevant to the later milk-meat rule.

48. An example, regarding Abraham, is given later in this chapter at p. 117.

49. The Hebrew word, like the Greek, Latin, modern English, and others, is from Persian. In Persian the word denoted a garden, and became used in that language then also for Heaven—this latter concept, of Paradise (along with that of Hell, and a Day of Judgement) becoming presently an innovating gift of the Persians to the Western (post-Biblical Jewish, and Christian), and the Islamic, worlds, with massive long-range consequence. The word itself in its Hebrew form (*pardēs*) does occur a few times in late portions of the Jewish Bible (Nehemiah 2:8, Song of Songs 4:13, Ecclesiastes 2:5), where it means not "paradise" but "garden" or "orchard" ("forest", in the King James Authorised and Revised Standard versions in the Nehemiah case). Xenophon introduced it from Persian into Greek, also in that meaning of "garden" or "park". The Greek form (*paradeisos*) was used then in the Septuagint to render the "garden" of Eden (translating the classical Hebrew word for "garden", *gan*, *gān*, Gen. 2:8, 9, 10, 15, etc.), and this led both Jews and Christians into adopting the Persian term and its derivatives to signify the eschatological garden, "paradise".

50. "Alas for the man who regards the Torah as a book of mere tales and everyday matters! If that were so, we, even we could compose a torah [*this might have been translated* 'a teaching'?] dealing with everyday affairs, and of even greater excellence"—The Zōhar (opp. citt. above, at our note

11 above), in its section on Bᵃhaʿᵃlōtᵉkā* (sc., Numbers 8:1ff.), Aramaic, vol. 3: f. 152 recto = p. [303]; Eng., vol. 5, p. 211.

51. Ibid.

52. "The problem was how to bring the reality of God closer to the warmth of the human heart. . . . It was the 'story' (*Haggadah*) based upon the Bible which supplied the need. The sages kept God close to the people by folkloristic transformation through the medium of the *Haggadah*. They brought God into the home and made him a member of the family." This quotation is from a study not of the Bible but of the Talmûd: Ernest R. Trattner, *Understanding the Talmud* (New York, Toronto, Edinburgh: Thomas Nelson, 1955), p. 91. The author does not explain why this was a "problem"; and his word "need" would seem to suggest that people *need* to live warm-heartedly close to God, rather than to suggest that this is a privilege, one that can certainly be lost. Another illustration of the foundational role of the Haggādāh would be the remark regarding its ". . . converting law to love and ritual to caress . . ." quoted in our chap. 2 above on The Song of Songs, p. 26, with its note 13, from Gerson D. Cohen, "The Rabbinic Heritage".

53. Over against this, however, is the point that to some degree the effect of Enlightenment intellectuality and the Emancipation socially has been to divert concern from the traditional overtones, and especially for many to undermine the vast apparatus claiming to be built upon scripture but in fact extending far beyond the Bible—Talmûd, Haggādāh, mystic orientations, and all; the worldview of which the Bible was in sizeable part both cause and effect—and to turn attention directly to that Bible in and of itself, perceived through a different worldview. "Archaeology has become the national pastime of Israel", it has been remarked, meaning Biblical archaeology, reconstructing the historical world of which the Bible primarily and literally speaks; and the Bible text is read rather than Rashi's or Nachmanides's or David Kimhi's commentaries. What is by some being lost, one might perhaps say, is what was traditionally involved in the Bible perceived as scripture. Not lost, indeed rather enhanced, is the powerful interest in history that the Bible, esp. the Pentateuch, has bequeathed—powerful because scripturally affirmed.

54. (New York and London: Funk and Wagnalls,1901–1906; many times reprinted.)

55. It does have articles on "Bible Canon", "Bible Editions", "Bible Exegesis", etc. The long exegesis article might be correlated with our point that we make a little further on in the present sector of this chapter, with regard to commentaries on the Bible as distinguishable from the Bible itself; in this case, there is an article on commentaries, none on the Bible.

56. These were set forth by Maimonides first in his Arabic commentary on the Mishnāh, entitled *Kitāb al-Sirāj*. They are found towards the end of the section treating the tenth chapter of the tractate *Ṣanhēdrin* of the order

Nᵉzîqîn—a chapter often named Ḥēleq, after a distinctive word at its opening, as has in general been a Jewish custom. In Hebrew—the version that
has been influential now for several centuries—this work is usually called
simply his Pêrûsh ha-m-Mishnāh or Pêrûsh 'al ha-m-Mishnāh. The Arabic
text, in Hebrew characters, in parallel columns along with a Hebrew rendering: Mishnāh, 'im Pêrûsh Rabbênû Mōsheh ben Maymôn: māqôr wᵉtargûm:—
tirgēm [*] mē-ᵃrābît 'al-pî kᵉtāb ha-y-yād ha-m-mᵉqôrî wᵉ-hôṣîp mābô' û-he'ārôt.
Yôṣēp ben Dāwid Qâpaḥ (Yᵉrûshälayim: Môṣad hā-Rab Qûq, 6 voll., '723–
'729/1963–1968), vol. Sēder Nᵉzîqîn (sc., vol. 4—'725/1964), pp. 210–217.
A rather disappointing English translation (made perhaps—see p. [95] of
Part I of the following—before this section in the above edn. had appeared,
although published shortly after it) is available in part III of Arnold Jacob
Wolf, tr., "Maimonides on Immortality and the Principles of Judaism", in
Judaism: a quarterly journal [New York], 15 (1966): [337]–342. Maimonides
returned to this matter in some of his later writings, in Hebrew—most
notably, but in substantially more elaborate and legalist-moralist fashion, in
his *Mishneh Tôrāh*, in the presentation on that same section, Ḥēleq; and he
dealt with the issues involved, in more general and philosophically elaborated fashion, in that work's opening chapter (Hilᵏkôt Yᵉṣôdê ha-t-Tôrāh) in
its first book, Maddā'—"What is Established as Incumbent re the Principles
of the Torah", in "The Book of Knowledge" (Hyamson, Mishneh Torah . . .
op. cit., our note 22 above), f.34a/p.34a. Already early last century this last
was published in Hebrew and Eng. trans.: Hermann Hedwig Bernard, *The
Main Principles of the Creed and Ethics of the Jews, exhibited in selections from . . .
Maimonides . . .* (Cambridge: [Cambridge University Press], MDCCCXXXII).

57. Immediately following The Ten Commandments. See *Sēder Tᵉpillôt
Kol Ha-sh-Shānāh . . . 'al yāday hā-R. Shim'ôn ben R. Yᵉhûdāh Ṣîng'er . . . /
The Authorised Daily Prayer Book of the United Hebrew Congregations of the
British Commonwealth of Nations:* [Hebrew text] *with a new translation by the
late Rev. S. Singer*, Nathan Marcus Adler, ed.; new edn., Israel Brodie, ed.
(London: Eyre and Spottiswoode, and New York: Bloch, 5722—1962), pp.
93–95. Cf. pp. 3–4 for a poetic affirmation of the Principles, the Yigdal,
which forms part of the standard Morning Service.

58. They do refer to the Tôrāh, which one might take as signifying
part, at least, of the Bible: namely, the Pentateuch—except that the Oral
Tôrāh as well as the Written is explicit more than once (and regularly in
Jewish reading would be tacitly understood); while at other points the more
wide-ranging meaning of "Tôrāh" is fairly clearly seen as intended, and in
any case would be received.

59. Louis Jacobs, *Principles of the Jewish Faith: an analytical study* (London: Vallentine, Mitchell, and New York: Basic Books, 1964). (Note the
opening sentence of the Preface, p. viii.) It is relevant to note that Rabbi
Jacobs later published another book specifically on *Jewish Biblical Exegesis*
(New York: Behrman, 1973), as well as works on general Jewish theology
and "belief" for modern Jews.

60. Although Jacobs speaks of "the Bible" frequently in his chapter on "The Eighth Principle: The Torah is Divine" (his chap. 9, pp. 216–301), he primarily there (and in the next chap., " . . . The Torah is Unchanging") understands *tôrāh* as "the Pentateuch" (pp. 218ff.) and writes evidently presuming that his readers will so understand it; and secondarily understands it as historically having included the Oral Tôrāh as well as the Written, indeed as the Pentateuchal laws as interpreted by the Rabbis in later centuries and also including new laws as introduced by them (pp. 282ff.). He also gives due space to the mystics' sense (and more generally that of the devout) of Tôrāh as far transcending the empirical text of what, implicitly, the word "Bible" signifies to many today. Although he himself is not explicit about this, I think that it would hardly be a distortion to sum up his long discussion by suggesting that the problem that he addresses arises from modern orientation to Bible—as distinct from traditional orientation to something else, which we in this study are exploring under the rubric "scripture".

61. Samuel C. Heilman, *The People of the Book: drama, fellowship, and religion* (Chicago and London: University of Chicago Press, 1983).

62. To be more precise: the Talmûd is constituted of two parts, the Mishnāh and the G^emārâ, the latter (the larger) being commentary on the former. (At least, this use of the word "Talmûd" has been dominant for a few centuries now; earlier it designated what is now the G^emārâ; and that usage is today a little coming back.) No doubt, the Talmûd as it discusses, and elaborates, items of the Mishnāh cites verses of the Bible in support of that discussion, that elaboration; it interprets those Biblical verses (sometimes quite ingeniously) in such a way as to ground its position on those Mishnāh items. On this, see esp. Jacob Neusner, "Accommodating Mishnah to Scripture in Judaism: the uneasy union and its offspring", in Michael Patrick O'Connor and David Noel Freedman, edd., *Backgrounds for the Bible* (Winona Lake, Indiana: Eisenbrauns, 1987), pp. 39–53, noting esp. p. 47.

63. *Mishnāh qôdem l^e-miqrâ'*—in the latter part of the third *pereq* of the tractate *Hôrayôt*, order *N^ezîqîn*, of the Jerusalem Talmûd. (Although one ineluctably translates *miqrâ'* here as "scripture", it is noteworthy that the word denotes not, as does that English term, what is written but what is "read aloud"—cf. in our first chapter above, specifically at its note 6 and its p. 8). I have used the following edition: *Talmûd Y^erûshalmî, ô Talmûd ha-m-ma'^arāb, w^e-yēsh qôrîn lô Talmûd Ereç Yisrā'ēl, û-ṣ^ebîbô y^ḥannû pêrûshîm* . . . (New York: M. P. Press, [1922]–1976, 7 voll.), vol. 7, where this passage is found on f. 19 recto = p. 37. In the English translation of Jacob Neusner, *The Talmud of the Land of Israel: a preliminary translation and explanation* (Chicago and London: University of Chicago Press, 35 voll., in process, 1982ff.—Chicago Studies in the History of Judaism, Jacob Neusner, ed.; later voll., William Scott Green and Calvin Goldscheider, edd.), the passage is designated Horayot 3/5/iii and is found at vol. 34, p. 125.

64. *La Mishna cite rarement un verset de l'Écriture, fait rarement allusion à l'Écriture comme entité, fait rarement le lien entre ses propres idées et celles de*

l'Écriture, et se réclame rarement de ce que l'Écriture a dit, même par allusion indirecte ou vague—Jacob Neusner, "L'Écriture et la tradition dans le judaïsme: l'exemple de la Mishna", in *SR: Studies in Religion / Sciences religieuses*, 9 (1980): 459, and indeed in many of his other writings (where he is often quite nuanced on the matter, bringing in caveats). Another example: "Mishnah hardly cites or otherwise acknowledges its dependence upon the biblical texts"—Jack N. Lightstone, "Scripture and Mishnah in Earliest Rabbinic Judaism", ibid., 15 (1985): 322 (although this passage recognizes that those texts—"particularly . . . the legal materials of the Pentateuch"—are presupposed, and that there is substantive though not formal dependence; loc. cit.).

65. "In many respects it was claimed that the *Mishnah* was more important than the Pentateuch (just as the claim was being set forth by Christians that the New Testament was in many respects more important than the entire Old Testament)"; again, "The shaping of the *Mishnah* took place during the years that Christianity was developing its New Testament. These were the years (the first and second century) when all peoples, who were in any manner touched by the ancient Judaic traditions, felt that it was necessary to possess some authoritative literature in addition to the Old Testament. . . . In other words, the *Mishnah*—not the Gospels—became the new testament of the Jewish people"— Trattner, *Understanding* . . . (op. cit. above, note 52), p. 20. Another example is Jacob Neusner, in various earlier writings and most recently at the beginning of his article MISHNAH AND TOSEFTA in *The Encyclopedia of Religion* (op. cit. above, our chap. 1, note 18), vol. 9, p. 560: "Viewed structurally, the two Torahs" (sc., Written and Oral) "may be compared to the conception of an old and a new testament in Christianity, thus:

$$\frac{\text{Old Testament}}{\text{New Testament}} = \frac{\text{Written Torah (Hebrew scriptures)}}{\text{Oral Torah (Mishnah and its continuators)}}$$

. . . The Mishnah . . . thus is as important to Judaism as the New Testament is to Christianity".

66. In the Jewish case this is true specifically of the Talmûd; much less so of the Mishnāh separately. The pattern of the Talmûd is to cite an item from the Mishnāh, to elaborate upon it, and then to adduce a Biblical proof-text to justify this. "The Talmud's sages . . . constantly cite verses of Scripture when reading statements of the Mishnah. These they read in their *own* way and framework. . . . References to specific verses of Scripture are as uncommon in the Mishnah as they are routine in the Talmud"— Jacob Neusner, "Accommodating Mishnah to Scripture . . ." (op. cit. above, our note 62), p. 47. Neusner contrasts the Talmûd's treatment of the two sources that it thus correlates, observing that its authors "rarely, if ever, set out to twist the meaning of a Mishnah passage out of its original shape. . . . they do not resort to deliberately fanciful or capricious readings of what is

at hand in the statement of the Mishnah's rule"—whereas in their citing of Biblical passages in support, a different "attitude. . . of mind appear[s]"—ibid., loc. cit.

67. Sc., religious authority. When first promulgated, it had political authority, being issued as a legally binding code by the Roman-Empire-appointed *patriarchos* (Hebrew, *nāsî*') Yᵉhûdāh bēn Shim'ôn ("Judah the Patriarch").

68. The tractate *Pirqê Ābôt* differs from the Mishnāh proper in style, pattern, and intent. Nonethless, it was presently incorporated into the larger work as if it were an integral part of it—though it is much more widely and intimately known to ordinary Jews than the remainder, and is separated out to be included in the Prayer Book. It suggests the new notion indirectly, by affirming that certain authorities (who are in fact the authorities presented in the Mishnāh as the latter's sources) carry on a tradition originating, from God, at Sinai through Moses, a tradition that is called *"Tôrāh"* ("instructing"). Well over a century later the Jerusalem Talmûd develops the outlook substantially. The Babylonian Talmûd, completed another couple of centuries still later, makes fully explicit the dual Tôrāh—written and oral—concept, with the oral as embodied in the Mishnāh and the Talmûd(s), and in the on-going living tradition. See primarily Neusner, *The Oral Torah* (op. cit., note 25 above), especially its chapters 3 and 8, noting particularly statements on its pp. 46, 47, and 186 (cf. also pp. 177–187).

69. Jack N. Lightstone, "The Role of Scripture in Judaism", unpublished paper presented to the annual meeting of the Canadian Society for the Study of Religion, 1980, pp. 7, 8.

70. *Ma'î Tôrāh? Mᵉdrash Tôrāh.* This is from the Babylonian Talmûd, tractate Qiddûshîn, 49b. I have used the following edn.: *Talmûd Bābᵉlî: mᵉnuqqād* [*] *'al-pî maṣṣôret Yᵉhûdê Têmān* . . ., Yôṣēp b. R. Ahᵃrôn 'Amar ha-l-Lēwî, ed. (Yᵉrûshālayim: Hôçᵉ'at ha-m-Mᵉnuqqād, 13 voll., 5740 [sc., = 1979–80), vol. 11, p. 98 [=folio 49 verso].

71. On the Hebrew phrase *kitᵉbê qōdesh*—or with the definite article, *kitᵉbê ha-q-qōdesh*, "the holy books"—cf. above, at our note 3; on the final point regarding student note-books, see the Rosenbaum article "Judaism" (op. cit. above, our note 28), p. 24.

72. Again, it has been fairly standard when a work has been translated into Hebrew from some other language—for instance Arabic—that the title-page will read: ". . . translated into our holy language [*lᵉshônēnû ha-q-qōdesh*]".

73. The last of the three mentioned, however, was forced towards the end of his life to leave Spain, where he had done most of his work, but where anti-Jewish policy was beginning by then to mount; and he spent his final years in Palestine.

74. It may be noted, however, that the Tôrāh Scrolls in the synagogue, constituting as it were the Jewish holy book in the most intense sense of

"holy", not only have no commentaries on or near them but also are not "pointed": do not have any vowels or punctuation marked. (It has been remarked that such pointing is indeed a sort of commentary.)

75. On this whole matter see James L. Kugel, "How Should the Bible Be Taught?", in *The Bible and the Liberal Arts: papers from a conference October 16–17, 1986* (Crawfordsville, Indiana: Wabash College, n.d.). Specifically on Abraham, see for instance pp. 13–15, where *inter alia* it is noted that even Abraham's being a monotheist is not in the Biblical account. It is noteworthy that Christian Church Fathers also adopted this embroidered image of the Patriarch.

76. Moshe Greenberg, "On Sharing . . ."—loc. cit above at our note 44 above.

77. Opp. citt. above, our note 11; *zōhar* is Aramaic for "radiance".

78. Scholem, the greatest modern scholar on the Qabbālāh, in his "Introduction" to his anthology *Zohar: the Book of Splendor, selected and edited by Gershom Scholem* (New York: Schocken Books, [1949], 1963), pp. 8, 7. More fully, the sentence from which the final clause in our quotation is taken reads that the Zōhar "determined the formation and development over a long period of time . . . of the widest circles in Judaism, and particularly of those most sensitive to religion" (p. 7). Again: he speaks of the Zōhar's becoming "a sacred text" and affecting "a new level of religious consciousness" (p. 8).

79. A modern who reads both the Biblical text and the Zōhar and considers them impersonally, unhistorically ("objectively"), sees that the relation between the two is purely formal; but does well to go on to recognize that seen more perceptively that formal relation tells us a great deal about both Bible and Zōhar, and about scripture in general, and about human nature in general.

80. *hᵃpok bah wa-hᵃpok bah di-kōllâ bah.* This is from *Pirqê Âbôt*, as read liturgically in the Sabbath service once a year (late summer), where it appears as 5:25 (in the Prayer Book—op. cit. above, our note 57—pp. 275). In other versions of this tractate, particularly in its original position within the Mishnāh, the passage is numbered 5:22, and appears with the spellings *hᵃpôk* and *kôllâ* (as in the Blackman edn.—op. cit., our chap. 2 above, note 5—the 2nd, New York, edn., vol. IV, p. 538).

81. In public ceremonies, "readings" are so called, as a noun, retaining the earlier sense.

6. The Hindu Instance

1. On the imprecision see, for instance, "The Devī-Māhātmya: a Purāṇa, a Portion of a Purāṇa, or 'purāṇa'?" in Thomas B. Coburn, *Devī-Māhātmya: the crystallization of the Goddess tradition* (Delhi: Motilal Banarsidass, and Columbia, Missouri: South Asia Books, 1985), Prolegomenon 4, pp. 51–69.

2. Although the work is endlessly elaborate and rich, it is perhaps fair to

mention three forms in which especially transcendence is made vivid: the-ist, moral—the presentation of both the importance and the ambiguities of the moral in human life is forceful and sustained—and an emphasis on human friendship.

3. The Rāmāyaṇa, like the Mahābhārata, is in classical Sanskrit, and has been in existence since the late first millennium B.C. In the sixteenth century A.D. an outstanding North Indian vernacular poet of the then flour-ishing *bhakti* movement, Tulsī (Tulasī) Dâs, produced a Hindi "version" of it, the *Rāmcaritmānas*, which has since been regarded by millions as its equivalent; it is often called simply The Rāmāyana, or *The Rámáyana of Tulsi Dás*, which latter is in fact the title of the first English translation, that by F. S. Growse, trans. (Allahabad: [North-Western Provinces Govern-ment Press, 1877], Ram Narain Lal, 7th edn., 1937). (The more recent version of W. Douglas P. Hill, *The Holy Lake of the Acts of Rāma*—Bombay etc.: Oxford University Press, [1952], 1971—uses as that title a translation of the Hindi, though it and his sub-title: *a translation of Tulasī Dās's Rāmacaritamānasa*, transliterate in semi-Sanskritic style.) For those millions this Hindi version has the same authority, the same cosmic status, as the original. In fact, however, it is not a translation but at most a paraphrase, with divergences fairly substantial, evident to anyone who compares them—but traditionally only one or other of the two has been read, or heard, has been engaged with, by any particular person; almost never, both. This work of Tulsī Dās, therefore, is a good instance of the sort of theoretically some-what informal scripture to which we give emphasis below in later parts of this chapter. It is what is presented annually in the Rām-Līlā mentioned in the next sentence in our text. Somewhat similar considerations apply, it seems, to the Bengali, Tamil, and a number of other versions. Recent scholarly work argues that even of the Sanskrit "original", variety of "tell-ings" has been characteristic. See Paula Richman, ed., *Many Rāmāyaṇas: the diversity of a narrative tradition in South India* (Berkeley, Los Angeles, Oxford: University of California Press, 1991), and especially its seminal article by A. K. Ramanujan, "Three hundred *Rāmāyaṇas:* five examples and three thoughts on translation", pp. 22–49.

4. Also, some might add, in limited ways Oberammergau today; although that is to a markedly restricted audience, and is in no way of comparable historical consequence. (Up to a hundred thousand may be in attendance at a given Rām-Līlā presentation, which goes on for several days.)

5. The curious will find an informative and illuminating introduction to the two epics, especially striking for the Rāmāyaṇa, in a lavishly illustrated issue of *The Unesco Courier* (to use the title of its English-language edn.) devoted to a popular presentation of them, December 1967, with brief explanatory and engaging articles by major scholars, beginning with the late historian Arthur L. Basham.

6. As already observed, for me the word "transcendence" connotes also

and always immanence. On this important matter, cf. our chap. 1 above, p. 10 at note 16. This is especially important for a consideration of India— decisively so. The sense of divine otherness is vivid for many Hindus— notably for Vedantins, both *Advaita* and *Visiṣṭhadvaita*. Yet characteristic even of these, let alone of widespread others, is a deep and striking sense also, and simultaneously, of the immanence of the divine—immanence of the transcendent, to describe the situation more carefully.

7. Our chap. 2, p. 34, with its note 43.

8. See especially John Carman and Vasudha Narayanan, *The Tamil Veda: Piḷḷāṉ's interpretation of the Tiruvāymoḻi* (Chicago and London: University of Chicago Press, 1989). It is this *Tiruvāymoḻi*, a long devotional poem of one of the *āḻvārs*—namely, Nammāḻvār—that is called "Tamil Veda".

9. On occasion, I am told, although I have not myself met this usage, the multivalent word *Āgama* may refer to what the West calls "the Vedas". More often, it serves to distinguish, rather, certain works from those; it has been used for texts particularly by Śaivas and Jains. The term (from *ā* + √*gam*) is literally: "what has come". It has been understood sometimes as "what has come down to us from of old" (and is sometimes translated "tradition"), and sometimes as "what has come down to us from on high". (The curious might wish to compare the Hebrew *Qabbālāh*, and the Arabic *tanzīl*). Further, the word was adopted into Indonesian—with the appropriate shift of accent—where it has come to serve as the standard equivalent for the Western concept "(a) religion". The term *Āgama* referring to scriptures was used especially in the Pāñcarātra tradition. It is sometimes seen as overlapping, or even co-inciding, with *śākta* (or *tantra*) in that term's (those terms') meaning when they are used similarly with scriptural reference.

10. We shall find counterparts to this in the Buddhist case, in our next chapter, with *sūtra*s presented as the cause, rather than result, of Buddhahood.

11. *Manu* in Sanskrit means "human being", as does *ādām* in Hebrew; and in both cases these have come to designate the primordial man, progenitor of the human race. (The word *manu* is cognate with German *Mensch* and English "man", and probably also with Latin *mens* and English "mind"; with this double reach, and the fact that as an adjective the Sanskrit means "wise", the concept might be compared to that of *homo sapiens*.)

12. See, for instance, Daniel H. H. Ingalls, "Authority and Law in Ancient India", *Journal of the American Oriental Society*, Suppl. #17, July-Sept., 1954, pp. 34-45. With regard to the Dravidian languages, the situation is, I understand, similar in classical Tamil and the others. It is certainly so in Arabic and classical Islamic life; and to some degree apparently also in Chinese? "Law" is indeed a specifically Western conceptualization. (Furthermore, in the Western "secular"/"religious" polarity, what it conceptualizes is envisaged as something secular.)

13. When the British legal system was introduced into India under the Rāj, this work with its voluminous commentaries and elaborate develop-

ments became officially operative in the courts, for what was called "Hindu law"; as, for "Muslim law", the Qur'ān and Sharī'ah (whereas "law" in general was British Common Law). *Dharma* has been fundamentally what the West, in its bifurcating outlook, would call a "religious" term—cf. the next sentence in our text. It has become the standard Hindi word for that Western notion, "a religion".

14. The proper inference from their choosing the term *śastra* is presumably nothing so subtle, but rather that they simply had got the impression that this was the Indian term for scripture. Our remark has to do with the impression made on others.

15. Many Westerners are still trapped within inherited assumptions and tend to be somewhat ill at ease with this word without a definite or indefinite article, and especially when spelled with a capital "G".

16. Set forth appreciatively in Diana L. Eck, *Darśan: seeing the divine image in India* (Chambersburg, Pennsylvania: Anima, 1981—Focus on Hinduism and Buddhism, Robert A. McDermott, series editor).

17. Sc., Tulsī Dās's mediæval rendering of the story in Hindi, the *Rāmcaritmānas* (cf. our note 3 above). Similar temples in Ayodhya and Mathura enshrining the Gītā may also be noted; and at Mirzapur the Vindhyacal temple has the entire Devī-Mahātmya Purāṇa on its walls.

18. In English (and other Western languages), as we shall be discussing presently, the Sanskrit word occurs almost exclusively in relation to this particular Indian meaning, with there the transcendental reference, while usually omitting in the West the transcendence. That is, it is used by English-speaking outsiders as referring to scriptures, understood merely as texts. In India it has continued also at less lofty levels, for example in *dhanurveda*, the science of archery; and one such instance does indeed get used in English: Ayurveda, denoting, in modern English, traditional Indian medicine, and in India traditionally, the science of medicine.

19. One example among many: the Bhāgavata Purāṇa, 3:12:39— *itihāsapurāṇāni pañcamam vedamīśvaraḥ*. I have used the edition *Śrīmadbhāgavatam*, with also English title . . . *The Holy Book of God*, Sanskrit and English, Swami Tapasyananda, trans. (Madras: Sri Ramakrishna Math, 4 voll., 1980–1982), vol. 1, p. 196.

20. By the general populace, certainly; but also in "the" Vedas (formally so-called) themselves—see at our note 29 below.

21. And, in theory, others of "the twice-born".

22. Including in their liturgical use, yet not only so. To the question of scripture in liturgy we return later in this and later chapters.

23. The phrase "rather than" in our preceding sentence, and "polarity" in this one, could appear tendentious. Many Westerners would find their own appreciation of an operatic aria, for instance, or other song, intolerant of being subjected to the bifurcation. Nevertheless, the analogy with the Indian situation is not close.

24. The term *mantra* is used to signify a range of matters in India of

which this is one. It is sometimes translated as "magic formula", but any characterization over-simplifies. *Mantra*s involve words used by human beings and seen as being related, or as relating us, to transcendence. For our purposes their pervasive use over the centuries in India could be perceived as a sub-variety of scripture worldwide; but also *vice versa*. An important recent group of studies, with bibliography, is Harvey P. Alper, ed., *Mantra* (Albany, N.Y.: State University of New York Press, 1989—SUNY Series in Religious Studies, Robert Cummings Neville, ed.).

25. The Māṇḍūkya Upaniṣad is a mystic commentary on the significance of this word. Its opening verse may remind us that this syllable, rather than not meaning anything, as some outsiders would have it, may better be characterized as meaning everything. It informs that all that has been, is, and will be, plus all that is beyond these three, beyond time, is indeed this syllable; and its second verse, that all this is indeed Brahman (*aum ity etad akṣaram idaṁ sarvam, tasyopavyākhyānam, bhūtam bhavad bhaviṣyad iti sarvam auṁkāra eva, yac cānyat trikālātītaṁ tad apy auṁkāra eva. Sarvaṁ hy etad brahma*). Text in S. Radhakrishnan, ed., *The Principal Upaniṣads* (London: Allen & Unwin, 1953—Muirhead Library of Philosophy, H. D. Lewis, ed.), p. 695. For outsiders, more illuminating than these verbal discussions is probably the experience of seeing and hearing a devout Hindu reverently pronounce it. We observed a comparable sentiment on the Jewish side in our preceding chapter. The statement in our text above, that it is not a lexical word and is without specific mundane reference, some might wish to modify by noting that later it came to be used at times for "Yes" (a term that has no direct equivalent in Sanskrit, Greek, Latin, and most Indo-European languages)—or "Amen".

26. The term "meaning" is often received in the current Western sense promoted in some philosophy and linguistics, of the referential signification of the words. Deeming this incomplete at best, unduly narrow (as we explore at greater length later in this study), I use "verbal meaning" to designate this. Texts can be, Vedic texts certainly to Hindus have been, enormously meaningful, in other senses—as music can be and has been meaningful to all of us. (Sound and meaning are not polarized!) What a set of words *means* to a given person (usually something at least slightly different for each person, as we contend) is far from exhausted, and may even be omitted and ignored, by what lexicographers might find in its words.

27. "[Many] Brâhmans at the beginning of this [sc., the nineteenth] century . . . knew it [sc., the Veda] or large portions of it by heart, and could recite the hymns at sacrifices and public or private gatherings, but they did not even profess that they understood it. They were proud to know it by heart and by sound, and there were some who actually thought that the hymns would lose their magic power, if recited by one who understood their meaning"—F. Max Müller, *Auld Lang Syne . . . My Indian Friends* (op. cit., our chap. 1 above, note 4), p. 170. Some might uncharitably

remark that Professor Müller is here in danger of veering close to those outsider scholars who neither understand, nor aim at understanding, the meaning of the Veda, as scripture (and what to understand the Veda means)? There is the story of the Christian who when challenged to say whether he really understood what is meant by the Trinity replied: "I could not believe in a God whom I could understand".

28. A somewhat wry and overtly ironic (some would say, charmingly naïve?) admission that the views on "the Vedas" of "most academic scholars" (sc. Western academic scholars) are indeed discrepant from Hindu understanding (and this author states quite forcibly that he himself considers the epics and *purāṇas* "non-Vedic", over against the Hindu presentation that he is introducing) may be found in Thomas J. Hopkins's "Foreword" to Satsvarūpa dāsa Gosvāmī, *Readings in Vedic Literature: the tradition speaks for itself* (New York, Los Angeles, London, Bombay: The Bhaktivedanta Book Trust, 1977), p. ix.

29. One example, among others: Chāndogya Upaniṣad 7: 1: 2, where the Itihāsa-Purāṇa complex is called so: *itihāsa-purāṇaṁ pañcamam*, following *ṛgvedam . . . yajurvedaṁ sāmavedam, atharvaṇaṁ caturtham*. Sanskrit text in Radhakrishnan edn. (op. cit., our note 25 above), p. 468. One might perhaps feel that in the Sanskrit here the first two words—the first compound—should be characterized not as "the" but rather as "an" Itihāsa-Purāṇa complex, as more probably the "original" meaning; and even that whichever article in English for that might be chosen (or, with a plural, no article at all), one should go on to render as "tales of ancient times" or the like, rather than as a proper name of works—the complex having not yet emerged as a formal object. Historically, in any case, it soon came to mean, to most hearers and readers, "the" works so named (though Radhakrishnan, careful and sensitive scholar that he was, translates as "the" [*sic*] "epic and the ancient lore"—pp. 468f.). A more succinct example of the general matter is Śatapatha Brāhmaṇa 13:4:3:12 and 13, which illustrates our point made in the next paragraph of our text, showing the term as, in our words, "not a proper noun so much as an attributive epithet". In that passage, *itihāsa . . . vedaḥ* and *purāṇam vedaḥ* are found in the two verses respectively. I have used the edn. *Śrīmad-Vājasaneyi-Mādhyandin-Śatapatha-Brāhmaṇam* . . . (Bombay: Gaṅgāviṣṇu Śrīkṛṣṇadās, 5 voll., Samvat 1997/Shake 1862/ San 1940), vol. 4, p. 89 of the pagination of the thirteenth *kāṇḍa* (that fascicule is dated 1996/1861/1939). These words have been translated as "the Itihâsa is the Veda . . . the Purâna is the Veda", as in, for instance, Julius Eggeling, trans., *The Satapatha-Brâhmaṇa, according to the text of the Mâdhyandina school* (Oxford: Clarendon Press, 5 voll., 1882–1900—The Sacred Books of the East . . . , F. Max Müller, ed., voll. XII, XXVI, XLI, XLIII, XLIV), Part V (sc. vol. XLIV, 1900), p. 369. I would suggest rendering, rather, "Itihāsa is *veda*" and "Purāṇa is *veda*", since the original, and still the contextual, meaning in this case presumably was, usually has been,

and is, that at this point in the sacrificial service the reciting of, as Eggeling himself puts it (ibid., in a subsequent clause), "some Itihâsa . . . some Purâna" is the (cosmically) proper prescribed ritual, if not also themselves inherently of cosmic status. That is, *veda* here is attributive, descriptive, is virtually adjectival. This sense of the clauses to present-day Hindu readers is surely evident—or at least, is available—in the Hindi version *Ratnadīpikā*, by Gaṇgāprasād Upādhyāy, which reads *itihās ved hai* and *purāṇ ved hai*. This Hindi work is available, along with the Sanskrit text, in *Śatapatha Brāhmaṇam* (New Delhi: Research Institute of Ancient Scientific Studies— Dr. Ratna Kumari Publications Series, Nos. [1]–3, 3 voll., Kali Samvat 5072/[1969]–1970), vol. 3, p. 1743.

30. See the second example (Śatapatha Brāhmaṇa) in our immediately preceding note, no. 29, just above. It was an epithet used to characterize, also, matters other than texts; as in the Upaniṣad as well as in the Brāhmaṇa phrase *ya evam veda*, concerning ritual ("*this* is veda"). We have previously instanced (note 18 above) such matters as "archery", where it is nominal rather than attributive yet still an abstract rather than a concrete noun. A significant and important doctoral dissertation that awaits being undertaken is an historical word-study of the term *veda*.

31. The term "most" could be deemed too strong in the light of the fact that in many parts of India the term *veda* is not particularly common at all. Intended in our sentence above is: most Hindus who have applied the term at all have applied it to these other matters.

32. *Satya*, which I have translated here as "truth", is from *sat*, "being". (It is chiefly modern Western culture that has bifurcated truth and reality; cf. Latin *verus*, signifying both "true" and "real", and other classical cultures, e.g., Islamic.) A modern Hindu scholar has wondered whether the conception that being and the word are one may not be compared "to *logos* in its pre-Socratic sense", so that "the word became poetry in the Veda, and 'flesh' in St. John's Gospel"—D. Prithipaul, in private conversation, after reading the above. On this, cf. further our chapter 8 below, its note 40.

33. J. L. Mehta, "The Hindu Tradition: the Vedic root", in Frank Whaling, ed., *The World's Religious Traditions: current perspectives in religious studies* . . . (Edinburgh: T. & T. Clark, 1984, p. 33–54), p. 40. His wording here, this scholar explains, "gathers together, in literal translation, thoughts scattered in the Ṛgveda" (ibid., p. 52).

34. C. Mackenzie Brown, "Purāṇa as Scripture: from sound to image of the holy word in the Hindu tradition", in *History of Religions*, 26 (1986): [68]–86. See esp. pp. 75–76.

35. Although quite early there were some studies such as the *Nirukta* of Yāska, treating difficult individual words (with etymologies that today are seen as at times rather fanciful), yet the first straight commentary on the Ṛg-Veda hymns was by a fourteenth-century-A.D. author, Sāyaṇa. A salient example of present-day study by a sophisticated (and in this case Western-

ized) Hindu is the striking, highly sensitive, article of J. L. Mehta, "The Hindu Tradition . . ." (op. cit. in our note 33 above). A full-fledged modern movement, fairly influential in North India especially in the last quarter of the nineteenth century, is the Ārya Samāj, with its cry "Back to the Veda (to the Vedas)!". In all these cases, as in many another, "Veda" means basically the Saṁhitas and chiefly—or simply—the Ṛg-Veda hymns.

36. For a latter-day Western expression of a somewhat comparable view, by—not surprisingly—a poet, see the remark of W. B. Yeats cited in our concluding chapter below (its note 42). An expression of such a view but without the negative (my "*not* in words . . ." above), without the polarizing of verbal and personal, would aver that truth may be communicated by a particular person's saying the words but not by another's saying even the same words. One present-day Hindu formulation: "For Hindus generally, scriptures play a secondary role . . . a Hindu is 'saved' by a guru rather than by a scripture. From this point of view I am rather inclined to claim that 'Hinduism' has no single scripture, but innumerable scriptures, since the teachings and instructions of the guru are absolutely binding on the disciple-student. . . . Access to the Veda or to any other religious sources, such as the purāṇas, epics, was usually given to a disciple through the guru, and even here the scriptures play only a supportive role and they functioned within the instructional framework of a guru"—K. R. Sundararajan, in my post-doctoral seminar at Harvard.

37. Brown, "Purāṇa as Scripture . . ." (op. cit., our note 34 above), pp. [68]–69.

38. *Vedam est, quidquid ad religionem pertinet, Vedam non sunt libri*—the Carmelite missionary Paulinus, reporting his experience when studying with Brahmans. Apparently he had reason to ask them whether the Vedic books really existed, since other missionaries had been reporting the above about no one having seen or known them; and he states that the answer to his question was as quoted here. This is cited from "Paull. a St. Barthol., Examen critico-historicum codicum indicorum bibliothecae sacr. congr. de propag. fide, Romae, 1792, pag. 50" in W. Caland, "De Ontdekkingsgeschiedenis van den Veda" in *Verslagen en Mededeelingen der Köninklijke Akademie van Wetenschappen, Afdeeling Letterkunde, 5de Reeks. 3de Deel* (Amsterdam: Johannes Müller, 1918), p. 303. In general this Caland article (ibid., pp. [261]–327) is of major importance for the light that it throws on the full matter of Hindu involvement with "the Veda" (in the Western sense) before Western scholarship's novel presentation of it last century. Further information, along with the gist of this article, is available in the long review of an offprint of it by Theodor Zachariae in *Göttingische gelehrte Anzeigen* (Königl. Gesellschaft der Wissenschaften), 183 (1921): 148–165. Of this review in German an amplified English translation by H. Hosten appeared in *Journal of Indian History*, 2 (1922–1923): [127]–157, under the title "The Discovery of the Veda". See also a more recent major article, of even more

central importance for our study here since it carries the story further by dealing with the impact of Max Müller's work within India after that novel presentation: Ludo Rocher, "Max Müller and the Veda", in *Mélanges d'Islamologie: volume dédié à la mémoire de* [sic] *Armand Abel* [the wording of both the title and the sub-title, and the editors, varies slightly in the successive volumes, and the editors change; offprints of vol. III bear the title *Mélanges Armand Abel* only], Pierre Salmon, A. Destrée, edd. (Leiden: E. J. Brill, 1974–1978), vol. III, pp. [221]–235.

39. Max Müller (on the title-pp. of voll. 5 and 6: "F. Max Müller"), ed., *Rig-Veda-Sanhita, the Sacred Hymns of the Brahmans; together with the commentary of Sayanacharya* (London: W. H. Allen, 6 voll., 1849–1874); 2nd edn., with more precise transliteration on the title-p., F. Max Müller, ed. (London: Oxford University Press, 4 voll., 1890–1892.) (On successive title-pp., political changes are interestingly reflected—in that of the first edn., voll. published before the 1857 Mutiny were "published under the patronage of the Honourable the East-India-Company", while subsequent ones' patronage was "of the Rt. Honourable Her Majesty's Secretary of State for India in Council"; the second edn. voll. appeared under that of "His Highness the Mahârâjah of Vijayanagara".) This is an edition of the Sanskrit, and has also a Sanskrit title-page; it may be noted that this English title, added as a separate page, does not actually call the work a book, nor scripture, nor refer it to Hindus (but to a restricted caste among them). We shall return to the point that to think of the Ṛg-Veda as a Hindu scripture, as became common in the West from the late nineteenth century, rather than as a collection of Brahman hymns, some might argue to be misleading—or more accurately, to be so especially until last century (after which the situation changed somewhat within India itself, as we have been noting—changed in part under influence of Western attitudes to scripture). Some years later in his edition of his English translation of a selection from the work, Müller called it a "sacred book" but only indirectly, by including it in the series with this title (F. Max Müller, ed., *The Sacred Books of the East*, Oxford: Clarendon Press, vol. 32, *Vedic Hymns* [1869, 1891²]; Delhi, etc.: Motilal Banarsidass, [1964], 1967). Müller himself was egregiously enthusiastic about the Ṛg-Veda, but essentially as an ancient document illustrating early Aryan (or indeed, early human) thought, language, and history. (For a succint and perceptive account, quoting some of Müller's own remarks on this, see Mehta, "The Hindu Tradition . . ." (op. cit.—our note 33 above—pp. 41–42.) Readers will recall that we saw, in our Qur'ān chapter above, a similar historicist attitude in Western treatment of that Muslim scripture for a time.

40. An engaging recent treatment of this matter is the posthumous article of Kendall W. Folkert, "The 'Canons' of 'Scripture'", in Levering, "Rethinking Scripture . . ." (op. cit. above, our chap. 1, its note 7), pp. 170–179.

41. See, as one illustration, the introduction (*avataraṇikā*—second range of pagination, following the 191–page prologue, *bhūrmikā*) of Rādhāgovindanāth,

Gauṛīya Vaiṣṇava Darśana . . ., vol. 1 (Calcutta: Sādhanā Prakāśanī, [1957], 2nd edn. 1980), pp. 8–10, from which are taken both the term *vedatva* cited here, and the (rather standard) characterizing of the Gītā as "the essence . . . ". I owe this (Bengali) reference to my colleague Joseph O'Connell.

42. The lack of split between humanism and theism in India means that all human gurus (and in another, lower, sense all human beings) are perceived as in some degree divine.

43. More strictly, thirty-nine. There is one repetition.

44. The Pañcvāṇī and the Sarvāṇī.

45. As in Muslim Persian poetry.

46. John Stratton Hawley, "Author and Authority in the *Bhakti* Poetry of North India", in *Journal of Asian Studies*, 47 (1988): 269–290; p. 273.

47. Loc. cit. Further, a number of parallel cases are cited, with other poets too whose works function scripturally for many, where the attributed names "point in the direction of authority rather than strictly of authorship" (ibid.).

48. Should one more cautiously read "many"? Who of us has counted? Yet even in the case of such villagers as have lived their lives more manifestly in relation to rites, gods, and so on, their lives have been not merely influenced but shaped by story; and the line between story and scripture is sufficiently tenuous that I have decided to let the text stand (with this annotation!).

49. Or, a significant portion of it; some have held that the supernal Veda is transcendingly vast, many times the size of its *śruti* version.

50. A further caveat is in order. (All general statements about the Hindu situation are over-simplifications, and omit the fascinating exceptions!) Some Hindus would say that in humanity divinity is not distorted, by worldliness and failings or approximations, so much as, rather, disguised—by *māyā* (which is somewhat mistranslated "illusion"); or is to be celebrated, as *līlā*—divinity at play. They have not failed to notice that transcendence transcends; nor, that it is immanent.

51. Cf. above, p. 138 and its note 36.

52. Less widespread is the ostensibly contrary notion that the Purāṇa in question is an elaboration of an original extremely brief utterance of the Supreme Him- or Her- or Itself. Yet in its own way this makes a same sort of point: that the final truth in its pure, inherent ("original") form is so simple as to be beyond our human apprehension, and has to be put in manageable articulated form if we are to grasp it (to be grasped by it).

53. Śaiva Siddhānta and Kaśmīrī Śaiva.

7. The Buddhist Instance

1. E.g., later in this chapter, p. 165, with its note no. 86.

2. Also in this chapter, for instance in some of our discussions below on the classical Chinese word for scripture, *ching*.

3. At least, not by outsiders. Sub-divisions, sects, groupings, within the Mahāyāna regularly have had a clear and definite sense of what counted for themselves as scriptural. The mutual recognition among such groups that gradually evolved, however, which included the awareness of diversity scripturally, and which we shall be considering presently, complicates the matter even for insiders.

4. Two persons are honoured in Japan for allegedly having done this. One is the twelfth-thirteenth-century leader Hōnen, of whom the legend goes that he had read the whole of the Tripiṭaka—but of course this would mean the Chinese Tripiṭaka; he would not have had anything to do with, for instance, the Tibetan. The legend, however, indicates both the esteem that such a feat is seen as deserving, and its rarity. The other person is an unusual modern scholar.

5. Individual movements and groups have at times been both clear and firm about what counted as scriptural works for them. They have been aware, however, that other movements, other groups, have had other choices.

6. Various monasteries in Tibet had made each its own collection of scripture translations. In the fourteenth century some scholar-monks "began to compile these . . . into an authoritative . . . canon", which was printed (in China) the following century; but with printed versions, further on-going development was profuse. "For most Tibetan Buddhists scripture was what one's own teacher and his tradition had defined as scripture"—Eva K. Dargyay, "The Process of Canonization in Tibet", paper (to be published presently) read at a conference in Toronto, 1988.

7. The Marxist has already begun to peter out as a discrete movement. Some find that the secularist also has already passed its peak and may not long endure. Whether a new era coming, currently recognized but not characterized in the non-descript phrase "post-modern", will be post-secular remains to be seen.

8. In the Islamic case, it is heinous blasphemy to imagine its needing repeating, or its being repeated. This was demonstrated, for instance, in the 1950's in Pakistan in the outrage over the Aḥmadīyah heresy of a new prophet. On the reaction see, for instance, the "Munir Report", sc. *Report of the Court of Inquiry Constituted under Punjab Act II of 1954 to Enquire into the Punjab Disturbances of 1953* (Lahore, 1954); also, Antonio R. Gualtieri, *Conscience and Coercion: Ahmadi Muslims and orthodoxy in Pakistan* (Montreal: Guernica, 1989).

9. One must not, however, allow stories of Mahāyāna Buddhists' (primarily Zen masters') reportedly saying "If you see the Buddha, kill him!" (meaning that truth transcends all mundane forms, to the point where these may distract) to divert one from a recognition that nonetheless these very Buddhists, as indeed all Buddhists, do in fact honour Siddhārtha Gautama. Or more exactly, they honour Sakyamuni (Sanskrit, Śākyamuni—"sage of

the Saka" tribe), a standard name for the historical figure, though for the Mahāyāna it is the Buddha of the legends that they have in mind when they hear or speak his name, or write or read it; and it is an engaging question as to how divergent that important Buddha has been, in the minds of each of them, from the mid-first-millenium-B.C. person whom the outsider sees living on earth in India. Those very Zen masters cited have a statue of Śākyamuni in their monasteries, and do reverence to it or him. Yet for them is it a statue actually of *him*? (Or should we more carefully phrase this: of what the rest of us perceive as him?)

10. (This is quite apart from the fact that new sūtras kept being added.) Even as regards the Pāli canon's sūtra texts, early Burma manuscripts, for instance, differ from the Sri Lanka ones accepted by outside scholars until recently as authoritative. Also, of the Sanskrit texts translated into Chinese, it has emerged that the translations sometimes represent an earlier form of the original than do the extant Sanskrit versions, from which until recently they were imagined by scholars to have diverged. See Lewis Lancaster, "Buddhist Literature: its canons, scribes, and editors", in Wendy Doniger O'Flaherty, ed., *The Critical Study of Sacred Texts* (Berkeley, Los Angeles, London: University of California Press, 1979—Berkeley Religious Studies Series), pp. 215–229, esp. pp. 221ff.

11. Lancaster, *ibid.* (our immediately preceding note just above no. 10), p. 228. Among Biblical scholars a growing number nowadays are noticing the "misleading" quality of that field's counterpart enthusiasms.

12. The Sanskrit word *pāramitā* (from *pāram*, "beyond", "across", "the other side of", and *itā*, "having gone") is virtually a literal equivalent of "transcendent" (from *trans*, "across, over, to the other side of", and *scando*, in compounds *scendo*, "to climb", "to rise" [as in "ascend", "descend"]). "Insight" to render *prajñā* in this instance, sound enough on general grounds, has been championed by Michael Pye, for instance in *Skilful Means: a concept in Mahayana Buddhism* (London: Duckworth, 1978)—*passim*; and see in particular his p. 4, note 6, and p. 103, note 1, where he mentions also Erich Frauwallner's *Einsicht*.

13. The *Prajñāpāramitāhṛdayasūtra* or Heart Sūtra, in ca. 25, or ca. 14, lines of verse in the two chief Sanskrit versions, a few hundred characters in the Chinese. Edward Conze, "Text, Sources, and Bibliography of the Prajñāpāramitā-hṛdaya", *Journal of the Royal Asiatic Society of Great Britain and Ireland*, 1948: [33]–51, is a careful study of its origins, early development, and its derivative place in the family of such sūtras—and with an opening indication of its massive importance: "The *Prajñāpāramitā-hṛdaya sūtra* is a religious document of the first importance. It carried *Hiuen-tsiang* through the Gobi desert, was reproduced, in writing, on stones, in recitation throughout Asia from Kabul to Nara, and formed one of the main inspirations of the Zen school, occupying in Buddhist mysticism about the same place the '*Mystical Theology*' of *Pseudo-Dionysius Areopagita* occupied in

Christian" (p. [33], with footnote reff. for each statement). See also Donald S. Lopez, Jr., *The Heart Sūtra Explained: Indian and Tibetan commentaries* (Albany: State University of New York Press, 1988—Kenneth Inada, ed., SUNY Series in Buddhist Studies), and cf. below, our note 108.

14. This last, consisting of only a single character—the Sanskrit letter "a"—was named the *Prajñāpāramitāsarvātathāgatamātā ekākṣara* ("the single-syllable Mother of all" these sūtras . . .). Christians will appreciate the force of this move perhaps more readily if they reflect on their own tradition's conceivably comparable (would some perhaps wish to insist, twice as extensive?) practice of speaking of God or Christ as the Alpha and the Omega.

15. Some forty are known, produced over a period of a thousand or so years. The 8,000-line one seems to have been the original. (We quote from it below, at our note 62.) It (along with perhaps the 25,000 one) and the shortest of the major ones, the widely popular "Heart Sūtra" (cf. above, our note 13) have been probably the most studied.

16. This longest is, indeed, the *Śatasāhasrikāprajñāpāramitāsūtra*.

17. "As long as Mahāyāna survived in India it continued to generate new *sūtras*, the total number of which is almost staggering"—Graeme Mac-Queen, "Inspired Speech in Early Mahāyāna Buddhism", in *Religion*, 11 (1981): [303]–319 and 12 (1982): [49]–65; part II, p. 60.

18. Chinese Buddhists themselves asserted that a *ching* (sūtra—cf. below, our note 20 and further reff. there) composed by one of themselves is properly so-called because its author was himself on the way to Enlightenment, so that, for instance, a particular monk's "preaching of [a work called in Chinese the *T'an-ching*, normally translated into English as] the *Platform Sutra* is basically no different from the Buddha's preaching of the sutras"—Ch'i-sung, *Chai-chu fu-chiao-pien T'an-ching yao-i*, as quoted in English in *The Platform Sutra of the Sixth Patriarch: the text of the Tun-huang manuscript, with translation, introduction, and notes by* Philip B. Yampolsky (New York and London: Columbia University Press, 1967—Records of Civilization: sources and studies, LXXVI), p. [125]. One presumes that the Chinese word translated here by Yampolsky as "sutras" at the end of this quoted sentence is again (as in the title) *ching*. (A similar assessment of "late" sūtras was evident in India.)

19. A notion emerged of "hidden scriptures" that were unearthed in later times. One of the forms that this idea took was of tortoises discovered with sūtras inscribed on their shell. Another source of newness was the notion of visionaries apprehending timeless truth—the latter idea formally recalling either shamanist traditions or Hindu-Vedic ones, or both.

20. Or in China, *ching*. Some so labelled were translations from Sanskrit whose original title did not include the term *sūtra*. The Chinese word was used also at times in comprehensive lists that embraced almost anything plausible. Some modern Western scholars hold that such catholicity means that we should not translate *ching* as "sūtra"; but one may feel that this is an

indication of how that originally Sanskrit word is heard by Western historical reductionists more than of how the Chinese one has historically been heard by Chinese Buddhists—as we have remarked. (Cf. also our note 18 above.) There is the consideration that *ching* in Chinese does, we would contend, mean "scripture" (cf. our note 23 below, and see more esp. our next chapter). It was consistently their word for translating *sūtra*, though that is not conclusive. In India the Pāli equivalent of *sūtra*—namely, *sutta*—denoted only one type of scripture for Buddhists, naming but one of the "three baskets" of the Pāli Canon, as we shall be noting. In Sanskrit, Hindu and Jain usage of the term was different, while among Mahāyāna Buddhists in India the Sanskrit term *sūtra* came to be used rather more loosely than its Pāli counterpart; as did also the concept *Buddhavacanam*, "word of the [a?] Buddha" (a matter to which we return more than once later in this chapter), justifying it. The matter is further complicated in that in English the word "sutra" has become familiar as signifying, for many, a Buddhist scripture without precision as to the type (as in, e.g., recent editions of the *Concise Oxford Dictionary*; *Webster's* are more restrictive). Given the imprecision of the Sanskrit, of the Chinese, and of the English, we have allowed ourselves rather substantial latitude in our use of the term in this study. By it we designate a Buddhist scripture, especially one ostensibly presenting a discourse of the or a Buddha, however "Buddha" may be understood.

21. A few Mahāyāna examples, from Japan and from China respectively, are given in our next paragraph with its notes. Some from Theravāda are offered below, pp. 151-152 with, in turn, their notes (nos. 33 to 39).

22. There are in Japanese two words regularly used for translating into that language the Western term "scripture", and in turn regularly translated into English by that term: *seiten* and *shōgyō*. (The first part of both words is written with the same Chinese character—"holy", "sacred"; the second word may be pronounced also *seigyō* [on such pronunciation, cf. below, our note 109]. The first word is, accordingly, "holy books", the second "holy teachings".) In Buddhist usage the latter, especially, appears, although also there both are common. The illustrative sect referred to is Jōdo Shin (True Pure Land). Its official presentations of its own "holy texts" have used all three of these two Japanese and one English terms as headings for its, collection. See *The Shinshu Seiten: The Holy Scripture of Shinshu* (Honolulu: the Honpa Hongwanji Mission of Hawaii, 1955; "second print", actually a considerably revised edn., 1961). A new edn., 1978, rather radically modified, was published (in San Francisco) by the Buddhist Churches of America, endorsed by that Hawaii Mission and the Buddhist Churches of Canada, with the same title (except for an added macron: *Shinshū*) and a modified wording in the subtitle: *Jōdo Shin Buddhist Teaching*. In the subsequent "Shin Buddhism Translation Series" (Yoshifumi Ueda, gen. ed., Kyoto: Hongwanji International Center, 1978ff., in process), half-a-dozen or more volumes have appeared thus far, all being

renderings in English of Shinran's own writings. In this series the English word "canon", as well as "scripture", is used. One may further note that over the last couple of centuries in the publishing by this organization of its scriptures, additional texts are included in successively later editions, while the Indian texts are reduced. On the sūtras included, see our note 74 below. On this whole matter, see especially an as yet unpublished seminar paper, 1984, of the late Minor L. Rogers, "A Founder's 'Teaching' as Scripture: Shinran Shōnin (1173–1262) and the Jōdo Shin Sect".

23. It would seem, however, that only a few works composed in China by Chinese, and not translations from Sanskrit, received the title *Ching*, "sūtra". The chief members of this class are the *Leng-yen-ching* (sixth cent.), the *Yüan-chue-ching* (eighth cent.), and the *T'an-ching* (the "Platform Sūtra of the Sixth Patriach"—see above, note 18, and below, note 49). Of these, only the last did not at least pretend to be from an Indian original—indeed to be by Śākyamuni himself. Although it seems that the first two have played only a small role in Japanese Buddhist developments, otherwise deeply dependent on the Chinese situation, in China itself all three have apparently been markedly popular and historically important. Other works known as *ching* in Chinese (examples are the *Fan-wang-ching*, and the *Ti-tsang-p'u-sa-pen-yüan-ching*) have been taken as translations from Sanskrit, but no original in Sanskrit has been found nor reference in Sanskrit to such, and some scholars are beginning to think that they too should be seen as original to China.

24. Judith A. Berling, "Bringing the Buddha Down to Earth: notes on the emergence of *Yü-lu* as a Buddhist genre", in *History of Religions*, 27 (1987): [56]–88, pp. 81, 83. This writer remarks of the "Recorded Sayings" (*Yü-lu*) in general that they "stress that the actions of masters, more than their words, are the means by which they transmit the Dharma" (p. 84).

25. Nonetheless the Chinese phrase *San* (three) *tsang* used as counterpart for the "Three Baskets" of the Sanskrit *Tripiṭaka* indicates that the collections were conceived formally, not casually compiled nor expected to be treated unscripturally. (Actually, *tsang* in Chinese is not exactly "basket", but any collection—or container for a collection, such as a chest or warehouse—of things stored together, esp. valuable things: in some contexts it is "treasury". Further, when used without *san*, "three", it served for what the West calls "canon": *Fo tsang* is the term for the Buddhist collection as a whole, *Fo* being "Buddha".)

26. *Aṅguttara Nikāya*, 7:9(79):2. In the Devanāgarī-script edition of the text, of the Pāli Publication Board (Bihar Government), vol. 3, *Aṅguttara Nikāya: Chakkanipāta, Sattakanipāta & Aṭṭhakanipāta*, Bhikkhu J. Kashyap, gen. ed. (Vārānasī: Mōtīlāl Banārsīdās, B[uddhist] E[ra] 2504 / V[ikram] E[ra] 2017 / [A.D.] 1960—Nālandā-Devanāgarī-Pāli-Series), this passage is at p. 263. In the roman-script edition of the Pāli text of the Pali Text Society, *Aṅguttara Nikāya, Part IV: Sattaka-nipāta, Aṭṭhaka-nipāta, and*

Navaka-nipāta, E. Hardy, ed. (London: Luzac, [1899], 1958), it is p. 143. An English translation is to be found in *The Book of the Gradual Sayings (Anguttara-Nikāya), or More-Numbered Suttas,* 5 voll., F. L. Woodward et al., trans. (London: for the Pali Text Society, Luzac, 1932–1936—Pali Text Society Translation Series, nos. 22 ff.); vol. IV (Series no., 26 [sic]), *(The Books of the Sevens, Eights and Nines),* E. M. Hare, trans., [1936] 1965, pp. 96–97.

27. *etaṃ Satthu sāsanam* (or: . . . *satthusāsanam*). This might be read as "this is the (*or:* a) word, or teaching, of the Buddha", or as ". . . of a Buddha"; or, taking *satthu* as the first member of a compound rather than as a genitive, one might read "this is Buddhist [i.e., supremely wise] teaching". (See s.v. *satthā* in Robert Cæsar Childers, *A Dictionary of the Pali Language*—[London, 1875] New Delhi: Cosmo, 1979, p. 469.) I should imagine that each of these ways of understanding the passage has in fact obtained among Buddhists of various sects over the centuries. (The Hare translation [op. cit., our immediately preceding note above, no. 26] gives "the word of the Teacher", which I have adopted in the text.)

28. The word *dharma* represents one of the ultimates in the Buddhist worldview. Non-Buddhists tend to understand it (even sometimes to translate it) as signifying what the historical Buddha taught. For Buddhists themselves, the Buddha taught it because it preceded him and is true, is final and salvific truth. Thus for them the word signifies rather Truth with a capital T, Reality with a capital R; I have discerned analogies between it and theists' concept verbalized as God, in the Buddhist chapter of my *Faith and Belief* (Princeton: Princeton University Press, 1979, pp. [20]–32). On some Buddhist meanings, and a comparing of these with non-Buddhist, see esp. John Ross Carter, Dhamma: *Western academic and Sinhalese Buddhist interpretations—a study of a religious concept* (Tokyo: Hokuseido Press, 1978). See further our note 99 below.

29. See our fuller discussion of the notion *Buddhavacanam* later in this chapter. In the meantime, one may note that this is not unlike a Christian's saying: "God is truth . . . . Wherever truth is found, there is God. And wherever truth is stated, there God is speaking". This remark was made several years ago in a discussion as to whether the Qur'ān, or the Bible, or whatever, is to be deemed "the word of God". See my *Questions of Religious Truth* (New York: Scribner's, and London: Gollancz, 1967), p. 85.

30. Chiefly in the *Mahāparinibbāna Sutta*. (This—which is to be distinguished from the unrelated Mahāyāna *Mahāparinirvāṇa Sūtra*—is one of the sūtras of the first section, *Dīgha-Nikāya*, of the second "basket" of the Tripiṭaka.) Several modern versions of the Pāli text have been published—each, as is the custom (Pāli having no script of its own), in the local script, whatever that be: in roman (London, 1890 ff.); in Sinhalese (Colombo, 2473/1929, and 2505/1962 [though I myself do not read Sinhalese script]); in Devanāgarī (Bombay, 2 voll., 1942–1936, and Pakāsitā, Bihar, 3 voll., 2502/

2015/1958), and so on. Although checking details with the later Indian edition, I have used primarily *The Dīgha Nikāya*, T. W. Rhys Davids and J. Estlin Carpenter, edd. (London: The Pali Text Society, 3 voll., [1890–1911], many times reprinted, by Oxford University Press and Luzac; some of the early printings had a hyphen between "Dīgha" and "Nikāya" on the title-page—e.g., the 1949 reprint of vol. 1). Here this "*suttanta*" is found at vol. 2, 1966, pp. 72–168. There are many translations of the sūtra, in English, French, German, Sinhalese, etc. Two of the English ones are mentioned (and discussed) in our note 99 below. Furthermore, "The Last Days", being chapter XI of Edward J. Thomas, *The Life of Buddha as Legend and History* (London: Routledge & Kegan Paul, [1927], 3rd edn., rev., [1949], 1960—The History of Civilization, C. K. Ogden, ed.), pp. [143]–164, is based on the account in this sūtra but gives also several further references, to the two other sūtras where such an account occurs and to modern studies.

31. Also, especially honoured. In Sinhalese, for example, the honorific word *vahansē*, used for the Buddha, one's parents and especially one's mother, and the Bo tree, is used also in naming the book of these tales (*Jātakapot vahansē*) and one other book (*Paritta*) of the Canon.

32. Indeed, development had been lively also outside what has become *that* group's canon—has become "the" Tripiṭaka—among other branches of Southern or non-Māhayāna Buddhist life before the Theravādins became predominant. Each sect, of which there were many (eighteen or twenty-four are traditionally noted; modern scholars report finding evidence for some thirty), had its scripture collection. Only the Theravādins' "Pāli canon" has survived, and for many centuries now has been seen as "the" scriptures of the movement. Cf. further our note 61 below.

33. *etaṃ pakaraṇaṃ Buddhabhāsitam eva nāma jātaṃ*—Edward Müller, ed., *The Atthasālinī: Buddhaghosa's Commentary on the Dhammasaṅgaṇi* (London: The Pali Text Society, [1897], distributed by Routledge & Kegan Paul, London, Boston, &c., 1979—Pali Text Society Text Series, no. 12), p. 4. The reference is to the book *Kathāvatthu*, written by Thera ("elder, presbyter, reverend") Tissa, son of Moggalī. Critics were contending that this should be rejected as merely *sāvakabhāsita* (p. 3), the word of a disciple; Buddhaghosa is here countering their arguments. The issue is whether this book is to be included—along with the *Dhammasaṅgaṇī* on which Buddhaghosa's work here is a formal commentary—in the *Abhidhamma*, the third of the Three Baskets of the formal Pāli canon. In the English translation the remark is found at vol. 1 p. 6 of *The Expositor (Atthasālinī): Buddhaghosa's commentary on the Dhammasangaṇī* [sic], *the first book of the Abhidhamma Piṭaka*, Pe Maung Tin, trans., Mrs. Rhys Davids, ed. and rev. (London: for the Pali Text Society, 2 voll., [Oxford, 1920–1921], Luzac, 1958—Pali Text Society Translation Series, nos. 8–9).

34. The Pāli text in Devanāgarī script: *Visuddhimagga of Buddha-*

ghosācariya, Dharmananda Kosambi, ed. (Andheri, Bombay: Bharatiya Vidya Bhavan, 1940). There is an edition also in roman script: *Visuddhimagga of Buddhaghosâcariya*, ed. by Henry Clarke Warren, rev. by Dharmananda Kosambi (Cambridge, Massachusetts: Harvard University Press, and London: Oxford University Press, 1950—Harvard Oriental Series, Walter Eugene Clark, ed., vol. 41); and two English translations: *The Path of Purity: being a translation of Buddhaghosa's Visuddhimagga*, by Pe Maung Tin (London, New York, &c: Oxford University Press, for the Pali Text Society, III Parts, 1923–1931—Pali Text Society Translation Series, nos. 11, 17, 21; to Part III "with an epilogue by Mrs. Rhys Davids"), and *The Path of Purification (Visuddhimagga) by Bhadantācariya Buddhaghosa, translated from the Pali by* Bhikkhu Ñāṇamoli (Colombo, Ceylon: R. Semage, 1956). A posthumous moderately revised 2nd edn. of this last (ibid., 1964), has the translator's name spelled Ñyāṇamoli on the title-page [although not in the reviser's "Foreword", p. vi].

35. Western scholars are just beginning to use the phrase "allegedly non-canonical", proffered recently in English by a Buddhist scholar, instead of the previously accepted "apocryphal", to characterize sūtras [*sic*] "not found in standard editions of the Pali Canon" but evidently widely used over many centuries, setting forth not, in the manner of new Mahāyāna sūtras, new ideas but "canonical" material simplified or re-arranged, in a way that has been historically effective in the transmission of the movement. See the forthcoming edition and translation of one such work, the *Nibbānasutta*: Charles Hallisey, "The Sutta on Nibbāna as a Great City". The quotation just given is from the introduction to this, where also Hallisey attributes his phrase to K. D. Somadasa, 1987. (I would add that the adjective "apocryphal" in English has, of course, in line with developments that we observed in our opening chapter above, changed its meaning over recent centuries from being positive and honorific to being negative and disparaging.)

36. It so happens that the name that this writer had been given, Buddhaghosa, already means (and was widely and legitimately received as meaning) something closely akin to this—*ghosa* ("sound") may be taken here as "voice". In addition, however, other etymologies were also formally proffered, for instance in the late pseudo-biographical work mentioned in the next sentence but one in our text: [Mahāmaṅgala], *Buddhaghosuppatti; or the Historical Romance of the Rise and Career of Buddhaghosa, edited by* James Gray (Pāli text, in roman script) and [Mahāmaṅgala], *Buddhaghosuppatti; or the Historical Romance of the Rise and Career of Buddhaghosa, translated* [into English] *by* James Gray (both, London: Luzac, 1892. Later the two volumes were bound together as one, each retaining its own pagination). This work links the word *ghosa* also (for this "also", cf. Pāli, p. 58; Eng., p. 26) to, *inter alia*, the name of a village near the great Bo tree (Pāli, p. 37; Eng., p. 4), and to the name of a prince of the *deva*s who surrenders heaven to be reborn on

earth as Buddhaghosa (Pāli, pp. 38–39; Eng., pp. 4–5). In the latter connection one may observe that although the English translation (p. 5) states that it was Sakka, the king of the *devas*, that gave up his heavenly life to become Buddhaghosa on earth, this seems to be an error, since in fact the original Pāli (p. 39) reads *Ghosadevaputta* here, rather; and indeed it is the latter that, a few lines earlier (Pāli, p. 38, Eng., p. 5), on being asked—by Sakka— to undertake this mission has said that much though he would prefer, and had hoped, to rise higher (than the *deva* realm) rather than to descend to the human world of great suffering and great distress (*manussoloke . . . bahudukkho bahupâyâso*), nevertheless for the sake of bringing the Lord's (Buddha's) message to those who have not effectively heard it he is willing to make such a sacrifice.

37. This work along with—to a lesser extent—the older *Questions of King Milinda* (*Milindapañha*) have together constituted the effectively dominant and authoritative texts for most monks in Sri Lanka, modern observers report, until the recent rekindled interest (mentioned in the next paragraph in our text) in the Pāli Canon. Cf. James P. McDermott, "Scripture as the Word of the Buddha", *Numen*, 31(1984): [22]–39, e.g. at p. 31; and Jack D. Van Horn, remarks in my post-doctoral summer seminar at Harvard, 1984, and his forthcoming *Scripture in Buddhist Life*. Many of the monasteries have in their libraries only a fraction of the formal Canon, plus some of these items that are in theory less scriptural but in practice, including ritual use, are more so; so that both the monks and the laity in fact do not know the full Pāli Canon—and in fact have had no way of knowing it. Yet the idea of it is nonetheless crucial. See also Steven Collins, "On the Very Idea of the Pali Canon", *Journal of the Pali Text Society*, XV (1990): [89]–126.

38. In Mahāmaṅgala, *Buddhaghosuppatti* (op. cit., our note 36 above) he is reputed, for instance, to have had a cosmically miraculous birth (see that earlier note). In that text (Pāli, p. 66; Eng., p. 35) it is also affirmed that when Maitreya, the messianically expected future-Buddha-to-be appears on earth, Buddhaghosa will be recognized as his foremost disciple; while in another text, the *Cūlavaṃsa*, the presentation sets him forth as being acclaimed, on proffering his teachings, as himself Maitreya— MacDermott, ("Scripture as the Word . . ." op. cit., in our note 37 immediately above), pp. 31–32. Comparativists will be interested to note also that in the Mahāmaṅgala account of Buddhaghosa's childhood there is an engaging parallel to the story of the young Jesus in the temple answering the scholars' questions (*Buddhaghosuppatti*, Pāli, p.39; Eng., p. 6).

39. J. D. Van Horn, as per our note 37 above.

40. The *Saddharmaratnāvaliya*.

41. The *Pūjāvaliya*.

42. G. D. Wijayawardhana, "Literature in Buddhist Religious Life", in John Ross Carter, ed., *Religiousness in Sri Lanka* (Colombo: Marga Institute, 1979), p. 71. On the popularity of this work cf. also his p. 68. Comparativ-

ists may note, in relation to these two works' role in Sri Lanka, that in Europe for some centuries Thomas à Kempis's *Imitatio Christi* circulated, we are told, considerably more widely than the Bible, and was a matter of major importance in Christian life and piety. Does this bear pondering for the matter of scripture and its counterparts in world history?

43. Although this canon is (in consciousness) closed, different parts within it are (unconsciously?) treated with differing degrees of hallowedness, as is illustrated in the use of the Sinhala honorific mentioned in our note 31 above.

44. E. Michael Mendelson, *Sangha and State in Burma: a study of monastic sectarianism and leadership*, John P. Ferguson, ed. (Ithaca and London: Cornell University Press, 1975), pp. 266–267.

45. Shortly after coming to the throne of Burma King Mindon built a new capital, Mandalay (1857), convened the "Fifth Buddhist Council" there (1871) which issued an authoritative text of the Canon, and had this then inscribed on 729 tablets set up for the purpose, each in a protective pagoda-like structure, with a 730th pagoda in a great square, constituting the Kuthodaw.

46. The writings of both the founder, Shinran, and the later leader Rennyo, two-and-a-half centuries later; the latter a couple of thousand years after the death of Siddhārtha. Cf. our note 22 above; and James C. Dobbins, *Jōdo Shinshū: Shin Buddhism in medieval Japan* (Bloomington and Indianapolis: Indiana University Press, 1989).

47. Already the Indian Mahāyāna sūtra the *Laṅkāvatāra* (fourth? century) had encouraged—stressed—one's going beyond the merely textual; and the Chinese movement adopted that sūtra's champions (esp. Bodhidharma and his disciples) as their heritage. For example, in this Indian sūtra at 3:63:14, the Buddha is presented as discriminating explicitly between Enlightenment ("realisation itself") and the teaching about it. The latter is said to be helpful towards the former, for those inclined towards that; but the "inner attainment . . . has nothing to do with words, discriminations, and letters" (*vāgvikalpākṣararahita*—"*rahita*" is more literally these matters "having been left behind"). Sanskrit text: P. L. Vaidya, ed., *Saddharmalaṅkāvatārasūtram* (Darbhanga [Bihar]: Mithilāvidyāpīṭapradhānena Prakāśitam) / Mithila Institute of Post-Graduate Studies and Research in Sanskrit Learning, Śakābdaḥ 1884/Samvat 2020/Ḗsaviyābdaḥ 1963—Sītāṃśuśēkhara Vāgachi Śarmā/Sitansusekhar Bagchi, gen ed., Bauddha-saṃskṛta-pranthāvalī—3/Buddhist Sanskrit Texts - No. 3), p. 60. An English version: *The Lankavatara Sutra: a Mahayana text, translated for the first time from the original Sanskrit by* Daisetz Teitaro Suzuki (London: Routledge, 1932; Routledge & Kegan Paul, 1968), p. 128. Adumbrations of this sort of attitude to verbalizing are found also in the highly influential Chinese "scripture" called *Ta-ch'eng ch'i-hsin lun* (The Awakening of Faith). Also in China, later Ch'an leaders adopted from a commentary on the Lotus Sūtra by one Pao-en

(sixth century) the phrase "non-reliance on words and letters", I am told, though I myself do not know the passage. With all this, one may compare the story of the Chinese Buddhist monk noted in the next paragraph in our text.

48. These terms are often said to be from, and even to be equivalent to, Sanskrit *dhyāna*, which is technically correct, lexically, but can be misleading religiously since the new movement that was developed under this name in East Asia was novel, significantly different from what had been so labelled in India.

49. *T'an ching*. This ninth-century (T'ang) work (some say eighth-century) has gone through many editions—one could say, versions—in China, and many translations in the modern West. The message of the Ch'an/ Zen movement's sixth patriarch, Hui-neng, conveyed in the text, has in many ways set the tone for developments in both China and Japan, until today. Our remark in the text above, on "the word *sūtra*", could be deemed tendentious in that this work, composed in Chinese, has of course had not that Sanskrit term but, rather, *ching* in its title, which (along with its Japanese rendering *kyō*) we are taking the liberty of considering as the Chinese counterpart. For an argument against the validity of this, see Roger J. Corless, "The Meaning of *Ching (Sūtra?)* in Buddhist Chinese", *Journal of Chinese Philosophy*, 3 (1975): [67]–72. For an argument in favour (of what after all is the standard practice), see for instance Kōgen Mizuno, "The Meaning of the Word Sutra" in his *Buddhist Sutras: origin, development, transmission*, Morio Takanashi et al., transs. (Tokyo: Kōsei, 1982), pp. 15–17 (cf. also its preceding two pp.). The Japanese original of this latter work appeared first serially in the monthly magazine *Kōsei*, and later in book form as *Kyōden: sono seiritsu to tenkai* (Tokyo: Kōsei, 1980). My own reason for choosing to render Buddhist *ching* as equivalent to "sūtra" is that I feel that this most reasonably represents Chinese perceptions.

50. Berling, "Bringing the Buddha Down to Earth" (our note 24 above), p. 79, the case of Yang-ch'i (from the early eleventh century). Berling remarks of the "Recorded Sayings" (*Yü-lu*) genre in general that they "stress that the actions of masters, more than their words, are the means by which they transmit the Dharma" (ibid., p. 84). With this one may interestingly compare a recent development among some Christian Biblical scholars— the inherited concept of verbal revelation being for them no longer tenable—to develop a thesis that revelation is to be found in or through the Bible in historical events. The view is nicely summed up in the title of a work by a leading representative of this school: G. Ernest Wright, *God Who Acts: Biblical theology as recital* ([Chicago: H. Regnery] and London: SCM, 1952—Studies in Biblical Theology, no. 8).

51. All such cases are ironic, but the Christian one doubly so. Jeremiah spoke of a personal inward relationship to (from? with?) the divine, a personalist quality, as superseding formal scripture; his doing so presently itself

became formal scripture (chap. 31 of the Biblical book under his name)—although among Jews, this was at a less elevated level than the previously accepted one ("the Prophets" were added as written scripture to, but were made not quite co-ordinate with, Tôrāh, as we have seen). St. Paul (who of course had no idea that he was writing scripture) urged on his fellow Christians (Romans 2:27–29, II Corinthians 3:6) that one go beyond, even leave behind, what has become in English the accepted phrase "the letter of the law" but could with more historicist accuracy perhaps be translated as "the text of Tôrāh". Or we may say, he was advocating going beyond scripture, urging leaving scripture behind. (He uses the words *gramma*, *nomos*; the Revised Standard and other modern versions render by "literal", "the written code".) To make his point Paul in these passages took from what were the scriptures, for him and those Churches to whom he was writing, the very wording of that similar concept in Jeremiah, in its Greek version; and in due course that wording became rather the name for a new scripture, the Christian "New Testament" (cf. above, our chap. 3, note 18).

52. "Pāli" signified originally the language of scripture. This may have been originally the dialect of Magadha spoken by Siddhārtha Gautama, but later the word signified rather a modified form of this in which the scriptures were a thousand years after his day written in Sri Lanka—in what has become known, then, as The Pāli Canon, a usage that we affect in this survey. Today "Pali" in English may be said to be the name of two things: that Theravādin canon, and the language in which it is written (has been written, since the time of Buddhaghosa). There is no specific script; Pali is written in whatever local script is in vogue.

53. Under Genghiz Khan (Chingīz Khān, Temūjin) and his successors, Buddhist influence in Mongolia was little felt outside the court; but Altan Khan, in the sixteenth century, who launched a new era generally, deliberately and formally fostered that influence among his people. Over against rather restricted Chinese cultural impingement on some of the clerical class it was chiefly Tibetan Buddhist influence that became dominant in Mongolia. At first, there was a subsantial production of Mongol versions of scriptures, from Tibetan, and even from Sanskrit. Under the Manchus, on the other hand, Tibetan was made the cultural language of the Buddhist order, and "[b]y the end of [their] regime there were many monks in Mongolia who were literate in Tibetan but not in their own language"—O. La. [sc., Owen Lattimore], "Mongolia: History", in *Encyclopædia Britannica*, 15th edn., 1986, 24:351.

54. In 1965 a well-to-do Japanese business man, Yehan Numata, set up a Bukkyō Dendō Kyōkai ("Buddhist Evangelism Institution"), with the stated goal of "the widespread propagation of Buddhism". It has published and distributed, particularly in hotel rooms, thus far in 36 languages, two million copies of a little selection of Buddhist scriptures; and has recently embarked on a translation into English of the Chinese Buddhist Canon,

establishing in 1984 a "Numata Center for Buddhist Translation and Research" in Berkeley, California. Their brochure on the setting up of this Center speaks of "the vast number of Buddhist scriptures, which are said to number 84,000", and of the first step in this venture, the publication of 139 works—"around 100 volumes in printed form"—for the first fifteen years of the project (viz, to the end of the current century), with the 'frank' expectation that "it will take perhaps one hundred years or more to complete the translation of the whole Chinese and Japanese Canon . . . into English". See *The English Translation Project of the Buddhist Canon in Chinese* (Berkeley: Numata Center for Buddhist Translation and Research, and Tokyo: Bukkyo Dendo Kyokai, [1985]). Quotations here are from pp. 2, 5, 14. For Jōdo Shinsū translation projects into English, see our note 22 above.

55. The translation is known, after the name of its patron, as *The Book of Zambasta*; the translator rather plaintively reports that "because of their *karma*" [because they are so benighted, so sunk in sin, a Westerner or Christian might have said?] "the Khotanese do not at all appreciate the Dharma [*dātu*] in Khotanese. . . . To them, in Khotanese it does not seem to be the Dharma" (23:4). He himself is resolute to render it into this vernacular (where it has since become among the oldest extant pieces of literature in that language), "for the benefit of all sentient beings" (23:2). The other group, in contrast, say that "'because it is spoken from above, it is all meaningful. The ultimate meaning (*paramārtha*) of the Dharma is effective even when no one perceives its [verbal, or immediate] meaning'" (23:10–11)—*The Book of Zambasta: a Khotanese poem on Buddhism*, ed. and trans. by R. E. Emmerick (London, New York, etc.: Oxford University Press, 1968), pp. 342, 344 (Khotanese text); pp. 343, 345 (English trans.). The above translations are mainly my own, following conversation with my former student Jan Nattier-Barbaro.

56. Dargyay, " . . . Canonization in Tibet" (op. cit. above, our note 6).

57. There is a tricky question as to what is meant by "translating" a written text from Chinese to Japanese, since the two languages, though radically different, use the same characters as non-phonetic ideographs. The Western concept "translation" is a product of the West and its use of alphabetic writing. It is directly applicable to oral/aural rendering in East Asia, as elsewhere, but less or more inapt there in the field of writing: there it becomes decidedly a metaphor that fits only in part, and at times not at all. The matter is too subtle and complicated to explore here, and in any case is beyond my competence. It would be a misleading, yet not a totally ridiculous, over-simplification to say that the matter is like asking what, if anything, might be meant by translating the written proposition "2+2=4" from English into German or Italian. The Japanese, however, did supplement their use of Chinese characters both by introducing certain reading marks (*kaeri-ten*) to help in reading the characters in Japanese word-order

and such, and also by developing specifically Japanese phonetic syllabaries (*hiragana*, and recently *katakana*). In the twentieth century some Buddhist texts have been published in Japan re-arranging the Chinese characters in Japanese word-order. (Is it overly fanciful to correlate the not strictly comparable point that for English "$4.16", the written French is regularly "4,16$"?) For an introductory survey of a few other aspects of historical development regarding Buddhist works, one may consult Joseph M. Kitagawa, "Buddhist Translation in Japan", in *Babel: revue internationale de la traduction*, . . . No. 1–2 (1963): 53–59—though our problem is not broached there, nor in other treatments of Chinese-Japanese "translation" that I have seen.

58. It is often remarked that an "indigenous 'Japanese Buddhism'" emerged in the Kamakura period (thirteenth century): "unlike previous Buddhists who wrote books in Chinese, Buddhist leaders of this period started writing their thoughts in the Japanese language"—Kitagawa, "Buddhist Translation . . ." (op. cit. above, our immediately preceding note, no. 57), p. 56. Shinran's hymns (*wasan*), to cite an example not of books, "were treated with as much reverence and honour as the great Mahāyāna scriptures of Indian origin. They were used liturgically, and were recited with awe; they were just as holy, emotionally just as deep"—notes on a private conversation with my colleague Masatoshi Nagatomi, 1980.

59. Also Sarvāstivāda and related groups, all of which were sometimes lumped together under the name Mahāsāmghika; they along with Theravāda were lumped together (by the Mahāyāna) under the disparaging designation "Hīnayāna". Mahāsāmghika literature was chiefly in Sanskrit; some of it might be deemed scriptural, or even thought of as constituting a sort of canon not altogether unlike the Theravāda Pāli one; but we do not pursue the matter since the subsequent history of these movements has been short, and in world terms not so major as those considered. Mahāyāna Sūtras were also in Sanskrit for several centuries.

60. Cf. our note 52 above.

61. By "surviving" is meant here, surviving actively as effective scripture in community life. Of other early movements' scriptures, modern French and Japanese scholars have been discovering Chinese versions of some that are surviving in the sense of being recoverable as texts. In Sri Lanka, also, it is becoming known that alongside the Mahāvihāra school of monks, whose product (late first century B.C.) the Pāli canon is, there was until ca. the twelfth century A.D. another, rival, school, the Abhayagiri, with a differing scriptural collection, the two being apparently of roughly equal strength there, but then the ruling monarchy suppressed the latter and favoured the Mahāvihāra, and (virtually?) no Abhayagiri texts have survived. Certainly none has survived as scripture. See Collins (op. cit. our note 37 above), pp. 96–102.

62. *kavikṛtam kāvyam*—one almost might render this as "poetry, con-

cocted by poets". Our grounds for citing this accusation are not a direct Theravādin source, the evidence being indirect rather: namely, Mahāyāna sūtras, relating that Māra, the Evil One—the Buddhist Devil —, hoping mischievously to mislead those attracted, insinuates in their ears this disparaging of new sūtras. The inference seems more than plausible that such a charge was in fact going the rounds. This account is found in several of the "Perfection of Wisdom" ("Transcendent Insight") sūtras. I have consulted specifically that in the 8,000-line version, using the edition of that Sanskrit text by P. L. Vaidya, ed.: *Aṣṭasāhasrikā Prajñāpāramitā* (Darbhanga: 1881/ 2016/1960, No. 4 in the Buddhist Sanskrit Texts series cited above, our note 47), p. 163. There is an English version (with the more literal "poetry, the work of poets"): *Aṣṭasāhasrikā Prajñāpāramitā / The Perfection of Wisdom in Eight Thousand Slokas*, Edward Conze, trans. (Calcutta: The Asiatic Society, 1958—Bibliotheca Indica, Work no. 284), p. 123; in the revised edn., *The Perfection of Wisdom in Eight Thousand Lines & its Verse Summary*, translated by Edward Conze (Bolinas, California: Four Seasons Foundation, [1973], 1975 —The Wheel Series, Donald Allen, ed., no. 1) this passage, its wording unchanged, is found at p. 202.

63. A salient example is afforded within the Qur'ān: when it was first being offered to the public in Arabia, detractors discounted Muḥammad as a mere poet (one instance, 21:5—*bal, huwa shā'ir*). The disparagement has become notorious in Islamic circles, Muslims vehemently rejecting the idea. Christians have in the past generally held some such view of the scriptures of all other peoples except the Jews'; and secularists, of all scriptures.

64. For example, a Sarvāstivādin monk named Saṃghadeva from Kashmir was active in China in the early days of Buddhist translating into Chinese, and disquieted the growing movement in China by denouncing Mahāyāna sūtras there.

65. —and not without residual formal disparagement occasionally. The sūtra cited in our note 62 above, including the verse there quoted, continued of course to be read and cherished. There were similar instances that went so far as to speak apparently of deliberately, malevolently, false—one might say "pseudo-Buddhist"—scriptures; although perhaps what is intended rather is false, pseudo-Buddhist, understandings of those scriptures. An example: Māra, the Buddhist Devil, may disguise himself as a Buddha and "expound, manifest, analyse, amplify and illuminate" such "scriptures" in his attempt to lead astray someone who appears to be on his or her way to Enlightenment—*Pañcaviṃśatisāhasrikā Prajñāpāramitā Sūtra* (sc., the 25,000-line version), Kāṇḍa 36/1:3:11b. In the edn. of the Sanskrit text by Nālinākṣadatta/Nalinaksha Dutt (London: Luzac, Śāka 1856/1934—Calcutta Oriental Series, no. 28), this passage is p. 158. In the English version *The Large Sutra on Perfect Wisdom: with the divisions of the Abhisamayālaṅkāra*—translated by Edward Conze (Berkeley, Los Angeles, London: University of California Press, 1975), it is p. 115. (Earlier versions

of parts of this last work had appeared in London: Luzac, in 1961, in [Madison, Wisconsin, in 1964] and [Seattle, Washington, in 1966].) I have used this Conze translation, except that he has rendered *prakāśayiṣyati* here as "reveal", and I have avoided that particular English word, since it tends to connote revelation from a higher source than the Devil!—and to have as its direct object something authentic.

66. Cf. our note 25 above.

67. This edition was produced by one Ŭich'ŏn, a monk who was a member of the royal family. The collection, we must acknowledge, did exclude scriptures of the *Ch'an/Zen*/Korean: *Son* schools, apparently on the personal preference of Ŭich'ŏn. On the other hand, again at his initiative, it explicitly included non-Indian Buddhist texts, from not only China but Japan. It must be noted, however, that when the blocks for printing this edition were later destroyed in war, the next edition omitted this "extension" of the canon. See Lewis R. Lancaster, in collaboration with Sung-bae Park, *The Korean Buddhist Canon: a descriptive catalogue* (Berkeley, Los Angeles, London: University of California Press, 1979), pp. xiii–xvi.

68. I owe these particular illustrations to my colleague Wm. A. Graham, reporting on his experience some years ago in Lebanon.

69. On a difference in current usage between the adjectives "holy" and "sacred" (to some extent a difference between first- and third-person implication), see the article "Holy (The Sacred)" by Willard Gurdon Oxtoby in *Dictionary of the History of Ideas: studies of selected pivotal ideas* (4 voll. plus Index vol., New York: Scribner's, 1968–1974), vol. 2 (1973), pp. 511–514.

70. In China, this sort of situation among Buddhists was attained after a period during which in that country two distinct branches of the movement had developed, but presently these merged again into a more comprehensive whole.

71. By the Chinese Buddhist Association. For these collections, see Miriam Levering, her note 45, p. 99, in Levering, "Scripture and its Reception" (op. cit., our chap. 2 above, its note 1).

72. Miriam Levering, in my 1982 post-doctoral seminar at Harvard. Cf. also her article mentioned in our immediately preceding note, just above.

73. See our note 22 above.

74. The three sūtras carry the Japanese titles *Daimuryōju-kyō*, *Kammuryōju-kyō*, and *Amida-kyō*. These are Japanese renderings of the Chinese titles. In Sanskrit, both the first and the third, although different, are named *Sukhāvatīvyūha sūtra*. Modern scholarship distinguishes by referring to them as *"The Larger . . ."* and *"The Smaller Sukhāvatīvyūha"*; the Chinese differentiated by calling the smaller one the "Amida" sūtra. The Jōdo Shinshū movement, in presenting its scriptures in English, has itself recently used as its three English renderings simply "The Larger Sutra", "The Meditation Sutra", and "The Smaller Sutra". Of the second, a Sanskrit original has not been found, which leads many scholars to infer that it originated,

rather, in Central Asia or China. Western orientalists late last century, before this point was accepted, concocted for it a Sanskrit title *Amitāyurdhyāna*, rather unfortunately because of the possible confusion then with the Chinese and Japanese third one; yet it has remained in vogue. Among the writings of the Seven Patriarchs (*shichiso shōgyō*) included in this official Japanese collection of the movement are some of Nagārjuna's from India. Shinran's writings occupy the largest sector of the whole. Of the sect's own later leaders, the chief one featured is Rennyo.

75. *upāya* comes from the root *i* "to go", in Sanskrit (as also in Latin, whence also in English "exit". "transit", "transient", etc). Its compound *upa-ī* (= *upe*) means "to approach, to come near" and "to reach". In modern Western secular culture, in which we are all immersed, with its drive to power and its technological spirit, the notion "means" suggests manipulation, and certainly control, whereas *upāya* would seem on careful scrutiny to be a less transitive, certainly a less exploitative, concept. The base idea here is not that the Buddha skilfully wields a technique by which he can control others' behaviour or thought, so much as that he can provide a route by which those others may attain the goal. The word *kauśalya* I would render here as "competence"—since "skill", the usual translation in this instance, is in present-day culture in danger of conjuring up an idea of artfulness; to be related not to wisdom so readily as to a knowledge that may be used to dominate and compel. (In fact, in early Buddhist usage it means "good" action in the sense of "righteous", and even specifically "non-*karma*-generating".) More crucial is *upāya*, which is a verbal noun. Its verb is an intransitive verb of motion, not a transitive verb of engineering. And the subject of the verb is not the Buddha but his auditor, moving from where he or she is to approach life's *telos*. Or alternatively, if it be the Buddha who is sensed as moving, then the point is his manifold ability to approach ordinary human beings, to enter into their lives, to "reach" their hearts. I am not in a position to speak about the nuances of the Chinese and Japanese versions of the technical term (*fang-pien* and *hōben* respectively); but I have the impression that as elements in the Buddhist tradition these hardly correlate with modern-day instrumentalism (at least, not in sensitive pious use). Apparently the Japanese case comes closer to being heard, popularly, as something devious (as to my ear the usual English translation implies); for Buddhist leaders in Japan have written explicitly against that, contending that this way of understanding the matter is inept. Apparently in at least modern Chinese the term is in danger of having been somewhat trivialized, rather, conveying a notion not of cunning but simply of what is convenient. Pye's careful and rather full study of the term in his *Skillful Means* . . . (op. cit., our note 12 above) is written without a distinction in mind such as I am proposing here—namely, that (from an outsider's perspective) it may be the Buddha who is wisely competent, but the follower who moves; yet most of the rich material that he presents reads more effectively, in my percep-

tion, if one bears that discrimination in mind. In later Mahāyāna, which developed in such a way as to give relatively little centrality to the historical personage whom the West calls "the Buddha", and in many of the instances that Pye cites, it is the follower to whom the skilfulness (or competence) as well as the "means", or as I would call it the avenue, are referred. Particularly on the Japanese situation that I have just mentioned, where I am largely following his data, see esp. his chapp. 6 and 8. I also have heard that in Japan the popular misconception enters into many jokes, and a denunciation of it as indeed a misconception into many sermons. I have said above "from an outsider's perspective" because in the Buddhist vision ultimately a person's movement to enlightenment (his or her own enlightenment, as it individualistically were), and that person's compassionate and efficacious regard for others so that they will attain enlightenment, not only converge but fuse. Moreover, the transcendent Buddha who (or: that) enables the Buddhist to attain (to reach Enlightenment) is not "another" person (certainly not "another person") but is the person's own true nature. In these interpretations even the "skill" or wise and compassionate effectiveness—which in the original perception is the Buddha's—and not only the "means" or movement, both become the devotee's. (This point is covertly evident from another recent work with the title *Skillful Means*, by Tarthang Tulku—n.p. [Odiyan?, Emeryville? Calif.]: Dharma Publishing, 1978—which unlike the Pye study is not concerned with the concept explicitly, does not mention the Buddha or anything specifically either religious or Asian or traditional or transcendent, and uses the phrase only once in the body of the book; it is simply a discussion of everyday work habits addressed to modern Americans and suggesting sensible ways to help people lead more fulfilling lives.) May I be allowed to hope that, in reference to Buddhist matters, presently in English "skilful means" will have been replaced with perhaps "effective avenues"? On the issue of what is involved here, some might find it evocative to compare the understanding in Christians' life of Christ's saying: "I am the way". (On *upāya* see further E. Conze "Skill in Means", in his "Buddhism: The Mahāyāna", op. cit., in Zaehner, in our note 86 below, pp. 306–308 of the 1959 printing.)

76. Some movements modestly and explicitly hold that other groups' truths are indeed higher than their own, but that their own is as far along the path as they themselves have yet got, or are for now capable of getting. An example of which I have been told, although I myself am not familiar with the Tibetan scene and know only a smattering of its history, is of two Tibetan Buddhist groups of which one apparently affirms that the texts of the other are at a higher level than its own. The two sects are the Kagyu-pa (Bka'-brgyud-pa) and the reputedly "higher" (sc., more esoteric) Nying-ma-pa (Rnying-ma-pa).

77. I have not ascertained the historically first use of this image, though it seems definitely to be of Chinese Buddhist provenance. In any case, it is

used in two of the Chinese *ching* mentioned above, our note 23: the *Leng-yen-ching* and the *Yüan-chue-ching*.

78. See the important scholarly article of Gregory Schopen, "The Phrase '*sa pṛthivīpradeśaś caityabhūto bhavet*' in the *Vajracchedikā*: Notes on the Cult of the Book in Mahāyāna", in *Indo-Iranian Journal*, 17 (1975): [147]–181, noting esp. its now widely quoted final sentence, stating as a tentative conclusion "that . . . early Mahāyāna (from a sociological point of view), rather than being an identifiable single group, was in the beginning a loose federation of a number of distinct though related cults, all of the same pattern, but each associated with its specific text" (p. 181).

79. *Stūpas* were the most important architectural forms of the early Buddhist movement, dome structures of stone or brick regularly housing relics of the Buddha and serving as devotional focus and memorial monuments to him. This passage goes on to say, however, that in such a case as this it is not necessary to deposit relics.

80. From the Lotus Sūtra (chap. 10). I have used the edition of the Sanskrit text of H. Kern and Bunyiu Nanjio, edd., *Saddharmapuṇḍarīka-sūtram / Saddharmapuṇḍarīka* (St.-Pétersbourg: Académie Impériale des Sciences, 5 tomes, 1908–1912—Bibliotheca Buddhica X), 3:231–232; my translation. In the translation from the Sanskrit of H. Kern, trans., *Saddharma-Puṇḍarīka, or The Lotus of the True Law* (Oxford: Clarendon Press, 1884; New York: Dover, 1963—F. Max Müller, ed., *The Sacred Books of the East*, vol. XXI), this passage is p. 220. There are many English versions of the Lotus Sūtra, both from the Sanskrit (as just given; and a rendering of this particular passage with discussion is given also in the Schopen article mentioned in our note 78 above—p. 164) and from the Chinese (our next note immediately below, no. 81; in the first of these mentioned there, this passage is p. 228). The Chinese has been the historically more influential.

81. In an English rendering of the version of this sūtra prevalent in China and Japan, one reads that a certain Boddhisattva "became a buddha" on receiving, keeping, reading, and preaching the Lotus Sūtra: *Myōhō-Renge-Kyō: the Sutra of the Lotus Flower of the Wonderful Law, translated by* Bunnō Katō, *revised by* W. E. Soothill, Wilhelm Schiffer (Tokyo: Kōsei, 1971), p. 365. Noticeable is that the phrase "became a buddha" is spelled in this rendering with a lower-case "b". The Nichiren sect's version uses upper-case, but retains the indefinite article: "was able to become a Buddha"— *Myō Hō Ren Ge Kyō/The Sutra of the Lotus Flower of the Wonderful Law, translated from Kumārajīva's version of The Saddharmapuṇḍarīka-Sūtra by* Senchu Murano (Tokyo: Nichiren Shu Headquarters, 1974), p. 261. Western students could understand rather "became *the* Buddha", since the passage is making the seemingly convoluted point that the author of this sūtra, reputedly the person whom the West calls *the* Buddha, when he was still that previous Bodhisattva was able "to attain to Perfect Enlightenment" (Kato et al., loc. cit.); Murano resorts to reproducing the Sanskrit: by taking full hold of and living by this very Lotus Sūtra which the speaker is now setting

forth, "I attained Anuttara-samyak-saṃbodhi" (p. 261). I do not know the Chinese here being translated; in the Sanskrit text (there this chap. is no. 19; in the Japanese, chap. 20), this Bodhisattva is affirmed to have gained this *uttarām samyaksaṃbodhim*—"ultimate perfect enlightenment", "ultimate perfect Buddhahood"—through this sūtra: Kern-Nanjio edn. (op. cit. in our preceding note immediately above, no. 80), tome 4, p. 381 (my trans.; cf. the Kern trans. [op. cit., ibid.], p. 359).

82. So, for example, again the tenth chapter of the Lotus Sūtra, in its opening verses. (Sanskrit, Kern-Nanjio, 3, p. 224; Eng., Kern, p. 213; Kato et al., pp. [222]–223—opp. citt., our notes 80 and 81 above). Although our last three examples are all taken from this particular sūtra, that work is by no means alone in proffering this fairly common-place Mahāyāna attitude.

83. Examples from Japan are provided in the lives of Kūkai (ninth century, from whom the Shingon movement arises), with the *Mahāvairocana sūtra* (Japanese: *Dainichikyō*) and other esoteric sūtras (although in his case his personal encounter with the teacher with whom he studied them was equally important, as befits that tradition's outlook); Nichiren (thirteenth century), with the Lotus Sūtra, as remarked above; Shinran (also thirteenth century) with three Sūtras (as also remarked). One might add Rennyo (fifteenth century) with the *Anjinketsujōshō*, an esoteric work that is not a sūtra (not a *ching*) but that served him scripturally. In all these cases, the results of their fresh readings of these scriptures laid the basis for major movements that continued for centuries and attracted multitudes.

84. To call him "the Japanese Asoka" would keep the analogy within the Buddhist movement.

85. In contrast, in India copyists were of low caste—and we have seen that their work would have utterly defiled the original Veda, which was indeed not copied or written at all.

86. The question is, however, a vexed one, and has been asked for a long while—e.g., last century by Arthur Lillie, *Buddhism in Christendom; or, Jesus, the Essene* (London: Kegan Paul, Trench, 1887). More recently, see, e.g., Roy C. Amore, *Two Masters, One Message* (Nashville, Tennesee: Abingdon, 1978); E. Conze, "Buddhism: The Mahāyāna", in R. C. Zaehner, ed., *The Concise Encyclopaedia of Living Faiths* (London: Hutchinson; and, with the spelling *Encyclopedia*, New York: Hawthorn Books, 1959), pp. 296–297. (In a 2nd edn., London: Hutchinson, 1971, in which also the spelling *Encyclopedia* in the title was used, it is pp. 293–294; in the Boston: Beacon Press edn., 1967, which (re-?)turns to *Encyclopædia*, pp. 296–297.) See also Étienne Lamotte, "Emprunts à des sources étrangères" in his *Histoire du Bouddhisme indien: des origines à l'ère Śaka* (Louvain: Publications universitaires / Institut orientaliste, 1958, pp. 739–752; and Edward J. Thomas, "Buddhism and Christianity", chap. XVII of his *The Life of Buddha* . . . (op. cit., our note 30 above), pp. [237]–248. We return to this matter briefly in a later chapter.

87. Above, p. 152.

88. The *Pātimokkha Sutta*, the earliest item in the Vinaya Basket, which is in turn the earliest sector of the Pāli Canon. See McDermott, "Scripture as the Word . . ." (op. cit. in our note 37 above), pp. 23–24.

89. Rogers, "A Founder's 'Teaching' . . ." (op. cit. in our note 22 above).

90. Cf. in modern North American English the use of the colloquial expression "I hear what you are saying" in the sense of "I grasp your point" (or: ". . . its inuendo", ". . . its implication"); although in Shinran's case there would seem to have been the added implication of taking it to heart and into one's living. Cf. the comment on Nichiren at our note 92 below.

91. See Thomas P. Kasulis, "Truth Words: the basis of Kūkai's theory of interpretation", in Donald S. Lopez, Jr., ed., *Buddhist Hermeneutics* (Honolulu: University of Hawaii Press, 1988—Kuroda Institute, Studies in East Asian Buddhism, no. 6), pp. 257–272. One may note esp., in his penultimate paragraph: "The truth of a statement depends not on the status of its referent, but on how it affects us" (p. 271).

92. Though not reified nor even denominated in Japanese, Nichiren's conception here converges with the deeper meaning of the English noun "faith" (Christian-derived though recently by many debased) now used for a globally-comparativist concept, as for instance in my *Faith and Belief* (op. cit., our note 28 above).

93. Nichiren observes that perception in general varies with the moral and spiritual quality of the perceiver. (His conceptualizing of this point was of course within a framework of Buddhist ideas: he phrased it in terms of *karma*.) In the water of the Ganges river, he analogizes, ghosts see fire, human eyes see water, celestials see ambrosia—because of their different *karma*, "though the water is one and the same". Similarly, with a scriptural text: the physically blind do not see even the written characters; the rest of us see these, but "those who are content with self-annihilation see therein emptiness; whereas the saint (bodhisattva) realizes therein inexhaustible truths, and the enlightened (Buddhas) perceive in each of the characters a golden body of the Lord"—Nichiren, *Works*, as translated and quoted in Masaharu Anesaki, *Nichiren, the Buddhist Prophet* (Cambridge [Massachusetts]: Harvard University Press, and London: Oxford University Press, 1916), p. 16. I have allowed myself to alter Anesaki's translation to substitute "characters" (referring to the ideographs) for his "letters".

94. Above, our chapter 2. Or, to stay within the Buddhist sphere, yet from the other end, as it were (in space, time, sect), of the Buddhist world: with this Japanese position one may perhaps compare the Theravādin thesis of the three stages of the disciple's progress, formulated in the *pariyatti, paṭipatti, paṭivedha* doctrine of, respectively, learning the truth (objectively, one might nowadays say), putting it into practice in one's living, and realizing its goal. See, for example, s.v. "Pariyatti" in Nyanatiloka, *Buddhist Dictionary: manual of Buddhist terms and doctrines*, third revised and enlarged edn., ed. Nyanaponika (Colombo, Ceylon: Frewin & Co., 1972), p. 127.

95. Recent work facilitating study of this matter, directly or indirectly, include: the double article of MacQueen, "Inspired Speech . . ." (op. cit. our note 17 above); Robert A. F. Thurman, "Buddhist Hermeneutics", *Journal of the American Academy of Religion*, 46 (1978): 19–39; George D. Bond, "History and Interpretation in Theravada Buddhism and Christianity", *Encounter*, [Colombo], 39 (1978): 405–434 , and "Two Theravada Traditions of the Meaning of 'The Word of the Buddha'", *Maha Bodhi*, 83 (2519/ 1975): [402]–413; José Ignacio Cabezón, "The Development of a Buddhist Philosophy of Language and its Culmination in Tibetan Mādhyamika Thought", University of Wisconsin-Madison doctoral dissertation, Ann Arbor, Michigan: University Microfilms International, 2 voll., 1987.

96. Of course, unlike the developments within later Buddhist history of which we are here speaking, Siddhārtha's sense was of a novel moon—if one may suggest a divergent version of that later Buddhist metaphor— worth pointing to, discerned in a somewhat different direction from what he sensed contemporary scriptures to be calling attention to. This was in addition to his perception that those scriptures themselves were distracting people from, not orientating them towards, what is ultimately significant. There is always more to transcendent reality (he realized, as may we) than even the best of our predecessors have discerned.

97. Pāli form of Sanskrit *dharma*. On this word see at our note 28 above and note 99 below.

98. The original meaning, it seems, of this word; it later came to refer specifically to the norms of conduct for the monks and nuns, the rules of the order.

99. The *Mahāparinibbāna Sutta*, 6:1. In the Rhys Davids/Carpenter edn. of the Pāli (op. cit., our note 30 above), this passage is p. 154. My translation. It is instructive to note how far outsiders may at times inadvertently misapprehend, and then even misrepresent, misrender, passages such as this—and misunderstand other people's scriptures generally—by omitting the transcendence denoted—not merely connoted—by the words that they (unreflectingly) choose. "Dharma" in English, for instance, has lent itself to being understood as the proper name of empirical Buddhist (or the Buddha's) teaching, whereas the word actually means "reality" or "truth"; it is cognate with the English word "firm", and refers to what finally holds, to what is absolute, utterly dependable (cf. our note 28 above). Similarly *desito* in this passage (my "pointed out" above) has often been translated as "taught", whereas, related to the Sanskrit root "to see", it means basically to make visible: not simply to propound, to instruct, but rather to point out, to demonstrate, to enable someone to see what is in fact there. Again, Pāli *paññatto* (my "made known" here) is connected with the Sanskrit term *prajña*, another of the fundamental concepts in the Buddhist worldview: wisdom or insight (cf. our note 12 above); it means to enable someone to be wise, insightful, to perceive, and in Buddhist contexts to perceive ultimate

transcendent reality. Thus the sentence in the text is in danger of coming across to outsiders as "the teaching that I have set forth", rather than "the truth to which I given access". Non-Buddhists need not, of course, agree that what Siddhārtha offered to his followers is absolute truth; but in translating texts that refer to it, it is important to recognize what those texts actually say, not what they would mean if spoken or heard, written or read, by a modern skeptic. Thus renderings from even an erudite scholar, who knows Pāli much better than do I, may miss these nuances. Coming closest to a sensitive English rendering was perhaps that in the Max Müller series, *The Sacred Books of the East* (our chap. 1 above, p. 6 and its note 4), its vol. XI: *Buddhist Suttas: translated from the Pâli by* T. W. Rhys Davids (Oxford, 1881), p. 112, when read with the caveats and hesitations expressed by his widow in the later reprint in *Dialogues of the Buddha, translated from the Pali by* T. W. and C.A.F. Rhys Davids (London: Luzac, for the Pali Text Society, 1951)—see pp. [vii], [ix], xi. Less effective is "The Doctrine . . . which I have taught" in Henry Clarke Warren, *Buddhism in Translations: passages selected from the Buddhist sacred books and translated from the original Pali into English* (Cambridge, Mass.: Harvard University Press, [1896] 1947; Charles Rockwell Lanman, ed., Harvard Oriental Series, vol. 3), p. 107—although one is grateful for the capital D.

100. Smaller and less enduring groups had stories of other Councils as well, similarly.

101. So, most influentially, Nāgārjuna; in his powerful philosophic system (on which, and esp. its central notion rendered as "emptiness", cf. the next paragraph in our text). Yet the point is found also—though rarely—in the scriptures themselves. One instance: the "Ārya" *Tathāgataguhya Sūtra* evidently avers that from the moment of his enlightenment until his *parinirvāṇa*—his earthly death, or passing on to 'the other shore'—the Buddha did not utter "even a single syllable"; "he did not speak, does not speak, and will not speak. But [*lege* And?] all beings, according to their own faith and diverse predispositions, recognize (*saṃjānanti*)" the Buddha teaching in different ways; each thinks, "'The Lord is teaching Dharma to us'". (The grounds for the Buddha's non-speaking are then given as that he, and his truth, are beyond articulations in [mundane] words and concepts.) This sūtra is extant only in Tibetan translation, which I do not read; my rendering here is from the Sanskrit of a fragment of the original that has survived by being quoted in the course of a seventh-century Sanskrit commentary on Nāgārjuna, given in Louis de la Vallée Poussin, ed., *Madhyamikavṛttiḥ: Mūlamadhyamakakārikās (Mādhyamikasūtras) de Nāgārjuna avec la Prasanna-padā commentaire de Candrakīrti* (St.-Pétersbourg: Académie Impériale des Sciences, 4 tomes 1903–1913—Bibliotheca Buddhica 4), p. 539 (I read *niścarantām*, rather than *niścarantom* as printed). There are somewhat unsatisfactory English translations of this passage in Th. Stcherbatsky, *The Conception of Buddhist Nirvāṇa* ([Leningrad: Academy of Sciences of the

USSR, 1927], The Hague, London, Paris: Mouton, 1965—Indo-Iranian Reprints), p. 210, and in *Lucid Exposition of the Middle Way: the essential chapters from the* Prasannapadā *of Candrakīrti, translated from the Sanskrit by* Mervyn Sprung, *in collaboration with* T.R.V. Murti *and* U. S. Vyas (London and Henley: Routledge & Kegan Paul, 1979), pp. 262–263. This carries to a final point the idea set forth in other Mahāyāna sūtras that—to quote a verse in the *Vimalakīrtinirdeśa*, l:10:12—"the Lord speaks with but one voice, Those present perceive that same voice differently, And each understands in his own language according to his own needs. This is a special quality of the Buddha". (Christians will be reminded of the Holy Spirit's inspiring this same result on the day of Pentecost: Acts 2:1–13.) This sūtra also has survived only in Tibetan, Central Asian, and Chinese versions (the last then also in Japanese), which have been markedly influential; I have used the English version of the Tibetan of Robert A. F. Thurman, *The Holy Teaching of Vimalakīrti: a Mahāyāna scripture* (University Park [Penn.] and London: The Pennsylvania State University Press, 1976), p. 14. There is a study and French version based on both the Tibetan and the Chinese in *L'Enseignement de Vimalakīrti (Vimalakīrtinirdeśa): traduit et annoté par* Étienne Lamotte (Louvain—Leuven: Publications Universitaires / Institut Orientaliste, 1962—Bibliothèque du *Muséon*, vol. 51), pp. 109–110. Furthermore, Lamotte, in a long footnote (no. 52, ibid.) on the above verse surveys several Buddhist positions on the varying ways (and varying languages, and absence of language) in which the Buddha imparted (imparts?) his message to all sorts and conditions of human beings: for instance, one may say that he speaks a variety of languages simultaneously; "if He expresses himself in Chinese, it is because that language is the best for the inhabitants of China"—ibid., p. 109, quoting the Vibhāṣā. Sentiments such as all these might be taken as a comment on scripture generally in human history, not merely on Buddhist scriptures? We shall return to this.

102. See also Raimundo Panikkar, *El Silencio del Dios* (Madrid: Guadiana, 1970—Colección «Tiempo al Tiempo»). There is, from the Italian version, an English trans. (which the author has "gone through . . . and introduced some modifications here and there"—p. xi; one wonders, however, whether he approved the English sub-title) by Robert R. Barr: *The Silence of God: the answer of the Buddha* (Maryknoll, New York: Orbis, 1989—Faith Meets Faith series, Paul F. Knitter, gen. ed.)

103. Much has been written on this multifaceted notion; see, for instance, Frederick J. Streng, *Emptiness: a study in religious meaning* (Nashville and New York: Abingdon, 1967). Cf. also our next note, just below, no. 104.

104. I am well aware that the phrase "lies beyond" is a metaphor, and is not one that sophisticated Buddhist philosophers would choose or perhaps even allow. Yet it is proffered here as a metaphor that to non-Buddhists may nonetheless prove helpful. The metaphor that among this group of Buddhists is established, and cherished, is of course the notion that is trans-

lated into English as "emptiness"—Sanskrit *śūnyatā* (would "vacuity" or "hollowness" be a better rendering? The term more literally designates swollenness). The term to them, of course, means not what "emptiness" means generally to English-speaking groups, but the transcendence that they have learned to apprehend as symbolized by it. Some Buddhists would resist this, since to them "transcendence" suggests something more specific and more remote than it means to, for instance, me who proffer it.

105. Dargyay, " . . . Canonization in Tibet" (op. cit., our note 6 above).

106. A careful and illuminating study of one particular sector of their work is Cabezón, "Buddhist Philosophy of Language . . ." (op. cit., our note 95 above).

107. In English and other Western treatment of Buddhist thought, "wisdom" and its equivalent in other Western languages are regularly used to render a technical term in Buddhist usage, *prajñā* (Sanskrit; Chinese, *po-jo*; Japanese, *hannya*)—though "insight" as a preferable rendering has been suggested, as we have observed at our note 12 above. In this sentence in our text, however, I am using "wisdom" in the normal English sense, which has its background, rather, both in Græco-Latin thought and in Biblical. Yet the Buddhist sense of *prajñā* is also relevant here—as the following summing up by a recent scholar of his observations on one of the "Wisdom" sūtras (the *Aṣṭasāhasrikā*) suggests: "'the word of the Buddha' means primarily the truth as revealed to man. One seeks this truth not by determining what a particular fleshly being once said, but by gaining access to it here and now. . . . [This] truth comes through liberating wisdom [sc. *prajñā*]. One can become intimate with this wisdom, embody it, put it into words"—MacQueen, "Inspired Speech . . ." (op. cit., our note 17 above), its Part II, p. 61—remarks that occur *à propos* of the Mahāyāna's cheerfully producing new scriptures as it went along—specifically, the various Wisdom sūtras.

108. A Japanese friend of mine, for instance, tells me that his mother has memorized the Heart Sūtra and recites it devoutly every night before she retires—without understanding a single word (or caring to understand). Similar examples could be cited from almost every century of Buddhist life (cf. the Khotanese instance mentioned above, at our note 55), and as well from almost every other religious tradition on earth (as my own experience in the Muslim world, for instance, attests; and as we shall exemplify further in our concluding chapter).

109. The title of this Sūtra is in Sanskrit *Saddharmapuṇḍarīkasūtra*, in Chinese *Miao-fa lien-hua ching*, in Japanese *Myōhō-renge-kyō*. These last two are the respective pronunciations of the same ideograms: visually the two titles are identical, while orally/aurally the two languages have quite different words represented by (their convergent or equivalent meaning represented by) the same characters (cf. our note 57 above). The Nichiren community today uses the Japanese pronunciation; Nichiren himself may have used the Chinese. Such considerations would seem to indicate amply that it

is not the title as such that is significant, but the (*or:* a) title as meaningful to the person concerned—the title treated scripturally, we might say.

110. Anesaki, *Nichiren* (op. cit. at our note 93 above), pp. 15, 16. One might be excused for wishing to modify the final sentence in this quotation as given in our text by suggesting that it is the act of pronouncing the formula (cf. "uttering" in his preceding sentence), or a presupposition of sincerity behind "*namu*" in it, rather than the bare title of the book, that legitimates Anesaki's remark. This correlates with my argument in our preceding note immediately above on the variations in wording of the title.

111. Along with these two in the *triratna* a third was included: the order of monks (and of nuns, originally—indeed continuingly, in the Mahāyāna); that is, the community set up by the Buddha and preserving (consecrated to preserving) for subsequent generations his memory and the contribution of his teaching. With this order also, of course, the scriptures were closely interlinked. To name this third here would convolute, but not invalidate, the language of the remainder of our sentence in the text.

112. In English the adjective "this-world", and even for many the noun "symbol", stand for specifically Western concepts, more out of place here perhaps than usual, since for example the Lotus Sūtra presents itself as having existed for thousands of myriads of æons before it led the Buddha to Enlightenment. On the other hand, Western traditions also, which do use the this-world/other-world distinction, have at times postulated pre-existence and final transcendence for their scriptures. Rather than symbolic, and certainly rather than mundane, we might see scriptures both East and West as being perceived as "cosmic"? Our personal view, however, continues to see them as symbolic—which leaves room for the diverse perceptions.

113. See the quotation of MacQueen given in our note 107 above. The next sentence in MacQueen's statement, following his "One can become intimate with this wisdom, embody it, put it into words" reads: "The person who does this—the *dharma*-preacher, the inspired speaker—is the delegate of liberating wisdom and is hence presented as a speaker of extended *buddhavacana*" (p. 61).

114. We shall address in our concluding chapter the issue that arises from the diversity of specific shapes: diversity both among the world's several such movements and within each, including the diversity amply found, as we have stressed, within the Buddhist. In our preceding sentence in the text we suggested that Buddhists for all their divergence on shapes found their various scriptures indicating that transcendence "matters more than anything else in our life"; it would not be legitimate to suppose that they felt (or that we feel) that it does not matter whether it be perceived rightly, as being indeed of "this or that specific shape"—or that it has not mattered historically that Buddhists have perceived it in the specific ways that they have. It will not do to avoid this question. Neither will it do to avert it by failing to recognize the transcendence that is in any case primary.

8. The Classics:
Chinese and Western

1. In this study I use a capital initial for "Classics" and "Classical" when referring to what may be called the Confucian tradition in China and specifically its books, and to the Græco-Roman tradition in the Western world and especially its books; and "Classicist" for persons who orient themselves to or by these. This is to indicate that in these two cases it is the proper name of a particular tradition. The word "classic" in English, and other Western languages, is used also as a common noun or its adjective, applied attributively to books (and other matters), of undefined range, that the speaker or writer discerns as of a particular quality. (As we shall be noting later—in our next chapter—this usage in European languages was historically, by a small interval, the more original of the two.) Thus the writings of Chaucer or Longfellow or Goethe may be called classics. This, for which I use lower case, and the the works to which it is applied, are in the Western case discussed in our next chapter. There is also in Chinese a quite different word other than *ching* for a sort of Chinese literature that has come to be regarded as a counterpart to this Western category: see our p. 206 below.

2. This is one of several names used by the Chinese for the complex tradition; another is *ching hsüeh* ("study of the *ching*" ['Classics'? 'scriptures'?]), and other more honorific appellations, some of them of recent currency. *Ju chia* is also standard, designating the Classicist "school", or the group of the Classicists. On the meaning of *Ju*—translated here "literati", the scholarly class, the learned élite—specifically in its early era, which later became symbolic and almost legendary, and on the subsequent meaning then of *Ju chiao*, see the doctoral dissertation of Diane Burdette Obenchain, "Ministers of the Moral Order: innovations of the early Chou kings, the Duke of Chou, Chung-ni and *Ju*", Harvard Unversity, 1984, and some of this scholar's subsequent writing. *Chiao* is "teaching", transmission of teaching, tradition. (It was wrestling with what in China this term designated, and the place of "three religions" in Chinese' life, while I was thinking out my book *The Meaning and End of Religion*—op. cit., our chap. 2 above, note 3—thirty years ago, that in significant part led me to propose "cumulative tradition", along with "faith", as better alternative concepts to the reified Western idea of "religion", usually used for *chiao*.)

3. After "Confucius", the Latin version concocted to render the name of the person, K'ung Fu-tzu, whom the West has—somewhat misleadingly—thought of as the "founder" of the tradition.

4. The distortions have to do with their neglect—or at best, subordination—of temporal, regional, and personal perceptions and responses, which in their on-going and often major diversity and development in fact constitute each cumulative [*sic*] tradition. They have to do also with their neglect or subordination of the transcendent dimension, that tradition's *raison d'être*

and *de continuer d'être*. See further the remark on reductionism in our note 6 below. From the ineptitude of the reifying quality of the concept "Confucianism", something of the on-going development is salvaged—or an attempt is made to salvage it—by the imposing of the other name, "Neo-Confucianism", on phases of that continuing evolution that are recognized as obviously resisting the uniformity implied in the simpler, more comprehensive, notion. Yet this half-hearted and begrudging admission of something awry in the old conceptualizing is not good enough.

5. These have to do with the substantial and accepted permeability of the three major traditions recognized by the Chinese: "Confucian", "Taoist", and "Buddhist". In contrast, the three major traditions recognized by the West when it was recently forming its conceptual patterns for pluralism, namely Christian, Jewish, and Islamic, have all been notoriously rigid in erecting theoretical boundaries around themselves and insisting on exclusivist attitudes to each other. Without the either/or separatism embedded in this Western mood, and given instead the general openness in China to mutuality (more pronounced in some ages than in others; cf. our note 11 below), it simply distorts the Chinese scene still further to import into it such reifications. (In the Western case also there has been permeability. It has, however, not been recognized and certainly not accepted: each tradition, once formed, has been supposed to be independent.)

6. "Ethnocentric" because modelled on the neologism "Christianity". This term was a reification formed on the name of the central figure and concept in the Christian tradition, Christ. In the Islamic case, the central figure and concept are God; it has been offensive to Muslims to suggest that they are making the very mistake that, in their view, Christians have made, of worshipping the messenger instead of properly heeding the message—particularly that message's emphasis on worshipping God alone. They see their religion, "Islām", as founded—and named—by God on the day of creation, with Adam the first messenger, Moses and Jesus as subsequent ones, and Muḥammad as the final one who, late in time, effectively revived it on earth. The case of the Chinese Classical tradition is interestingly parallel, since for its devotees the importance of Confucius, though immense, is ultimately derivative. He, like Muḥammad, has been considered great because he recognized, personally embodied, effectively articulated, and transmitted—but did not originate—the supreme wisdom about the human condition in the cosmos. For both, the high status in which they are held rests on their association with that transmission—not least, in book form. The term "Muhammadanism", apart from being ethnocentric, was also reductionist. It names the tradition by referring to something in this world; whereas the whole point of the Islamic tradition is that it is oriented to God, at a level above the mundane, to which level Muḥammad is honoured for pointing. Even in the Christian case, and the Buddhist, the tradition's name (recent though it be, and problematic) is not "Jesusism"

nor "Gautamaism", after the name of the mundane aspect of the central figure, but derives rather from the recognized cosmic dimension: from the title by which that central figure's transcendent status is affirmed. Chinese Classicists, similarly, see their "Way of the Sages" as having absolute priority over its articulation by K'ung Fu-tzu—the man "Confucius". In this they are, of course, following that thinker himself. He did not originate the pattern to which his role was to call attention.

7. It has been fairly standard for commentators in the tradition to turn, with regard to the books that they were cherishing, to the metaphor of the net and the fish (the metaphor comes from the Taoist sage Chuang-tzu: the purpose of the net is the fish, and once it has been caught it is the fish that is important, the net becoming, if not relatively negligible, at least recognizedly secondary). Thus the words of the Classics gain their significance and value from their meaning, from the truth that they convey; they are important for a reader only insofar as he or she can by means of them catch hold of that truth. (The exception of course is that they may lead that reader to a partial grasp, and continue then important insofar as they go on leading to a more and more substantial apprehension. It was a subject of debate as to whether it was conceivable that the fish could be caught without the net—with one's bare hands, as it were.) (An alternative metaphor was the hare and the trap.)

8. And on which we have already remarked, in our note 5 above.

9. The use of this term *ching* has had a complicated history. A thousand years after the tradition's "canon", to import a Western concept, had been formed in Han times, it was enlarged in the Sung, following Chu Hsi in the twelfth century, with The Four Books (*Ssu Shu*) placed alongside The Five (or Six) *Ching*—and in fact over-arching them in actual importance. (It is this somewhat revolutionary development that gives rise to the Western term "Neo-Confucianism".) The word *shu*, "book", is basically more akin to the Western term "scripture" in its denotation; in connotation, for those who choose the Western term "Classic" for this tradition's *ching*, these four *shu* deserve equally to be called "Classics" for this "Classical" movement once they became canonized. Since these considerations do not, we feel, affect our argument, we ignore throughout this presentation the distinction between these two Chinese terms, allowing ourselves to do so partly on the grounds that two of the four *shu* are in fact sections, at that point objectified for the first time, of the original *ching*. Besides, the phrase *shih san ching*, "thirteen *ching*", comprising these four "books" along with certain others, in due course became current.

10. One example would be a traditional library-classification system, where the Confucian "Classics" were the only set of *ching* to constitute a special class. What the West calls the "scriptures" of the other religious movements in China—Taoist, Buddhist—including such works as Lao-tzu's *Tao Te Ching* and others with the title *ching* were grouped along with

various other works under various other headings. (In some imperial libraries set up in early Manchu times, Buddhist scriptures were omitted altogether, it seems.)

11. The development of the Buddhist tradition in China and its place in Chinese life from the time of its arrival from India about the beginning of what in the West is the Christian era and now the international era over the next thousand years or so are far too complex and subtle to be summarized hastily, of course. Yet it is hardly misleading to say that at least until the ninth century of this era, increasingly under the Six Dynasties and especially in the T'ang, China found itself much attracted to the new movement; and many of the literati, to say nothing of the populace at large, lived in some sort of consciously positive relation to Buddhist teaching. A few voices dissented on principle from this and from the amalgam of "The Three Teachings" (Classical or "Confucian", Taoist, and Buddhist) that had come into vogue. These minority views begin notably with Hsün Chi in the sixth century, Fu I in the seventh, Han Yü in the ninth; and by the time the second millennium was well under way the literati had become largely critical of the other two movements. These other movements were, and continued, much more "popular" than the *Ju chiao*, and the criticism tended to be that of an élite deploring the waywardness of the uncultured. The Classicists were at this point not primarily in dialogue with Buddhist and Taoist intellectuals, yet in fact had absorbed—unconsciously, no doubt—a great deal from them. This is evidenced for instance by Chu Hsi (twelfth century), whose novel and powerful interpretation of the Classical tradition, which he championed against the Buddhists, is in fact deeply imbued with Buddhist spirit—a point that both he and especially his followers might be surprised, or embarrassed, to acknowledge. Apart from such matters in substance, also formally the Buddhist imprint had become significant, not least in the area that is our special concern, since the Classical tradition henceforth had an enlarged place for scripture and commentary, illustrated for example in the voluminous and important *yü lu* literature of the "Neo-Confucians", with its title as well as some of its orientations a quiet borrowing. On the whole, the targets of the expressed criticism of the "foreign importation" were thus only indirectly these movements' scriptures as such; and I am not aware of any challenge putting forth the idea that these pertained to a different category from their own "Classics", however much they might feel that the teachings set forth in them might be less worthy. That is, they do not seem to have called into question that the sacred books of all three groups come under the one heading of *ching*. This observation does not conflict with another: that admittedly the Classicists ("Confucians") in China have at times perceived their *ching* as diverging from the Buddhist ones not only obviously in content but also formally in that they were seen in a different light. Presumably one might say that for them the word *ching* had differing meanings in the two cases? It is also true,

less self-consciously of course yet markedly, that their *ching* have been seen by their own group at some times in a different light from at other times. That is, one may say, with assurance, that the word *ching* has had meanings for them in some eras different from those that it has had for them in others. One may even be sure that the word has meant something different to different individual Classicists; and even to the same person at different phases in his, or in this particular case less strikingly her, life—just as the word "Bible", for instance, or "Gita", of course resonates differently for various people depending on a thousand idiosyncratic factors. We have already noted that the word "scripture" has for many been shifting its meaning recently from a metaphysical concept to an earthly sociological one. It is obvious that for devout Christians, for example, the word "scripture" although used for both has a radically different meaning in their minds—and hearts—when referring to the Bible and when referring to the Qur'an—apart from the variations in the meaning even of "Bible" for different individual Christians. A careful investigation of the meanings and uses of the term *ching* in the process of Chinese history has only begun.

12. Women adherents, though often loyal, were seldom among those who stressed, or even recognized, distance. Both men and women, and especially the latter, have participated in the standard mood of appreciation.

13. Unconsciously, on the other hand, the West was involved in this very issue from the time that it turned Christian (or Jewish), in regard to its two traditions, one from Palestine and one from Greece and Rome. As an explicit problem to be wrestled with, however, religious pluralism has surfaced only recently, and philosophic pluralism among civilizations still more recently; and even the religion-philosophy Western dilemma is relatively modern. We shall be looking at this last important matter later in this present chapter. Here we may simply observe that historically the relation of Confucian to Buddhist and Taoist has been richly comparable to that of Western Classicist to Christian and Jewish.

14. The Henderson work mentioned in our note 73 below is relevant here, one of its virtues being its interrelating of Classical and scriptural commentarial traditions. Its comparative view is a good deal wider than the sub-title suggests, embracing "besides the Chinese Confucian: . . . Vedānta, Qur'ānic exegesis, rabbinic Judaism, ancient and medieval Christian biblical exegesis, and the classical epic (mainly Homer)" (p. 4), and adducing several observed parallels with these.

15. This concept too (Chinese: *sheng*) has, of course, had a history. In early times, there was a high sense of the status—metaphysical, mythological—of the sage; in the Han, of K'ung Fu-tzu and the authors of the Classics. Thus in the earlier phase the sage was widely seen as more unlike the rest of us (though for instance Meng-tzu—"Mencius"—noted for his optimistic perception of human nature—and Hsün-tzu, for instance, already championed a less differentiated view). By Sung times, the sage is generally

regarded as what we others can become if we do (or are) this and that; is what we all ideally are aiming at. Earlier, persons of ordinary status but of high attainment were called *hsien*, standardly translated "worthies" (or sometimes also were designated by another word—a distinct Chinese term, though it happens to have the same pronunciation, and therefore transliteration, as the other—rendered as "immortals", which latter some Taoists aimed—and worked—at becoming). For a discussion of, chiefly, early usage, see for instance Julia Ching, "Who Were the Ancient Sages?" in Julia Ching and R. W. L. Guisso, edd., *Sages and Filial Sons: mythology and archaeology in Ancient China* (Hong Kong: Chinese University Press, 1991), pp. [1]–22; note esp. pp. 8–9.

16. This point, and also the word "awe" two sentences previous, I owe to personal conversation with a Confucian friend.

17. Wen T'ien-Hsiang, as quoted in Donald W. Treadgold, *The West in Russia and China: religious and secular thought in modern times*, (Cambridge: Cambridge University Press, 2 voll., 1973), vol. 2, *China, 1582–1949*, p. [v].

18. Typical is the formulation of the leading historian of Chinese philosophic thought, the late Feng Yu-lan: ". . . the entire two thousand years from Tung Chung-shu down to the present century [sc. the beginning of the twentieth century, when he was writing] has belonged to the Period of Classical Learning, and . . . all its philosophers, irrespective of their own originality or non-originality, could gain a hearing for their ideas only by attaching themselves to one or another of the philosophic schools of antiquity—which, for most of them, meant the Confucian classics"—Fung Yu-lan, *A History of Chinese Philosophy*, trans. [from the Chinese, Shanghai, 1931–1934] by Derk Bodde, 2 voll. (vol. 1, [Peiping: Henri Vetch, 1937], Princeton: Princeton University Press [1952], 1973[7]; vol. 2, [1953] 1973[7]), vol. 2, p. 720. The work includes discussion of Buddhist and Taoist thought, while giving the chief emphasis to Confucian. The above quotation is from the Conclusion of the work, and goes on to say that this process may be "described as . . . filling old bottles with new wine".

19. The Chinese terms are usually *cheng* ("right", "straight") and *cheng-tao* ("right way", "straight path") for the position proffered as correct, and *i-tuan*, *tso-tao*, *hsieh* for deviations from it. See, for instance, Paul A. Cohen, *China and Christianity: the missionary movement and the growth of Chinese antiforeignism, 1860–1870* (Cambridge, Mass.: Harvard University Press, 1963), pp. 4–5. Memorials to the emperor would often offer him arguments as to why the authority of the state should be used to back specific contemporary instances of the former and to suppress those of the latter. When these arguments proved persuasive, the analogy with the "religious" side of the Western dichotomy, with its authoritative enforcements, becomes that much closer.

20. The Yi dynasty was fifteenth through nineteenth century. The rites performed were in honour of Confucius and the founder of the particular

sŏwŏn and their teachings. The tablets (which were not themselves the object of ceremonies or direct veneration) were often the writings of one or another particular interpreter, often Korean, whose school of thought the *sŏwŏn* taught and advanced, rather than the Chinese Classics which they interpreted. The *sŏwŏn* are called "private academies" by Western scholars—e.g., Edwin O. Reischauer, John K. Fairbank, *A History of East Asian Civilization*, vol. 1, *East Asia: the great tradition;* vol. 2, *East Asia: the modern transformation* (Boston: Houghton Mifflin, [1958], 1960–[1962], 1965—of the 1965 edn. of vol. II, Albert M. Craig is third author), vol. I: p. 441. They were "named and patterned after the *shu-yüan* of Sung China" (ibid.). Matteo Ricci is felt to have had these in mind when reporting to the authorities in Rome (a letter of 1596) his decision not to open a church, at least for the time being, but to use for conversation with élite Chinese friends the substantial house that he had been permitted by the city governor, despite his being a foreigner, to buy, and his own visits to their homes: *non faremo in questo principio chiesa e templo, ma una casa da predicare, come fanno i suoi più eminenti predicatori—Opere storiche del P. Matteo Ricci S.I., ed. a cura del* Comitato per le Onoranze Nazionali, *con prolegomeni note e tavole dal* Pietro Tacchi Venturi (Macerata: Filippo Giorgetti, 2 voll., 1911–1913), vol. II p. 230; cf. also his letter of three days earlier to a confrère in Rome, vol. II p. 215: *Non credo per adesso faremo chiesa, ma una casa di predicare. . . .* This correspondence with the *shu-yüan* is stated explicitly, and a contrast is drawn between them as secular (*laïc*) and church, temple, and bonze (Ricci himself uses this last word) as religious, by Jacques Gernet, *Chine et christianisme: action et réaction* (Paris: Gallimard, 1982), pp. 27–28 (although his two reff. are incorrect). Other modern scholars, however, note that in fact the *shu-yüan* were "characterized by a solemn, almost sacral atmosphere", and their meetings involved rituals and singing of hymns—E. Zürcher, "The First Anti-Christian Movement in China (Nanking, 1616–1621)", in *Acta Orientalia Neerlandica: proceedings of the congress of the Dutch Oriental Society held in Leiden on the occasion of its 50th anniversary, 8th-9th May 1970,* P. W. Pestman, ed. (Leiden: Brill, 1971), pp. 188–195, p. 193.

21. (We shall be returning to these two matters later in this chapter, for their significance in European developments.) For the views of two from among the more significant European thinkers involved in the European intellectualist response to the new awareness of Confucian China, see a study by Julia Ching and Willard G. Oxtoby, *Moral Enlightenment: Leibniz and Wolff on China* (Nettetal: Steyler, 1992—Monumenta Serica Monograph Series, 26); similarly, for an anthology of others' studies, see Ching and Oxtoby, *Discovering China: European interpretations in the Enlightenment,* 1992 (Rochester, N.Y.: University of Rochester Press, 1992—Library of the History of Ideas, vol. 7). See also the reff. given in our note 71 below.

22. Cf. our note 15 above, on the concept of "sage". Even "humanism", Western and Chinese, has implied the metaphysical assumption that there

is an ideal of what it means to be truly [*sic*] human, in addition to the empirical actuality of what various human beings observably have been and currently are; that each of us in fact approximates to, or deviates from, what humanity ultimately *is*. Hence, in the West, are terms like "humane" (which not everyone is); or remarks such as that so-and-so acted inhumanly. Humanism in the Chinese case has been "anthropocosmic, definitively not anthropocentric", in the words of a modern Confucian friend. This classical dimension is included in my own use of the word and concept "human", also in this study.

23. We shall be noting later that Sinological scholarship in the West has recently shifted towards an increasing recognition of the "religious" qualities of the tradition. See p. 195 and its note 72 below. To say that it is or is not religious, or is more religious or less than one has previously held or than others have or do hold, is to aver that it is more like one of the West's two traditions than like the other; the extent, however, to which those concerned understand those Western two, together and discretely— let alone, the relation between them—varies enormously.

24. Not only in the Hindu and Buddhist cases, where such diversity is manifest and acknowledged, but in fact even, for a modern who looks critically, among discrete parts of a single volume such as the Bible, or even a single sector of it, the New Testament, so far as content and subject matter are concerned. To diversity in metaphysical vision of status, we return in a moment.

25. David Tracy, *The Analogical Imagination: Christian theology and the culture of pluralism* (New York: Crossroad, 1981). I do not wish to under-estimate the quality of Tracy's argument in that significant book; nor to overlook the point that he is using the word "classics" as referring not to "The Classics" as the traditional Græco-Roman written legacy to the West, but to more recent undefined writings that are culturally recognized as having been given an especially high status and worth. We return in our next chapter (cf. also our note 1 above) to considering this other of these two chief Western meanings of our word, two meanings that are distinct yet of course not unrelated. From among the several responses and comments that Tracy's thesis has evoked, one may mention for instance Krister Stendahl, "The Bible as a Classic and the Bible as Holy Scripture", *Journal of Biblical Literature*, 103 (1984): [3]–10.

26. "*transporté d'admiration . . . tressaillir de joye . . . l'enthousiasme divin*"— in a 1766 letter to Falconet, reprinted in Denis Diderot, *Correspondance*, Georges Roth (and for later voll., Jean Varloot), edd. (Paris: Éditions de Minuit, 16 voll., 1955–1970), vol. 6, p. 261.

27. In a letter to Mirabeau dated March 22, 1740: ". . . *je pleurais de joie lorsque je lisais ces* Vies [sc., of Plutarch]; *je ne passais point de nuit sans parler à Alcibiade, Agésilas et autres; j'allais dans la place de Rome pour haranguer avec les Gracques* [sic], *et pour défendre Caton quand on lui jetait des pierres. . . . Il me*

tomba, en même temps, un Sénèque dans les mains, je ne sais par quel hasard; puis, des lettres de Brutus à Cicéron . . . : ces lettres sont si remplies de hauteur, d'élévation, de passion, et de courage, qu'il m'était bien impossible de les lire de sang-froid . . . j'en étais si ému, que je ne contenais plus ce qu'elles mettaient en moi; j'étouffais, je quittais mes livres, et je sortais comme un homme en fureur . . ."—*Œuvres complètes de Vauvenargues: préface et notes de* Henry Bonnier ([Paris]: Hachette, 1968, 2 voll.), vol. 2, p. 562.

28. *"trasporto di grida, di pianti, e di furori"*—Vittorio Alfieri, in his posthumous *Vita scritta da esso* [Francesco Tassi, ed.; "London"—sc. Florence, 1804]: epoca terza, cap. settimo. I have used the edition of Luigi Fassò, ed., *Vita, Rime e Satire di Vittorio Alfieri* (Torino: Unione Tipografico-Editrice Torinese, 1949—Classici Italiani, Ferdinando Neri, dir., vol. 71), where this passage is p. 141. More fully, it reads: *"con un tale trasporto . . . pur anche, che chi fosse stato a sentirmi nella camera vicina mi avrebbe certamente tenuto per impazzato"*.

29. *". . . je m'enflammois . . ."*—having remarked *"Plutarque surtout devint ma lecture favorite. Le plaisir que je prenois à le relire sans cesse . . . . Sans cesse occupé de Rome et d'Athènes"*. He goes on: *"je me croyois Grec ou Romain, je devenois le personnage dont je lisois la vie; le récit . . . me rendoit les yeux étincelants . . ."*—From his *Confessions* (Part I, Book I, 1719–1723) as in *Œuvres complètes de J. J. Rousseau, avec des notes historiques par* G. Petitain (Paris: Lefèvre, 8 voll., 1839), vol. 1, p. 19.

30. To a series of enthusiastic, indeed rapturous, comments of the sort offered here, given at much greater length, my attention was drawn by the illuminating work of Peter Gay, *The Enlightenment: an interpretation—the rise of modern paganism* (New York: Knopf, 1966 and [London: Weidenfeld & Nicolson, 1967]). (A sequel appeared presently: Peter Gay, *The Enlightenment: an interpretation—Volume II: the science of freedom*, New York: Knopf, 1969 and London: Weidenfeld & Nicolson, 1970, whereupon the former work began to be referred to as vol. 1, although its many subsequent re-impressions by a variety of publishers in both New York and London seemingly never designated it so formally, on title-pp. etc.) In that earlier work see esp. §II of part 2 of its first chap., pp. 42–58. Cf. its first three chapters generally, which constitute its "Book One: The Appeal to Antiquity", pp. [29]–203; not least, chap. 1, with its significant title "The Useful and Beloved Past", pp. 31–71. For my quotations, the originals that I here cite of the eighteenth-century writers are in some cases drawn from editions different from those that Gay has used, and the translations that I give are my own; yet for being directed to them I am indebted to him.

31. Gibbon in his autobiography, of his trip to Italy 1764–1765. This work was first published posthumously under the title "Memoirs of My Life and Writings" as the opening section of *Miscellaneous Works of Edward Gibbon, Esq.*, John Holroyd (first Earl of Sheffield), ed. (London, 2 voll., 1796). Our quotation is from the recent version, substantially improved

over that first one: Edward Gibbon, *Memoirs of My Life: edited from the manuscripts by* Georges A. Bonnard (London &c: Nelson, 1966; also, New York: Funk & Wagnalls, 1969), p. 134.

32. Nonetheless, quietly rather than with that erstwhile exuberant enthusiasm, there are still today scholars and others of the older generation who owe to their Classical education a devotion to the truth and to its pursuit, a resolve to know and to understand, and commitments to intellectual integrity and to living rationally. (Some might prefer to say, who owe to that education the form, the intensity, and the nurturing of such devotion, resolve, commitment.) Some owe to it also the ability to recognize the rationality that deserves our loyalty as an affair much grander than the impoverished latter-day post-Enlightenment rationality that distinguishes itself from poetry, from art, from moral virtue—and from wisdom.

33. Classical *mimesis*, particularly as set forth by Plato, was a powerful concept; applying the idea to literature, and to art generally, developed by Aristotle, has also had a major history in subsequent Western life, including in the early modern period. A recent article on its early appropriation into the Christian movement is Thomas Louis Brodie, "Greco-Roman Imitation of Texts as a Partial Guide to Luke's Use of Sources", in Charles H. Talbert, ed., *Luke-Acts: new perspectives from the Society of Biblical Literature Seminar* (New York: Crossroad, 1984), pp. 17–46. This provides also a convenient survey of bibliography on the whole matter, both for Classical times and for modern; see the endnotes, esp. no. 5, pp. 38–39, for modern studies, and 6–11, p. 39, for Classical references. On Classical imitating and emulating within literature, see in our note 50 below on Milton, Pope, Bacon.

34. Even the style of our language here in presenting this point seems today unduly ornate, so far has our culture moved from the ornateness of their time.

35. Or at least, comparison has been pointed out between the role in Western life of the Græco-Roman tradition as a whole and the Christian, or between the former and religion, if not specifically between their respective writings or the treatment of these. (Yet such differentiation is hardly crucial for our concerns.) For examples see: A. D. Nock, "Conversion to Philosophy", being chap. XI of his *Conversion: the old and the new in religion from Alexander the Great to Augustine of Hippo* (Oxford: Clarendon, 1933; London &c: Oxford University Press, [1952,] 1963), pp. [164]–186; A.-J. Festugière, *Épicure et ses dieux* (Paris: Presses Universitaires de France, 1946, 2ème édn. corrigée 1968; Collection "Mythes et Religions", dir. P.-L. Couchoud, 1946, G. Dumézil, 1968) (there is an English version of the first Fr. edn.: *Epicurus and his Gods*, C. W. Chilton, trans.—Oxford: Blackwell, 1955); Werner Jaeger, "Über Ursprung und Kreislauf des philosophischen Lebensideals", in *Sitzungsberichte der preussischen Akademie der Wissenschaften—Jahrgang 1928: Philosophisch-historische Klasse* (Berlin: Verlag der Akademie der

Wissenschaften / Walter de Gruyter, 1928), pp. 390–421; Werner Jaeger, *Humanism and Theology* (Milwaukee, Wisconsin: Marquette University Press, 1943—"The Aquinas Lecture, 1943"). I was guided to these writings by my former colleague Zeph Stewart.

36. "G.P.G." (sc., Georges Gusdorf), "HUMANISTIC SCHOLARSHIP, HISTORY OF", *Encyclopædia Britannica*, 15th edn., 1974, p. 1170 column 2. (In more recent versions of this 15th edn., this article has been dropped. Is this dropping an index of the waning in our time of the Classic meaning of humanism?)

37. Gusdorf, "Humanistic Scholarship . . ." (op. cit., our immediately preceding note no. 36), p. 1176 col. 1.

38. In contrast to the modern development noted in our first chapter above, in this context the "values" are absolute, not merely subjective, referring to transcendental realities independent of whether, or how far, human beings perceive or pursue them. (Their conceptualization as Truth, Beauty, and Justice or the Good, has been, we recognize, a human response; the concepts are, as ever, particular human constructs.)

39. Cf. my "Philosophia, as One of the Religious Traditions of Humankind: the Greek legacy in Western civilization, viewed by a comparativist", in *Différences, valeurs, hiérarchie: textes offerts à Louis Dumont, et réunis par Jean-Claude Galey* (Paris: Éditions de l'École des Hautes Études en Sciences Sociales, 1984/Maison des Sciences de l'Homme—Bibliothèque), pp. [253]–279.

40. Given our concern here with scripture—as a verbal form for registering a society's apprehending of ultimacy—it is not uninteresting to note that the term *logos*, chosen by the Greeks for their concept of rationality, means "word". One might wonder about adding, then, to Professor Prithipaul's observation noted in our Hindu presentation, our chap. 6 above, its note 32: that the Word became poetry in the Veda, became flesh in the Gospel, became Reason in the Classics—and became scripture all over the world. This begs several questions, however, hardly resolvable short of a fuller understanding of language in human life, of our capacity to speak, and of the role of these in our reaching out towards what is higher than we have grasped yet have dimly perceived.

41. Cf. above, our note 22.

42. I have felt that there is little reason to use the French term for what was, more specifically, Italian and, more generally, Western-European. This is despite the Swiss whose work effectively introduced the concept to Europe, and did so in its French form in his German title with reference explicitly to Italy: Jacob Burckhardt, *Die Cultur der Renaissance in Italien: ein Versuch* (Basel: Schweighauser, 1860, with dozens of reprintings, many translations, and extensive influence).

43. We speak of "the most recent"; of course this has a long history. Salient was the attack even before the eighteenth century on the Classicist

position, as when Charles Perrault presented in the Académie Française in 1687 a widely-echoing poem on the then polarity in the literary world between "the ancients and the moderns".

44. It is acknowledged that Marx took over on the philosophic side the conceptual outlook of the Christian Hegel and modified it radically but did not reject it *in toto* by any means; less widely recognized is that although he modifed the Biblical outlook of his own Jewish background radically he nonetheless unwittingly retained elements from it, of which the eschatological Armageddon conflict is one example, and of course the prophetic proclamation of a call to social justice is another. For an interesting and useful bibliographic essay, although of course partial in scope, on the issue generally one may note Donald W. Treadgold, "Introduction" to the first translation into English of a turn-of-the-century Russian essay: Sergei Bulgakov, *Karl Marx as a Religious Type: his relation to the religion of anthropotheism of L. Feuerbach*, Virgil R. Lang, ed., Luba Barna, trans. (Belmont, Massachusetts: Nordland, 1979), pp. 11–33.

45. Gilbert Highet, *The Classical Tradition: Greek and Roman influences on Western literature* (Oxford: Clarendon Press, 1949), pp. 227–228; and see in general the chapter from which the quoted sentence is taken, esp. pp. 227ff.

46. A brief popular study illustrating this particular example is Howard Clarke, *Homer's Readers: a historical introduction to the* Iliad *and the* Odyssey (Newark: University of Delaware Press; London, Toronto: Associated University Presses; 1981).

47. See, for example, Reuben Arthur Brower, *Alexander Pope: the poetry of allusion* (Oxford: Clarendon Press, 1959), pp. 172–173 (where an original Horace passage to which Pope is parallel is quoted) and that chapter generally.

48. ". . . *les défenseurs de tout mouvement pro-classique, quel qu'il soit, s'intéressent invariablement à leur propre culture plutôt qu'à celle du modèle, et à eux-mêmes plutôt qu'à leurs héros*"—Gustave E. von Grunebaum, "Le concept de classicisme culturel" in R. Brunschvig et G. E. von Grunebaum, edd., *Classicisme et déclin culturel dans l'histoire de l'Islam: Actes du symposium international d'histoire de la civilisation musulmane (Bordeaux 25–29 Juin 1956)* (Paris: Librarie G.-P. Maisonneuve, Éditions Besson * Chantemerle, 1957), p. 16. This pertains, as von Grunebaum insists, not only to post-Classical Islamic developments; one could give, of course, many illustrations from European history, most strikingly from the eighteenth century ("The *philosophes* liked to . . . popularize Newton wrapped in the toga of Cicero or Lucretius"—Peter Gay, *The Enlightenment* . . .—op. cit., our note 30 above—p. 32; italics mine). An illustration that we might take for present purposes from early China (late third century B.C.) would be the recommendation to the Ch'in emperor Ch'in Shih-huang from his prime minister Li Ssu that in order to preserve his (unpopular) imperial power he should suppress the Classics since their enthusiasts " 'make mention of the *past*, so

as to blame the *present*'"—quoted in Young-chan Ro, "The Significance of the Confucian Texts as 'Scripture' in the Confucian Tradition", *Journal of Chinese Philosophy*, 15 (1988): [269]–287, at p. 276. (The prime-minister's advice was taken, and the infamous "Burning of the Books" ensued—though the Classics one way and another survived, while the dynasty did not, being overthrown within a few years to be succeeded by the Han, the empire that perceived the Classics as providing, rather, a potentially great theoretical base for the country and took steps that are often described by Western scholars as "establishing Confucianism as the state religion", and that certainly laid the foundation for China's largely Confucian culture and polity for the next two thousand and more years.)

49. In addition to the innumerable instances in Europe, one may cite Benjamin Franklin in the realm of journalism, who in his *New-England Courant* informed his "Gentle readers" that he designed "never to let a paper pass without a Latin motto, which carries a charm in it to the Vulgar, and the Learned admire the pleasure of construing"—cited in Richard M. Gummere, *The American Colonial Mind and the Classical Tradition: essays in comparative culture* (Cambridge, Massachusetts: Harvard University Press, 1963), p. 16. Gummere's book altogether is well worth pondering as illustrative for our thesis in this sector of our chapter here.

50. Gay, *The Enlightenment* . . . (op. cit. in our note 30 above), p. 43. The remark is made about *les philosophes*. On the matter of "invisible quotations", see our quotation at the end of the present paragraph in our text. It may be noted further that writers of the early modern era in Europe not only quoted the Classics, explicitly and implicitly, but also imitated them: Milton's *Paradise Lost* is in twelve books, a number clearly modelled on the twelve of Virgil's *Aeneid* (itself patterned on the twenty-four of Homer's *Iliad* and *Odyssey*); Pope presumed (rightly) that his poems' close formal and other likeness to those of his beloved Horace would of course be recognized as such—and be therefore esteemed. In somewhat similar vein, one might note that the modern scientific movement also, sometimes contrasted with the classical, had its important early innovating manifesto, that of Francis Bacon, though explicitly novel, cast formally in relation to what it was proffered to replace, by being entitled *Novum Organum*, recognizedly echoing Aristotle.

51. A Christian Arab student from Beirut, back in the days when that was a pleasant and friendly town, on studying the Qur'ān in my seminar for his first time remarked to me in astonishment, "I never realized how full it was of clichés, from beginning to end". He had grown up hearing—and doubtless himself using—snatches of that Muslim scripture every day, but unaware, being Christian, of where they came from.

52. Graham, *Beyond the Written Word* (op. cit. our chap. 1 above, note 7), p. 165. Italics original. For one Christian example of this from among many, cf. our chap. 2 above, p. 31 and its note 34.

53. I might here mention my "Religion as Symbolism", being the *Propæ-dia* introduction to the section on Religion in the current 15th editions (1974 ff.) of the *Encyclopædia Britannica* (in the 1986 printing, this is *Propædia* pp. 299–301). A later retrospective on this and further development is my "Symbols in Religion", *Symbols in Life and Art: the Royal Society of Canada symposium in memory of George Whalley / Les Symboles dans la vie et dans l'art: la Société Royale du Canada, colloque à la mémoire de George Whalley*, James A. Leith, ed./réd. (n.p. [sc. Montreal]: McGill-Queen's University Press for The Royal Society of Canada, 1987), pp. [89]–104; revised version, "Symbolism in World Religions and in Inter-Religious Discourse", *World Faiths Insight*, New Series 16 (June 1987), pp. 2–19.

54. An additional minor yet interesting point of comparability between the ever-changing place in Western life and history of the Classics and of the Bible is the important role of the printing press when it emerged in giving both sets of writings a new importance and effectiveness. One may also perhaps mention that the Church had introduced the use of the book as a symbol, something that the Classics had not done but that became not insignificant in the role also of Classical books in Western sensitivity. On this latter point see Ernst Robert Curtius, *Europäische Literatur . . .* (op. cit., our chap. 1 above, note 18), Kap. 16, "Das Buch als Symbol", pp. 304 ff. (English, pp. 302 ff.), not least the concluding paragraph of its §4, p. 313 (English, p. 311).

55. See the references given in our note 35 above. In addition, one might mention the observation that, for the great German Classicists, *"La foi dans le modèle grec a assumé des traits religieux"*—von Grunebaum, *Classicisme . . .* (op. cit., our note 48 above), p. 7, which is another way of saying that the attitude of active participants in this tradition was at that time and place more manifestly similar than usual to that customary among participants in the Palestinian one.

56. The idea of "belonging" to a religion is itself odd, certainly—however common the phrase may have become in recent times. The remainder of the phrase given here was somewhat current not long ago—and that remaining part would be quite appropriate if the word "religions" were legitimate. The formulation was the title of a fairly influential book in the earlier part of this century: William Edward Soothill, *The Three Religions of China: lectures delivered at Oxford* ([London: Hodder & Stoughton, 1913]; 2nd edn., London &c: Oxford University Press, 1923; 3rd edn., 1929, 1930, with several subsequent reprints, continuing into quite recent times, by these and other publishers). The phrase appeared earlier in a sub-title: Hampden C. DuBose, *The Dragon, Image, and Demon: or, the three religions of China . . .* (London: S. W. Partridge, 1886).

57. This wording modifies slightly the title of my "Philosophia" piece (above, our note 39).

58. One is tempted to say that it coined the term "religion" in this

sense, given the radical innovation involved in the new conception that in modern times it forged to be served by its traditional Latinate word. Western civilization in its pre-secular phases, as considered below later in this chapter, had not bifurcated the two traditions, and had not used the word "religion" (and its cognates in other Western languages) in this way. On the history of the word and the cognates see Ernst Feil, *Religio: die Geschichte eines neuzeitlichen* [sic] *Grundbegriffs vom Frühchristentum bis zur Reformation* (Göttingen: Vandenhoeck & Ruprecht, 1986—Forschungen zur Kirchen- und Dogmengeschichte, Band 36) (a second volume is awaited, for the later period); Michel Despland, *La religion en occident: évolution des idées et du vécu* (Montréal: Fides, 1979—Héritage et Projet, 23); my *Meaning and End of Religion* . . . (op. cit., our chap. 2 above, note 3); and, repondering these three and the issue, Michel Despland and/et Gérard Vallée, edd./dirr., *Religion in History: the word, the idea, the reality / La religion dans l'histoire: le mot, l'idée, la réalité* (Waterloo, Ontario: Wilfrid Laurier University Press for the Canadian Corporation for Studies in Religion / Corporation canadienne des sciences religieuses, 1992—Editions SR, vol. 13).

59. For example, the Christian West has its philosophy, law, grammar, from Greece & Rome, whereas in India, for instance, and then also in the Buddhist movement, the distinction has not obtained between philosophy and theology (nor between philosophy and religion generally); nor in the Islamic case, for instance, that between law and religion; and so on. Just as English-speaking children may begin by feeling that the French are funny people who call something a *fenêtre* when in fact it is quite obviously a "window", so some Westerners have felt that Muslims are exceptional people who "mix up" politics and religion, as if these were two manifestly distinct things that it is normal to separate. Whether one sees them as separate depends on one's worldview. (This in turn depends partly on historical experience. The Christian movement spent its formative centuries in a social structure for the operating of which its members were not responsible, and this has given both Christians and secularists the specific notion that politics, and garbage collection, are not "religious" tasks. Other civilizations have had other experience.)

60. Now that science has become firmly established on inherited principles, the pursuit of truth is perhaps for a time not so essential to its development as previously. Many a practitioner these days is in pursuit rather of research grants, or of promotion, or of advancing a "discipline". Yet a sense of fairness (at least in the promoting dean? the granting body? the public at large?) is widely presupposed. Certainly there is no scientific, "objective", basis for a love of truth (nor love of anything else), nor even for a passing preference for it over self-serving lying. Similarly, there is no scientific, "objective", basis for justice (or "fairness"). There would seem no scientific reason why society should not be organized in a fascist form with science totally controlled by the rulers and used solely to ensure and to increase

their power. It could be argued that only in a free society can science flourish; but there is no scientific reason why it should flourish. (There is no scientific reason why human life should continue, either in general or in the case of any particular individual; let alone, why it should be or become better rather than worse.) A totally amoral science in a totally amoral society would be a nightmare. The prodigious Western drive to know, about the world and indeed about the universe and reality altogether, has been given form, and nurture, through the tradition from Greece. The Western response to other facets of transcendence have been given form and nurture through it and still others through that from Palestine; or, through both. In each case the ability to respond, with less or more zest, is of course inherently human—as the history of the rest of the world richly though diversely demonstrates.

61. Cf. above, note 22. In general, of course, this is a subtle and immensely elaborate matter. Cf. further our chap. 1 above, p. 10 and specifically its note 16, with the reff. there, for clarification of the intent of the above sentence and of the way that words are being used here. See also the "Symbolism" pieces mentioned in our note 53 above.

62. Without exception. "What has Athens to do with Jerusalem?" asked Tertullian. The Church's answer, at the time and since, has overwhelmingly been: "Much". (Tertullian himself had an exceptionally thorough Classical education, and was perhaps an expert in Roman law.) Few moderns are as stunned as they might be that the New Testament—as it were, the manifesto of the nascent Christian movement—was in Greek. (So also was the Jewish Bible for probably the majority of Jews at that time.) Two foundational ideas in Greek thought, *logos* and *sophia*, were integrated into early Christian. (That the former category became foundational for Christian theology is one illustration. Another is that after the latter concept the greatest of all Orthodox Christian churches was named. This is apart from the point that "Wisdom Literature" is an integral element in both the Jewish and the Christian Bibles.) The Catholic Church has throughout thought in Latin. Still today, Christian theologians normally presume that they must be—or simply, that they of course are—in dialogue with Western philosophy; only painfully are they being pushed into paying attention to the other "religious" traditions of the world, obvious though it might seem that this would be the more normal context in relation to which they would do their thinking.

63. Or, less often, deliberately as distinct yet important to be taught. See, for example, Curtius, *Europäische Literatur* . . . (op. cit., our chap. 1 above, note 18), German, pp. 263–267 / English, pp. 260–264.

64. Notably by Friedrich August Wolf, in an historicizing and analytic rather than in the traditional reverential and holistic fashion of treating Homer; in Frid. Aug. Wolfius, *Prolegomena ad Homerum: sive, de operum homericorum prisca et genuina forma variisque mutationibus et probabilii ratione*

emendandi (Halis Saxonum: Libraria Orphanotrophei, [1795], 1859², and many further editions). This has recently become available also in an English version of the Latin, as F. A. Wolf, *Prolegomena to Homer, 1795: translated with introduction and notes by* Anthony Grafton, Glenn W. Most, and James E. G. Zetzel (Princeton: Princeton University Press, 1985). Wolf has been called "the founder of modern philology"; and indeed, to use our earlier phrasing, he was a present-day-type academic in that he was resolute to learn about, more than oriented to learning from, the Classic texts.

65. The important and justly famous Anglo-Irish scientist Robert Boyle—one of the founders of the Royal Society and a devout Protestant who *inter alia* gave money for the translating and publishing of the New Testament in Irish and Turkish and wrote on the theological imperative to study the world scientifically—left funds in his will for "The Boyle Lectures" (still being given today), a series of what might nowadays be called sermons, to "vindicate" "the Christian religion . . . against notorious infidels, such as atheists and deists". The first lecturer appointed to deliver the series (in a London church, 1692) was Bentley. To support his argument for Christian truth he appealed not, as he himself put it, to the authority of sacred (sc. Christian) books but on the scientific side (using a scripturalist metaphor) to "the mighty volumes of visible nature and"—in Classicist vein—"the everlasting tables *[sic]* of right reason". He calls on Newton's *Principia* of five years earlier. Further, in an eloquent peroration to the last of the eight lecture-sermons he draws a beguiling parallel between the marvellous structure of human anatomy and that of Virgil's *Aeneid*; he speaks too of the human frame's "syntax" and metric qualities. On this see Rudolf Pfeiffer, *History of Classical Scholarship* (Oxford: Clarendon, 2 voll., 1968–1976), vol. 2, pp. 146–147. On Bentley generally see the standard sources for seventeenth-century intellectual developments and the history of humanism.

66. Above, our notes 5 and 11, and pp. 178–179.

67. The new Christian enthusiasm for "dialogue" has found Buddhists, especially East Asian, the most responsive and the most engaging, by far; and some Christian missionaries—particularly Roman Catholic in Japan—have proposed Christian-Buddhist *rapprochement* at a quite serious level, notably with Zen. Cf. also the active quarterly journal *Buddhist–Christian Studies* (University of Hawaii Press, 1981ff.; David W. Chappell, ed.), with members of both communities on its Editorial Board and among its contributors. There are many further illustrative examples.

68. Encyclopædia Britannica, 1986 version of the 15th edition, 10:39, s.v. RICCI, MATTEO

69. It would take us too far afield—into matters outside our scriptural focus—to advance and to substantiate the argument for such an interpretation of Ricci. Yet the facts of his life, it seems to me, can certainly be read in such a way as to support (even to push) this view, over against the

traditional notion that he was primarily interested in spreading the Gospel, and used his great competence in the other fields and his observation of the situation in China to "accommodate Christianity" as a strategic means to arrive at an ulterior end. My reading of his life and interests at least has the merit of absolving him of duplicity, not to say downright dishonesty, in his dealings with the Chinese with whom he hobnobbed and whose extraordinary respect he earned. It also coheres with his family upbringing, with his studies in the West, and with the fact that he first studied theology and became an ordained priest only after he had reached the Orient under Jesuit auspices. It also exonerates his Chinese friends from gullibility and obtuseness. (There is the further point that so far as some of his Western-Classical loyalties were concerned, he showed himself less ready for accommodation: he evidently thought that the Chinese *literati* with whom he discoursed—and who were otherwise engaging—were silly folk, certainly just plain wrong, in that they did not think "rationally" on various points, by which he actually meant, did not think in Western philosophic categories.)

70. Internally within Europe, this is clear; further, one may note that it was in the eighteenth century—not the seventeenth, when this issue arose—that the Vatican pronounced against the Confucian tradition.

71. Although it was not actually the first presentation in a European language, the first widely known and the uniquely influential work informing the West about the Chinese Classical tradition designated "Confucius" (this book is the basis of K'ung Fu-tzu's Latinate name in the West) as a "philosopher": *Confucius Sinarum Philosophus, sive scientia sinensis latine exposita*, by the four Jesuit missionaries Prosper[us] Intorcetta, Christian[us] Herdtrich, François [. . . ciscus] Rougemont, Philip[pus] Couplet, *jussu Ludovici Magni* (Paris: Danieles Horthemels, MDCLXXXVII). For a discussion of the little-known earlier Jesuit publications to introduce the West to what they were finding, see the discussion of Knud Lundbaek, "The First Translation from a Confucian Classic in Europe", in *China Mission Studies (1550–1800) Bulletin*, 1(1979): 2–11. Of some relevance to this matter is also Paul A. Rule, *K'ung-tzu or Confucius?—the Jesuit interpretation of Confucianism* (Sydney: Allen & Unwin Australia, and London, Boston: George Allen & Unwin, 1986—East Asia Series of Australian National Univ. Department of Far Eastern History and Asian Studies Association of Australia).

72. See, for instance, Diane B. Obenchain, "Confucianism and Modernity: Confucian practice as religious practice", paper read at a conference on "Religion in China: past and present" sponsored by the International Academy of Chinese Culture and the New Ecumenical Research Association, Beijing, 1989 (forthcoming), which traces this development carefully; and two works of Rodney L. Taylor, "The Study of Confucianism as a Religious Tradition: notes on some recent publications", *Journal of Chinese*

Religions, no. 18 (Fall 1990), 143–159, which, as a "Review Article", focusses on the latest phase of the development, and *The Religious Dimensions of Confucianism* (Albany [New York]: State University of New York Press, 1990—SUNY Series in Religion, Robert Cummings Neville, ed.), which illustrates it. The history of calling the tradition a philosophy, or a religion, has gone through stages that are related to developments in Western intellectual and cultural history, much more significantly than to matters in China. We have earlier commented on the fact that most strikingly no doubt in India but generally outside the West (and the related Islamic complex), a distinction between religion and philosophy manifestly does not hold.

73. After this present study had first been completed, a comparative investigation with primary emphasis on the Chinese tradition appeared: John B. Henderson, *Scripture, Canon, and Commentary: a comparison of Confucian and Western exegesis* (Princeton and Oxford: Princeton University Press, 1991). This is a valuable work, especially for China, on which its information far outdistances our meagre discussion here. It is valuable also in throughout fully correlating scriptural and Classical traditions (cf. our note 14 above). Differences in outlook, however, affecting the treatment of the world situation historically are substantial between that study and this present one; notably so on two matters. One of these has to do with what Henderson (*passim*) calls the "assumptions" of commentators traditionally towards their Classics and scriptures (as if they had no good reason to adopt the positions that they did, but simply approached them with *a priori* gullibility?), and the "strategies" or "stratagems" that they then "devised" to "support" these "assumptions" (as if they were cunning, but lacked intellectual honesty and an authentic spirit of inquiry?). The second major divergence is between his and my perception of the relation between modern Western and other cultures (for him, Western modernity *is* modernity, and is the standard by which the others are judged). Readers will assess whether that book's interpretation, or this one's, of roughly the same sort of material worldwide presents the more reasonable inferences from, and the more plausible hypothesis to render intelligible (*verstehen* as well as *erklären*), the empirical data. However one decides, the most important matter as we have repeatedly affirmed is to consider those data, and to form an understanding of humanity and of world history illumined by them and that gives them due weight. There is a question also about the future—for which, criticism without appreciation seems not enough. With a perhaps unlikely yet crucial combination of sufficient intelligence and sufficient goodwill, the coming world culture may move towards modifying and thereby to some degree superseding both the modern West and the pre-modern others, avoiding the deficiencies of the others which he sees so sharply, and of the West, whose deficiencies some among us see so sorrowfully.

9. Brief Further Considerations

1. Scholars differ, or may be seen as differing, as to whether through uncovering more of the historical material it will be confirmed that "the community" made this decision, as I have written, or whether one should say rather that the tenth Guru so decided, somewhat unilaterally. Since the community had until then felt that authority lay with its leader, and also— except for a few dissidents—richly accepted the new decision once it was made (whether "by" or "through" the leader), I have not felt that my phrasing requires modifying. It is also noteworthy that from the start a reverence for the written word had in fact been in evidence, in that Guru Nānak himself carried a hymnary (*pōthī*), and Guru Arjun, the fifth of the ten leaders, began the task of collating the materials of what has become the community's scripture.

2. *Bhagat*s—this Panjābī word is the counterpart to Sanskrit *bhākta*, adjective or adjectival noun relating to the mediæval "Bhakti" movement.

3. There have been also a few other names for it, such as Ādī Granth ("Primordial Book").

4. On annual festival days, and on particular family occasions, there is a ceremonial recitation, known as *akhaṇḍ pāth*, of the entire scripture over a two-day period wherein it is uninterruptedly intoned, by relays.

5. W. Owen Cole, *The Guru in Sikhism* (London: Darton, Longman & Todd, 1982), p. 56. His "in a manner" here can hardly elicit cavil; every religious group—and sub-group—is involved with its scriptures in a manner that diverges less or more from others'. "To an extent", however, is more problematic. Although Dr. Cole no doubt has studied the Sikhs more carefully than have I, yet my own observation would suggest that over against the Islamic case this could hardly be maintained without difficulty. One wonders whether he does not have in mind for his comparison Hindu and other Indian movements, rather, with which indeed most students tend to link the Sikh (and indeed within a few paragraphs of the above remark he does draw a comparison on this matter by placing "Sikhism . . . within the bhakti tradition of Indian religion", noting its scriptural uniqueness there— p. 58).

6. This is true particularly of that history from the eighth to the eighteenth century. (For the period before the seventh, the issue does not arise.)

7. I qualify the adjective "fixed", since it applies more formally to the situation following the Meiji restoration than to the earlier period.

8. Outside students may see these as scriptures of Kokkai (State) Shintō. Before World War II there was a rite in the public schools for honouring the Rescript in a manner closely similar to Shintō rites in the home before the *kamidana* (*kami*-shelf; altar). I owe this observation to my friend Wilbur M. Fridell.

9. A good general introduction is Padmanabh S. Jaini, *The Jaina Path of Purification* (Berkeley, Los Angeles, London: University of California Press, 1979); see chapter 2 (pp. 42–88), "The First Disciples and the Jaina Scriptures". Also valuable: L. Alsdorf, "Jaina Exegetical Literature and the History of the Jaina Canon", in A. N. Upadhye et al., edd., *Mahāvīra and his Teachings* (Bombay: Bhagavān Mahāvīra 2500th Nirvāṇa Mahotsava Samiti, 1977), pp. 1–8.

10. My former student Kenneth W. Folkert was at work on this entrancing matter when his life was suddenly brought to an end by a deplorable road accident during field study in India. Most of his discoveries and careful exposition of their details have not been published, and perhaps now never will be; a little of his thinking on the former of our two points in our text appeared posthumously in his "The 'Canons' of 'Scripture'" in Levering, *Rethinking Scripture* . . . (op. cit. our chap. 1 above, note 7), pp. 170–179.

11. Recent scholarly study is uncovering material indicating that the development of the Chinese script and that of the Phœnician consonantal alphabet were interlinked in ways not previously recognized. The primary investigator in this matter is Victor H. Mair, whose elaborate research on it will be published in due course. In the meantime his paper "West Eurasian and North African Influences on the Origins of Chinese Writing" presented at the 33rd International Congress of Asian and North African Studies, Toronto, 1990, broached the matter significantly; it has appeared in the Proceedings of that conference: *Contact between Cultures* (Lewiston, New York: Edwin Mellen Press, 4 voll., 1992) in vol. 3 *(Eastern Asia: Literature and Humanities)*, Bernard Hung-Kay et al., edd., pp. 335–338. On contacts involving religious matters but not the question of writing, see also this scholar's "Old Sinitic **Mᵢag*, Old Persian *Maguš*, and English 'Magician'", in *Early China: the annual journal of the Society for the Study of Early China*, 15 (1990): [27]–47.

12. See also above, in our chap. 3.

13. See my "The Crystallization of Religious Communities in Mughul India", in Mujtabai Mīnuvī and Īraj Afshār, edd., *Yād-nāmeh'-e Īrānī-ye Mīnūrskī: shāmel-e maqālāt-e taḥqīqī marbūṭ be-muṭāla'āt-e Īrānī* (Tehrān: Enteshāt-e Dāneshgāh-e Tehrān, 1348/1969—no. 1241—Ganjīneh'-e Taḥqīqāt-e Irānī, 57/Publications of Tehran University, no. 1241), pp. 197–220 of the Western-language segment; reprinted in *On Understanding Islam* (op. cit., our chap. 3, note 2 above), pp. 177–196.

14. Some details on this matter are available in William J. Watson, "İbrāhīm Müteferriḳa and Turkish Incunabula", *Journal of the American Oriental Society*, 88 (1968): 435–441.

15. On this point see Rogers, "A Founder's 'Teaching' . . ." (op. cit. above, our chap. 7 note 22).

16. One may, for instance, refer back to the Jain case, above, where the

change involved the (imported) concept of "canon"; and to the Max Müller transmuting of the Veda into a printed book (above, our chap. 6, p. 139, at note 39), in the new objectifying mood—in comparable fashion to the on-going mutual impingement in China of Confucian, Taoist, and Buddhist scriptural developments on each other (above, our preceding chapter). More subtle examples—there are many—deserve a study on their own; not only in the scriptural field, but in the general realm of the world's religious history. This last matter has been explored in some of my seminars at Harvard, and is touched upon briefly in my "Traditions in Contact and Change: towards a history of religion in the singular", in *Traditions in Contact and Change: selected proceedings of the XIVth congress of the International Association for the History of Religions*, Peter Slater and Donald Wiebe, edd. (Waterloo, Canada: Wilfrid Laurier University Press, for the Canadian Corporation for Studies in Religion, 1983), pp. [1]–23. See also the first chapter, "A History of Religion in the Singular", of my *Towards a World Theology: faith and the comparative history of religion* (London: Macmillan, and Philadelphia: Westminster, 1981; Maryknoll, N.Y.: Orbis, 1989, pp. 3–20).

17. Cf. our chap. 5 above.

18. *Sunnah* names the recognized and authoritative "custom" (of the Prophet; of the Islamic community) that is set forth in the Ḥadīth, that "decisive, yet secondary . . . group of materials in the Islamic complex" to which reference is made in our chap. 3 above, at page 46.

19. Cf. our chap. 6 above, p. 137.

20. (In the Christian case, the Old-Testament/New-Testament distinction is related to this "pair" phenomenon in ways that some might see as comparable, along with interesting difference.)

21. The slogan of the Ārya Samāj, founded in 1875 by Dayānand Saras-vatī and developing into a sizeable movement in esp. north-western India.

22. And roughly contemporary; also in north-western India.

23. So far as I am aware, the first time that this important issue was raised was—engagingly—by Thomas B. Coburn, in a paper read to the Boston 1987 meeting of the American Academy of Religion. The substance of the presentation has now appeared in his *Encountering the Goddess: a translation of the Devī Māhātmya and a study of its interpretation* (Albany: State University of New York Press, 1991), in its chapters 4–5–6. Cf. also Henderson, *Scripture, Canon, and Commentary*, noted at the end of our preceding chapter (chap. 8 above, its note 73).

24. A still further refinement is made in the Folkert proposal, set forth in his ". . .'Canons'. . ." (op. cit., our note 10 above), suggesting that such liturgical usage might well be recognized as constituting a distinct category of canonized scripture.

25. Cf. our chap. 8 above, esp. its notes 1 and 25.

26. The Greek terms that the Alexandrians had developed for their new concept (*enkrinomenoi, enkritoi*, etc.) "defied Latinization" (*ließ sich nicht*

latinisieren—Ernst Robert Curtius, *Europäische Literatur* . . . , op. cit., our chap. 1 above, note 18), (German, p. 253; Eng., p. 249), or anyway were not followed by a specific term in Latin.

27. *Es war ein folgenreicher, aber auch fragwürdiger Schritt, daß um 1800 das griechisch-römische Altertum* en bloc *als «klassisch» erklärt wurde*—ibid, p. 254 (Eng., p. 250).

28. The powerful role of a shared scripture in bonding a community comes again to mind.

29. This is the similarity that engaged Tracy in his comparison of scripture with (modern) classics. See above, our preceding chapter, p. 184 and its note 25. Once again, it will be noticed that on this matter I am preferring to approach classics by way of scripture; he, *vice versa*. Whichever way an observer goes at the authoritativeness common to both types, the sense is decisive that one meets in each what is higher than one has yet oneself reached: that they are superior to us, and provide us with an opportunity to rise above our current selves (nearer to our potential selves; and to use classical terms, to our true selves).

30. The phrase "oral scripture" sounds more paradoxical to our modern ears than it would have to earlier ages. For the noun now suggests something written *rather than* oral. It does this not only because the two modes have become quite separated in our experience and our thinking, in a way whose invalidity for earlier times we have observed in the course of our study; but also because moderns tend to think in mundane terms, forgetting the transcendent reference whereby what is oral on earth may be honoured as having been written (or existing in written form) in heaven. (The use of *katabnā* and *kutiba* in the Qur'ān illustrates this point compellingly; cf. our note 32 below.)

31. For a good recent bibliography on this subject, see Graham, *Beyond the Written Word* (op. cit., our chap. 1 above, note 7), p. 174, the first part of his note 9.

32. In the case of the Qur'ān, for instance, that work is called *kitāb*, an Arabic word equivalent (etymologically) to (written) "scripture" in significant part in that it is conceived as having been written [*sic*] from all eternity by God (on a tablet in heaven). People on earth may write it or hear it read, read it or recite it, enshrine it or parts of it in their memories, but none of that affects its primordial quality. Similarly, the Decalogue vouchsafed to Moses at Sinai was "written by the finger of God", a point of powerful importance even to those among its cherishers who might themselves be illiterate, let alone to the "tradents" who handed on the tradition. (Cf. the Ancient Near East "Tablets of Destiny" remarked in our chap. 3 above, pp. 59–60. Furthermore, in other cases also, what is delivered, or received, orally/aurally may be honoured for being written mundanely somewhere by someone, a mark of special seriousness (cf. our chap. 3 above, p. 49—the Zarathushtrian scriptures on tablets of gold—and p. 60 and its note 61—

Hammurabi's law inscribed in stone; and the remarks in our opening chapter above on the literal sense of the word "scripture").

33. One has in mind such instances as Joseph Smith's *The Book of Mormon* (1830) and his "inspired revision" of the Bible; and Mary Baker Eddy's *Science and Health: with key to the scriptures* (1875). In the twentieth century, a process is discernible, although it is not yet consolidated, whereby starting with Sun Myung Moon's *Divine Principle* (1952) a scriptural corpus is emerging for his movement ("The Unification Church"). Regarding *The Book of Mormon* it may be noted this work was put forth as having been given to Joseph Smith—by an angel—inscribed on tablets of gold, recalling the Zarathushtrian case mentioned in our immediately preceding note just above no. 32.

10. Conclusion: Scripture and the Human Condition

1. The Merchant of Venice, Act 1 scene 3.
2. As well as serving as support *for* some of those movements.
3. Biblical examples are embarrassingly many.
4. Among Biblical scholars the salient leader here has been Brevard S. Childs, whose pioneering work—beginning notably with his *Biblical Theology in Crisis* (Philadelphia: Westminster, 1970)—is visible in especially his two outstanding more recent publications, *Introduction to the Old Testament as Scripture* and *The New Testament as Canon: an introduction* (see above, in our chap. 1, p. 15 and its note 23 and in our chap. 3, note 18, respectively), and increasingly now also in some of his students'. Another development within the academic Biblical-scholarship field is that of "canon criticism" led by James A. Sanders; see his works listed in our chap. 3 above, note 43, with bibliography in the 1987 one of this development to that date, pp. 195–200. Illustrative of expressions of the sense within the field that something has been or has become seriously wrong with what has previously been in vogue, is Walter Wink, *The Bible in Human Transformation: toward a new paradigm for Biblical study* (Philadelphia: Fortress, 1973); see esp. his first two brief chapters: "The Bankruptcy of the Critical Biblical Paradigm" (note the opening two sentences), and "Is Biblical Study Undergoing a Paradigm Shift?". (In the substantial remaining section the author proffers his own Jungian alternative.) From academic scholarship in other fields of religion, especially the comparative, again there has been a good deal not only of careful studies of particular scriptures and scriptural traditions, and also some reflective juxtaposing of several or all, yet general theories have just begun to be attempted, and the move from a study of texts to a study of scripture(s) is even more incipient. One may mention among recent items Miriam Levering, ed., *Rethinking Scripture* (op. cit., our chap. 1 above, note 7); Harold Coward, *Sacred Word and Sacred Text: scripture in world religions*

(Maryknoll, N.Y.: Orbis, 1988); William A. Graham, *Beyond the Written Word* (op. cit., our chap. 1 above, note 7), and id., "Scripture", in *The Encyclopedia of Religion* (op. cit., chap. 1 above, note 18) 13: 133–145; Denny & Taylor, edd., *The Holy Book* . . . (op. cit., our chap. 5 above, note 28); Wendy Doniger O'Flaherty, ed., *The Critical Study of Sacred Texts* (op. cit., our chap. 7 above, note 10); F. F. Bruce and E. G. Rupp, edd., *Holy Book and Holy Tradition* (op. cit., our chap. 3 above, note 9); etc. Of earlier studies notable are Günter Lanczkowski, *Heilige Schriften: Inhalt, Textgestalt und Überlieferung* (Stuttgart: Kohlhammer, 1956)—English translation, *Sacred Writings: a guide to the literature of religions*, Stanley Godman, trans. ([London: Collins, 1961] and New York: Harper & Row, [1961] and, slightly abridged, Harper Chapelbook, 1966); Johannes Leipoldt and Siegfried Morenz, *Heilige Schriften* (op. cit., our chap. 3 above, note 20); and Gustav Mensching, *Das heilige Wort: eine religionsphänomenologische Untersuchung* (Bonn: Ludwig Röhrscheid, 1937).

5. In particular, there are certain voices in literary criticism that have been arguing for an appreciation of the richer and more subtle values, and of human engagement in them, in great works of literature than seemed to be allowed by a strictly mundane-empirical study of the text as such; and these on occasion take note of the devaluation of scripture inflicted by such modern-day absence of this appreciation. An outstanding example is the work of Northrop Frye, considered below (pp. 223–224). Others are C. S. Lewis and Frank Kermode, quoted at, respectively, our notes 21 and 38 below.

6. On this, cf. our chapter 1 above at pp. 9–10.

7. This is from my Introduction to Religion in the Encyclopædia Britannica (op. cit. above, our chap. 8, note 53).

8. And even then, on a small scale. On the whole, Muslim culture was notably more tolerant of its 'superseded' Jewish and Christian communities within its borders than Christian culture has been of its 'superseded' Jewish. On the other hand, the emergence in the nineteenth century of the Bahā'ī movement in Iran and of the Aḥmadī in India, claiming in turn to supersede traditional Muslims', elicited from these a fierce intolerance. (On the latter instance, cf. above, our chap. 7, note 8.) Muslim theological attitude to the Sikh phenomenon has been less clearly defined, but was fiercely negative in the early eighteenth century and again in the 1947 turmoils.

9. With its doctrines of *naskh* and *taḥrīf*.

10. This reference is to the long and to some degree inconclusive debate as to whether Zarathushtrians-Gabr-Parsis, Hindus, Buddhists, and others should be recognized as *ahl al-kitāb*. The question was recognized as having both political and cosmological consequences.

11. Among Muslims there has been vehement rejection of Western treatment and interpretation of the Qur'ān; among Sikhs, resentment of Western academic studies of the Granth Ṣāḥib; among certain Christians one notes the increasing movement to repudiate academic liberalism gener-

ally and its critique of the Bible in particular; and so on. Secular theorists have tended to dismiss these complaints as in each case one more instance of the obtuseness of the religious mentality to truth, truth being represented in their minds by the secularists' "objective" views. It has hardly occurred to them that these views might indeed be valid so far as they go yet still leave out something—and indeed something integral, and foundational.

12. To say nothing of the dubious consequencess of the "common lore" (below, our p. 239) that one may perhaps think of as substituting in the role once played by scripture.

13. This was so in each of the Christian and the Jewish cases; along with an un-transcendentalized view of other, Asian, scriptures insofar as they were aware of them.

14. We re-iterate the point indicated in our opening chapter (p. 10, and its note 16) and held throughout this study and my other writings, that the term "transcendence" in my usage connotes always and also immanence. We return to this later in this present chapter.

15. It has been said that Descartes having constructed this polarity, Western philosophy ever since has been struggling to put the two fragments together again—thus far, with little success. The issue, of course, is not to put them together, but not to take them apart in the first place.

16. Apart from the intellectual error of "subject/object", also the separating, fragmenting, have been powerfully abetted, even established, practically by the economic system. Free-market capitalism has been conspicuously successful at dealing with things, notably poor in what has become the 'other' matter of human relations. It both has distanced persons from things (the worker—now the employee, but also even the employer—from his or her work, and from the "product" that they play a part in producing, with little if any personal integrity involved, or even personal interest in that thing) and also has alienated persons from one another, turning persons into individuals, explicitly competitive with one another and explicitly supposed to be driven by self-interest. (In modern culture humankind feels lonely even in the universe.)

17. Since in addition to objects it includes us, and community and beauty and scripture and so on.

18. Yet on this characteristically Western (basically Christian) term one would have to struggle with the Buddhist *anatta* doctrine, taking into account the convergence on the point at issue and the divergence of conceptual analysis.

19. For a somewhat fuller treatment of this matter see my "Objectivity and the Humane Sciences: a new proposal", in *Symposium on the Frontiers and Limitations of Knowledge/Colloque sur les frontières et limites du savoir* ([Ottawa]: Royal Society of Canada/Société Royale du Canada, 1975), pp. [81]–102; reprinted in slightly abridged form in Oxtoby, ed., *Religious*

Diversity . . . (op. cit., our chap. 4 above, note 18), pp. 160–180. The issues involved in all this demand, however, a much more sustained inquiry than was available then or than is feasible here.

20. Buber saw something of this, and developed his point in his thesis of "I-Thou" being as basic as "I-it". Dilthey saw our following point, in his thesis of *verstehen* and *erklären*. The people who talk of "post-modernism" seem to see merely the negative point that what was recently celebrated as modern will not do.

21. On this point it is interesting to compare a critic's remark on literature: "Literary experience heals the wound, without undermining the privilege, of individuality"—C. S. Lewis, *An Experiment in Criticism* (Cambridge: at the University Press, 1961), the opening sentence of that book's culminating paragraph, p. 140. That full paragraph and its preceding one (pp. 139–141) regarding "literature considered as Logos" which "admits us to experiences other than our own" are—*mutatis mutandis*, and provided that one give due weight to this qualification—pertinent to our higher concerns here.

22. On the theory that "believing" is what religious people do, its recentness, and its woeful fallacy, see my *Belief and History* (Charlottesville: University Press of Virginia, 1977) and *Faith and Belief* (op. cit., our chap. 7 above, note 28).

23. Notably in his two recent works on the Bible: *The Great Code: the Bible and literature* (New York: Harcourt Brace Jovanovich, and Toronto: Academic Press Canada, 1982), and *Words with Power: being a second study of "The Bible and Literature"* (Toronto, London, New York, &c: Viking—Penguin, 1990); of these two a brief synopsis (in part, "something of a shorter and more accessible version", as he himself puts it—p. [xvii]) is his posthumously published *The Double Vision: language and meaning in religion* (Toronto, Buffalo, London: University of Toronto Press, 1991). Cf. his Norton Lectures at Harvard, *The Secular Scripture: a study of the structure of Romance* (Cambridge, Massachusetts and London: Harvard University Press, 1976). Also important for this matter was his earlier *The Educated Imagination* (Toronto: Canadian Broadcasting Corporation, [1963], 1980—The Massey Lectures, Second series; and many subsequent editions, in the U.K. and the U.S.), with *inter alia* its memorable remark (p. 24): "You wouldn't go to *Macbeth* to learn about the history of Scotland—you go to it to learn what a man feels like after he's gained a kingdom and lost his soul".

24. *Passim*, in the works mentioned in our immediately preceding note, no. 23, esp. of course the 1963 one. Comparable is one of his expressive phrases in the 1982 volume, where he speaks of the mind's moving "from the closed fortresses of believer and skeptic to the community of vision" (p. 230).

25. To some readers he conveys the impression that while his discernment raises the Bible to a higher level than modern skeptics have tended to

appreciate, namely to the level of imaginative literature at its best, nonetheless he leaves it there rather than perceiving it as still higher ("the Bible is like Shakespeare", they hear him as saying—"merely"). Occasionally, however, he writes explicitly that there is, indeed, more to it than that—even though it be obtuse not to recognize that it is at least that. Illustrative here is his wording of his sub-title in his 1982–1990 pair; in the former, note his comment (pp. xii–xiv) on its difference from the familiar "Bible as Literature" treatment. I have a sense that he would have taken quite positively to my "prose, poetry, and scripture" theme below. I know that he actively approved my comparative inquiry.

26. . . . and in what we appreciate of others' imaginative constructs.

27. The modern notion of instrumental reason is a sorely debased substitute, approaching the subjective.

28. Or, as one of India's delightful stories puts it, two more; or one half more . . . .

29. Cf. also from another realm the nineteenth-century American philosophic theologian C. C. Everett: "the imagination, first the explorer and then the poet of the race, becomes at last its seer, its prophet, and its priest". This sentence follows his remarking that "the imagination . . . is the eye of the soul . . .—only [the imagination] shows us God. We receive Him through the imagination, just as we receive the outward world through the imagination". From Everett, *Poetry* . . . (op. cit., our chap. 4 above, note 2), pp. 44–45. The first two chapters of this work (pp. 1–49) are entitled "The Imagination", within its Part I: "Poetry" (pp. 1–154). With regard to our later discussion in this chapter regarding truth, one may note once again his further comment, which we previously (ibid.) cited: "when poetry is true, it is truer than anything beside" (p. 44).

30. The word "positivist" is no longer used by those who hold the position (rather, chiefly now by its opponents), although they still fit the description that Auguste Comte gave to the term.

31. "People throughout the world have found words to provide a frame for the sacred, to mediate knowledge of truths and to have moving or transforming power"—opening sentence of Levering, ed., *Rethinking Scripture* . . . (our chap. 1 above, note 7). She goes on: "Some Hindus, for example, have recognized speech as a goddess (Vāc), even as creative divinity itself, while certain sounds/words (*śabda*) are themselves seen by Hindus as channels of the divine energy of creation. Many communities affirm unambiguously that certain words (the Ten Commandments, the Qur'ān) come directly from God. Others understand the Word as the best metaphor for the self-revelation of what is ultimate, even if that Word takes the form not of words but of persons or deeds". This and the first sentence quoted here constitute the opening paragraph of her "Introduction" to her volume of essays constituting the book cited.

32. Some would find this suggestion less troublesome, perhaps, if I

wrote of three modes of human use of or involvement in language; of ways in which persons read or hear language—rather than three modes of language itself. I myself would find this an unnecessary refinement, since I do not perceive language as something in itself, to which human beings are related from as it were the outside; but rather, somewhat like sight or hearing, as an aspect or component of humanness. Our involvement in it constitutes its existence and its nature. In any case, the "suggestion" is meant to be illuminating, and perhaps need not be taken as descriptive or classificatory. An aside: of three "principal" modes of language we speak here in order to leave room for sundry minor modes. One example might be the charmingly opaque and bizarrely whimsical style of English in London *Times* crossword puzzles. In general, puns, subtle *double entendre*, sly allusions, may play a non-negligible part in human relations through language with one another and with the world. Our involvement in language is endlessly rich.

33. Is Lewis Carroll's "Jabberwocky" an exception? (Or would some see it as merely verse, not poetry?)

34. The difference between poetry and prose is not the same as that between scripture and the other two; some would say, is not even of the same order. Our "suggestion" to be toyed with is offered not to affirm such sameness, but to intimate that they might nonetheless prove fruitfully comparable.

35. Robert Burns, the opening line of one of his poems. Original spelling: "my luve". (For those who feel that the comparison's being a simile, not a metaphor, absolves it from not being literally untrue, one could offer instead the line from the popular song, "Life is just a bowl of cherries".)

36. With the result that true courage, a true note in music, being true to oneself or to a friend, becoming more truly human, are neglected—or dismissed outright.

37. And with non-fiction prose, at that. Another instance of de-transcendentalizing!

38. Similarly, it is by no means obvious that social-science prose descriptions of personality, a society, or an era can always proffer truth more effectively than a good novel. On the relation to truth of literature—or *vice versa*—cf. the literary critic Kermode (he deals particularly with poetry, great fiction, and extensively, the Bible), noting esp. his remark regarding "the radical and never fully understood truth" of life and the world, to which great literature gives access; truth that is contained in one of the two worlds (the empirical and a further one) of which he speaks as depicted in such literature. Such depicting constitutes what he sees as those works' "dual force" (—Jean Sudrann, in the Phi Beta Kappa *Key Reporter*, Winter 1990–91, p. 4). One may, furthermore, question whether myth may not well on occasion proffer truth more effectively than literalism, or especially may not have been done so back in pre-scientific days when literalist knowledge

of the world was less. The modern requirement is not to confuse a given myth with literalism.

39. Actually, there has been a tendency, championed also by certain philosophers, finally to drop the word and concept "truth" as a noun, retaining only its corresponding adjective, "true", which along with "false" are deemed to be predicates of only sentences, statements, or propositions. Many literary critics, as we have been observing, have discerned a relation of language to truth that at least supplements such a narrow view. It sorely needs supplementing; or outright challenging.

40. For a less condensed presentation of this pivotal point, see my "A Human View of Truth", in *SR: Studies in Religion/Sciences religieuses*, 1 (1971): [6]–24, published also in John Hick, ed., *Truth and Dialogue: the relationship between world religions* (London: Sheldon, 1974—Studies in Philosophy and Religion, [no. 2], P. R. Baelz, gen. ed.; the American edn. has a divergent title, *Truth and Dialogue in World Religions: conflicting truth-claims*, Philadelphia: Westminster, 1974), pp. [20]–44 (cf. also ". . . A Rejoinder", pp. [156]–162).

41. So, for example, the most widely known recent historian of the scientific movement: Thomas S. Kuhn, *The Structure of Scientific Revolutions* (Chicago: University of Chicago Press, [1962], 2nd edn., 1970—*International Encyclopedia of Unified Science*, vol. 2, no. 2). See esp. pp. 170–173. (One may consult also his revisionary 1969 "Postscript", esp. p 206.) (This is one more illustration of the point that modern Western culture has been losing its capacity to discern transcendence historically and partially accessible in immanence.)

42. William Butler Yeats, in "a letter written . . . shortly before his death", according to the caption reproduced in a drawing by Robert Baldock printed in a limited edition as a broadside by Wesley Tanner and published 1974 by The Druid Press, Berkeley, California. His "to put it . . . in a phrase" is teasingly consonant with the notion that his words express.

43. Hence our word "evidently" in the latter part of the sentence at the conclusion of our chapter 1 (p. 19), to which reference is made in the second half of our paragraph above, the final paragraph of page 230. That earlier sentence, one may recall, reads in full: "Yet after all, it is a surprising thing to do: to take a piece of literature and evidently to elevate it to a very special status, and then to live . . . accordingly".

44. Terms such as "Qur'an", "Veda", "Perfection of Wisdom Sutras", and the rest have as we have previously remarked tended in outsiders' usage to serve as specific terms that denote specific texts. No doubt it is a major step forward, towards intellectual accuracy as well as towards justice, when the realization is added that for participants in the groups for whom they have been scripture they in addition [sic] connote [sic] transcendence. Yet this is still not adequate, not yet fully accurate. For on the contrary, as we have repeatedly seen in the course of our study, fundamentally what makes

them scripture is that they *denote* transcendence, and connote empirical matters wherein or whereby that transcendence has become available. It is not that the devout's empirical encounter with certain texts has led them, gratuitously, upwards to a transcendent presumption, but rather, basically, the other way around. (On this, one might perhaps cf. above, note 73 of our chap. 8.)

45. To take examples from the Buddhist instance, we noted their calling their scriptures by a transcendent name, *Buddhavacanam* (our chap. 7 above, pp. 150, 151, and esp. 172–173); further, their averring that the scriptures' teachings are in turn the source of transcendent Buddhas themselves (ibid., p. 164 with its notes 81, 82).

46. We have already met this same point expressly in the Jewish case (cf. our chap. 5 above, e.g. p. 118 with its note 80), and in the Hindu, where a particular scripture is affirmed to be an almost infinitesmal part of its huge prototype (our chap. 6 above, e.g. note 49). Similarly in the Islamic: the Qur'ān (18:109) tells its readers: "If the sea were ink for the Words of my Lord, yet the sea would be exhausted before the Words of my Lord were exhausted, even if We were to bring another like it as reinforcement" (my trans.).

47. I like, too, the Jewish image, re-iterated down the centuries, that the Tôrāh was written in black fire on white fire (*bā-ēsh sheḥôrāh 'al-ēsh lebānāh*). For instance, in the Midrash on Psalm 90: 3, ¶ 12—*Midrash Tehillîm* (opp. citt., our chap. 2 above, note 16), Hebrew, p. 196 recto = p. [391]; Eng., vol. 2, p. 94.

48. Zōhar 3: 152a (opp. citt., our chap. 5 above, note 11—Aramaic, vol. 3, p. 152 recto / [303]; English, vol. 5, pp. 211–212). Although this way of putting the matter has to do with the human ascent from lower to higher in apprehending Tôrāh, in other instances (as illustrated in our notes 47 immediately above and 53 below) the point is forcefully made that Tôrāh begins first on high and gradually descends, not merely in the obvious sense of becoming eventually available to human beings on earth, but gradually having moved from a pre-differentiated form into the form of words, having begun at a metaphysically higher level.

49. Leonard J. Bowman, "Bonaventure's Use of Apocalyptic Scripture in the Collationes in Hexaemeron", unpublished paper read to the twentieth International Congress on Medieval Studies May 11, 1985—Western Michigan University. The reference is to Bonaventura's *lignum vitae, scilicet fidem* and *lignum scientiae, scilicet legem*, the latter of which is to be seen, and read, but not eaten. He quotes the threat in the Garden of Eden about not eating *that* tree (which indeed is called *lignum scientiae . . .* in the Vulgate), *quia destrueres quidquid Christus fecit.* That Eden tree was indeed fateful, but we might almost speak of it as "fatal" in the matter of a literal reading of scripture, since Bonaventura goes on to quote II Corinthians 3:6: *littera occidit*—"the letter killeth [but the spirit giveth life]". I have used the edition

S.R.E. Cardinalis S. Bonaventuræ . . . Opera Omnia (Paris: Ludovicus Vivès, 1864–1867, 14 voll.), where this passage, from *Sermo* 16 of "Illuminationes Ecclesiæ in Hexaemeron", is found at vol. 9 pp. 107–108 (Bowman refers to a different edn., with the differing wording of that title). The opening subordinate clause of the Bowman sentence that I have cited in our text refers to an unpublished doctoral dissertation, University of Chicago 1979, of Dominic Vincent Monti, "Bonaventure's Interpretation of Scripture in his Exegetical Works", p. 162. This dissertation adduces passages to support his argument that Bonaventure is to be recognized as one of the pioneers in mediæval times of seeking the *intentio auctoris* of a scriptural book if we are to understand what it says.

50. From "Break Thou the bread of life . . .", an 1877 hymn by Mary Artemisia Lathbury, written originally for The Chautauqua Vesper Hour, and sung with deep feeling by many millions in various English-speaking Protestant circles throughout the latter part of last century and the first half of this. (It was rendered also into French.) The particular wording here plays on the Christian practice of having the phrase "The Word" referring both to the Bible and to Jesus Christ, and indeed to the metaphysical *Logos*.

51. Cf. above, our chap. 3, pp. 59–60.

52. *Tanzīl*, with this meaning, has been not merely a technical theological term, but is in everday use among the populace in referring to their scripture.

53. Furthermore, the remainder of the sentence quoted above (our note 47) about writing in black fire on white fire, helps us to sense the primordiality and transcendence of scripture in the perception of Jews: the Tôrāh, " . . . as it lay on the lap of" God, *became* written so, two thousand years before the creation of the world (loc. cit.).

54. Another significance is that unfortunately for our purposes, the innovative "Fundamentalist" attitude to a particular scripture has coloured, even formed, many outside observers' sense of what scripture or a particular scripture means generally in human affairs. This is drastically different from what they have normally meant over preceding centuries. It has given involvement with scripture a bad name—one that is only partly deserved, even in the modern world. It is engaging to note that what Fundamentalists, historicist scholars, and radical skeptics share in common is a lack of appreciation of the transcendence involved. They all imagine that the meaning of that scripture lies in itself, rather than in something beyond both it and us to which it points.

55. In a situation of this kind, some are inclined to resort to Wittgenstein's proposal of "family resemblance". I have never been impressed by that notion, however; it seems to me not helpful. For one thing, the metaphor gains its plausibility from being based on a fundamental and quite "objective" linkage underlying the observed diversities of a literal family: namely, the genetic commonality of blood kinship with certain genes that

constitutes the family (and gives rise to some resemblances). For another, in the case of "games", which Wittgenstein cites as an example, the force of the proposal is based on his appeal to us to "look at" games to see how diverse they in fact are even though we call them all "games"; whereas actually what they have in common lies not in the games themselves, but derives from the fact that they are all treated by human beings in a comparable way. To see why we call them all "games" we should look not at those games but at the people playing them: it is a human attitude to, involvement in, games that constitutes their being such, not anything formal—nor substantial—inhering in them objectively. (Some persons make a business of hockey; and some make a game of what for others is not play but work.) A much more perceptive philosophic treatment of games has been set forth by Gadamer, relating the players to them. He writes of *Spiel als Leitfaden der ontologischen Explikation* ("Play *[but one could equally well, both in general and in this context, say 'game']* as the clue to ontological explanation*"): Hans-Georg Gadamer, *Wahrheit und Methode: Grundzüge einer philosophischen Hermeneutik* (Tübingen: J.C.B. Mohr [Paul Siebeck], 1960, 2. Auflage, 1965 [and subsequent reprints]), p. [97]; see the section *Der Begriff des Spiels*—pp. [97]–105, being the first section of §1, "*Spiel als Leitfaden . . .*", of chap. II of his Part I, *Die Ontologie des Kunstwerks . . . .* There is an English trans.: *Truth and Method* ([London: Sheed and Ward, 1975], New York: Continuum, 1975), where this passage ("The Concept of Play") is pp. 91–99.

56. In the West, this has named something historically perceived as intertwining with scripture but not identical with it. It is in danger, however, of inducing many to presuppose an identifiable revealer (such as God) as a concept to go with it, whereas many scripturalists conceptualize both transcendence, and its being made accessible, in other ways. Islamic thinking has discriminated between two types of what the West embraces under its single term "revelation": namely, *waḥy* and *ilhām*, the former more absolute, the latter more personalist. This would make it easier for some Muslims to include all that we are subsuming under "scripture", by retaining a special status within the whole for their own, while regarding the effectiveness of the Qur'ān (*waḥy*) in the life of distinct given individuals—their varying ability to understand, to appreciate, to receive—as multiple instances coming under the heading of *ilhām*?

57. For Christians, "the Word of God" sometimes refers to the Bible; sometimes to the person of Christ; sometimes (as in *logos spermatikos*, for instance with Clement and Origen) to the universal self-disclosure of the divine of which the historical Jesus Christ is one instance ("late in time"). (Hindus would feel the force of this conception.)

58. Cf. above, our chap. 3, p. 47 and its note 4.

59. Even this might be deemed an over-simplification. We insisted on the point, in our Judaica chapter above (pp. 120–121), that for Jews the

concept "God" cannot be understood as a separate matter, but derives its meaning from taking its (however dominant) place within the dynamic complex of the whole pattern of Jewish life; and of course the same thing applies for the Buddhist, Hindu, and other communities to their particular major concepts—and to "scripture" (or their counterpart thereto) similarly for every religious group (or century, or . . .). In each case, accordingly, "scripture" might be dubbed, if one looks carefully enough, at least a quadrilateral notion, being related to the three matters mentioned in our text and further to all the other items in that specific case. One may, however, subsume all these last under the heading of the "human" in the triangle proffered: every human being is unique, and is what he or she is in that uniqueness as within a particular context (including a religious context)—as well as all of us participating in humanity, and in our common world.

60. More fully on this, see my "Symbols in Religion" (op. cit. above, our chap. 8, note 53).

61. The Reformed churches might then take to speaking of "The Word and the other Sacraments"?

62. Might the point about Buddhist sūtras made in the concluding three paragraphs of our Buddhist chapter above be seen perhaps as comparable to the analogy here of "sacrament" in the Christian case?

63. Nor did he much put his mind to the question of how we are encouraged to pursue such ideals as we perceive; nor whether some people's ideals are "better" or "truer" than others, and what it would mean for us to move towards sharpening our discernment.

ACKNOWLEDGEMENTS

I AM FORMALLY, and morally, obliged to acknowledge certain financial support given me at certain points towards work on this book over several years, and I am happy to do so: the U.S. National Endowment for the Humanities, for making possible two rewarding summer seminars for post-doctoral scholars; the Canada Council, for a two-year Senior Fellowship after my retirement; the Rockefeller Foundation, for an unforgettable and remarkably productive month at their incomparable Bellagio villa on Lake Como, where I started the writing. One is indeed grateful for these matters.

It is neither required nor customary to proffer enthusiastic thanks to certain other institutions, yet without them the writing of this or various other books would be quite impossible. To them I am deeply grateful: the university as an idea and as an actuality in our tradition and our society, and specific universities that for over fifty years have provided an environment and resources, enabling me to learn, plus an income enabling me to live—specifically Forman Christian College and the University of the Panjab, Lahore (financially, the Canadian Churches that underwrote my time there), then McGill, Dalhousie, and Harvard (and, not financially but otherwise, since my retirement as during my undergraduate days, the University of Toronto). The honour and privilege of serving in these and the opportunities that they have provided are precious. One could go on.

When it comes from institutions to persons to whom I am indebted for help in producing this work, the number is so large and indefinite as to be bewildering. Even if restricted to those of major help, it is unmanageable. Must one not include Bernard of Clairvaux, Rashi of Troyes, Ramanuja, and counterparts from other centuries and civilizations, who manifestly have helped me immensely to understand what scripture has involved; Muslim friends in Lahore half a century ago whose life or casual remarks helped me to understand; and a host of others. The colleagues and students in those academic institutions, the participants in those summer seminars, the church sermons that I have heard, even the reported activities—good and bad—of scripturally inspired groups throughout the world; a listing would indeed not be feasible. At another level, I have always been markedly grateful to, for instance, one John T. Platts, whom I never met and know almost nothing about, but whose admirable *Hindustani Dictionary* helped me to learn Urdu when I first went to India; and to the many other scholars who have compiled instruments enabling us to enter the discourse of groups beyond our own. Not only scholars, of this and many other sorts, but teachers, poets, musicians—from whom do we not learn?

Certain contributors to understanding are of course cited or mentioned in the notes and references; others are not. More immediately, various friends, former students and colleagues, have been generous enough to read through drafts of specific chapters, matters that they know much more thoroughly than do I. I have profited from their encouragement, and from their suggestions leading to amendments; my indebtedness to them is profound, and readers of the book will share in that indebtedness.

I have, of course, thanked each privately; not to do so publicly here is odd. Yet I confront a dilemma faced in some degree by many authors: how can one name a few people and omit a great host of others who, in my case over the course of my long lifetime from childhood, have helped me towards such understanding as I have managed to attain. Indeed, were it not for the corrosive individualism of our modern culture, no one could presume that a book is the work simply of its author. Every book is significantly a product of its context, a response however innovative to and in that context. Certainly this one is *inter alia* a product of the Harvard Center for the Study of World Religions, by which I chiefly mean, as I meant at the time, the persons constituting that Center during the years that I was a member. To them, and to the wider circle of my companions in the journey through the years—friends, and critics, and the indifferent—I am happy to acknowledge forcefully that I, and "my" book, owe immeasurably much.

INDEX

A (Sanskrit letter), 310 n.14
Abhayagiri school, 321 n.61
Abhidhamma(pitaka), 151, 314 n.33
Abraham, 107, 117, 152, 292 n.48, 298
  n.75
Acts (Biblical book), 331 n.101
Adad, 59–60, 275 n.60
Adam, 300 n.11
Adam, James, 273 n.48
Adi Granth, 353 n.3. *See also* Guru
  Granth Sahib
Aeschylus, 57, 188
Aesop, 151
Agama(s), 129, 135, 300 n.9
Ahl-i-Quran, 204
Ahmadi(yah), 308 n.8, 358 n.8
Ahura Mazda, 63
Akhand path, 353 n.4
Akkadian language, 245 n.13
Albright, W. F., 276 n.70
Alcuin, 268 n.27
Alexandria, 53, 57–59, 273 nn.44,46
Alfieri, Vittorio, 184, 342 n.28
Allegorical interpretation, 59
Alpha and Omega, 310 n.14
Alphabet. *See* Writing
Alsdorf, L., 354 n.9
Altan Khan, 319 n.53
Alvar, 128, 135, 300 n.8
Amida, 167
Amida-kyo, 323 n.74
Amitayurdhyana, 324 n.74
Amore, R. C., 327 n.86

Amos, prophet, Book of Amos, 207, 208
Anatta, 359 n.18
Andrew of St. Victor, 259 n.57
Anesaki, Masaharu, 328 n.93, 333 n.110
Anglican, 205, 247 n.19
Anguttara Nikaya, 312 n.26
Anjinketsujosho, 327 n.83
Antitheses (Marcion), 54
Apocalyptic literature, 275 n.64
Apocrypha(l), 13, 247 nn.19–20, 268
  n.25, 274 n.54, 315 n.35
Apotelesmatika, 271 n.40
Aqiba, Rabbi, 23, 38, 249 n.5, 257 n.54
Arabic language, chap. 4 *passim*, 154
Aranyaka, 134
Aristeas to Philocrates, Letter of, 274
  n.51
Aristotle, 33, 57, 188, 189, 255 n.41,
  274 n.49, 343 n.33, 346 n.50
Armageddon, 345 n.44
Art (and scripture), x, 19, 227, 233, 343
  n.33
Arya Samaj, 305 n.35, 330 n.101, 355
  n.21
Ascension of Muhammad, 76, 278
  nn.6–7
Ashurbanipal, 272 n.44
Astasahasrika, 332 n.107
Astrology, 55, 270 nn.37–38
Augsburg (Lutheran Conference), 13
Augustine, 269 n.29
Augustus, 274 n.50
Aural. *See* Oral/aural

The author expresses his thanks to Fortress Press and its associates for providing
the index, as for the many other ways in which they have been remarkably consider-
ate throughout the publication process.

Avesta, 7, 49–50, 262 n.9
"Awakening of Faith", 317 n.47
Ayurveda, 301 n.18

Babylon(-ian), 48, 53, 55, 57, 59. *See also* Writing: cuneiform
Bacon, Francis, 346 n.50
Baha'i, 358 n.8
Bailey, H. W., 263 n.9
Baldock, Robert, 363 n.42
Baraitot, 101
Barth, Karl, 5
Basham, A. L., 299 n.5
Baydawi, 72
Bedjan, Paul, 263 n.11
Behistun/Bisitun inscription, 63, 276 n.71
"Belief theory", 105, 222–23, 360 n.22
Benares, 130
Bencheikh, J. E., 278 n.7
Bengali language, 141
Bentley, Richard, 193
Berit, 265 n.18, 282 n.1. *See also* Covenant
Berling, J. A., 312 n.24, 318 n.50
Bernard of Clairvaux, chap. 2 *passim* with its notes, 167, 368
Bhagat, 353 n.2
Bhagavad Gita, 5, 10, 18, 22, 34, 86, 128, 135, 141, 202, 243 n.3, 246 n.15, 248 n.2, 301 n.17, 338 n.11
Bhagavata Purana, 127, 141, 301 n.19
Bhakti, 129, 140, 141, 299 n.3, 353 n.2
Bickermann, E., 274 n.51
Bka'-brgyud-pa, 325 n.76
Bleeker, C. J., 272 n.44
Bodhidharma, 317 n.47
Bodhisattva, 151, 326–27 n.81, 328 n.93
Bonaventura, 233, 364 n.49
Bond, G. D., 329 n.95
Book of Common Prayer, 205
Book of the Dead, 290 n.37
Bowman, John, 263 n.10
Bowman, L. J., 364–65 n.49
Boyce, Mary, 263 n.9
Boyle, Robert, 350 n.65
Brahman, 11n., 140–41, 302 n.25
Brahmana, 134, 303–4 n.29, 304 n.30
Brahmin, 131–32, 302 n.27, 305 n.38
Braude, W. G., 253 n.16
Brodie, T. L., 343 n.33
Brower, R. A., 345 n.47
Brown, C. M., 304 n.34, 305 n.37
Buber, Martin, 360 n.20

Buddha, 51, 84, chap. 7 *passim* with its notes, 240, 258 n.55
Buddhaghosa, 151–52, 314 n.33, 315–16 n.36, 316 n.38
Buddhavacana(m), 150, 151, 172–73, 311 n.20, 313 n.29, 333 n.113, 364 n.45
Budge, W. A. Wallis, 276 n.71
Bukkyo Dendo Kyokai, 319 n.54
Bulgakov, Sergei, 345 n.44
Burckhardt, Jacob, 344 n.42
Burma, 152
Burns, Robert, 362 n.35

Cabezon, J. I., 329 n.95, 332 n.106
Canaan(-ite), 48, 53, 57, 60
Canon(-izing), 39, 58, 246 nn.17–18, 257 n.52, 266 n.18, 269 n.32; Chinese, 157, 201, 312 nn.22,25; consolidating of, 13, 263 n.9, 273 n.44; criticism, 357 n.4; fixed/closed, 152, 317 n.43; Hebrew, 268 n.25, 272 n.43; Jaina, 354 nn.9,16; Korean, 147, 158; Muratorian, 269 n.31; New Testament, 265 n.18, 268 n.25, 269 n.29, 270 n.32; Pali, 152, 157, 309 n.10, 311 n.20, 312 n.26, 313 n.30, 314 n.31, 314 nn.32–34, 315 n.35, 316 n.37, 319 n.52, 321 n.61, 328 n.88; Tibetan, 147, 156
Canterbury, Archbishop of, 247 n.20
Canticum Canticorum. See Song of Songs
Carman, John, 300 n.8
Carpenter, J. E., 314 n.30
Carroll, Lewis, 362 n.33
Carter, J. R., 313 n.28
Cassiodorus, 268 n.26
Cassirer, Ernst, 256 n.47
Chaitanya, 140, 141
Ch'an, 154
Charles the Great, 268 n.27
Chaucer, 334 n.1
Cheng, 339 n.19
Chiao, 334 n.2
Childers, R. C., 313 n.27
Childs, Brevard, 248 n.23, 265 n.18, 270 n.32, 272 n.43, 357 n.4
Ching, 176, 178–79, 182, 307 n.2, 310 nn.18,20, 311 n.20, 312 n.23, 318 n.49, 334 n.2, 336 n.9, 337–38 n.11
Ching hsueh, 334 n.2
Ching, Julia, 339 n.15, 340 n.21
Christ, 46, 110, 125, 148, 173, 234, 236, 262 n.4, 310 n.14, 335 n.6., 366 n.57. *See also* Jesus

Chuang-tzu, 336 n.7
Chu-ching jih-sung, 160
Chu Hsi, 337 n.11
Cicero, 188
Clarke, Howard, 345 n.46
Classicism(-ists), 188, 195; Christian, 193
Classics, 48, 57, 59, chap. 8 *passim* with its notes, 200, 206–7, 208, 216, 224, 272 n.44, 273 n.45, 274 n.50, 356 n.29, 360 n.25
Clement of Alexandria, 366 n.57
Coburn, T. B., 298 n.1, 355 n.23
Codex Amiatinus, 268 n.26, 269 n.28
Cohen, G. D., 252 n.13, 293 n.52
Cohen, P. A., 339 n.19
Cole, W. O., 353 n.5
Coleridge, W. C., 225
Collins, J. J., 275 n.64
Collins, Steven, 316 n.37
Comte, Auguste, 361 n.30
Confucian. *See* Classics
Confucius, 177, 207, 334 n.3, 335–36 n.6, 339 n.20, 351 n.71
Conze, Edward, 309 n.13, 325 n.75, 327 n.86
Corinthians, Epistles to, 269 n.29, 283 n.1, 319 n.51, 364 n.49
Corless, R. J., 318 n.49
Corpus Hermeticum, 55, 270 n.36
Council of Javneh (Jamnia), 56, 271 n.42
Council of Jerusalem, 13
Council of Trent, 13, 247 n.19
Covenant, 92–93, 265 n.18, 282–83 n.1; Ark of, 290 n.37
Coward, Harold, 357 n.4
Craig, A. M., 340 n.20
Craigie, P. C., 257 n.53
Crusades, 280 n.13
Culavamsa, 316 n.38
Curses, 63, 276 n.72, 277 n.73
Curtius, E. R., 247 n.18, 273 n.46, 347 n.54, 356 n.26
Cyrus, Edict of, 95

Dadu Panth, 141
Daimuryoju-kyo, 323 n.74
Dainichikyo, 327 n.83
Damasus, Pope, 269 n.29
Danby, Herbert, 258 n.54
Daniel, Book of, 268 n.25, 287 n.18
Daniel, Norman, 280 n.13
Dante, 77, 278–79 n.8

Dargyay, E. K., 308 n.6, 320 n.56, 332 n.105
Darius, 63, 277 n.73
Darwin, 11
David, King, 26, 142, 154
Davids, T. W. Rhys, 314 n.30
Deal, W. E., 243 n.3
Decalogue. *See* Ten Commandments
Deists, 194
Denny, F. M., 245 n.9
Descartes, 359 n.15
Despland, Michel, 348 n.58
Deuteronomy, 62, 277 n.73, 283 n.2, 290 n.37
de Vaux, R., 290 n.37
Devi-Bhagavata, 127
Devi-Mahatmya, 127, 301 n.17
Dhamma. See Dharma
Dhammapada, 152
Dhammasangani, 314 n.33
Dhanurveda, 301 n.18
Dharma, dhamma: Buddhist, 151, 164, 170, 173, 174, 234, 312 n.24, 313 n.28, 318 n.50, 320 n.55, 329 nn.97,99, 330 n.101, 333 n.113; Hindu, 129–30, 301 n.13
Dhorme, Paul, 275 n.58
Dhyana, 318 n.48
Diatheke, 282 n.1
Diderot, 184
Digha-Nikaya, 313–14 n.30
Dilthey, 360 n.20
Diringer, David, 276 nn.66–67
Dob Ber, Rabbi, 260 n.65
Dobbins, F. S., 279 n.13
Dobbins, J. C., 317 n.46
Dravidian languages, 300 n.12. *See also* Tamil language
Driver, G. R., 275 n.59
d-r-sh, 290–91 n.38
DuBose, H. C., 347 n.56
Durkheim, Emil, 252 n.12

Easter, 95
Ecclesiastes, Book of. *See* Qoheleth
Ecclesiasticus, Book of, 282 n.1
Eck, D. L., 301 n.16
Eddy, M. B., 357 n.33
Egypt, 48, 95, 109, 121
Eisegesis, 16
Emptiness, 170–71, 330 n.100, 332 n.104. *See also* Silence of the Buddha
Enuma Elish, 273 n.44
Episcopalian. *See* Anglican

Esther, Book of, 268 n.25
Eucharist, Christian 70
Euripides, 57
Everett, C. C., 277 n.2, 361 n.29
Exegesis, 291 n.38, 338 n.14; rules of, 67; Islamic (*tafsir*), 71
Exodus, Book of, 28, 95–97, 121, 275 n.63, 282 n.1, 292 n.47

Fairbank, J. K., 340 n.20
Fang-pien, 324 n.75
Fan-wang-ching, 312 n.23
Fatalism, Islamic (*qismat*), 6
Feil, Ernst, 348 n.58
Feng Yu-lan, 339 n.18
Festival(s), Buddhist, 152; Iranian, 272 n.44; Ram-Lila, 127, 299 nn.3–4; Sikh, 353 n.4; seasonal, 109–10, 273 n.44
Festugiere, A.-J., 343 n.35
Feuerbach, 241
"Fingers pointing to moon", 162, 168–69
Finnegan's Wake, 206
Five Scrolls, 99, 109
Folkert, Kendall W., 247 n.21, 306 n.40, 354 n.10, 355 n.24
Fo tsang, 312 n.25
Four Books (Chinese), 336 n.9
Franklin, Benjamin, 346 n.49
Frauwallner, Erich, 309 n.12
Freedman, D. N., 271 n.43
Fridell, W. M., 353 n.8
Frye, Northrop, 223–24, 358 n.5
Frye, Richard N., 263 n.9
"Fundamentalist", "Fundamentalism", 3, 41, 217, 235, 243 n.2, 365 n.54
Fung Yu-lan. *See* Feng Yu-lan

Gadamer, H.-G., 366 n.55
Gaudiya Vaisnava movement, 140, 141
Gautama Buddha. *See* Siddhartha Gautama
Gay, Peter, 342 n.30, 345 n.48, 346 n.50
Gelasian Decree, 269 n.29
Gemara, 295 n.62
Gematria, 42
Genesis, Book of, 2–3, 5, 11, 99, 109, 276 n.65, 291 n.40
Genghiz Khan, 319 n.53
Gerhardsson, Birger, 264 n.17
Gernet, Jacques, 340 n.20
Ghandi, M. K., 22, 248 n.2

Ghosa, 315 n.36
Gibbon, Edward, 184, 342 n.31
Gideon project, 202
Gita. *See* Bhagavad Gita
Gnostic, 267 n.22. *See also* Mandaean
Goethe, 206, 334 n.1
Golden calf, 28
Gospel(s), 5, 23, 53, 155, 245 n.13, 262 n.3, 268 n.25, 296 n.65, 344 n.40
Graham, W. A., 244 nn.7–8, 245 n.12, 264 n.14, 323 n.68, 346 n.52, 356 n.31, 358 n.4
Grammatikoi, 57
Granth Sahib, 48. *See also* Guru Granth Sahib
Greenberg, Moshe, 291 n.44, 298 n.76
Greenspahn, Frederick, 291 nn.39,41
Gualtieri, A. R., 308 n.8
Gummere, R. M., 346 n.49
Gurdwara, 197
Guru, 141, 196, 305 n.36, 307 n.42, 353 n.1
Guru Granth Sahib, 141, 196–97, 200, 270 n.33, 358 n.11. *See also* Granth Sahib; Adi Granth
Guru Ravidas Granth, 141–42. *See also* Ravidas
Gusdorf, G. P., 186, 273 n.46, 344 nn.36,37
Gutenberg Bible, 201; era, 8, 13, 246 n.17

Hadas, Moses, 274 n.51
Hadith, 46, 90, 281 n.20
Haftarah, Haftarot, 99, 109
Haggadah, 112, 293 n.52
Hagiographa, 23, 93, 249 n.5, 287 nn.17,20. *See also* Ketab/Ketuvim
Halakhah, 112, 287 n.17
Halflants, M. C., 254 n.22
Hall, Isaac, 279 n.13
Hallisey, Charles, 315 n.35
Hallo, W. H., 272 n.44
Haloun, G., 266 nn.19–20
Hammurabi, 60, 275 n.59, 357 n.32
Hanukkah, 292 n.47
Haqq, 76
Harnack, Adolf, 269 n.32
Hawley, J. S., 307 n.46
Heart Sutra, 309 n.13, 310 n.15, 332 n.108
Heavenly tablets. *See* Tablets
Hebrew language, 117, 154, 298 n.74
Hebrews, Book of, 283 nn.1–2

Heilman, S. C., 295 n.61
Henderson, J. B., 338 n.14, 352 n.73
Henning, W. B., 266 nn.19–20
Henrichs, Albert, 266 n.19
Hephaestus of Thebes, 55
Heraclides Ponticus, 57
Hesiod, 57, 59
Hewart, Lord, 254 n.30
Hieroglyphics. *See* Writing: hieroglyphic
Highet, Gilbert, 345 n.45
Hill, W. D. P., 299 n.3
"Hinayana", 321 n.59
Hiuen-tsiang, 309 n.13
Hoben, 324 n.75
Hoffmann, R. J., 269 n.32
Hokmah, 267 n.24. *See also* Wisdom
Holdrege, B. A., 268 n.24, 286 n.12
Homer, 57, 59, 188, 193, 338 n.14, 346 n.50, 349 n.64
Honen, 308 n.4
Hopkins, T. J., 303 n.28
Horace, 185, 189, 345 n.47, 346 n.50
Hsien, 339 n.15
Hsun-tzu, 338 n.15
Hui-neng, 318 n.49
Humash. *See* Pentateuch
Humanism, 186–87, 190, 240, 281 n.22, 340–41 n.22
Huxley, T. H., 11

Ibn Aqnin, 34, 250 n.8
Ibn Ezra, 101, 250 n.8
Ilham, 366 n.56
Iliad, 127
Images graven/written, 138, 139
Imagination, Frye and Coleridge on, 223–25
Imitatio Christi, 206
"Immortals" (Taoist). *See Hsien*
Ingalls, D. H. H., 271 n.39, 300 n.12
Inscriptions. *See* Behistun; Safaitic, *etc.*
Instrumentum, 54
Isaiah, Book of, 8, 95, 99, 110
Isma'ilis, 67
Itihasa, 127, 303–4 n.29

Jacobs, Louis, 294 n.59, 295 n.60
Jaeger, Werner, 343–44 n.35
Jain, Jaina, 198, 300 n.9, 354 nn.9,16
Jaini, P. S., 354 n.9
Jamnia/Javneh. *See* Council of Javneh
Japanese language, 156, 245 n.13, 320–21 n.57
Jataka, 151, 314 n.31

Jeffrey, Arthur, 263 n.10
Jellicoe, Sidney, 274 n.53
Jeremiah, Book of, 154, 253 n.16, 265 n.18, 318 n.51
Jerome, 53, 251 n.9, 256 n.50, 268 n.25
Jerusalem, 13, 62, 110, 290 n.38
Jesuits, 181, 194, 351 n.71. *See also* Ricci
Jesus, 51, 53, 173, 246 n.13, 262 nn.3–4, 316 n.378. *See also* Christ
Jodo Shinshu. *See* True Pure Land
John, Gospel of, 5, 23
John of the Cross, 43
Joshua, 109
Josiah reform, 62, 276 n.70, 291 n.38
Joyce, James, 209
Ju, ju chia, ju chiao, 177, 180, 194, 195, 334 n.2
Judah ha-Nasi, 61
Judith, Book of, 268 n.25

Kabbalah. *See* Qabbalah
Kagyu-pa, 325 n.76
Kalam, 236, 262 n.4
Kammuryoju-kyo, 323 n.74
Karma, 320 n.55, 328 n.93
Kasulis, T. P., 328 n.91
Kathavatthu, 314 n.33
Kausalya, 161, 324 n.75
Kent, R. G., 276 n.71
Kermode, Frank, 358 n.5
Ketab/Ketuvim (Ketubim), 7, 23, 109, 249 n.5
Khotanese language, 155
Kimelman, Reuven, 259 n.57, 260 n.61
Kimhi, David, *See* Radak
King, L. W., 276 n.71
Kings (Biblical books), 276 n.68, 282 n.1, 291 n.38
Kitab, 356 n.32. Cf. *Katabna, Kutiba*, 356 n.30
Kitagawa, J. M., 321 n.57
Kitve qodesh, 116, 284 n.3, 297 n.71 [variant spellings]
Koester, Helmut, 265 n.18
Kogen Mizuno, 318 n.49
Kojiki, 198
Kokutai no Hongi, 198
Kotodama, 198
Krishna, 127, 140–41, 144
Kugel, J. L., 298 n.75
Kuhn, T. S., 363 n.41
Kukai, 167, 327 n.83
Kümmel, W. G., 265 n.18, 269 n.29
K'ung Fu-tzu. *See* Confucius

Kuthodaw, 317 n.45
Ku-tien, 206

Lafontaine, Jean de, 151
Lambert, W. G., 272 n.44
Lamentations, Book of, 253 n.16
Lamotte, Etienne, 327 n.86, 331 n.101
Lancaster, L. R., 309 nn.10–11, 323 n.67
Lanczkowski, Günter, 358 n.4
Landy, Francis, 256 n.49
Lankavatara, 317 n.47
Laodicaeans, Letter to, 269 n.29
Lao-tzu, 336 n.10
Lathbury, M. A., 365 n.50
Latin language, 349 n.62
Lattimore, Richmond, 277 n.73
Law(s), 103–4, 129, 234, 275 n.59, 301 n.13; and Prophets, 53, 271–72 n.43; Islamic (*shari'ah*), 71, 301 n.13, 348 n.59; Jewish, 26, 93, 103. *See also Nomos;* Torah; letter of, 319 n.51; Western concept, 129, 300 n.12
Leclercq, Jean, 249 n.4, 253 n.18
Leiman, S. Z., 271 nn.42–43
Leipoldt, Johannes, 266 n.19, 272 n.44, 358 n.4
Leng-yen-ching, 312 n.23, 326 n.77
Lesky, Albin, 273 n.46, 274 n.55
Levering, Miriam, 248 n.1, 323 nn.71,72, 354 n.10
Lewis, C. S., 358 n.5, 360 n.21
Lewis, J. P., 271 n.42, 283–84 n.7
Lieberman, Saul, 264 nn.11,17; 270 n.35
Lightstone, J. N., 271 nn.42–43, 296 n.64, 297 n.69
Lila, 307 n.50
Lillie, Arthur, 327 n.86
Loewe, Raphael, 256 n.49
Logos, 186, 236, 262 n.4, 304 n.32, 344 n.40, 349 n.62, 360 n.21, 365 n.50, 366 n.57
Longfellow, H. W., 334 n.1
Lopez, Jr., D. S., 310 n.13
Lotus Sutra, 5, 160, 165, 167, 172, 203, 224, 244 n.3, 317 n.47, 326 nn.80,81; 327 nn.82,83; 333 n.112
Luke, Book of, 53, 54, 154, 264 n.18, 283 n.1
Lundbaek, Knud, 351 n.71
Luther, Martin, 188, 247 n.19

Maccabean Revolt, 95
Maccabees, (Biblical books), 282 n.1, 284 n.6
MacLeish, Archibald, 87, 280 n.15
MacQueen, Graeme, 310 n.17, 329 n.95, 332 n.107, 333 n.113
Madina, 149
Madrasah, 67
Mahabharata, 128
Mahamangala, 316 n.38
Mahaparinibbana Sutta, 313 n.30, 329 n.99
Mahasamghika, 321 n.59
Mahavairocana sutra (Dainichikyo), 327 n.83
Mahavihara, 321 n.61
Mahayana, 6, chap. 7 *passim* with its notes
Maimonides, 103, 113, 193, 288 n.22, 289 n.31, 293–94 n.56
Mair, V. H., 354 n.11
Maitreya, 316 n.38
Mandaean(s), 48, 52, 61, 267 nn.22-23
Mandalay, 166
Mani, Manichee movement, 22, 48, 51–52, 61, 248 n.3, 266 n.19
Mann, Jacob, 286 n.15
Mantra, 132, 301–2 n.24
Manu, 129, 300 n.11
Manyoshu, 198
Mara (evil one), 322 nn.62,65
Marcion, 54, 270 n.32
Marduk, 60
Mariaselvam, Abraham, 257 n.53
Mark, Book of, 283 n.1
Markwart, J., 262 n.7
Marx, Karl, 188, 345 n.44
Marxist, 147, 308 n.7
Masnavi, 208
Masoretes, 251 n.9
Matthew, Book of, 13, 30, 254 n.26, 283 n.1
Maya, 307 n.50
McDermott, J. P., 316 nn.37,38
Mecca, 149
Mehta, J. L., 279 n.12, 304 n.33, 305 n.35
Mencius (Meng-tzu), 338 n.15
Mendelson, E. M., 317 n.44
Mendenhall, G. E., 283 n.1
Mensching, Gustav, 358 n.4
Messiah, Messianic, 27, 95, 258 n.55. Cf. Maitreya
Miao-fa lien-hua ching, 332 n.109
Micah, Book of, 291 n.38

Midrash, 26, 253 n.16, 283 n.2, 287
    n.22, 291 n.38, 364 n.47
Midrash Rabbah, 256 n.49
Miles, J. C., 275 n.59
Milton, John, 206, 346 n.50
Mimesis, 343 n.33
Mindon, King, 317 n.45
Miqra, 8, 120, 244 n.6, 295 n.63
Mishnah, 55, 61, 100, 111, 114–16, 249
    n.5, 270 n.35, 288 n.22, 290 n.36,
    293 n.56, 295 n.62, 296 nn.64–66,
    297 n.68; Horayot, 295 n.63;
    Sanhedrin, 293–94 n.56; Ta'anit,
    290 n.38
Missionary movements, 55, 84, 147,
    159, 163, 164–65, 181, 194, 202,
    246 n.14, 280 n.13, 305 n.38,
    350 n.67
Mongolian language, 155
Monti, D. V., 365 n.49
Moon, Sun Myung, 357 n.33
Morenz, Siegfried, 266 n.19, 272 n.44,
    358 n.4
Mormon, Book of, 48, 357 n.33
Moses, 53, 60, 62, 98, 100, 105, 110,
    115–16, 151, 154, 193, 283 n.2, 290
    n.37, 297 n.68, 356 n.32; The Five
    Books of. *See* Pentateuch; Torah
Moses de Leon, 285 n.11
Mount Sinai. *See* Sinai
Mughul empire, 201
Muhammad, 46–47, 70, 76, 77, 84, 88,
    110, 262 n.3, 278 n.7, 280 n.13, 322
    n.63, 335 n.6
Mullen, Jr., E. T., 275 n.64
Muller, Max, 8, 139, 244 n.4, 279 n.12,
    302–3 n.27, 306 nn.38–39, 326 n.80,
    330 n.99, 355 n.16
Muqallid, 72
Murano, Senchu, 326 n.81
Muratorian canon, 269 n.31
Murid, 72
Murti, 130
Myoho-renge-kyo, 332 n.109. *See also*
    Lotus Sutra

Nachmanides, 101, 117, 293 n.53
Nagarjuna, 324 n.74, 330 n.100, 330
    n.101
Nagatomi, Masatoshi, 321 n.58
Namu, 172, 333 n.110
Narayanan, Vasudha, 300 n.8
Naskh, 358 n.9
Nattier-Barbaro, Jan, 320 n.55

Nau, François, 263 n.8
Nayanmar, 128
Nehemiah, Book of, 292 n.49
"Neo"-Confucian, 177, 335 n.4, 336
    n.9, 337 n.11
Neo-Platonic, 33
Neusner, Jacob, 258 n.54, 270 n.35, 289
    nn.25–26, 290 nn.33,35; 295 n.62,
    296 nn.64–66, 297 n.68
New Testament, 51, 59, 110, 114, 260
    n.61, 264 n.18, 265 n.18, 268 n.25,
    269 n.29, 270 n.34, 296 n.65,
    319 n.51, 341 n.24, 349 n.62, 350
    n.65, 355 n.20. *See also* individual
    books
Newton, Isaac, 350 n.65
New Year festival. *See* Festivals
Nibbanasutta, 315 n.35
Nichiren, 160, 167, 172, 233, 326 n.81,
    327 n.83, 328 nn.90,92–93, 332
    n.109
Nicholas of Lyra, 259 n.57
Nicholson, E. W., 276 n.69
"Night Journey" of Muhammad.
    See Ascension
Nihongi, 198
Nirukta, 304 n.35
Nirvana, 151
Nock, A. D., 343 n.35
Nomos, 104
Norito, 198
Numata, Yehan, 319 n.54
Numbers (Biblical book), 293 n.50
Nying-ma-pa, 325 n.76

Obenchain, D. B., 334 n.2, 351 n.72
Oberammergau, 299 n.4
Objective-subjective. *See* Subject-object
O'Connell, Joseph, 307 n.41
Odyssey, 127
"Old Testament", 51, 58–59, 92, 93, 94,
    114, 218, 259–60 n.61, 265 n.18,
    268 n.25, 270 n.34, 284 n.5, 296
    n.65, 355 n.20. *See also* chap. 5
    passim
Olmstead, A. T., 276 n.71
Om, 132
Oral/aural, 7–9, 49–50, 61, 120,
    130–31, 138, 165, 199–200, 209,
    245 nn.9,12; 264 n.17, 320 n.57,
    353 n.4, 356 nn.30,32. *See also*
    Torah: Oral
Origen, 38, 251 n.9, 256 n.50, 259
    nn.57,61; 366 n.57

Oxtoby, W. G., 277 n.74, 323 n.69, 340 n.21

Pahlavi language, 49. *See also* Avesta
Palacios, M. A., 278 n.8
Pali, 319 n.52. *See also* Canon: Pali
Panikkar, Raimundo, 331 n.102
Pan Tadeusz, 208
Pao-en, 317–18 n.47
"Paradise", 112, 292 n.49
Paramita, 309 n.12. *See also* Prajnaparamita
"Para-scripture", 152, 204–6
Pardes, 112
Parinirvana, 151, 330 n.101
Pariyatti, 328 n.94
Park, Sung-bae, 323 n.67
Parsis, 50. *See also* Zarathushtrian
Passover, 26, 95–97, 109
Patimokkha Sutta, 328 n.88
Patipatti, 328 n.94
Pativedha, 328 n.94
Paul, St., 54, 154, 260 n.67, 319 n.51
Paulinus, 305 n.38
Pe Maung Tin, 315 n.34
Pentateuch, 54, 58, 61, 93, 98, 105, 106, 115, 118, 151, 264 n.17, 284 n.5, 286 n.13, 287 nn.16–18,21; 291 n.40, 293 n.53, 294 n.58, 295 n.60. *See also* Torah
"People of the Book", 47, 107, 114
Pepìn, Jean, 274 n.56
"Perfection of Wisdom". *See* Prajnaparamita
Perrault, Charles, 345 n.43
Pfeiffer, Rudolf, 273 n.46, 274 n.55, 350 n.65
Philo of Alexandria, 59
Philosophes, 188, 194, 195, 345 n.48, 346 n.50
Pingree, David, 270 n.38
Pir, 72
Pirqe Abot, 116, 297 n.68, 298 n.80
"Platform" Sutra, 154, 167, 310 n.18, 312 n.23, 318 n.49
Plato, 33, 57, 188, 343 n.33
Platts, J. T., 369
Plotinus, 33
Polotsky, H. J., 266 n.19
Pope, Alexander, 189, 209, 345 n.47, 346 n.50
Pope, M. H., 38, 252 n.11, 255 n.40, 257 n.53, 259 n.58, 260 nn.64–65
Positivist, 12, 225, 361 n.30

Posnanski, Adolf, 285 n.8
"Post-modern", 243 n.1
Prajna, 329 n.99, 332 n.107
Prajnaparamita, 149, 309 n.13, 310 n.14, 322 n.62, 363 n.44
Printing, 8, 99, 130, 150, 165, 201, 202, 246 n.17, 286 n.16, 347 n.54, 355 n.16. *See also* Gutenberg
Prithipaul, D., 304 n.32, 344 n.40
Promised Land, Biblical, 95, 109
Prophets, Biblical, 5, 62, 93, 109, 284 n.5, 287 n.17, 319 n.51. *See also* particular books
Proverbs, Book of, 291 n.42
Psalms, Book of, 23, 53, 142, 205, 253 n.16, 284 n.5, 287–88 n.22, 364 n.47
Puech, Henri-Charles, 266 n.19
Puja, 130
Pujavaliya, 316 n.41
Purana, 126–27, 129, 130, 131–32, 135, 138, 141, 144, 298 n.1, 301 n.19, 303–4 nn.28–29, 307 n.52
Pure Land. *See* True Pure Land
Pusey, E. B., 244 n.4, 285 n.9
Pye, Michael, 309 n.12, 324–25 n.75

Qabbalah, 99, 118, 287–88 nn.19–20, 298 n.78, 300 n.9
Qimhi, David, 101
Qismat, 6
Qoheleth, Book of, 58
Qumran, 275 n.64
Quran, 5, 46–47, 61, 66–90, 204, 210, 224, 234, 264 n.17, 275 n.62, 363 n.44; *Ahl-i-*, 204; and Bible, 46, 49, 338 n.11; and Christ, 46; community (*ummah*) aspect of, 86, 261 n.1; dynamic process, 89–90; effect of, 82, 346 n.51; human and divine in, 6, 262 n.4, 366 n.56; *katabna* and *kutiba* in, 356 n.30; meaning, 8, 49–50, 87–88, 90, 120, 244 n.8, 281 n.22; origin, 78, 81, 356 n.32; revelation in, 59, 60, 361 n.31; scholarship, 71; *surahs*, 80; translations, 80, 154; Western interpretation, 358 n.11; Word of God. *See* Word of God: in Islam

Rabin, Chaim, 257 n.53
Rabinowitz, L. I., 287 nn.17,20
Racine, Jean, 206
Radak, 117, 293 n.53
Radha, 140

Radhagovindanath, 306–7 n.41
Radhakrishnan, 303 n.29
Ramanuja, 128, 368
Ramanujan, A. K., 299 n.3
Ramayana, 18, 127, 130, 299 nn.3,5
Ramban. *See* Nachmanides
Ram-Lila, 127
Rashi, chap. 2 *passim* with its notes;
   101, 117, 249–50 n.5, 283 n.2, 287
   n.21, 293 n.53, 368
Ravidas, 141–42
Recitation. *See* Oral/aural
Reformation (Protestant), 63, 84, 164,
   205; and Hebrew Bible, 58, 274
   n.54; as Biblical period, 108; histori-
   cal orientation, 84; Preaching em-
   phasis, 8; *sola scriptura* in, 13, 205
Regensburger, Reinhold, 276 n.66
Reischauer, E. O., 340 n.20
Renascence, Renaissance, 188, 273 n.46
Rennyo, 317 n.46, 327 n.83
"Rescript on Education", Japan, 198
Retna, 263 n.11
Revelation, Book of, 277 n.73
Rg-Veda, 84, 132, 134, 136, 139, 143,
   234, 304 n.33, 304–5 n.35, 306
   n.39
Ricci, Matteo, 195, 340 n.20, 350–51
   nn.68,69
Richardson, Peter, 289 n.32
Rig-Veda. *See* Rg-Veda
"Rites Controversy", 181
Rivington, C. R., 247 n.20
Rnying-ma-pa, 325 n.76
Ro, Young-chan, 346 n.48
Rocher, Ludo, 306 n.38
Rogers, M. L., 312 n.22, 328 n.89, 354
   n.15
Rosenbaum, Jonathan, 289 n.28, 297
   n.71
Romans, Epistle to, 5, 31, 254 n.31, 319
   n.51
Rome, 184–85, 191
Rosenbaum, Jonathan, 289 n.28, 297
   n.71
Rosenthal, E. I. J., 291 n.44, 292 n.45
Rouse, M.A. and R. H., 268 n.28
Rousseau, J. J., 184, 342 n.29
Rsis, 132, 137, 144, 234
Rufinus, 256 n.50
Rule, P. A., 351 n.71
Rumi Jalalu-d-din, 208
Rupa, 130

Sa'adyah Ga'on, 252 n.11
Sabbath, Jewish, 108–9

Sabda, 361 n.31
Sacrament, 240, 241, 367 n.61. *See also*
   Eucharist
Sacred Books of the East, 6–8, 244 n.4
Saddharmapundarikasutra, 332 n.109.
   See also Lotus Sutra
Saddharmaratnavaliya, 316 n.40
Safaitic inscriptions, 63, 277 n.74
Sage, Chinese, 180, 338–39 n.15, 340
   n.22
Sa'id, Labib al-, 245 n.9
Saivas, 300 n.9, 307 n.53
Sakka, 316 n.36
Sakta, 300 n.9
Sakyamuni, 308–9 n.9, 312 n.23
Samas, Shamash, 59–60, 275 n.60
Samghadeva, 322 n.64
Samhita, 134, 138, 305 n.35
Samuel, Book of, 291 n.38
Sanders, J. A., 272 n.43, 357 n.4
Sankara, 128
Sanskrit language, 55, 129, 133, 141,
   155, 172, 262 n.7, 299 n.3, 301
   n.18, 303 n.29, 306 n.39, 309 n.10,
   324 n.75
San tsang, 157, 312 n.25. *See also* Three
   Baskets
Sarasvati, Dayanand, 355 n.21
Sarvastivada, 321 n.59
Sastra, 129, 130, 301 n.14
Satapatha Brahmana, 303 n.29
Sayana, 304 n.35
Schechter, Solomon, 249 n.5, 256 n.49,
   289 n.32
Scherman, Nosson, 250 n.6, 252 n.14
Schmidt, Carl, 266 n.19
Scholem, Gershom, 291 n.43, 298 n.78
Schopen, Gregory, 326 n.78
Scribes, Biblical, 273 n.47. Cf.
   grammatikoi, 57
Secularist, 147, 191–92, 216, 217,
   218–20, 223, 231, 308 n.7
Seiten, 311 n.22
Sepher, 7. Cf. *Soperim*, 273 n.47
Septuagint, 48, 51, 53, 58, 251 n.9, 268
   n.25, 274 n.53
Setton, K. M., 280 n.13
Shah-nameh, 208
Shakespeare, William, 207–9, 361 n.25
Shamash. See Samas
Shari'ah. See Law: Islamic
Shelley, Percy B., 188
Shema, 283 n.2
Sheng, 338 n.15

Sheppard, G. T., 247 n.18
Shi'ah, 67
Shimun, Rabbi, 287 n.22
Shingon movement, 327 n.83
Shinran, 160, 167, 312 n.22, 317 n.46, 321 n.58, 324 n.74, 327 n.83, 328 n.90
Shinto, 197–98, 353 n.8
Shogyo, 311 n.22
Shotoku Taishi, 165
Shu-yuan, 340 n.20
Siddhartha Gautama, 150–51, 157, 167, 168–70, 173–74, 258 n.55, 280 n.14, 308 n.9, 317 n.46, 319 n.52, 329 n.96, 330 n.99
Sikh(s), 48, 55, 141, 196–97, 200–201, 262 n.5, 270 n.33, 353 n.5, 358 nn.9,11
Silence of the Buddha, 170, 240, 330 n.101
Silver, D. J., 285 n.7
Simpson, W. K., 272 n.44
Sinai, 60, 96, 106, 109, 115–16, 149, 297 n.68, 356 n.32
Siva [Shiva], 129
Smith, J. K., 243 n.3
Smith, Joseph, 48, 357 n.33
Smith, W. C., 347 n.53, 367 n.60
Smrti, 137, 204, 206
Social Gospel, 5
Soderblom, Nathan, 261 n.2
Sola scriptura, 13, 205
Solomon, King, 25, 26, 142
Solomon ben Isaac. See Rashi
Somadasa, K. D., 315 n.35
Son (Korean Zen), 154
Song of Songs, chap. 2 passim with its notes; 58, 142, 207, 292 n.49
Sonne, Isaiah, 286 n.15
Soothill, W. E., 347 n.56
Soperim, 273 n.47. Cf. Sepher, 7
Sophia, 268 n.24, 291 n.42, 349 n.62. See also Wisdom
Sophocles, 57
Southern, R. W., 280 n.13
Sowon, 181, 340 n.20
Spinoza, 38, 64, 255 n.47
Sruti, 137, 204, 307 n.49
Ssu Shu, 336 n.9
Stcherbatsky, Th., 330 n.101
Stendahl, Krister, 257 n.51, 277 n.2, 341 n.25
Stevenson, R. W., 243 n.3
Stewart, Zeph, 270 n.37, 344 n.35

Strack, H. L., 288 n.24
Streng, F. J., 331 n.103
Stupa, 164, 326 n.79
Subject-object polarity, 221–23, 359 nn.15,16
"Suffering Servant", 95
Sufi, 67, 72, 73, 215
Sukhavativyuha sutra, 323 n.74
Sukkoth, 109
Sumerian literature, 245 n.13, 272 n.44, 275 n.58
Sundararajan, K. R., 305 n.36
Sundberg, Jr., A. C., 269 n.30, 272 n.43
Sunnah(-i), 204, 206, 355 n.18
Sunyata, 332 n.104. See also Emptiness
Sutra, 6, 10, chap. 7 passim with its notes; 300 n.10, 318 n.49. See also Heart Sutra; Lotus Sutra; Platform Sutra, etc.
Sutta pitaka, 150
Swanson, T. M., 272 n.43
Synagogue, 58, 297 n.74; service, 98, 108, 120, 298 n.80
Synoptic Gospels, 5

Tabari, al-, 71
Tablets, heavenly/scriptural, 49, 57, 59–60, 107, 234, 262 n.3, 275 n.64, 290 n.37, 317 n.45, 340 n.20, 356 n.32, 357 n.33
Ta-ch'eng ch'i-hsin-lun, 317 n.47
Tafsir, 71
Tahrif, 358 n.9
Talmud, 101, 111, 114–16, 186, 204, 206, 256 n.49, 264 n.17, 287 n.21, 288 n.24, 290 n.36, 292 n.46, 295 n.62, 296 n.66; Babylonian, 51, 61, 101, 260 n.63, 297 nn.68,70; Jerusalem, 61, 295 n.63, 297 n.68
Tamil language, 128, 300 nn.8,12
T'an Ching, 318 n.49. See also "Platform Sutra"
Tanakh, 7, 93, 98, 284 n.4
Tanna, 264 n.17
Tanzil, 365 n.52
Tao Te Ching, 6, 336 n.10
Taoist, 6, 178, 197, 199, 335 n.5
Targum, 38, 256 n.49
Tawhid, 83
Taylor, R. L., 351 n.72
Ten Commandments, "Ten Words", Decalogue, 61, 107, 294 n.57, 356 n.32, 361 n.31
Tennyson, Alfred Lord, 209

Teresa of Avila, 43
Tertullian, 349 n.62
Testament. *See* Covenant; New Testament; Old Testament
Tetrabiblos, 55, 271 n.40
Theravada, chap. 7 *passim* with its notes
Theron, D. J., 265 n.18
Thirty-Nine Articles, 247 n.19
Thomas a Kempis, 317 n.42
Thomas Aquinas, 193
Thomas, E. J., 314 n.30
Thompson, R. C., 276 n.71
Thoth, 290 n.37
"Three Baskets", 147, 150–51, 158, 166, 311 n.20, 313 n.30, 314 n.33. *See also* T(r)ipitaka; and the particular Baskets (*Abhidhamma*, etc.)
Thurman, R. A. F., 329 n.95, 331 n.101
Tibetan language, 155–56
Time, patterns of/structuring of, 109. *See also* Festivals: seasonal
Tipitaka, Tripitika, 150–51, 152, 308 n.4, 314 n.32. *See also* "Three Baskets"
Tiruvaymoli, 300 n.8
Tissa, son of Moggali, 314 n.33
Ti-tsang-p'u-sa-pen-yuan-ching, 312 n.23
Tobit, Book of, 268 n.25
Torah, 18, 43, 94, 97–107, 186, 205, 210, 233, 234, 249 n.5, 264 n.17, 273 n.47, 285 nn.11–12, 287–88 n.22, 290 n.33, 291 n.40, 296 n.65, 297 n.68, 364 n.48, 365 n.53; and wisdom, 267 n.24, 295 n.60; Oral, 18, 61, 100–101, 115, 205, 260 nn.61,64; 264 n.17, 288 n.22, 294 n.58, 295 n.60; text of, 319 n.51, 364 n.47. *See also* Law; Pentateuch
Tosapot, 101
Tosepta, 257 n.54, 288 n.23
Touger, Eliyahu, 288 n.22
Tracy, David, 341 n.25, 356 n.29
"Transcendent Insight". *See* "Perfection of Wisdom"
Translation, 9, 80, 129, 145–55, 156, 245–46 n.13, 246 n.14, 311 n.20, 320–21 n.57
Trattner, E. R., 293 n.52, 296 n.65
Treadgold, D. W., 339 n.17, 345 n.44
Tree of life, tree of knowledge, 234
Trent, Council of. *See* Council of Trent
Trinity, Christian doctrine of, 262 n.4, 286 n.11, 303 n.27
Tripitaka. *See Tipitika*

True Pure Land (Jodo Shin[shu]), 153, 166, 202, 311 n.22, 323 n.74
Tulka, Tarthang, 325 n.75
Tulsi Das, 299 n.3, 301 n.17

Uich'on, 323 n.67
Ummah. See Qur'an: community
Upanishad, 67, 134, 138, 141, 302 n.25, 303 n.29, 304 n.30
Upaya(-kausalya), 161–62, 324-25 n.75
Urbach, E. E., 252 n.11, 259 n.57

Vac, 361 n.31
Vacanam, 172. *See also* Buddhavacanam
Vaisnava, 127
van der Leeuw, G., 46, 261 n.1
Van Horn, J. D., 316 nn.37,39
van Unnik, W. C., 265 n.18, 277 n.73
Varanasi/Benares, 130
Vauvenargues, Luc de Clapiers, 184, 341–42 n.27
Veda, 7, 18, 22, 124–25, 130, 141, 210, 234, 258 n.55, 279 n.12, 301 n.20, 304 nn.29–31, 305 n.36, 355 n.16, 363 n.44; Atharva-, 134; Ayur-, 301 n.18; "Back to the", 204, 305 n.35; *dhanur*-, 301 n.18; meaning of, 130; number of, 133, 303 n.28; oral/aural emphasis, 7, 139; recitation of, 132, 302 n.27; Rg-Veda. *See* Rg-Veda; Sama-, 134; Sanskrit word, 133; supernal, 307 n.49; Tamil, 128, 300 n.8; verbal meaning, 133, 303 n.27; words as, 135; Yajur-, 134. *See also sruti*
Vedantin, 300 n.6
Vimalakirtinirdesa, 331 n.101
Vinaya (pitaka), 150, 170, 328 n.88
Virgil, 346 n.50, 350 n.65
Visnu [Vishnu], 129
Visnu Purana, 126–27
Visuddhimagga, 151
von Campenhausen, H. Fr., 265 n.18, 269 n.30, 270 n.32
von Grunebaum, G. E., 345 n.48, 347 n.55
Vulgate, 53, 155, 251 n.9, 254 n.31, 268 nn.25,26; 269 n.29, 364 n.49

Wahy, 366 n.56
Walzer, Michael, 285 n.10
Warren, H. C., 330 n.99
Watson, W. J., 354 n.14
Wen T'ien-Hsiang, 339 n.17

Werblowsky, R. J. Z., 287 n.21
Westerholm, Stephen, 289 n.32
Widengren, Geo, 263 n.9, 264 n.12, 266 n.19, 267 n.23, 274 n.57, 275 n.58, 278 n.6
Wigoder, Geoffrey, 287 n.21
Wijayawardhana, G. D., 316 n.42
Williams, S. W., 279 n.13
Wink, Walter, 357 n.4
Wisdom, 33, 52, 171, 267 n.24, 284 n.5, 291 n.42, 329 n.99, 332 n.107, 335 n.6, 349 n.62. *See also Sophia*
Wittgenstein, Ludwig, 51, 266–67 n.21, 365–66 n.55
Wolf, F. A., 349–50 n.64
Word, 344 n.40, 365 n.50; of God, 3, 11, 35, 41, 154, 232, 236, 313 n.29, 331 n.101, 361 n.31, 366 n.57 *(see also Logos;* Torah); in Islam, 47, 68, 70, 72, 88, 262 n.4, 281 n.18 *(see also Kalam);* of the Teacher (Buddha), 151, 154, 170, 172, 313 n.27, 316 n.36, 317 n.47, 329 n.99, 332 n.107 *(see also Buddha-vacanam)*
Words, 171, 198, 231, 234, 281 n.19, 304 n.35, 305 n.36; framing sacred, 361 n.31; non-reliance on, 154, 318 n.47. *See also* Writing
"Worthies", 339 n.15
Wright, G. E., 318 n.50
Writing, 61–63, 354 n.11; alphabetic,

62, 354 n.11; cuneiform, 59, 62, 276 n.66; hieroglyphic, 62, 276 n.66; in India, 130, 138–39; *See also* Oral/Aural
Writings. *See* Hagiographa; *Ketubim*

Yang-ch'i, 318 n.50
Yaska, 304 n.35
Yavanajataka, 271 n.39
Yeats, W. B., 230, 305 n.36, 363 n.42
Yehudah ben Shimon, 297 n.67
Yigdal, 294 n.57
Yohanan, Rabbi, 259 n.57
Yuan-chue-ching, 312 n.23, 326 n.77
Yu-lu, 312 n.24, 318 n.50, 337 n.11

Zachariae, Theodor, 305 n.38
Zafren, H. C., 286 n.15, 287 n.18
Zambasta, Book of, 320 n.55
Zanj, 72
Zarathushtra, 51, 264 n.11
Zarathushtrian, 7, 48, 49, 50, 61, 200, 263 n.9, 356 n.32, 357 n.33
Zen, 154, 308 n.3, 309 nn.9,13; 318 n.49, 350 n.67
Zionist, 95
Zlotowitz, Meir, 250 n.6, 259 n.59, 260 n.63
Zohar, 118, 233, 234, 285 n.11, 287 n.22, 292 n.49, 298 nn.77–79, 364 n.48
Zurcher, E., 340 n.20